IN THE BEHAVIORAL SCIENCES

SCIENTIFIC INQUIRY

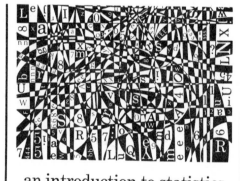

an introduction to statistics

GERALD L. ERICKSEN
St. Olaf College

SCIENTIFIC INQUIRY
IN THE
BEHAVIORAL SCIENCES

an introduction to statistics

SCOTT, FORESMAN AND COMPANY

Library of Congress Catalog No. 75–95031
Copyright © 1970 by Scott, Foresman and Company, Glenview, Illinois 60025.
Philippines copyright 1970 by Scott, Foresman and Company.
All Rights Reserved.
Printed in the United States of America.
Regional offices of Scott, Foresman and Company are located in Atlanta,
Dallas, Glenview, Palo Alto, Oakland, N. J., and London, England.

PREFACE

This book is intended for undergraduate behavioral science students encountering, for the first time, quantitative methodology, measurement, and statistics. It is an outgrowth of a one-semester course offered to sophomore students who have generally approached the subject with such thoughts as "I hated mathematics in high school and have avoided it ever since" or "I just don't like the idea of applying numbers and formulas to people in fields like psychology and sociology." It is understandable that such students view with considerable trepidation the notion of making inquiries about behavior through quantitative methods.

The presentation of material employed herein was developed in the belief that the nonmathematically inclined student can at least develop an appreciation for the utilization of data as a basis for behavioral inquiry. An attempt has been made to achieve a balance between the student's intuitive view of behavior and a readable rationale for the structure of inquiry that is presented.

It is the author's experience that the student's enthusiasm is too often quenched by seemingly endless computational details. Therefore, attention has been given only to formulas necessary to define concepts, with the thought that the details of massive calculations are best carried out by digital computers. It is felt that the student should, at this point in his education, concentrate on the proper planning of behavioral inquiries and the interpretation of results rather than on details of the several so-called computing formulas. The problems in the text are correspondingly designed to require a minimum of machine calculations.

Quantitative methodology somehow seems to be more palatable when viewed as a way of supplementing and checking on the student's common-sense notion of behavior. Therefore, extensive use of examples has been made in order to encourage the transition from intuitive thinking to systematic inquiry. These examples are intended to appeal to the student's intuitive notion of relevant issues concerning human behavior and, at the same time, to help integrate the specific analysis being presented into the general structure of the text. It is felt that the use of limited artificial data is justified in order to achieve these purposes. At the end of each chapter, there are summaries and review questions. Supplementary discussions, inserted throughout the text, are indicated by vertical rules placed prominently along the margins of the relevant pages. Summary charts are presented in Chapter 13 to provide the student with ready references to the techniques discussed throughout the text. The final chapter is devoted to related topics in the hope of encouraging the student to look ahead to more sophisticated techniques of inquiry in upper division courses and in graduate work.

In completing this book, I wish to express my appreciation to Miss Jean Havlish for typing the original manuscript. Further, I am indebted to the Literary Executor of the late Sir Ronald A. Fisher, F.R.S., to Dr. Frank Yates, F.R.S., and to Oliver & Boyd Ltd., Edinburgh, Scotland, for permission to reprint Table VI in this book, which is taken from Table III of their book *Statistical Tables for Biological, Agricultural, and Medical Research*.

G. L. Ericksen

CONTENTS

CHAPTER 1

THE NATURE OF
BEHAVIORAL INQUIRY

FROM INTUITION TO INQUIRY

Undoubtedly, one of the reasons that you are a behavioral science student is that you have an interest in questions concerning behavior. Initially this interest was probably of an intuitive nature, or, in terms of Alfred North Whitehead's *Aims of Education,* this was the romantic stage of your developing interest in behavior. For example, you may have been motivated by a desire to "do something about" civil rights issues, the poverty program, education of the underprivileged, the emotionally ill, etc. This motivation and interest may be a result of a variety of factors, such as your own background, experiences of those close to you, or a conviction concerning certain social problems. Certainly the individual who has such interests and desires is welcomed to the behavioral sciences, for without any intuitive thoughts to generate new hypotheses and new plans of action any *structure of inquiry* becomes at once sterile and tedious. Intuitive interest in behavioral problems is an important aspect of the approach to the structure of inquiry presented here, since the primary purpose of this book is to provide you with specific skills in order that you may formulate your inquiries and plans of action in a somewhat more precise manner.

Quite understandably, there has been considerable concern about this transition from the intuitive view of behavior to the relatively precise structuring of questions about it. Moroney, in his book *Facts from Figures,* recalls a story about Christ which might indicate to some that the whole field of methodology really got off on the wrong foot:

> *Had it not been for the statisticians Christ would have been born in the comfort of a cottage in Nazareth instead of a stable in Bethlehem. . . . They simply didn't think of the overcrowding there would be in a little place like Bethlehem.*

This story, according to Moroney, serves as a symbol of the blindness of planners of all ages to individual comforts. It is hoped that you will realize that learning a structure for your inquiries does not mean that you will be required to turn your back on individual needs, nor will you necessarily become a major threat to Christianity.

Begging the fanciful question of whether or not statisticians were responsible for Christ's original discomfort, there still remain serious philosophical issues concerning the so-called scientific investigation of the wide variety of behavior that interests behavioral scientists. First of all, there is a problem of the meaningful *description* of behavior, since the appropriateness of a measure depends on the type of behavior under study. For example, describing an individual's average bowling score is a considerably different problem from describing his attitude toward legalized marijuana or the United States' involvement overseas. We shall consider this matter in some detail in the next chapter. Second, and perhaps more important from a philosophical point of view, is the question of attempting to draw *inferences* or generalizations about a total group or population from information gained from observing a sample of individuals. For example, we are all familiar with statements such as

> *On the basis of our experience,* children with a "head start" in nursery school seem better prepared for kindergarten than those remaining at home.

> *On the basis of our experience,* culturally deprived children show greater reading proficiency with computer-based instruction.

> *On the basis of our experience,* modular scheduling of academic subjects seems to produce better note-taking in preparation for college, greater individual initiative, and an improved ability to discuss issues in small groups.

In drawing any inference about behavior, we attempt, then, to reason from experience. As pointed out by Hammond and Householder (1962), Whitehead does not give us a great deal of comfort in making such generalizations in his statement, "The theory of induction is the despair of philosophy—and yet all our activities are based upon it." Hammond and Householder furthermore remind us that David Hume, the Scottish philosopher, wrestled with this problem of inference in the middle of the eighteenth century. Hume held that the sum of our experimental conclusions is that "...From causes which appear similar we expect similar effects ... all inferences from experience suppose, as their foundation, that the future will resemble the past...." Hume argued that if the course of nature changes, "...all experience becomes useless," and, in true philosophical fashion, posed the question: "What logic, what process of argument secures you against this supposition?" (Hendel, 1927). This is a question that is still very pertinent today. It is typically handled by a *leap of faith* based on practicality or common sense rather than on any logically tight statistical argument. Illustrations of this leap of faith are all around us: Both doctor and patient are satisfied with tests conducted on only a sample of blood; farmers feel no great compulsion to send in an entire field to be soil-tested; defense plants do not instruct their inspectors to shoot up their entire output of ammunition to insure a high quality of production.

Aside from the older philosophical issues involved in establishing this linkage from intuition to inquiry to inference, modern man still resents and obstructs the precise investigation of human behavior. To some individuals, the collection of data concerning human behavior is associated with endless credit cards, tax levies, military quotas, and other systems whereby individual differences are minimized. To others *data* may connote advertising tricks designed to hide the truth about a product's packaging and quality. Overwhelmed by numbers or exasperated by the clever statistical tricks of the advertising trade, many conclude that although figures might not lie, sure as anything liars figure, and that, as Mark Twain remarked, the result is lies, damned lies, and statistics in that order. In the extreme case of precise structuring of human behavior, one is reminded of George Orwell's *1984*, of the Congressional hearings on testing and public policy (Amrine, 1965), and of Martin L. Gross' *The Brainwatchers*, where rigid adherence to control and quantification might be considered a major threat to individual liberty. Writings such as these point out a fear that quantitative methods in the behavioral sciences have grown from a dreary science to a national menace in a few short years.

The federal government is the major source of financial support for behavioral research. As such, it is confronted with the problem of determining, in the light of our constitutional freedoms, the nature and quantity of data concerning each citizen that may be reasonably collected and maintained. On the one hand, for example, increasing federal support of public education and the culturally impoverished calls for improved assessment and evaluation of the effectiveness of these various spending programs. This assessment seems to be pointing toward an extended *data bank* for retrieval of both subject matter information and individual information. On the other hand, in proposing a general data bank that would include details such as police records, mental health records, and education and tax information, the government is faced with the understandable negative public reaction to the construction of a "push-button dossier" for the American population.

We seem, in the United States, to be quite willing to accept governmental support in conducting behavioral experimentation. Pilot cities, model neighborhoods, preschool training, curriculum reform, and megalopolis planning provide sufficient evidence of our acceptance of this federal involvement. At the same time, however, we jealously guard against a public invasion of our *private* information. Undergraduate students conducting research projects under training grants from the National Institute of Mental Health are familiar with the regulation requiring a committee of responsible lay people to review any research proposal involving human subjects in the experimentation. So, as in the case of the philosophical issue of inference, an intuitive, common-sense approach is necessary when one attempts to resolve the problem of maintaining a reasonable balance in the complex manipulation of environments and individuals. The application of a *structure of inquiry* is not only sterile and tedious unless guided by intuition; it may well be dangerous, as evidenced by experimentation involving the "mind-expansion" drugs.

In the hostile rejection of quantitative inquiry as being philosophically sterile, computationally tedious, and socially dangerous, it seems a shame that the deep beauty of inquiry is scorned. The purpose of a structure of inquiry may be closely aligned with Jacob Bronowski's view expressed in his book, *Science and Human Values:* "When Coleridge tried to define beauty, he returned always to one deep thought: beauty, he said, is 'unity in variety.' Science is nothing else than the search to discover unity in the wild variety of nature—or more exactly, in the variety of our experience. Poetry, painting, the arts are the same search, in Coleridge's phrase, for unity in variety." This same thought of unity in variety motivates our search for a structure of behavioral inquiry. In behavioral research we really need both unity and variety to progress very far. That is, if before and after all of our efforts everything remains constant, there is little to say from an experimental point of view. However, if there were no uniformity whatsoever in behavior, a search for explanation with any structure of inquiry would be futile. An introduction to this structure, to be developed in the succeeding chapters, is designed to aid you in the study of a wide variety of behavior and, more importantly, to leave you with a sense of the unity in that variety. A structure of inquiry can provide you with a beautiful and enlightening set of techniques for advancing your personal, creative efforts in the behavioral sciences.

HISTORICAL DEVELOPMENTS

Any complete history of the quantitative methods used in conducting behavioral inquiries would take us far from the purpose of this book. Good historical reviews of statistical methods are provided by Walker (1929) and Boring (1957), as well as by Hammond and Householder (1962). One has only to refer to *The Sixth Mental Measurements Yearbook* to see, for example, that the mental testing movement has shown considerable expansion since Simon Binet first developed his intelligence test in France in 1904. Likewise, the 1963 *Handbook of Research on Teaching* is sufficient evidence of the growth of educational research since E. L. Thorndike did his work on the effects of reward and punishment at the turn of the century. Of course, the general field of statistical analysis shares a history with mathematics that is, indeed, a ponderous study in itself. In the face of the "knowledge explosion," shared by the behavioral sciences, there are, nevertheless, certain particularly significant developments that help to provide a perspective for the study of behavioral inquiry.

Probably the first major work in the applied study of individual variations arose from Charles Darwin's intuitive observations. Darwin noted that there seemed to be a common inheritance among the various species of finches found in the Galapagos Islands. At the same time he observed that there were consistent differences among the species as he moved from island to island. An article by Roger T. Peterson (1967) entitled "The Galapagos: Eerie Cradle of New Species" contains excellent photographs to illustrate the specie differences that, it is now claimed, resulted in part from the varying ways in which food is obtained by the finches living among the islands. Peterson recalls Darwin's statement of 1845: "Seeing this graduation and diversity of structure in one small intimately related group of birds, one might really fancy that from an original paucity of birds in this archipelago, one species had been taken and modified for different ends." From this intuitive observation of the underlying unity in the variety of individual cases came Darwin's famous work *On the Origin of Species by Means of Natural Selection* published in 1859.

As Ferguson (1966) has noted, "Variation was a central concept in the theory of natural selection because evolution couldn't occur without it." In the life struggle for adaptation and survival an organism will tend to be "naturally selected" if it varies in any profitable way. Ferguson quotes the first issue of *Biometrika* in 1901.

> ... *The first condition necessary, in order that any process of Natural Selection may begin among a race, or species, is the existence of differences among its members. ... The unit, with which such an inquiry must deal, is not an individual but a race, or a statistically representative sample of a race....*

Ferguson furthermore states: "Darwin made no direct contribution to statistical method. He did, however, create a theoretical context ... which made the study of variation meaningful ...."

Following Darwin's breakthrough there came a fairly rapid succession of developments in the study of individual variability. Francis Galton and his student Karl Pearson made significant, if controversial, contributions through the application of mathematical concepts to social and biological events. Out of this effort came, for example, Galton's application of the *normal law of error* to these events. Virtually everyone today is familiar with this so-called "normal" or "bell-shaped" curve so often used for grading students in the classroom. From Galton's work also came the concept of correlation now so widely used in describing the strength of a relationship between two variables. Furthermore, Galton's work, in 1885, "The Regression Toward Mediocrity in Hereditary Stature" still is of consequence in the interpretation of the "before-after" type of research study. We shall consider the problem of correlation and regression in Chapter 11.

Another Englishman, Sir Ronald A. Fisher, developed "a method capable of analyzing the variation to which experimental and observational material is subject so that an assessment of the various components of variation can be made." This method, known as the *analysis of variance*, is one of the most powerful tools for behavioral inquiry available today; we shall consider it in detail in Chapter 10.

Another technique, known as *factor analysis*, was developed to isolate and identify essential factors or traits underlying a particular set of observations. Two of the better-known works in the area of factor analysis are Charles Spearman's *Abilities of Man, Their Nature and Measurement* (1927) and L. L. Thurstone's *Multiple Factor Analysis* (1947). The now-popular "structure of intellect" proposed by J. P. Guilford is actually a factor analytic extension of Thurstone's concept of the primary human abilities of verbal comprehension, memory, spacial visualization, numerical facilities, etc.

By the mid-1940's a new approach to decision-making was taking form. Abraham Wald was one of the foremost men in this field, known as *statistical decision theory*, an approach used increasingly for making inquiries in the behavioral sciences. Chapter 14 includes a brief introduction to the concepts of factor analysis and statistical decision theory.

RECENT DEVELOPMENTS

The following areas are just a few of those in which the problems of behavioral inquiry are being attacked with quantitative approaches:

Education. We are in a period of innovation in our public educational system. The school of the future described by Trump in 1961 is rapidly becoming a reality. The key to this change in what Conant terms our "comprehensive" schools appears to be flexibility. This flexibility demands variations in school arrangements of scheduling, facilities, staff use, and instructional organization. A great deal of effort is being given to inquiries concerning such innovations as the "modern" mathematics programs, modular scheduling, with its varying class sizes and varying formats of student/teacher/subject matter interaction, computer-based instruction for subjects ranging from basic reading to advanced mathematics, and the structuring of knowledge by such methods as Bloom's *Taxonomy of Educational Objectives*. The essential question is: Are these innovations sufficiently effective to justify the investment of a large portion of our available educational resources? In answering this question educators are turning to controlled structures of inquiry.

Sociology. We are pressed, as never before, to implement action programs in the ghettos of our cities in order to make at least part of the "American dream" a reality for the underprivileged. Although countless federal, state, and local programs have been and are being proposed, the issue is still whether or not they are effective. To avoid the irrationality of an already explosive emotional situation, a rational structure of inquiry is essential in carrying out such an assessment of the desired changes in health standards, in preschool through adult educational programs, in civic responsibility and social awareness, as well as in income levels and in utilization of welfare services.

Psychology. Exciting and at the same time frightening paths are being explored concerning the way our minds function, the nature of our emotions, and how we relate to other human beings. The appearance of the electronic digital computer has turned the psychologists' attention to such things as cybernetics and computer-based instruction. The need for carefully controlled and responsible clinical research is pointed up by the public concern about the misuse of various "mind-expansion" drugs. Our increased industrial productivity has, in addition, placed emphasis on carefully controlled studies in marketing as well as in working conditions and methods.

It is thus apparent that, although the historical roots of behavioral inquiry lie in the area of biology, the principles have been applied in many fields. In fact, the beauty of a structure of inquiry is that it remains uniform over the wide variety of fields that interest behavioral scientists.

CHAPTER 2

STRUCTURING BEHAVIORAL INQUIRIES

THE NEED FOR A STRUCTURE OF INQUIRY

Although intuitive insight is an important source for generating new hypotheses and plans of action, it can only take us so far in our attempt to reach objective decisions about behavior. This is because intuition is private and therefore varies from individual to individual.

Much of the early behavioral inquiry was carried on in this *personal* manner, resulting in various "schools" of thought; one followed the "authority" deemed most convincing at the time. For example, at the turn of the century, an educator might be known as a "Deweyian," "Thorndikean," or whatever. In the extreme case, such as with the Freudians, a type of mystical cult developed in which the tenets of the "authority" were not open to objective, rational inquiry. The principle of self-correction of modern experimental methodology simply was ruled out. The usual manner of bringing new ideas into the light under this approach was to break from the cult and form yet another "school" based on those new ideas, much as Alfred Adler did from the Freudians.

An outgrowth of the strictly personal approach to behavioral inquiry was the so-called *deliberative* method. In this approach a consensus among several "authorities" was developed through a sort of committee agreement. Although this did result in at least a crude check on private intuition, the resulting decisions were seldom verified in any objective public way. For example, as Kerlinger (1964) has pointed out,

> It was self-evident to many educators of the last century—it was only common sense—to use punishment as a tool of pedagogy. Now we have evidence that this older, common-sense view of motivation may be quite erroneous. Reward seems more effective than punishment in aiding learning.

Other time-honored common-sense truths such as "The world is flat," "The classics strengthen the mind more than other more practical subjects," and "Babies should be fed every four hours whether they need it or not," have also met their downfall in the face of other common-sense experience or controlled experimentation. Repeated findings such as these leave one with an uneasy feeling about the infallibility of a consensus of intuition as a guiding principle for inquiry.

In order to free ourselves from the shortcomings of private intuition we turn to methods of behavioral inquiry that are public. Specifically, we wish publicly to describe behavior, to test hypotheses about behavior, and to measure the strength of association among various kinds of behavior. By a *public structure of inquiry* it is meant that the measures of behavior are objective enough to allow an interchanging of investigators without significantly altering the resulting data. For rather elementary forms of behavioral data this interchangeability does not pose much of a problem— our height, our weight, our objective test results, and our score after an evening of bridge would generally be the same, regardless of who records them. However, in other, more delicate, matters of human behavior, such as preferences, attitudes, prejudices, and complexes, the interpretations of behavior may show little, if any, agreement from observer to observer.

The first step in investigating behavior with a public structure of inquiry is the establishment of operational definitions. An operational definition spells out the meaning of a concept by denoting the measuring operations involved in it. For example, intelligence may be operationally defined as that score obtained on the Stanford-Binet intelligence test. Although operational definitions have proved to be very helpful in making otherwise vague concepts open to public investigation, a word of caution is necessary. There is no law requiring operational definitions to make literary sense. This distinction between operational and literary definitions can be the source of considerable confusion and suspicion about inquiries concerning human behavior. Simply to state that one is measuring some aspect of behavior such as happiness, love, or hostility is to leave room for endless speculation as to what the investigator means by these terms. Surely they mean different things to different people. Operational definitions at least permit intelligent debate over the reasonableness of the definitions to be used in the inquiry. Consider the problem of arriving at workable, operational definitions of success for a community improvement program. For example, will a score on a *reading readiness* test be accepted as an objective measure of success in a nursery school program? Will the *number of books checked out* from the school library be accepted as a measure of success in a reading resource project? Will *income* and *years on the job* be accepted as measures of success in an employment services project? Arriving at mutually agreed upon operational definitions for all the desired outcomes (i.e., dependent variables) is always of primary concern in the evaluation phase of such behavioral inquiries.

In general, the closer together operational and literary definitions are, the smaller the chance for misunderstandings in interpreting the results of an inquiry for lay persons. Nevertheless, many intuitive, literary interpretations of behavior are so vague as to be of little value for the behavioral scientist. In any case, the distinction between the operational and literary worlds must be clarified before one proceeds with the kind of objective inquiry presented here.

TYPES OF BEHAVIORAL RESPONSES

We have seen that one of the first stages of behavioral inquiry involves focusing on some identifiable phenomenon and arriving at an acceptable operational definition for it. B. J. Underwood (1957) states, "Human activities, behavior, or more simply, responses, constitute the universe of phenomena which psychologists describe and attempt to understand." These responses of human beings are of varied forms, depending, in part, on the relative precision with which we can operationally measure them.

At times, the most we can do with an individual's response is to label it. Simply tagging or categorizing events such as either visiting or not visiting a counsellor, or being for or against the United States' foreign involvement is termed *nominal scaling*. The essential characteristic of this lowly scale, if indeed it can be considered a scale at all, is that an individual's response falls into one and only one category. That is, a student either takes a course for credit or he does not—he does not take it for partial credit. Since the differences among the various categories of a nominal scale are qualitative in nature, there is a limit to the number of quantitative approaches that are appropriate for analyzing nominal data. Nevertheless, there are techniques, to be considered following this chapter, that are available for making decisions about categorical human responses. Some examples of behavioral inquiry dealing with categorical responses are

> A public opinion analyst may classify people as favoring or opposing certain ideas, propositions, candidates, etc.
>
> A sociologist may classify people as "inner-directed" or "other-directed," as having a rural rather than an urban residence, as conservative or liberal, as atheistic or religious, etc.
>
> An educator may describe a classroom as "student-oriented" or "teacher-oriented."
>
> A clinical psychologist may diagnose a patient as "schizophrenic" or "paranoid," etc.

When numbers may be assigned to the individual responses such that it is possible to place them in a *rank order* from low to high, we have what is termed an *ordinal scale*. Many of the experimental scales of esthetics as well as the sociological scales of social status are of this type. Some of the techniques that are appropriate for rank ordered data will be presented in Chapter 12. Some examples of behavioral inquiry with rank ordered responses are

A clinical psychologist observes mental patients in a hospital for a period of six months and then ranks them according to their degree of improvement.

A sociologist ranks members of a citizens' committee in order of their stated concern for certain social issues.

A group of children is ranked, by a counselor, according to their aggressive behavior.

Notice that in the ordinal scale nothing is said about the distance between two numbers; they may be close together or far apart. All that is said is that one number represents a higher, stronger, or greater response than another number.

If, in addition to the order of the response magnitude's being represented by numbers, the size of the difference between the numbers has meaning, such that the numbers may be added or subtracted from one another, we have what is called an *interval scale*. Examples of inquiry that might be considered at this level of quantification are

A sociologist studying job suitability by means of an aptitude test.

A physiological psychologist studying the effects of temperature in space research.

An educator comparing classes by means of various standardized achievement or intelligence tests.

If the ratio of the numbers also has meaning, permitting us to multiply and divide the numbers, we have a *ratio scale*. For example, weight is measured on a ratio scale. That is, an individual weighing 200 pounds may properly be considered as weighing twice as much as someone weighing 100 pounds. However, a person with an intelligence test score of 150 (on an interval scale) is not considered twice as intelligent as someone with a score of 75. Distance is also ratio in nature. It is an accepted fact that the precision of behavioral measurement lags behind that of the physical sciences. The large majority of behavioral research deals with phenomena more properly considered at the *nominal, ordinal,* or *interval* level than at the *ratio* level. For a discussion of this issue, see Torgerson (1960).

Regardless of the level of precision with which we can measure the responses under study, we generally wish to accomplish the following: describe the behavior, test hypotheses about the behavior, and finally establish the degree of association existing among various behaviors. There are two general approaches to the basic problem of analysis. One widespread approach has been to classify the techniques of analysis according to the distinction of nominal, ordinal, and interval scales. There is increasing resistance to this practice, however, on the part of statisticians. They feel that the theoretical problems of measurement are, in essence, distinct from the theory of statistical analysis. Rather than organizing the many available statistical techniques under the levels of measurement, statisticians are increasingly viewing phenomena as *categorical* or *metric*. The categorical metric distinction views behavioral phenomena as either falling into distinct qualitative categories or as differing along a continuum. This latter organization is generally respected in this book, with some of the more widely used, so-called *order statistics* introduced separately in Chapter 12. There are no hard and fast rules concerning at what level any particular phenomenon of interest should be placed. At times it might be helpful to treat a particular kind of behavior or test data as ordinal and at other times as interval. The point is that, although the various techniques of the structure of inquiry were developed under somewhat different assumptions about the underlying scale, no suggestion is being made here that an investigator must slavishly adhere to one interpretation of the scaling assumptions of his behavioral measures. Nevertheless, a flagrant disregard of this matching of the scale of measurement and the type of analysis employed can only be a disservice to the rational inquiry of behavior. For example, by adopting highly questionable operational definitions and by disregarding the scaling problem it is possible, as in some "personality quizzes" of popular magazines, to convey the impression that people can be "2.4 happy" or "6.8 well adjusted." Such practices have led some to describe statistics, not altogether facetiously, as "starting from an unknown premise, utilizing unwarranted assumptions to arrive at a foregone conclusion." However, from a practical point of view, as Games and Klare (1967) have pointed out, "We have yet to see a college student say that the mean of a basket of mixed fruit is an orange, even when oranges predominate in the basket . . . . The several meaningless operations you *could* perform are so illogical that you will automatically reject them. Who would decide that the mean (arithmetic average) of a set of mixed animals in a zoo is a monkey? Inappropriate operations on nominal scales are exceedingly rare in our experience."

THE QUALITY OF RESPONSE MEASURES

Once we are satisfied with the operational definition of a response and have determined that some level of quantification is possible, we are confronted with a question concerning the *quality* of the response measure. By quality we mean, in part, the extent to which the measure is reliable and valid. A response measure is considered to be perfectly reliable if it generates consistent data free from error. For example, we hope that the measuring instruments of our inquiry will remain fairly stable over time. Thus, if an incoming patient at a state school were estimated to have an intelligence quotient of 40 one day and one of 140 two weeks later, we would have a most disconcerting situation. Either the patient has improved remarkably or our response measure is unreliable. The latter seems to be closer to the truth. Furthermore, as Guilford (1965) has indicated, "One should speak of the reliability of a certain instrument applied to a certain population under certain conditions."

It is quite possible for a response measure to be highly reliable and yet to be of little value to the behavioral scientist in the problem of predicting other behavior from it. General problems of relating specific measures or tests to other factors of behavior (such as outside criteria, similar tests, etc.) involve the work of measurement validation. Again one must ask the question, "Valid for what purpose?" as a measure that is valid in one situation cannot be expected to be valid in all situations. Particular caution is required in describing a particular measure as valid. Simply because two response measures demonstrate a high degree of relationship, one must resist the lure of post hoc reasoning—namely, that because one response occurred before the other, the former is the cause of the latter (Kerlinger, 1964). It is always well to keep in mind that virtually any two response measures may be matched in this manner, and there is no logical justification for inferring causality from a strength of relationship. Seder (1948) refers to this as the "rabbit's foot" fallacy, indicating that one might have simply been lucky in obtaining two sets of response measures that just happened to go together. The popular "correlational studies," in which searches are made of past records in an attempt to uncover relationships among various traits, fall in this category. The long debate over the relationship of lung cancer and heart disease to smoking testifies to the complexity of this issue.

The topics of measurement reliability and validity are generally considered separately from the methodology of inquiry, for the theory of measurement and test theory constitutes a vast field of technical knowledge in and of itself. Throughout the discussion in this book, it is assumed that questions of reliability and validity are answered to the satisfaction of the research worker before he proceeds with his investigation. The concepts are mentioned here only to point out their legitimate position in the whole spectrum of behavioral inquiry.

PRINCIPLES OF EXPERIMENTATION

In objectively studying behavior we have seen that considerable effort is required even before we actually begin our inquiry in the field. Operational definitions, levels of quantification, and measurement quality all pose important questions for the behavioral scientist. From this point there are various ways to proceed with the inquiry. We shall consider two fairly common approaches: one is known as *ex post facto* and the other *experimental*.

The ex post facto approach to behavioral inquiry is mentioned both because it is so commonly used and because of its major weaknesses. In ex post facto inquiry, the usual procedure is to compare two known groups of individuals with respect to some characteristic. For example, nursery school children might be contrasted with non-nursery school children on a speech test of articulation. Should there turn out to be a significant difference in articulation in favor of the nursery school children, the ex post facto conclusion might be that the nursery school environment results in better articulation than does the home environment. Of course, the fallacy is that the children were "self-selected" for nursery school, and the investigator has no real assurance that other factors were the same. That is, the children who attended the nursery school could well have had other characteristics that could be the "true" reason for the articulation differences. These other factors are in no way controlled in ex post facto inquiry. Kerlinger presents a thorough case against this approach, and in general the fact that it is so popular and is done under the name of "scientific case study" research in no way elevates its lowly position in the behavioral sciences.

A much more acceptable approach to making decisions in the face of uncertainty in the behavioral sciences is the so-called experimental approach, which is really an application of the classical scientific method. There is, of course, an enormously important field of study known as the philosophy of science, and we can only touch on some of the more obvious principles here. Fisher (1937) is generally credited with setting down in a systematic fashion the principles of experimentation followed in experimental inquiry in the behavioral sciences today.

First, there is the principle of proper *control*. In essence this principle requires that the conclusions of the inquiry be based on similar subjects. The author has had the experience of attempting to contrast two methods of teaching mathematics in secondary schools: one a so-called new or modern mathematics curriculum, and the other a traditional or conventional curriculum. Obviously an important factor is the pupils' initial ability. Keeping the principle of control in mind, we attempted to have comparable classes under both curricula. However, a check on the classes' fall pretesting resulted in the situation illustrated in Figure 2.1. In her enthusiasm for teaching the new mathematics, the teacher had also selected the best students for this class, leaving the average and below-average students for her conventional class, thus violating the fundamental principle

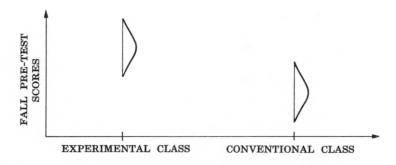

FIGURE 2.1
An illustration of poor experimental control

of control. Although this example is an illustration of poor experimental control, there are numerous reported case studies and experiments carried on with no control group at all. Such inquiries, where there is no comparable group with which to compare the experimental results, are of limited value to the behavioral scientist.

A second principle of experimentation is that of *randomization*. In effect, the principle of randomization assures that every subject in the study has an equal (or known) chance of receiving any given treatment. It is implied that the investigator has the power to assign subjects to the various treatments (sometimes referred to as the ability to "manipulate" the independent variable) before the experiment begins. This ability on the part of the investigator largely separates ex post facto and experimental research. Random selection and assignment of individuals provide rich rewards for the experimenter. These include improved generalization of results and counterbalancing of extraneous factors. One certainly feels better about generalizing to an entire school district from the results of a study based on a sample of students scattered throughout the district than from one based on students, all of whom come from one neighborhood. Studies in which an attempt is made to generalize to a larger group or population beyond the sample actually studied are sometimes referred to as *random effects* designs. Where no attempt at inference is made, beyond the sample actually analyzed, the study is referred to as a *fixed effects* design. To illustrate the concept of *counterbalancing*, suppose that in a prison rehabilitation program, the relative merits of group therapy and individual therapy sessions are to be studied. In order to make the two groups comparable, the investigator might attempt to select prisoners with similar lengths of sentence, occupational levels, previous income, intelligence, etc. However, even after a fairly exhaustive list of individual characteristics has been prepared, there are still many more potentially significant factors in a person's background that could be prejudicial in favor of either the group therapy or individual therapy approach. By randomly assigning the selected sample of prisoners to the two treatments there is a much better chance that these unknown, extraneous factors will be counterbalanced and will not build up to unforeseen systematic differences in the initial characteristics of the two groups.

A third principle of experimentation is that of *replication*. This means repeating the treatment under study on more than one subject. The primary condition for the development of a quantitative structure of inquiry is the ability to assess the variability of measurements used in the field. However, without replication there is no way to estimate this variability. Suppose, for example, that we wish to compare the effects of two treatments in a hospital setting. Let treatment A be given to group 1 and treatment B be given to group 2. If we were told only that the average score on the test used to measure the effectiveness of the treatments was 50 for group 1 and 45 for group 2, would we be justified in supporting the treatment given group 1? Here the question is one that concerns the variability within each treatment. If experience has shown that the scores within a given treatment range only two or three points, we would have a different interpretation of our results than if the normal spread were 15 or 20 points. A failure to replicate within a treatment leaves one in the dark as to the extent of variability. Some of the early studies on extrasensory perception were guilty of a "one-shot approach" with no opportunity for replicating the reported findings. Variability will always exist in any practical situation, and therefore an attempt is usually made to manipulate the experimental conditions in such a way that they are as different as possible so that the average treatment differences show up above and beyond any variability within a given treatment.

Finally, an objective inquiry should be *self-contained*. That is, the statistical conclusions should be based on the data of the inquiry itself and not on "expert" opinion. Johnson (1949) has made the discouraging, but nonetheless astute, observation, "The common procedure of consulting a statistician on statistical principles after an experiment or investigation has been completed is equivalent to holding a post-mortem analysis."

Plans of inquiry carefully laid out in conjunction with these fundamental principles of experimentation can do much in the way of overcoming the problem of *confounded* results. The results of an inquiry are said to be confounded when, in manipulating what we think is the relevant factor, one or more other factors also change so that it is not clear which change was responsible for the observed differences in the results. B. J. Underwood (1957) gives a good discussion of the general problem of the manipulation of environmental, task, or subject variables and the possibility of confounding caused by these same variables. For example, had the study illustrated in Figure 2.1 actually been carried out, any observed achievement differences favoring the new curriculum (task) would have been confounded by pupil ability (subject). Furthermore, whenever individual subjects change (by virtue of new knowledge, motivation, etc.) during the course of an experiment, unless the experimenter takes this change into account in the study design, there is the danger of confounding by subjects. As another illustration, if one method of structuring a group discussion has the advantage of good lighting, adequate ventilation, proper heating, and pleasant surroundings, the comparative results of the method of structuring (task) would be confounded by the room conditions (environment). As a final example of Underwood's paradigm, suppose that a method of group therapy were tried on some prisoners in the prison setting. Even though the prisoners involved in the experimental program turned out "better" by some criterion, it is still an unfortunate truth that a good adjustment in prison is no guarantee of good adjustment in society. The environmental factor is, in a sense, confounded by the fact that it took place within the larger prison environment. That is, one environment is confounded by another environment. *Confounding*, then, can be a considerable obstacle to arriving at an unambiguous interpretation of the results of any behavioral inquiry.

SAMPLING

After the necessary and sufficient information for the inquiry has been determined and the overall experimental plan laid out, the next step is to specify the sample of individuals to be included in the analysis.

A distinction is made between a *sample* and a *population*. *Population* refers to the entire group of individuals about which we are making our inquiry, e.g., all the children of kindergarten age in a specified school district, all of the patients classified as paranoid in a specified set of state mental hospitals, all of the incoming freshmen at a specified college, etc. It is essential to be precise in specifying the population; otherwise, there is no clear way to select a random sample from it. The principle of randomization, as we have seen, is a requisite for making reasonable inferences or generalizations concerning the population.

There are several reasons for selecting only a sample of individual cases from the specified population and analyzing only this sample in making inferences about the population from which the sample came. First of all, it is generally impractical to collect data from the entire group of interest. It may cost too much or take too much time. Second, when the measurement of the behavioral response is tedious, recording errors by the investigator may well increase as the number of observations increase. Furthermore, in certain types of animal research where the inspection process may permanently alter the animal, there is an obvious need not only for sampling but also for keeping the sample size within reason.

There have been some rather recent developments supporting the perhaps surprising notion that a sample size can be too large. This idea, which is related to the distinction between "practical" and "statistical" significance, will be discussed in Chapter 14. Essentially, the chance of declaring a result statistically significant is inversely related to the sample size, and one can, in a sense, "force" statistical significance by making the sample size arbitrarily large. The general concept of sample size is an issue of considerable importance in making statistical inferences and one that we shall encounter repeatedly.

The proper mechanics for sampling are aimed at reducing reporting errors and also avoiding biased samples. M. J. Solin, in his humorous book, *Sampling in a Nutshell*, reports several kinds of reporting errors such as "It is a statistical fact that the reported age of women over 40 is under 40"; "In establishing TV ratings a housewife might not want to say she watched three 'washboard wailers' in a row and might check off a more educational program just to make it look good." Solin states, "The so-called 'telephone-coincidental' method of TV rating is appropriately named since any resemblance between what is actually being watched and the answer given over the telephone may well be purely coincidental."

Nonrandom, biased samples are quite common, particularly when the so-called "quota sampling" technique is employed. In this method an interviewer is simply told the number of responses he is to collect. However, whether the individuals are randomly drawn from the population or all taken from the baseball park, for example, is unknown. The famous Kinsey report findings on sexual behavior have been criticized from the standpoint that individuals who are willing to discuss the intimate details of their sexual experiences may well be rather different from the general population in the United States.

Sampling, then, constitutes a critical link between the design of an inquiry and the final data analysis. No amount of careful planning or extensive analysis can make a good study out of data collected from a poorly constructed sample. Furthermore, the word "haphazard" is in no way a synonym for the word "random."

ANALYSIS

Once the sample data has been collected according to the predetermined experimental plan, the process of analysis begins. There are several aspects to the general structure of data analysis, including condensation, comparison, significance determination, and finally decision making based on the data.

The condensation of the data normally takes two forms, graphical and numerical, and is aimed at presenting the data in a more easily comprehensible form. The appropriate graphical presentation (e.g., tables, pie charts, bar charts, frequency diagrams, etc.) and numerical summarization (e.g., frequencies, means, medians, range of data, etc.) vary according to the level of scalability ascribed to the response measure. The numerical summarization of a mass of data is the view most people have of statistics—endless hours of tedious calculations carried out to a disturbing degree of precision. Fortunately, the modern electronic digital computers free us from this tedium and allow us to concentrate on other, more exciting, aspects of behavioral inquiry.

The summary values (e.g., means, medians, ranges, etc.) computed from a sample of data are termed *statistics*. The corresponding values for the entire population are termed *parameters*. Thus sample statistics are used to shed light on population parameters. More will be said about this later on.

The next phase of the analysis involves comparing the summary statistics with some standard values or making a relative comparison between, say, an experimental group and a control group. The procedures of comparison in order to determine the significance of the results are highly systematized and form the major focus of the remainder of this book. Suffice it to say, at this point, that the purpose of the comparisons is to compare the obtained results with chance expectations. If our particular results are rare, in the sense that it is unlikely that chance alone could account for them, our results are said to be statistically significant; otherwise, they are not. It is common practice to define a statistically significant event as an event that would happen only about one to ten percent of the time by the operation of chance alone. The significance of a result or the lack of it, in turn, permits a rational decision concerning the hypothesis originally posed in the inquiry.

Data analysis is really the only means for handling large masses of numerical information. It applies, however, only to statements reducible to quantitative form, and, although the analysis is objective for all levels of data scales, the final decisions are often affected by subjective interpretations.

With this introduction we turn in the remaining chapters to the business of describing behavioral responses, testing hypotheses about the responses, and studying the relationships among various responses.

SUMMARY

An attempt has been made to demonstrate the need for a structure of inquiry and to emphasize the fact that not all behavioral responses can be measured with equal precision. Furthermore, the quality of a measure in terms of reliability and validity depends not only on the purpose of the measure but also on the particular situation to which it is applied. Basic principles of experimentation are introduced as a means of distinguishing "experimental" inquiry from ex post facto research as well as a way to avoid confounding the results of the inquiry. The notion of a sample of data (as opposed to a population of data) is introduced as a link between designing an experiment and analyzing the results in order to reach a rational, public decision regarding the inquiry. The following terms and expressions are introduced in this chapter:

Personal inquiry
Deliberative inquiry
Public structure of inquiry
Operational definitions
Nominal, ordinal, interval, and
    ratio scales
Analysis
    Condensation
        Graphical
        Numerical
    Comparison
    Significance determination
    Decision making

Reliability
Validity
Post hoc reasoning
Ex post facto research
Experimental inquiry
    Control
    Randomization
    Replication
    Self-contained
Confounding
Sample
Population
Statistics
Parameters

REVIEW QUESTIONS

1   Discuss the major shortcomings of the so-called *personal* approach to behavioral inquiry.

2   What are three objectives of public inquiry about human behavior?

3   What is meant by an *operational definition*?

4   What are the characteristics underlying nominal, ordinal, and interval scales?

5   Contrast the qualities of *reliability* and *validity* of a measuring device.

6   What is meant by *post hoc reasoning*?

7   Describe a so-called *ex post facto* type of inquiry.

8   What is a major defect in ex post facto inquiries?

9   Describe four basic principles of experimental inquiry.

10   What is meant by *confounded results* in experimental inquiry?

11   A *sample* comes from a larger set of observations. What is this larger set called? How large may a sample be?

12   What two forms does the condensation of data usually take?

13   Distinguish between a *statistic* and a *parameter*.

14   Data analysis applies to what type of statements?

CHAPTER 3

DESCRIBING
BEHAVIORAL RESPONSES

DESCRIBING CATEGORICAL RESPONSES

The most elementary way to describe a human characteristic is simply to categorize it into one of several classifications. Thus an individual is either male or female; either institutionalized or not; born either in Germany, the United States, China, or somewhere else. You will recall that, in this simple process of categorization, nothing is said of the scale underlying the classifications other than that an individual characteristic or response is either in a given category or it is not. The simple rule underlying the collection of categorical data is: The various categories or events should be *mutually exclusive*, which means that an individual cannot be in two categories at the same time. Correspondingly, the description of any sample of categorical responses is also very simple: Merely record the number of individual cases observed in each category or event. For example, we might observe that in a sample of ten people:

Two were born in Germany, three in the United States, four in China, one elsewhere.

Three are institutionalized, seven are not.

Five are male, five are female.

The resulting frequencies for each category are often presented graphically by means of the well-known pie charts or bar graphs. Normally pie charts are constructed to show the relative percentages in each category. The birthplace data are presented in Figures 3.1 and 3.2. David Ogilvey, in his book, *Confessions of an Advertising Man*, gives an example of how such a categorical description might be utilized in decision making.

In conducting a survey of why women buy face cream, the following categories were set up: cleans deep in pores, prevents dryness, complete beauty treatment, recommended by skin doctors, younger-looking skin, prevents make-up caking, contains estrogenic hormones, pasteurized for purity,

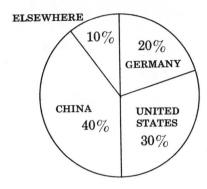

FIGURE 3.1
Birthplace percentages shown in a pie chart

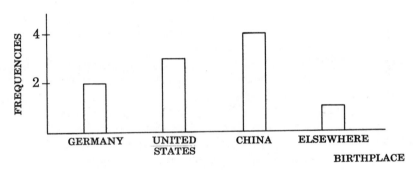

FIGURE 3.2
Birthplace frequencies shown in a bar chart

prevents skin from aging, smooths out wrinkles. In describing *the sample of data it was discovered that the greatest number of women responded to the "cleans deep in pores" category. From this voting came one of Helena Rubenstein's most successful face creams. We christened it Deep Cleanser, thus building the winning promise into the name of the product.*

The ease of description for categorical data is one reason for its popularity; one need not compute such statistics as the mean, median, mode, range, etc., as in the case of metric phenomena.

FREQUENCY DISTRIBUTIONS

As we mentioned in the last chapter, metric data assume that the various possible responses vary along a continuum rather than merely falling into mutually exclusive categories. However, since all behavioral measuring instruments (tests, scales, etc.) are of limited precision, our observations are recorded as though we were dealing with discrete data. For example, reporting mechanical ability test scores of 40 and 41 would seem to convey the impression that the ability of individuals somehow "jumps" from 40 to 41. It is more reasonable to believe that were our measuring instrument more precise we would also observe individuals' scores falling between 40 and 41. For this reason, a discrete score or response is usually interpreted as meaning that the individual's measured characteristic falls somewhere in an interval surrounding the reported score. In this manner, a score of 40 represents an interval on the continuum from 39.5 to 40.5, a score of 41 the interval 40.5 to 41.5, and so on.

GRAPHICAL REPRESENTATION

There are several ways to present a sample of metric data in graphical or tabular form. The simplest procedure is merely to prepare an *arbitrary listing* of the response measures, as illustrated by the hypothetical test scores of Table 3.1. The order of presentation may be determined by the order in which the test papers were turned in, by an alphabetical listing of the students, or by any other arbitrary rule.

TABLE 3.1   **ARBITRARY LISTING OF 110 TEST SCORES (ARTIFICIAL DATA)**

55	70	08	41	57	21	33	52	59	69	18
79	42	23	54	98	32	63	11	17	27	31
72	55	22	15	66	53	35	65	30	67	84
62	44	27	50	64	39	68	49	33	01	19
35	47	56	81	88	49	20	12	73	85	61
36	48	76	31	14	91	54	41	24	62	64
60	06	43	52	28	51	78	58	29	45	80
46	56	87	26	37	60	66	34	50	93	44
82	71	25	42	77	58	43	68	72	46	37
38	51	74	39	57	48	53	40	47	75	45

The listing in Table 3.1 tells us no quick story about the distribution of scores, since it is extremely difficult to comprehend all of them at one time. A scanning of Table 3.1 reveals a low score of 1 and a high score of 98, but little else. Therefore, as a graphical aid for summarizing a sample of data, an arbitrary listing is of limited value. Consider, for example, the following situations:

A teacher attempting to assign grades based on the distribution of test scores.

A social worker trying to understand the distribution of family incomes in a particular area of a city.

A clinical psychologist attempting to determine if the spread and average of intelligence test scores obtained from a select group of children are in line with published norms.

In situations such as these, even with considerable subject matter expertise, it would be extremely difficult to get a good picture of the mass of data presented in an arbitrary listing.

If the data are arranged in order of magnitude, the resulting list is referred to as an *array*. The array of the scores of Table 3.1 is presented in Table 3.2. Although an array is still not the clearest visual summarization for a set of data, it is definitely an improvement over an arbitrary listing. It is much easier to see, for example, that the range of scores is from 1 to 98 by looking at Table 3.2 than from Table 3.1. However, one normally still feels somewhat overwhelmed by a list of 100 or more numbers, regardless of their arrangement.

TABLE 3.2   **AN ARRAY OF THE 110 SCORES OF TABLE 3.1**

01	20	29	36	42	47	52	57	64	71	80
06	21	30	37	43	48	53	58	64	72	81
08	22	31	37	43	48	53	58	65	72	82
11	23	31	38	44	49	54	59	66	73	84
12	24	32	39	44	49	54	60	66	74	85
14	25	33	39	45	50	55	60	67	75	87
15	26	33	40	45	50	55	61	68	76	88
17	27	34	41	46	51	56	62	68	77	91
18	27	35	41	46	51	56	62	69	78	93
19	28	35	42	47	52	57	63	70	79	98

An *ungrouped frequency distribution* is a simplification of an array wherein we simply tally the number of individuals receiving each score. The ungrouped frequency distribution for the scores of Table 3.1 is given in Table 3.3. From the standpoint of a visual summary an ungrouped frequency distribution has few advantages over an array if the data have a wide range of values, as in our example. This is because the frequencies tend to be rather small for each individual value, and therefore there are nearly as many numbers to look at as there are in an array. This is also the case with continuous data, since there is little likelihood of observing several scores rounded to exactly the same value. In general, little is to be gained in most practical situations involving continuous data or discrete data having a wide range of values by constructing an ungrouped frequency distribution.

TABLE 3.3   **AN UNGROUPED FREQUENCY DISTRIBUTION OF THE SCORES OF TABLE 3.1**

Score	Fre-quency	Score	Fre-quency	Score	Fre-quency	Score	Fre-quency
01	1	30	1	50	2	70	1
06	1	31	2	51	2	71	1
08	1	32	1	52	2	72	2
11	1	33	2	53	2	73	1
12	1	34	1	54	2	74	1
14	1	35	2	55	2	75	1
15	1	36	1	56	2	76	1
17	1	37	2	57	2	77	1
18	1	38	1	58	2	78	1
19	1	39	2	59	1	79	1
20	1	40	1	60	2	80	1
21	1	41	2	61	1	81	1
22	1	42	2	62	2	82	1
23	1	43	2	63	1	84	1
24	1	44	2	64	2	85	1
25	1	45	2	65	1	87	1
26	1	46	2	66	2	88	1
27	2	47	2	67	1	91	1
28	1	48	2	68	2	93	1
29	1	49	2	69	1	98	1

A much more helpful tabular presentation is the *grouped frequency distribution*, which involves groups of scores rather than individual scores. This results in a considerable visual simplification of the sample of data. The steps in constructing a grouped frequency distribution are as follows:

Step 1 / DETERMINE THE NUMBER OF DESIRED GROUPS OR INTERVALS

If there are too many intervals, we achieve little improvement over the ungrouped frequency distribution. With too few intervals, on the other hand, the grouping is too coarse to adequately reflect the general shape of the distribution.

The exact number of intervals used varies widely in reported research, although most are within the range of five to 20. The number depends largely on the purpose of the frequency distribution. For example, although five may be adequate for a visual presentation, it is probably too coarse a grouping upon which to base further summary calculations.

Step 2 / DETERMINE THE WIDTH OF EACH INTERVAL

This is accomplished by simply dividing the range of the data by the desired number of intervals. The result, rounded to the nearest whole number, is the appropriate interval width.

Step 3 / TALLY THE SCORES IN EACH INTERVAL

Consider the construction of a grouped frequency distribution for the scores of Table 3.1.

Step 1 / LET US SELECT 10 INTERVALS TO DESCRIBE OUR DATA

Step 2 /

$$\text{Range of the data} = 98 - 1 = 97$$

$$\text{Number of intervals} = 10$$

Therefore,

$$\text{Interval width} = \tfrac{97}{10} = 9.7$$

Since an interval of 9.7 is not convenient, we shall round to the next whole number. Thus we shall construct intervals of width 10.

Step 3 / THE TALLIES WITHIN EACH INTERVAL ARE SHOWN IN
TABLE 3.4

TABLE 3.4   A GROUPED FREQUENCY DISTRIBUTION OF THE
SCORES OF TABLE 3.1

Interval*	Tallies	Grouped frequency distribution
0–9	///	3
10–19	⊬⊬ //	7
20–29	⊬⊬ ⊬⊬ /	11
30–39	⊬⊬ ⊬⊬ ⊬⊬	15
40–49	⊬⊬ ⊬⊬ ⊬⊬ ////	19
50–59	⊬⊬ ⊬⊬ ⊬⊬ ////	19
60–69	⊬⊬ ⊬⊬ ⊬⊬	15
70–79	⊬⊬ ⊬⊬ /	11
80–89	⊬⊬ //	7
90–99	///	3

* The interval end points are assumed to extend one-half unit beyond the interval, forming what are termed *real interval limits*. Thus the real limits corresponding to the apparent limits (0–9), (10–19), etc. are (−0.5–9.5), (9.5–19.5), etc., respectively.

Often the grouped frequency distribution is extended to include cumulative distributions showing the number and percentage of scores contained in or falling below a particular interval. Table 3.5 gives the grouped frequency distribution, the *cumulative frequency distribution*, and the *cumulative percentage distribution* for the data of Table 3.4. The cumulative frequency distribution thus merely indicates the number of scores contained in or falling below each of the intervals. That is, three scores in Table 3.5 are in the interval 0–9, 10 scores are either contained in or fall below the interval 10–19, 21 scores are either contained in or fall below the interval 20–29, etc. The cumulative percentage distribution, on the other hand, translates each of the numbers in a cumulative frequency distribution into a percentage of the total number of scores. Hence the three scores in the interval 0–9 represent 2.7 percent (i.e., $100 \times \frac{3}{110}$) of the entire 110 scores; the 10 scores contained in or falling below the interval 10–19 represent $100 \times \frac{10}{110} = 9.1$ percent of the entire 110 scores, etc.

TABLE   3.5   **GROUPED FREQUENCY, CUMULATIVE FREQUENCY, AND CUMULATIVE PERCENTAGE DISTRIBUTIONS FOR THE DATA OF TABLE 3.4**

Interval	Grouped frequency distribution	Cumulative frequency distribution	Cumulative percentage distribution
0–9	3	3	2.7
10–19	7	10	9.1
20–29	11	21	19.1
30–39	15	36	32.7
40–49	19	55	50.0
50–59	19	74	67.3
60–69	15	89	80.9
70–79	11	100	90.9
80–89	7	107	97.3
90–99	3	110	100.0

The pictorial representation of a grouped frequency distribution is known as a histogram. The histogram for the data of Table 3.5 is shown in Figure 3.3. It is generally agreed that the height of a histogram should be approximately three-fourths of the horizontal distance. This convention helps overcome visual illusions created by distortions of either the frequency scale or the scale of scores. Certainly you would agree that Figure 3.3 represents a considerable improvement over Table 3.1 in providing a visual summary of the data.

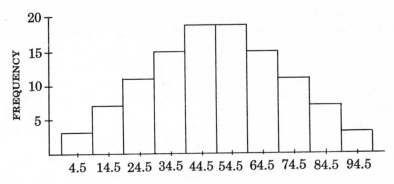

FIGURE 3.3
Histogram for the data in Table 3.5

The ultimate simplification in the graphical presentation of interval data is the *frequency polygon*. Here, instead of constructing rectangles corresponding to the frequencies in each interval, we draw a set of connecting lines through the tops of the rectangles at their center. The frequency polygon corresponding to the histogram of Figure 3.3 is presented in Figure 3.4. It is common practice to draw a smooth line to approximate the rather jagged appearance of the frequency polygon.

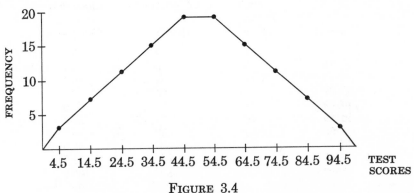

FIGURE 3.4
Frequency polygon for the data in Table 3.5

There are three types of frequency polygons frequently resulting from data collected in the behavioral sciences: symmetrical, skewed, and bimodal.

By far the most widely discussed frequency polygon is the symmetrical one, such as that in Figure 3.4.

The most common nonsymmetrical distribution is represented by the skewed frequency polygon. A frequency polygon may, of course, be skewed in either direction, as indicated in Figures 3.5 and 3.6. We would expect, for example, to find a positively skewed distribution for scores on:

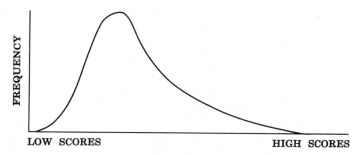

FIGURE 3.5
Positively skewed frequency polygon

Tests that are quite difficult for the group, such as a sixth grade reading test given to a fourth grade class. Most of the children would be expected to be at the lower end of the scale with only a few at the upper end.

Incomes of families living in a poverty area.

Intelligence measures of children coming from culturally deprived homes.

It is not that high scores are impossible in these circumstances; it is just that they are rather unlikely.

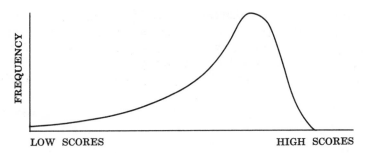

FIGURE 3.6
Negatively skewed frequency polygon

On the other hand, for example, we would expect to find a negatively skewed distribution in situations where the data represents

The heights of college basketball players.

Aptitude test scores of Ivy League college freshmen.

The incomes of families from a well-to-do section of a city.

Again, it is not that low values are impossible in these circumstances; it is just that they are rather unlikely.

A less frequently observed nonsymmetrical distribution is represented by the bimodal frequency polygon illustrated in Figure 3.7. A bimodal distribution often results from the "mixing" of two distinct populations. For example, if one were to draw a sample of reading test scores from both a sixth grade class and a junior high school class, it is reasonable to expect a bimodal distribution. In cases where such a distribution occurs it is usually wise to investigate the definition of the underlying population before proceeding with further analysis. It is much simpler in elementary behavioral analysis to study one population at a time.

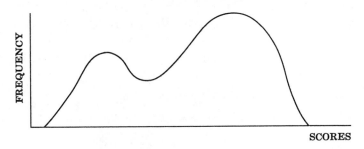

FIGURE 3.7
Bimodal frequency distribution

A frequency polygon that is constructed from a cumulative percentage distribution is called an *ogive* curve; it is quite helpful in quickly estimating the percentage of scores above or below a particular value. The ogive corresponding to the cumulative percentage distribution of Table 3.5 is shown in Figure 3.8. It should be noted in Figure 3.8 that the ogive curve

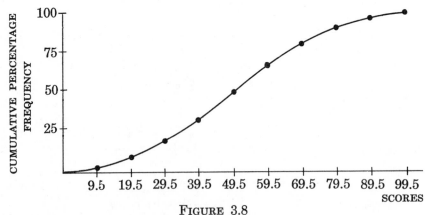

FIGURE 3.8
Ogive for the cumulative frequency distribution of Table 3.5

is constructed by lines connecting points corresponding to the cumulative frequency at the upper end of each interval, rather than at the interval midpoints. This is because the scores falling within an interval are assumed to be distributed equally throughout the interval. That is, 2.7 percent of the cases are below a value of 9.5; 9.1 percent are below a value of 19.5, etc. It is easy to see from Figure 3.8, for example, that about 80 percent of the scores fall below the value 69.5. It can also be seen that about 75 percent of the scores fall below 65, etc.

Although a fairly good appreciation for the meaning of a set of data may be obtained simply by examining it, a great deal still depends on interpretation, which may vary from individual to individual. Normally, in communicating our findings and in decision making we require a more objective and precise description of our data. We turn, therefore, to the *numerical description* of a set of data.*

NUMERICAL REPRESENTATION

You will recall that the frequency polygon, while showing the general shape of a distribution, provides only a rough, subjective estimate of the central tendency and the dispersion of the data. The numerical descriptions to be discussed now are objective, precise statements of the central tendency and the dispersion.

Measures of Central Tendency

Knowledge of the value or score around which a particular group of individuals tend to cluster can be very helpful. For example,

> The knowledge that one fifth grade class has an average intelligence quotient (I.Q.) of 120 while another centers around an I.Q. of 80 is certainly informative.

> An average income rise of $2000 per year for families supported under a given federal program might well be taken as a descriptive measure of the effectiveness of the program.

> An average reaction time of 0.7 second for a group of astronauts on a particular task might require a significant change in the design of related equipment.

There are three commonly employed measures of central tendency or average: arithmetic mean, median, and mode.

---

* Because the ordinary rules of addition, subtraction, and multiplication apply to a wide range of metric data, the numerical description of such data has been quite highly developed. See Appendix D for a review of the more extensively used rules of algebra necessary for analyzing metric data. In practice the resulting formulas are very simple to work with, as will be seen from the accompanying examples in the rest of this chapter.

MEAN

The arithmetic mean, or more simply the mean, being both easily under-stood and easily calculated, is the most commonly used measure of central tendency. Virtually everyone can and does compute means at one time or another. A mean score, such as in bowling, golf, classroom grading, etc., is obtained simply by adding up the individual scores and dividing by the number of scores.

Symbolically the arithmetic mean of a sample of data is written as $\bar{X}$.

DEFINITION   *Arithmetic Mean*

The arithmetic mean $\bar{X}$ is defined as follows:

$$\bar{X} = \frac{\sum\limits_{i=1}^{N} X_i}{N}$$

For example, if we have a sample of three I.Q. scores, 100, 105, and 110, the mean I.Q. is

$$\bar{X} = \frac{100 + 105 + 110}{3} = 105$$

From a physical point of view the arithmetic mean is the "center of gravity." That is, if we were to cut the corresponding frequency polygon out of a hard surface, the arithmetic mean would be the balancing point of the distribution.

The arithmetic mean is a "democratic" statistic, in the sense that its value is determined by every item in the distribution. It is said to be a calculated measure of central tendency and may be treated algebraically. Thus we may take, for example, the mean of means. Such would be the case if we had the mean incomes for three sections of a city (i.e., $\bar{X}_1$, $\bar{X}_2$, and $\bar{X}_3$). We could then compute an overall mean from the means of the three sections of the city. For example, if $\bar{X}_1 = \$4000$, $\bar{X}_2 = \$2000$, $\bar{X}_3 = \$3000$ are the means of the three sections, the overall mean is

$$\bar{X} = \frac{(4000) + (2000) + (3000)}{3} = \$3000$$

If no consideration is given to the differing number of cases for each individual mean calculation, the resulting overall mean is referred to as an *unweighted mean,* as in our example. On the other hand, when considera-tion is given to the differing number of cases, the resulting overall mean is referred to as a *weighted mean.* If there were 500, 300, and 200 individuals residing in the three respective sections of the city, the weighted composite mean income would be

$$\bar{X} = \frac{(500)(\bar{X}_1) + (300)(\bar{X}_2) + (200)(\bar{X}_3)}{1000}$$

$$= \frac{(500)(4000) + (300)(2000) + (200)(3000)}{1000}$$

$$= \$3200$$

The difference between the $3000 for the unweighted mean and the $3200 for the weighted mean reflects the fact that the single $4000 mean was based on 500 individuals and therefore received more weight than the other two means.

The major disadvantage of the arithmetic mean is that it is greatly distorted by extreme values and therefore may not be typical. For example, we might decide to seek special poverty aid for a particular section of a city if the mean annual income were below $3000 per family. If there were an eccentric millionaire who just happened to live in the area, his income would have a disproportionate effect on the calculation of the arithmetic mean. Such a mean would not be typical of the group of interest, as indicated in Figure 3.9 by means of a frequency polygon. It is probably best to define the population in such a way that extreme values are not included. In spite of this drawback, the algebraic manipulations permissible with the arithmetic mean make it the most useful measure of central tendency for drawing inferences from a sample of data.

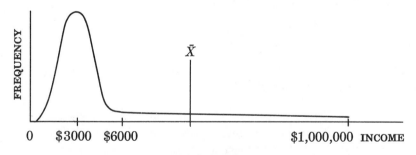

FIGURE 3.9
Illustration of the mean's being greatly affected by extreme values

There are so-called "simplifying formulas" available for computing an estimated mean from grouped frequency distributions (see Appendix B). However, these simplifying formulas appear neither simple to the beginning student nor essential to the practical research worker with modern computing machines. In any case, we shall find the simple defining formula of the mean of a sample of data

$$\bar{X} = \frac{\sum\limits_{i=1}^{N} X_i}{N}$$

adequate for our needs here. Using this formula, we see that the mean of the data given in Table 3.1 is

$$\bar{X} = \frac{55 + 79 + \cdots + 37 + 45}{110} = 49.5$$

MEDIAN

A measure of central tendency that is not affected by extreme values is the median. The median is a measure of position of a set of N scores. It is that value at which 50 percent of the scores are above it and 50 percent of the scores are below it. The steps in computing the median are

Step 1 / ARRANGE THE VALUES ACCORDING TO MAGNITUDE

That is, form an *array* of the data.

Step 2 / THE SIZE OF THE MIDDLE VALUE IS THE MEDIAN

If there is an even number of values, the mean of the two middle values is taken as the median.

For example, assume that we have the numbers 52, 68, 100, 50, and 51. We form an array (50, 51, 52, 68, 100); the size of the middle value is 52, which is, therefore, the median. For the six numbers 50, 51, 52, 54, 68, 100, the mean of the two middle values is

$$\bar{X} = \frac{52 + 54}{2} = 53$$

which is the median. In the same manner the median of the data given in Table 3.2 is easily seen to be 49.5.

> *   A distribution whose midpoint value has a frequency greater than one presents a special problem. For most practical applications in such a situation, it is usually sufficient to define the median as the value of the repeated number. Thus in the four examples below, the median would simply be taken as 8, 3, 4, and 3, respectively. However, should a more precise determination of the median be desired, the assumption is usually maintained that the cases are evenly distributed throughout a range extending from one-half unit below the value to one-half unit above the value. The following examples should help make this clear.

---

* NOTE: These vertical lines will be used throughout the text to indicate material that is considered supplementary and may be bypassed, at the instructor's discretion, without interrupting the continuity of the book.

Example 1

$$5, 6, 6, 7, 8, 8, 8, 11, 13, 15$$
$$1 \quad 2 \quad 3 \quad 4 \quad 5 \quad 6 \quad 7 \quad 8 \quad 9 \quad 10$$

Assume that the three scores (8, 8, 8) are spread equally through the interval 7.5–8.5; i.e., pretend that each 8 occupies one-third of a unit. Five scores fall below the median value, since there are 10 scores. If we count from the lower end, however, the fifth score (i.e., the first 8) is considered to extend one-third of the way into the interval 7.5–8.5. Thus we have

$$\text{Median} = 7.5 + 0.33 = 7.83$$

Example 2

$$1, 2, 2, 3, 3, 3, 3, 5, 6$$
$$1 \quad 2 \quad 3 \quad 4 \quad 5 \quad 6 \quad 7 \quad 8 \quad 9$$

Assume that the four scores (3, 3, 3, 3) are spread equally through the interval 2.5–3.5; i.e., pretend that each 3 occupies one-fourth of a unit. Four and one-half scores fall below the median value, since there are nine scores. If we count from the lower end, the four and one-half scores include 1, 2, 2, together with the first 3 and one-half of the second 3. Since each of the 3's is assumed to occupy one-fourth of the interval (2.5–3.5), we require $(\frac{1}{4} + \frac{1}{8})$ of the interval (2.5–3.5). Thus we have

$$\text{Median} = 2.5 + 0.375 = 2.875$$

Example 3

$$1, 2, 4, 4, 4, 4$$
$$1 \quad 2 \quad 3 \quad 4 \quad 5 \quad 6$$
$$\text{Median} = 3.5 + 0.25 = 3.75$$

Example 4

$$1, 3, 3, 3$$
$$1 \quad 2 \quad 3 \quad 4$$
$$\text{Median} = 2.5 + 0.33 = 2.83$$

In addition to the fact that it is not distorted by extreme values, the median has the advantage of being an appropriate measure even when the distribution is "open-ended." For example, consider the distribution of Table 3.6. The arithmetic mean is not an appropriate measure for such "open-ended" distributions.

TABLE   3.6   **AN EXAMPLE OF AN OPEN-ENDED DISTRIBUTION**

Number of children	Frequency
0	3
1	6
2	7
3	19
4	8
Over 4	10

The primary disadvantages of the median are that it is not as familiar as the mean and it cannot be treated in the same algebraic fashion as the mean. Thus we cannot compute separate medians for, say, three groups of data and then calculate a mean of the three medians to arrive at some sort of an overall median that would be descriptive of all three groups. This latter restriction is a major reason for the superiority of the mean over the median in the analysis of metric data.

As with the mean, there are formulas for estimating the median for grouped frequency distributions (see Appendix B).

The median is also referred to as the *fiftieth percentile*. Figure 3.10 illustrates the median position by means of an ogive curve. Thus the median estimated from the ogive of Figure 3.8 agrees with the calculated value 49.5. Other percentiles may be found in the same manner. Thus the twenty-fifth percentile (commonly called the lower quartile) is that value below which 25 percent of the cases fall. Likewise, the seventy-fifth percentile (commonly called the upper quartile) has 75 percent of the cases below it. For example, the seventy-fifth percentile of the data of Figure 3.8 is seen to be approximately 65.

The percentile rank of a score may likewise be found from the ogive by referring first to the score of interest and then locating the corresponding percentage value. Thus the percentile rank of the median score of 49.5 is 50. In the same manner, the percentile rank of a score of 65 in Figure 3.8

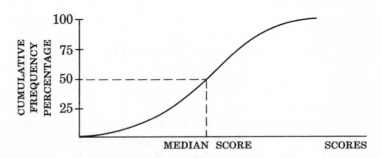

FIGURE   3.10
Median location on an ogive curve

is seen to be approximately 75. Such a graphic determination of the percentile rank is usually sufficient. However, the percentile rank of a particular score may be determined algebraically by the following formula based on an array of the original scores.

Percentile rank

$$= \frac{\text{cumulative frequency including the score of interest}}{\text{total number of scores}} \times 100$$

For example, the percentile rank corresponding to a score of 65 in the data of Table 3.2 would be

Percentile rank $= \frac{83}{110} \times 100 = 75.4$

which compares favorably with the result obtained graphically by means of Figure 3.8. Where more than one score equals the score of interest, the cumulative frequency may be taken to include one-half of them. Thus, for example, the *percentile rank* corresponding to a score of 66 would be estimated as

$$\frac{84}{110} \times 100 = 76.3.$$

For grouped frequency distributions the percentile rank may be estimated by the formula given in Appendix B.

> In most distributions of behavioral data, such as those in Table 3.5, differences between raw scores located near the center of the distribution correspond to larger differences between the corresponding percentile ranks than do the same raw score differences located at the end of the distribution. For example, in Table 3.5 the difference of the percentile ranks corresponding to the interval end points 9 and 19 is seen to be
>
> $$9.1 - 2.7 = 6.4$$
>
> whereas the difference of the percentile ranks corresponding to the interval end points 49 and 59 is
>
> $$67.3 - 50.0 = 17.3$$
>
> Therefore, particular caution should be exercised when one is attempting to compare the performance of two groups on the basis of average percentile ranks. That is, for the common unimodal distribution the conversion of raw scores to percentile ranks does not generally result in a scale of equal intervals.
>
> There are, nevertheless, techniques appropriate for comparing groups on the basis of rank information only, some of which will be discussed in Chapter 12.

MODE

The mode is simply the most frequent value. Thus for the values 3, 6, 4, 3, 2, 6, 7, 6, 1 the modal value or mode is 6.

The mode is, of course, simple to calculate and gives a quick measure of central tendency, unaffected by extreme values, without the necessity of forming an array. However, the limitations of the mode are great. First of all, there may be no unique mode for a set of data. Such is the case for the values 3, 9, 9, 4, 7, 6, 6, 5. Furthermore, the mode, like the median, cannot be treated algebraically as can the mean. Again, there are formulas for estimating the mode for grouped frequency distributions (see Appendix B).

If the frequency distribution is symmetrical, the mean, median, and mode will be identical. However, for skewed frequency distributions they will not correspond. Figures 3.11 and 3.12 illustrate, by means of frequency polygons, the relationship of the three measures of central tendency for skewed distributions.

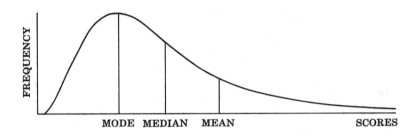

FIGURE 3.11
Measures of central tendency in a positively skewed distribution

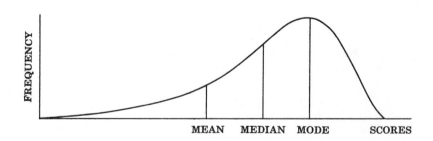

FIGURE 3.12
Measures of central tendency in a negatively skewed distribution

Measures of Dispersion

Having reduced our entire sample of data to a single number representing the central tendency, we ask: Have we lost something by this summarization? The answer is yes, as can be seen from the following examples:

Suppose that the mean I.Q.'s for two fifth grade classes were both 110. Judging only from this information, we would conclude that the two classes were comparable in intelligence. However, it could well be that the distributions of intelligence scores for the two classes are as illustrated in Figure 3.13. Even though the two class means are identical, it is clear that a

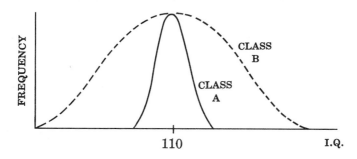

FIGURE 3.13
Contrasting dispersions for distributions with identical means

teacher facing class B has a much more difficult task because of the wide dispersion of abilities.

Suppose that the difference between the mean annual incomes of two occupational categories is $2000. Certainly our interpretation of this difference depends on the dispersion or variability of incomes within the two occupations. Figure 3.14 illustrates the case in which the two occupations are quite homogeneous with respect to income. On the other hand, when

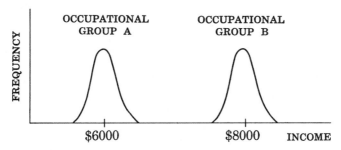

FIGURE 3.14
Two homogeneous occupational groups

the two occupational categories are quite heterogeneous with respect to income, knowledge of the occupational category may tell us very little about an individual's income because of the extensive overlap. This is illustrated in Figure 3.15.

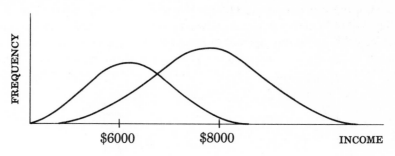

FIGURE 3.15
Two heterogeneous occupational groups

Any complete description of interval data must, then, take the dispersion or variability into account. Of the several indices available to reflect the dispersion of a distribution, the *range* and the *standard deviation* are the most widely used.*

RANGE

The range is, of course, merely the difference between the highest and lowest values. It provides a quickly computed index of dispersion, but since it has the disadvantage of being dependent on only two values, it is greatly affected by isolated, extreme values. Furthermore, the range has limited utility in the process of drawing inferences from a sample of behavioral data.

STANDARD DEVIATION

A much more useful index of dispersion than the range is the standard deviation, symbolically written as S for a sample of data.

DEFINITION   *Standard Deviation*

The standard deviation S of a set of N values is**

$$S = \sqrt{\frac{\sum\limits_{i=1}^{N} (X_i - \bar{X})^2}{N}}$$

---

* The *mean deviation* and the *semi-interquartile range* are other, infrequently used measures of dispersion (Spiegel, 1961).
** A table of square roots is given in Table I of Appendix A.

The formula for the standard deviation may be clarified as follows: Let us consider N values $X_1, X_2, \ldots, X_N$ with mean

$$\bar{X} = \frac{\sum\limits_{i=1}^{N} X_i}{N}$$

One way to express the dispersion about the mean would be to simply list the individual deviations. That is,

Individual values	*Deviation from the mean*
X_1	$(X_1 - \bar{X})$
X_2	$(X_2 - \bar{X})$
$\vdots$	$\vdots$
X_N	$(X_N - \bar{X})$

Such a listing can be tedious, however, and does not result in an easily comprehended summary of the dispersion for a mass of data. A reasonable solution to this problem would seem to be to simply take the average of the individual deviations as our measure of dispersion. That is,

$$\text{Measure of dispersion} = \frac{\sum\limits_{i=1}^{N} (X_i - \bar{X})}{N}$$

This expression is an unsatisfactory index of dispersion, since it will always be zero for every distribution. This can be seen from the following relationships:

$$\frac{\sum\limits_{i=1}^{N} (X_i - \bar{X})}{N} = \frac{\sum\limits_{i=1}^{N} X_i - \sum\limits_{i=1}^{N} \bar{X}}{N} \qquad \text{by Rule 3 of Appendix D}$$

$$= \frac{\sum\limits_{i=1}^{N} X_i - N\bar{X}}{N} \qquad \text{by Rule 2 of Appendix D}$$

$$= \frac{\sum\limits_{i=1}^{N} X_i - \sum\limits_{i=1}^{N} X_i}{N} \qquad \text{by the definition of the mean } \bar{X}$$

$$= 0$$

The resulting zero value is caused by the canceling out of the positive and negative deviations. To overcome this problem of the signs, each deviation may be squared (the negative deviations are thus eliminated) before the average is computed. That is,

Individual values	Deviations from the mean	Squared deviations
X_1	$(X_1 - \bar{X})$	$(X_1 - \bar{X})^2$
X_2	$(X_2 - \bar{X})$	$(X_2 - \bar{X})^2$
$\vdots$	$\vdots$	$\vdots$
X_N	$(X_N - \bar{X})$	$(X_N - \bar{X})^2$

Thus

$$\text{Measure of dispersion} = \frac{\sum_{i=1}^{N} (X_i - \bar{X})^2}{N}$$

However, the operation of squaring has changed our units of measurement. Therefore, to express the index of dispersion in the original units of measurement, the square root of this average is taken. The resulting expression is known as the standard deviation S. Thus

$$S = \sqrt{\frac{\sum_{i=1}^{N} (X_i - \bar{X})^2}{N}}$$

For example, consider a sample of only three intelligence scores.

Individual	Score	Deviation from the mean	Deviation squared
1	100	-5	25
2	105	0	0
3	110	$+5$	25

Thus

$$\bar{X} = \frac{\sum_{i=1}^{N} X_i}{N} = \frac{100 + 105 + 110}{3} = 105$$

and

$$S = \sqrt{\frac{\sum_{i=1}^{N} (X_i - \bar{X})^2}{N}}$$

$$= \sqrt{\frac{(100 - 105)^2 + (105 - 105)^2 + (110 - 105)^2}{3}}$$

$$= \sqrt{\frac{(25) + (0) + (25)}{3}} = \sqrt{\frac{50}{3}} = 4.08$$

An alternate computing formula, often used in evaluating the standard deviation for a set of data, is

$$S = \sqrt{\frac{\sum_{i=1}^{N} X_i^2}{N} - \bar{X}^2}$$

The equivalence of the two formulas may be seen as follows:

$$S = \sqrt{\frac{\sum_{i=1}^{N} (X_i - \bar{X})^2}{N}} = \sqrt{\frac{\sum_{i=1}^{N} (X_i^2 - 2\bar{X}X_i + \bar{X}^2)}{N}}$$

$$= \sqrt{\frac{\sum_{i=1}^{N} X_i^2 - 2\bar{X} \sum_{i=1}^{N} X_i + N\bar{X}^2}{N}}$$

$$= \sqrt{\frac{\sum_{i=1}^{N} X_i^2 - 2N\bar{X}^2 + N\bar{X}^2}{N}} = \sqrt{\frac{\sum_{i=1}^{N} X_i^2}{N} - \bar{X}^2}$$

For our example we have

$$S = \sqrt{\frac{(100)^2 + (105)^2 + (110)^2}{3} - (105)^2}$$

$$= 4.08$$

Applying this formula to the data in Table 3.1, a value of 21.37 is obtained for S.

The standard deviation is affected by every value in the sample and has several properties that are extremely helpful not only in describing sample dispersions but also in making inferences from a sample of data. We shall consider these properties in some detail in Chapter 6 in studying the relationship of the standard deviation to the normal curve.

As with the measures of central tendency, formulas have been developed for estimating the standard deviation from a grouped frequency distribution (see Appendix B).

The square of the standard deviation, as we have defined it here, is called the *biased sample variance* and is denoted by S^2. If $N - 1$ rather than N is used in the denominator in the definition of S, the square of the standard deviation is called the *unbiased sample variance* and is denoted by $\hat{S}^2$. The distinction between S^2 and $\hat{S}^2$ is maintained in the estimation of population variance by sample variances. S^2 is said to be the biased sample variance because it tends to underestimate the "true" population variance by the factor $N - 1/N$. However, for large values of N this distinction becomes negligible. Unless we specify otherwise, we shall use the simpler form of

$$S = \sqrt{\frac{\sum_{i=1}^{N} (X_i - \bar{X})^2}{N}}$$

Higher-order Descriptive Measures

Indices of *skewness* and *kurtosis* (i.e., the peakedness of a distribution) have been developed. However, they are not widely used in behavioral inquiries because of their rather unstable nature when one attempts to estimate characteristics of populations from them (Hoel, 1954).

STANDARD SCORES

We have seen that we may describe the central tendency of a sample by the arithmetic mean and the dispersion by the standard deviation. These two statistics help us to answer another question: How can we compare scores obtained from tests where different units of measurement are used? For example,

Suppose that we have a set of test scores on both mechanical knowledge and manual dexterity for a group of industrial employees. Suppose further that the summary statistics for the scores of the two tests are as follows:

Test of mechanical knowledge	Test of manual dexterity
$\bar{X} = 50$	$\bar{X} = 100$
$S = 10$	$S = 20$

Obviously, a score on the test of mechanical knowledge cannot be directly compared with a score on the test of manual dexterity. The two scores are measured on different scales. Furthermore, a particular score does not represent the same relative position of the individual on the two tests. For example, a score of 50 is average on the mechanical knowledge test but considerably below average on the manual dexterity test.

What we would like is a score that would reflect an individual's relative standing in a group, regardless of the scale used and independent of the mean and standard deviation of the test scores. That is, if, in our example, the employee's relative standing in the group remained unchanged on the two tests, we would like his score to remain unchanged also. One method would simply be to compute the percentile ranks of the scores on the two tests. This is a frequently used method of comparing the relative position of individuals on two different scales.

Another approach, which we shall find even more useful, is to use *standard scores*.

DEFINITION   *Standard Score*

Corresponding to each original (frequently called *raw*) score X_i in a sample of scores with mean $\bar{X}$ and standard deviation S, a standard score is denoted Z_i and is defined in general as follows:

$$Z_i = \frac{\text{original values} - (\text{mean of the distribution of original values})}{(\text{standard deviation of the distribution of original values})}$$

Thus we have

$$Z_i = \frac{X_i - \bar{X}}{S}$$

Notice that for every raw score there is a standard score. Therefore, there will be a distribution of standard scores, just as there is a distribution of the original test scores.

What, then, do we gain by changing our scores on the two tests from their original values to standard scores? The answer is that we create a common scale for the interpretation of the scores. Standard scores have a mean of zero and a standard deviation of one, regardless of the mean or standard deviation of the original distribution. Therefore, each distribution can be reduced to a distribution with a mean of zero and a standard deviation of one. Furthermore, the scale underlying the standard score distribution is always in standard deviation units, regardless of the scale of measurement of the original scores.

The mean and standard deviation of the standard score distribution (i.e., of Z_i scores) may be derived as follows:

$$\bar{Z} = \frac{\sum\limits_{i=1}^{N} Z_i}{N} = \frac{\sum\limits_{i=1}^{N}\left(\dfrac{X_i - \bar{X}}{S}\right)}{N} = \frac{\sum\limits_{i=1}^{N}(X_i - \bar{X})}{NS}$$

$$= \frac{\sum\limits_{i=1}^{N} X_i - N\bar{X}}{NS} = \frac{N\bar{X} - N\bar{X}}{NS}$$

$$= 0$$

S (of Z_i scores)

$$= \sqrt{\frac{\sum\limits_{i=1}^{N}(Z_i - \bar{Z})^2}{N}} = \sqrt{\frac{\sum\limits_{i=1}^{N} Z_i^2}{N}}$$

$$= \sqrt{\frac{\sum\limits_{i=1}^{N}\left(\dfrac{X_i - \bar{X}}{S}\right)^2}{N}} = \sqrt{\frac{\sum\limits_{i=1}^{N}\left(\dfrac{(X_i - \bar{X})^2}{S^2}\right)}{N}}$$

$$= \sqrt{\frac{\sum\limits_{i=1}^{N}(X_i - \bar{X})^2}{N} \cdot \frac{1}{S^2}} = \sqrt{\frac{S^2}{S^2}}$$

$$= 1$$

Referring to our example, we can see that if the individual scored 50 on the mechanical knowledge test and 100 on the manual dexterity test, his score was at the mean on both tests. The standard scores should reflect this relative position, which they do. That is,

Mechanical ability $Z_i = \dfrac{X_i - \bar{X}}{S} = \dfrac{50 - 50}{10} = 0$

Manual dexterity $Z_i = \dfrac{X_i - \bar{X}}{S} = \dfrac{100 - 100}{20} = 0$

In this case both scores are zero standard deviations away from the mean. On the other hand, a score of 80 would place an individual in a much better relative position on the mechanical knowledge test than on the manual dexterity test. This fact is reflected by the standard scores as follows:

Mechanical ability $Z_i = \dfrac{X_i - \bar{X}}{S} = \dfrac{80 - 50}{10} = 3$

Manual dexterity $Z_i = \dfrac{X_i - \bar{X}}{S} = \dfrac{80 - 100}{20} = -1$

In this case a mechanical ability score of 80 is three standard deviations above the mean of the mechanical test. A manual dexterity score of 80 is one standard deviation below the mean of the dexterity test.

There is one essential point to remember about standard scores. Converting the original scores to standard scores does not alter the shape of the distribution, even though the mean and standard deviation are changed to zero and one, respectively. Essentially what this means, for comparative purposes, is that the two distributions should have approximately the same shape even though the scales of measurement, means and standard deviations, might differ. Where the distributions do differ in form, the percentile ranks provide a better method of comparing the relative position of individuals in the two distributions.

LINEARLY DERIVED SCORES

We have seen that a raw score of 80 on the manual dexterity test results in a standard score of -1. In fact, any raw score below the mean of the test will correspondingly result in a negative standard score. Describing someone's manual dexterity as minus one is odd indeed. The worst he could do, the individual might well reason, is to receive a score of zero. To be "in the hole" on an ability test is a difficult concept to explain to the layman. Zero would seem, then, to be a more acceptable lower limit for ability scores.

In order to avoid the interpretation of negative standard scores corresponding to raw scores falling below the mean we use linearly derived scores.

DEFINITION   *Linearly Derived Score*

Given a standard score

$$Z_i = \frac{X_i - \bar{X}}{S}$$

a linearly derived score may be formed as follows:

$$L_i = M + \text{S.D.}(Z_i)$$

where M is an arbitrarily selected mean and S.D. is an arbitrary standard deviation.

A widely used linearly derived score is the so-called T score, which has a distribution with mean of 50 and a standard deviation of 10. That is, $T_i = 50 + 10(Z_i)$. For example, in the case where the individual scored 80 on the manual dexterity test, the standard score was -1. The corresponding T score would be

$$T_i = 50 + 10(Z_i)$$
$$= 50 + 10(-1)$$
$$= 40$$

A manual dexterity score of 40 is easier to explain than a score of -1, although they both imply that the individual's manual dexterity score was one standard deviation below the mean. As a second example of a T score, consider a raw score of 95 on the manual dexterity test. In this case,

$$Z_i = \frac{X_i - \bar{X}}{20} = \frac{95 - 100}{20}$$

$$= -0.25$$

and

$$T_i = 50 + 10(Z_i)$$

$$= 50 + 10(-0.25)$$

$$= 47.5$$

The particular mean and standard deviation is arbitrary in linearly derived scores. The graduate record examination uses a mean of 500 and a standard deviation of 100; the army general classification test uses a mean of 100 and a standard deviation of 20; the Stanford-Binet intelligence test uses a mean of 100 and a standard deviation of 16, etc. Thus, for example, a child with an I.Q. of 116 is considered to be one standard deviation above the mean I.Q. for his age group. Again, the primary purpose of linearly derived scores is to avoid the interpretation of the negative standard scores. The shape of the original distribution is not altered in the transition first to standard scores and then to linearly derived scores.

SUMMARY

In this chapter we have been concerned with describing behavioral responses. Categorical responses are described numerically by simple tallies and shown graphically as a pie or bar chart. So-called metric responses are assumed to fall along a continuum, even though observations are recorded discretely. The several possible methods of representing metric information graphically include: arbitrary listing, array, ungrouped frequency distribution, grouped frequency distribution, histogram, frequency polygon, and a cumulative frequency polygon. Frequency polygons have an unlimited number of forms; however, three fairly common general shapes are known as symmetrical, skewed, and bimodal polygons.

The numerical description of a frequency distribution usually involves measures of central tendency—mean, median, and mode—and measures of dispersion—range and standard deviation. The advantages and disadvantages of each of these measures are discussed, and reference to the various computing formulas for grouped data is restricted to Appendix B.

The concept of a standard score is introduced in order to provide a basis for comparing scores obtained from different distributions. The two primary characteristics of interest regarding the distribution of standard scores are (1) The distribution has a mean of 0 and a standard deviation of 1, regardless of the magnitude of the original scores. (2) Converting the original scores to standard scores does not alter the shape of the distribution (that is, a skewed distribution is not made symmetrical by standardizing the scores). Finally, the idea of linearly derived scores is introduced to avoid the interpretation of negative standard ability scores. Additional terms and expressions encountered in this chapter are

Mutually exclusive categories
Discrete *vs* continuous data
Ogive curves
"Mixing" of data from two distinct populations
Mean as the center of gravity
Weighted mean
Percentile
Percentile rank
Dispersion or variability
Biased *vs* unbiased sample variance
Kurtosis
Relative standing
Standard score
Standard deviation units
Negative standard scores
Linearly derived score

REVIEW QUESTIONS

1   A variable that can theoretically assume any value in a specified range is called a _____ variable. One that can assume only certain values, such as 0, 1, 2, ... is called a _____ variable.

2   An array is (a) a sequential order, (b) a summarization, (c) a measure of dispersion, (d) all of these.

3   A _____ may be obtained by connecting midpoints of the tops of the rectangles in a histogram.

4   If *two* widely different populations are sampled, the resulting descriptive curve would most likely be a _____ curve.

5   If a junior high school test in mathematics were administered to a group of high school seniors, what shape would the resulting distribution of test scores most likely be?

6 In the following diagram indicate the measure of central tendency indicated by a, b, and c.

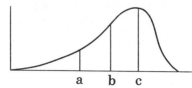

a. _ _ _ _ _ _

b. _ _ _ _ _ _

c. _ _ _ _ _ _

7 In a positively skewed distribution the mean lies on which side of the median?

8 Evaluate the mean, median, and mode for the following set of observations: 5, 2, 10, 1, 3, 11, 10.

9 Show that for any set of numbers, the sum of the differences from the mean is equal to zero.

10 What is a major disadvantage of the arithmetic mean and the range?

11 Find the standard deviation for the following data: 2, 3, 4.

12 In order to compute a standard score, what two characteristics of a distribution must one know?

13 What is the relationship between the *shape* of the *raw* score distribution and the standard score distribution?

14 If $\bar{X} = 60$ and $S = 10$, evaluate the corresponding Z_i and T_i scores for the following raw scores:

    (a) $X_i = 60$, $Z_i =$ _ _ _ _ _ _ , $T_i =$ _ _ _ _ _ _ .

    (b) $X_i = 30$, $Z_i =$ _ _ _ _ _ _ , $T_i =$ _ _ _ _ _ _ .

    (c) $X_i = 50$, $Z_i =$ _ _ _ _ _ _ , $T_i =$ _ _ _ _ _ _ .

15 What effect does a linear transformation have on the general *shape* of the distribution of original scores?

16 What is the primary motivation for transforming standard scores to so-called *linearly derived* scores?

17 Express the following as a single expression involving a summation sign.

    (a) $2X_1 + 2X_2 + 2X_3 + 2X_4 =$ _ _ _ _ _ _ .

    (b) $X_{19}^2 + X_{20}^2 + X_{21}^2 + X_{22}^2 =$ _ _ _ _ _ _ .

    (c) $(X_1 - \bar{X})^2 + (X_2 - \bar{X})^2 + \cdots + (X_N - \bar{X})^2 =$ _ _ _ _ _ _ .

18   Evaluate the following terms if:

$$X_1 = 2, \qquad X_2 = 1, \qquad X_3 = 2$$
$$Y_1 = 1, \qquad Y_2 = 2, \qquad Y_3 = 3.$$

(a) $\sum\limits_{i=1}^{3} X_i = $ ------- .

(b) $\sum\limits_{i=1}^{3} Y_i = $ ------- .

(c) $\sum\limits_{i=1}^{3} X_i^2 = $ ------- .

(d) $\sum\limits_{i=1}^{3} X_i Y_i = $ ------- .

(e) $\left(\sum\limits_{i=1}^{3} X_i\right)\left(\sum\limits_{i=1}^{3} Y_i\right) = $ ------- .

(f) $\left(\sum\limits_{i=1}^{3} X_i^2\right)\left(\sum\limits_{i=1}^{3} Y_i^2\right) = $ ------- .

CHAPTER 4

A BASIS FOR EXPERIMENTATION WITH CATEGORICAL RESPONSES

Although categorical responses constitute the most rudimentary form of human measurement, it is still possible to carry out experimentation and to reach decisions in a rational manner concerning this type of behavioral inquiry.

There is both a strength and a weakness in the statistical techniques designed for categorical responses. The strength lies in the fact that since little is said about the scale underlying the categories, the results of the inquiry have a fairly wide range of generalizability. However, the increased generalizability resulting from the liberal assumptions underlying non-parametric tests comes at a price. The price is that the statements made are weaker statements than could be made if more precise measures were appropriate for the behavioral response under study. For example, to say, "The child has an acceptable level of intelligence" is a weaker statement than "The child has an I.Q. of 155 as measured by the Stanford-Binet intelligence test." It is easy to be lured by the simplicity and generalizability of the categorical approach and therefore to "throw away information" by treating metric responses as categorical. However, a developing field such as the behavioral sciences can ill afford any loss of information in seeking to make as strong statements as possible regarding the complexities of human behavior. Again, while the measurement issue should not be the single master of behavioral inquiry, neither should the research worker routinely turn to techniques requiring the fewest assumptions simply because they are easier to work with. As a matter of fact, with the prevalence of electronic computers, computational differences among the statistical techniques are no longer a crucial issue.

While there are several statistical techniques that have developed for analyzing categorical data, two are most widely used. One involves the *binomial distribution*, and the other is known as *the chi-square goodness of fit test*. The remainder of this chapter is devoted to the development of some of the "building blocks" underlying these techniques. There are two reasons for taking the time to develop these basic concepts. First of all, many elementary inquiries can be adequately handled with one or more of these basic tools without reference to the more involved techniques. Second, an understanding of the essential elements provides a better appreciation of the rationale underlying the more highly developed approaches to inquiry. Certainly an appreciation of the underlying rationale permits a more intelligent application of the techniques used in behavioral inquiries.

PROBABILITY STATEMENTS AND CATEGORICAL RESPONSES

Although the description of categorical responses is very simple and somewhat informative, we are normally more interested in the probability of occurrence of these categories or events. The question that we constantly face is: Have we observed something commonplace and unimpressive in our inquiry, or did our "experiment" yield an unusual, rare event or set of events such that it is quite unlikely that our observations could have resulted from chance alone? More specifically, we would like to know if our sample could have reasonably come from a population where a particular set of conditions exists. Consider, as an illustration, the following situations:

A sample of children in a poverty area was selected to receive special instruction in personal hygiene and health. Is the percentage of children with dietary deficiencies in this sample significantly lower than would be generally expected for the entire population of these poverty area children?

A community action council was appointed by the mayor. Is there a significantly lower number of foreign-born citizens on this council than would be expected on the basis of the census data for the city?

A school board is debating the question of whether or not to invest in a student driver-training program. Is the number of reportable accidents among those individuals having had such a program significantly below that reported by the National Safety Council for the comparable age group in the population as a whole?

To answer those kinds of questions it is necessary to introduce concepts of probability appropriate for categorical data. We need, furthermore, a general approach to these kinds of questions, i.e., a way of looking at the situation. With this in mind we turn to the following four-part *formal statement of a basis for probability appropriate for categorical data:*

    I. First of all, describe or take as known two things:
        1. A fundamental experiment.
        2. The meaning of an outcome of the experiment.

The specification of the fundamental experiment and meaningful outcomes should be agreed upon before the inquiry is begun. For example:

Fundamental Experiment	*Meaningful Outcome*
A Better Chance (ABC) program	College entrance
"Culture Mobile" for underprivileged children	Recognition of cultural objects
Head Start nursery schools for preschool children	Reading readiness success
Model city programs	Frequency of specific type of crimes

II. Next, it is necessary to prepare a list of all the possible outcomes. This list of outcomes should be both mutually exclusive and exhaustive. That is, any given result should fall into one and only one category, and furthermore there should be a category for every possible result. For example, consider the possible outcomes following any year of college:

Outcome	*Description*
O_1	Graduated
O_2	Continued for another year
O_3	Left to get married
O_4	Left to join the military service
O_5	Left for some other reason

The entire collection of all the possible "outcome points" or results of a study or experiment is given a name. It is called the *sample space* of the experiment and is sometimes simply labeled **s**. For the above college "experiment" the following notation would be used to describe the sample space:

$$\mathbf{s} = (O_1, O_2, O_3, O_4, O_5)$$

In general, for an experiment with, say, n outcomes we would have

$$\mathbf{s} = (O_1, O_2, \ldots, O_n)$$

The sample space **s** is thus merely the set of all outcome points, where n denotes the total number of possible outcomes. Let us relate the notions of a *fundamental experiment, meaningful outcomes,* and **s** by means of the following example:

Fundamental experiment	A request for money from home by a college student at two different times.
Meaningful outcomes	Success (receiving the money) or failure (not receiving the money).
Possible outcomes	The possible outcomes of this "field study" or "experiment" are O_1 = success on both requests. O_2 = failure on first request, success on second request. O_3 = success on first request, failure on second request. O_4 = failure on both requests.
Sample space	n, the number of outcome points, is four. Therefore, $$\mathbf{s} = (O_1, O_2, O_3, O_4)$$

As an illustration of a slightly more involved setup, consider the following:

Fundamental experiment	Administer one of three drugs to a patient and assign the patient to one of five wards.
Meaningful outcomes	A patient has a particular drug and is housed in a particular ward.
Possible outcomes	The results of this experiment may be placed in the form of Table 4.1.

III. Generally in our inquiry we are interested in some particular set of outcome points, not all of them. That is, our interest might be in achieving success of any kind in the first example above (i.e., O_1 or O_2 or O_3) or in receiving drug 1 and being placed in an odd-numbered ward in the second example (i.e., O_1 or O_7 or O_{13}).

We call the set of outcome points of interest an *event* and label it E. In general, an event is made up of, say, h points. Thus if the event E were defined to be success on both requests in the above example, it is clear that $h = 1$. However, if the event E were defined to be success on only one request, $h = 2$.

DEFINITION

An event E is a set of h outcome points in the sample space $\mathbf{s}$.

TABLE 4.1   **SAMPLE SPACE OF EXPERIMENTAL OUTCOMES**

Drug

		1	2	3
	1	O_1	O_2	O_3
	2	O_4	O_5	O_6
Ward	3	O_7	O_8	O_9
	4	O_{10}	O_{11}	O_{12}
	5	O_{13}	O_{14}	O_{15}

Sample space

n, the number of outcome points, is 15. Therefore,

$$\mathbf{s} = (O_1, O_2, \ldots, O_{15})$$

Of course, h can be no larger than n, and each outcome point is either in E or not. In any case, regardless of what event is being defined, n remains unchanged.

IV. Finally we can define the probability of an event E. The common notation for this probability is $P(E)$.

DEFINITION   *Probability*
_____

The probability of an event, $P(E)$, is

$$P(E) = \frac{h}{n}$$

that is, the number of outcome points defining the event divided by the total number of outcome points in the sample space.

This definition of the probability of an event assumes the outcome points to be equally likely. That is, any outcome has just as great a chance as any other to occur. In the above example, if the assignments of drugs and wards were made randomly, this would certainly be a reasonable assumption. Under this equally likely assumption, the probability of the event of being given drug 1 and being assigned to an odd-numbered ward would be:

$$P(E) = \frac{h}{n} = \frac{3}{15}$$

since there are three outcome points defining this event and the total number of points in the sample space is 15.

In circumstances where it is not reasonable to assume that the outcome points are equally likely, an alternative definition, which does not make this restriction, is often used.

ALTERNATIVE
DEFINITION *Probability*

$P(E)$ is the relative frequency with which the event E occurs over a long series of trials.

Many of the computer simulation techniques being developed in industry and military systems are designed to provide estimates of the probabilities of various events by simulating real-life situations. Thus if a particular type of manual radar tracking system resulted in a misclassification of an unidentified aircraft five times out of 100 trials, $P(E)$, the probability of misclassification of this type of aircraft, would be estimated as

$$P(E) = \tfrac{5}{100} = 0.05$$

If the outcomes of an experiment are, in fact, equally likely, the above two definitions of probability will converge. The age-old coin-tossing problem illustrates this convergence. The probability of a head (event E) on the toss of a fair coin is, by the first definition,

$$P(E) = \frac{h}{n} = \frac{1}{2}$$

since there are only two possible outcomes in the sample space. Also, if one took the trouble repeatedly to toss a fair coin, a head would appear approximately half of the time. Out of 1000 tosses probably very close to 500 of them would turn up heads. As the number of tosses increases without limit, the ratio of heads to the total number of tosses will converge on one-half, which by the second definition is the desired probability.

At any rate, either the probabilities associated with each outcome point are assumed known by the nature of the experimental setup, or an attempt is made to generate empirical estimates of the desired probabilities by conducting successive trials of the experiment.

In summary, the formal basis of probability involves a fundamental experiment, meaningful outcomes, definitions of events, and definitions of probability.

JOINT EVENTS

Having defined a single event E and the probability of a single event $P(E)$, we turn to more interesting questions concerning two events.

The basic question is: *What is the chance of some later event, labeled E_2, happening given that an earlier event, labeled E_1, has already happened?* The interest in this kind of question stems from the fact that after causing one event to occur, we can also, at times, find some other event that is more likely to occur as a result. The existence of such a relationship between two events is, of course, invaluable for bringing about behavioral changes. Consider, for example, the following questions relating pairs of events:

What is the relative frequency or chance of poor articulation	*given*	Speech correction in nursery school?
What is the chance of an experimental subject's solving a finger maze in one trial	*given*	A period of adaptation?
What is the chance of a patient being assigned to an understaffed ward	*given*	That treatment was conducted by an inexperienced counselor?

A general notation is used to express this type of conditional probability:

$$P(E_2 \mid E_1)$$

which is read, "The probability of event E_2 happening given that event E_1 has already happened."

Sometimes, of course, the two events will have no relationship in the sense of one event's affecting the occurrence of the other. Such events are termed *independent*. If, on the other hand, one event does affect the occurrence of the other, the events are called *dependent*. This leads us to the following definition:

DEFINITION

If $P(E_2 \mid E_1) = P(E_2)$, E_1 and E_2 are said to be independent events; otherwise, they are dependent events.

Consider the following situation as an illustration of independent events.

In the above drug/ward assignment example, let

E_1 = administration of drug 1

and

E_2 = assignment to ward 1

Now from inspection of the sample space given in Table 4.1, we see that

$$P(E_2) = \frac{h}{n} = \frac{3}{15}$$

and

$$P(E_2 \mid E_1) = \frac{h}{n} = \frac{1}{5}$$

thus

$$P(E_2 \mid E_1) = P(E_2)$$

and we conclude that the two events are independent. That is, the administration of a particular drug in no way affects the assignment of wards.

On the other hand, the following situation is an illustration of dependent events.

In an experimental study, a subject is to guess the "proper" button to push. There are three square buttons and two round buttons. Let

E_1 = event of being told the proper button is square

and

E_2 = event of pushing the proper button

Thus

$$P(E_2) = \frac{h}{n}$$

$$= \tfrac{1}{5}$$

since there are five outcome points in the sample space, and only one button is the proper one.

However,

$$P(E_2 \mid E_1) = \frac{h}{n}$$

$$= \tfrac{1}{3}$$

since there are only three outcome points in the sample space associated with "knowing" that the proper button must be square. Therefore,

$$P(E_2 \mid E_1) \neq P(E_2)$$

The two events are dependent. Knowledge of the shape of the button improves the chance of selecting the proper button.

Aside from the above question of conditional probabilities whereby one event may affect the probability of the occurrence of a later event, there is a second question: *What is the chance of both E_1 and E_2 happening at the same time?* There are two simple cases to consider in answering this question.

CASE 1   *Independent Events*

If E_1 and E_2 are independent events, the probability of both occurring is the product of their separate probabilities. This is written symbolically as

$$P(E_1 E_2) = P(E_1) P(E_2) \tag{1}$$

As an example, consider again the drug/ward assignment problem, where

$E_1 =$ administration of drug 1
$E_2 =$ assignment of ward 1

E_1 and E_2 have been shown to be independent events; thus the chance of being administered drug 1 *and* being assigned to ward 1 is

$$P(E_1 E_2) = P(E_1) P(E_2)$$

$$= \left(\tfrac{5}{15}\right)\left(\tfrac{3}{15}\right) = \tfrac{15}{225}$$

$$= \tfrac{1}{15}$$

This result can be directly verified by an inspection of the sample space in Table 4.1.

CASE 2   *Dependent Events*

If E_1 and E_2 are dependent events, the probability of *both* occurring is the product of the probability of the first event and the conditional probability of the second event. This is written symbolically as

$$P(E_1 E_2) = P(E_1) P(E_2 \mid E_1) \tag{2}$$

To illustrate this type of joint event, suppose that, in the button-pushing experiment, the chance of being told that the proper button was square was determined by the flip of a coin. Thus the probability of being told that the proper button is square is $\frac{1}{2}$. That is,

$$P(E_1) = \tfrac{1}{2}$$

Recalling that

$$P(E_2 \mid E_1) \neq P(E_2)$$

we conclude that E_1 and E_2 are dependent events. Therefore, the probability of being told that the proper button is square *and* also of pushing the proper button is

$$P(E_1E_2) = P(E_1)P(E_2 \mid E_1)$$
$$= \left(\tfrac{1}{2}\right)\left(\tfrac{1}{3}\right)$$
$$= \tfrac{1}{6}$$

In the consideration of joint events there is a third logical question: *What is the chance of one event or a second event's (or both) happening?* Here the key word is *or* rather than *and*. There are, again, two rather simple cases to consider for this type of question.

<u>CASE 1</u>   *Mutually Exclusive Events*

If E_1 and E_2 are mutually exclusive events—that is, they cannot happen together—the probability of one or the other's occurring is the sum of their separate probabilities. This is written symbolically as

$$P(E_1 + E_2) = P(E_1) + P(E_2) \tag{3}$$

In the drug/ward assignment problem, let

E_1 = administration of drug 1

and

E_2 = administration of drug 2

E_1 and E_2 are, therefore, clearly mutually exclusive events, since one and only one drug is administered to an individual patient. Now

$$P(E_1) = \tfrac{5}{15}$$

and

$$P(E_2) = \tfrac{5}{15}$$

Therefore, the probability of being administered drug 1 *or* drug 2 is

$$P(E_1 + E_2) = P(E_1) + P(E_2)$$
$$= \tfrac{5}{15} + \tfrac{5}{15}$$
$$= \tfrac{10}{15}$$

CASE 2   *Non-mutually Exclusive Events*

If E_1 and E_2 can happen together—that is, they are not mutually exclusive events—the chance of either (or both) happening is the sum of their separate probabilities minus the probability of their happening together. This is written symbolically as

$$P(E_1 + E_2) = P(E_1) + P(E_2) - P(E_1E_2) \qquad (4)$$

The reason for this somewhat more complicated expression may be clarified by the following situation in the drug/ward problem: Let

E_1 = administration of drug 1

and

E_2 = assignment to ward 1

Now the probability of E_1 or E_2 (or both) happening can be deduced from the sample space given in Table 4.2.

TABLE 4.2   SAMPLE SPACE OF EXPERIMENTAL OUTCOMES

		Drug		
		1	2	3
	1	✕	✕	✕
	2	✕		
Ward	3	✕		
	4	✕		
	5	✕		

Thus by direct application of the definition of the probability of an event (in this case being administered drug 1 or being assigned to ward 1, or both) we have

$$P(E_1 \text{ or } E_2 \text{ or both}) = \tfrac{7}{15}$$

However, if we had used the formula appropriate for the mutually exclusive case, the outcome point corresponding to both drug 1 and ward 1 would have been added in twice. In order to correct for this, we subtract the probability of both events' happening. Thus in this case of non-mutually exclusive events we have

$$P(E_1 + E_2) = P(E_1) + P(E_2) - P(E_1E_2)$$

$$= \tfrac{5}{15} + \tfrac{3}{15} - \tfrac{1}{15} = \tfrac{7}{15}$$

which corresponds to the solution obtained directly from the sample space diagram.

A diagram, known as a Euler or Venn diagram, is sometimes used to show this type of situation graphically. In our case the Venn diagram would be as shown in Figure 4.1. Each oval represents an event, and the overlap

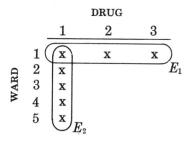

FIGURE 4.1
Venn diagram

clearly demonstrates that they are non-mutually exclusive events.

In summary, for answering probability questions about joint events, we have the following helpful rules:

For *independent* events

$$P(E_1E_2) = P(E_1)P(E_2) \tag{1}$$

For *dependent* events

$$P(E_1E_2) = P(E_1)P(E_2 \mid E_1) \tag{2}$$

For *mutually exclusive* events

$$P(E_1 + E_2) = P(E_1) + P(E_2) \tag{3}$$

For *non-mutually exclusive* events

$$P(E_1 + E_2) = P(E_1) + P(E_2) - P(E_1E_2) \tag{4}$$

Thus for rather simple inquiries involving categorical data with known probabilities we can report the impressiveness of a particular outcome by computing the probability of its occurrence from the above formulas.

COMBINATORIAL ANALYSIS

There are at least two important reasons for understanding the sample space underlying an inquiry; that is, of being aware of all the possible results or outcome possibilities.

The first reason is one we have already studied. We used the sample space in deriving reasonable statements about the chance of some particular event's (or combination of events) occurring by means of the definition

$$P(E) = \frac{h}{n}$$

The second reason for our interest in the sample space of a behavioral inquiry is that each separate, individual outcome point in the sample space may require our special attention. That is, to insure that we are equipped to handle each possible result of an inquiry, it is necessary to know what the results are before we make the inquiry.

For rather simple situations, the possible outcomes are obvious, such as in accepting or refusing an offer, winning or losing the toss of a coin at the start of a football game, etc. However, for more complex situations the number of possible outcomes may not be intuitively obvious. Since it is necessary to know what the possible outcomes are, we turn to what is known as *combinatorial analysis*.

We shall consider three rather general rules that are helpful in determining the total number of possible outcomes under various conditions where the nature of the sample space might not be immediately clear.

RULE 1

The number of arrangements (called *permutations*) of n objects is $n(n-1)(n-2)\ldots(1)$. This is written symbolically as

$$_nP_n = n! \tag{5}$$

where

$$n! = n(n-1)(n-2)\ldots(1)$$

and is read "The number of permutations of n objects taken n at a time equals n factorial." The factorial symbol ! has the additional conventions associated with it that

$$0! = 1! = 1$$

It should be remembered in using Rule I that all the objects are taken into account.

Two examples will demonstrate the utility of Rule I in both probability questions and in identifying each possible outcome.

As a probability problem consider the following situation involving the judging of intelligence by photographs: Suppose that, so far as measured I.Q. is concerned, three children are ranked in the order child A, child B, and child C.

The *experimental subject* is to order these children by I.Q. on the basis of their pictures.

Now, as a research question, we might inquire: If there is no true association between intelligence and appearance, what would be the chance of the subject's placing all three children in the proper rank position? In other words, if our subject does place them all correctly, is this a statistically impressive result in the sense that it would be expected to occur, say, less than 10 percent of the time by chance alone?

To answer this question we must arrive at the total number of arrangements possible. We notice that the first position can be filled by any of the three pictures, the second position by either of the two remaining pictures, and the third position by the single remaining picture. By enumeration the six possible arrangements are

$$ABC \quad BAC \quad CAB$$
$$ACB \quad BCA \quad CBA$$

More simply, by Rule I,

$$_nP_n = n!$$
$$_3P_3 = 3\cdot2\cdot1$$
$$= 6$$

The probability, then, of the subject's placing the photographs in the "correct" ABC order by chance alone would be

$$P(\text{ABC}) = \tfrac{1}{6} = 16.7\%$$

which is still not an impressive result. What is needed? The obvious answer is to include more photographs. Thus if four photographs were used, the total number of arrangements possible would be

$$_4P_4 = 4\cdot3\cdot2\cdot1 = 24$$

and the corresponding probability of getting all four placed correctly by chance alone is

$$P(\text{ABCD}) = \tfrac{1}{24} = 4.2\%$$

which would certainly be a statistically significant result by our above standard of 10 percent.

The second example of Rule I will demonstrate its use in cases where each possible result requires our attention.

In observing a small group therapy session, consisting of one counselor and three patients, one variable that we might find to be of clinical interest is the *order of arrival*. That is, the first patient to arrive might gain a sense of support from the counselor, whereas the last to arrive might feel "threatened" by being faced with the entire group.

In order to equalize this dimension, how many group sessions should be planned? From Rule I the total number of arrangements of arrival of the three patients is

$$_3P_3 = 3!$$

$$= 6$$

Thus it would be necessary to structure, through a receptionist or some other mechanism, six unique arrival orders. In this case each outcome point is important in its own right, independent of questions of probability.

There is a special case of Rule I that arises frequently enough to deserve our attention.

RULE 1   *Special Case*

Of the n objects let

n_1 of them be alike or indistinguishable

n_2 of them be alike or indistinguishable

$\vdots$

n_k of them be alike or indistinguishable

Then

$$_nP_n = \frac{n!}{n_1!\, n_2! \ldots n_k!} \tag{6}$$

This special case of Rule I is illustrated with the following experimental situation: Two experimental "stooges" are instructed to sit with a naïve subject on a bench and to pressure the subject into agreeing with them as part of a suggestibility study. Of interest is whether or not the seating arrangement of the stooges has any significant effect on the responses given by the subject. How many unique arrangements are possible if one treats the two stooges as alike or indistinguishable?

Placing subscripts on the notation a used to denote the stooges, we find that the total number of arrangements (from Rule I) is

$$_3P_3 = 3! = 6$$

These six may be enumerated as

(1) a_1a_2b	(3) a_1ba_2	(5) ba_1a_2
(2) a_2a_1b	(4) a_2ba_1	(6) ba_2a_1

However, since a_1 is indistinguishable from a_2, (1) and (2) are indistinguishable, as are (3) and (4) as well as (5) and (6). So there are really only three distinguishable arrangements.

By direct application of the special case of Rule I we have

$$_nP_n = \frac{n!}{n_1!\, n_2!\, \ldots\, n_k!}$$

$$_3P_3 = \frac{3!}{2!\, 1!} = 3$$

RULE 2

If out of n objects, r objects are to be arranged, the total number of possible arrangements is

$$_nP_r = \frac{n!}{(n-r)!} \qquad (7)$$

The reasoning behind this expression may be seen by noting that there are

n	possibilities for selecting the first object
$(n-1)$	possibilities for selecting the second object
$(n-2)$	possibilities for selecting the third object
$\vdots$	$\vdots$
$(n-r+1)$	possibilities for selecting the rth object

Thus the total number of possible arrangements of the r objects is

$$n(n-1)(n-2)\, \ldots\, (n-r+1)$$

which in turn is equal to

$$\frac{n(n-1)(n-2)\, \ldots\, (n-r+1)(n-r)(n-r-1)\, \ldots\, (1)}{(n-r)(n-r-1)\, \ldots\, (1)}$$

$$= \frac{n!}{(n-r)!}$$

For example, suppose that an industrial psychologist is asked to work out a sales strategy based on the inferred interests of prospective clients. The client's interests in four areas are ranked following an initial visit. These areas might be A, sports; B, politics; C, introverted interests; D, company problems.

The sales strategy is to be directed at the two strongest interests, in order of their strength. Thus if the inferred interests of a prospective client were ranked B, D, C, A, the desired sales strategy (BD) would center mainly on politics and secondly on company problems. Sports and introverted interests would be ignored. The question, of course, is how many strategies must the salesman carry in his arsenal?

There are four possibilities for the client's strongest interest. There are three possibilities for the client's second strongest interest—or a total of 12 situations that have to be met. Enumerated, the 12 sales strategies would be

AB, AC, AD, BA, BC, BD, CA, CB, CD, DA, DB, DC

More simply, from Rule II we have

$$_nP_r = \frac{n!}{(n-r)!}$$

$$_4P_2 = \frac{4!}{(4-2)!} = \frac{4!}{2!} = 12$$

RULE 3

If we wish to ignore the order or arrangement (i.e., interest pattern AB is the same as BA, CD the same as DC, etc. in the previous example) we work with *combinations* rather than *permutations*. The number of combinations of n objects taken r at a time is

$$_nC_r = \frac{n!}{(n-r)!\,r!} \tag{8}$$

The rationale for this expression is that for each group of r objects selected from the n objects there are $r!$ ways of ordering them. That is, in the above example, there are two ways of ordering AB, two ways of ordering AC, etc. Now the total number of possible arrangements $= _nP_r$, and since combinations ignore order we have

$$_nC_r = \frac{_nP_r}{r!} = \frac{n!}{(n-r)!\,r!} = \frac{n!}{(n-r)!\,r!}$$

For example, consider selecting two of three individuals for some purpose such that the order of selection of the two individuals is of no importance. That is, $n = 3$ and $r = 2$. The total number of arrangements is

$$_3P_2 = \frac{3!}{(3-2)!} = 6$$

Enumerated, these arrangements are

(1) AB   (3) AC   (5) BC

(2) BA   (4) CA   (6) CB

However, if we ignore order, (1) and (2) become the same, as do (3) and (4), as well as (5) and (6). Thus there are only three combinations.

More simply, by Rule III we have

$$_nC_r = \frac{n!}{(n-r)!\,r!}$$

$$_3C_2 = \frac{3!}{(3-2)!\,2!}$$

$$= 3$$

With these "building blocks" we are now able, in the next chapter, to study the widely used *binomial distribution* and the *chi-square goodness of fit test* for analyzing categorical responses.

SUMMARY

This chapter has presented some of the fundamentals underlying experimentation with categorical responses. The first is a *formal statement of a basis for probability appropriate for categorical data* including the fundamental experiment, meaningful outcomes, definition of events, and definitions of probability. The second involves joint events to answer the question: What is the chance of some later event's happening given that an earlier event has already happened? Here a distinction is made between independent and dependent events and also between mutually exclusive and nonmutually exclusive events. Finally, combinatorial analysis is introduced in order that the number of possible outcomes in more complex situations can be determined. General rules are discussed which deal with permutations and combinations. The formulas and rules for joint events and combinatorial analysis are

$$P(E_1E_2) = P(E_1)P(E_2) \tag{1}$$

$$P(E_1E_2) = P(E_1)P(E_2 \mid E_1) \tag{2}$$

$$P(E_1 + E_2) = P(E_1) + P(E_2) \tag{3}$$

$$P(E_1 + E_2) = P(E_1) + P(E_2) - P(E_1E_2) \tag{4}$$

$$_nP_n = n! \tag{5}$$

$$_nP_n = \frac{n!}{n_1!\,n_2!\,\ldots\,n_k!} \tag{6}$$

$$_nP_r = \frac{n!}{(n-r)!} \qquad\qquad (7)$$

$$_nC_r = \frac{n!}{(n-r)!\,r!} \qquad\qquad (8)$$

Additional new terms and expressions encountered in this chapter include:

Mutually exclusive and exhaustive outcomes
Sample space
Particular set of outcome points
Equally likely outcome points
Relative frequency
$P(E_2 \mid E_1)$
$P(E_2 \mid E_1) = P(E_1)$
$P(E_2 \mid E_1) \neq P(E_1)$
Euler or Venn diagram
Indistinguishable objects

$$_nC_r = \frac{_nP_r}{r!}$$

REVIEW QUESTIONS

1   What is one strength in statistical techniques designed for categorical data?

2   In our formal statement of a basis for probability we first describe (or take as known) a fundamental experiment and also the _____ .

3   The set of all possible "outcome points" in an experiment is known as the _____ _____ of the experiment.

4   If an individual case is either in E_1 or E_2 (but not in both), E_1 and E_2 are said to be _____ _____ .

5   In probability problems, how is an *event* defined?

6   If we assume equally likely outcome points in an experiment, how is the *probability of an event E* defined?

7   Assume that an animal may choose any of four equally likely paths labeled A, B, C, D. Consider a *single* trial and let E be the event of choosing path A.

    (a) Describe **s**.   ------
    (b) What is n?   ------
    (c) What is h?   ------
    (d) What is $p(E)$?   ------

8   *Fundamental experiment:* A company may hire or not hire each of two applicants. Let E be the event of choosing one or the other or both.

$$n = \text{------} , \qquad h = \text{------}$$

9   *Fundamental experiment:* A subject may or may not be given a drug. He may also be housed in one of six wards. Let E be the event of a subject's being given a drug and coming from an even-numbered ward.

$$n = \text{------} , \qquad h = \text{------}$$

10   *Fundamental experiment:* A family may be classified into one of six sociological categories for both *income* and *number of children*. Let E be the event of being in the lowest income category.

$$n = \text{------} , \qquad h = \text{------}$$

11   In order to use the definition of probability, $P(E) = (h/n)$ for each of the above events, what assumption is necessary for each of the outcome points in **s**?

12   What might be an alternative approach to establishing the probabilities for each of the points in **s**?

13   In order that $P(E_2 \mid E_1) = P(E_2)$, what must be true about the events E_1 and E_2?

14   If E_1 has no effect on E_2, $P(E_1E_2) = \text{------}$.

15   If E_1 and E_2 are dependent events, $P(E_1E_2) = \text{------}$.

16   If $P(E_1 + E_2) = P(E_1) + P(E_2)$, E_1 and E_2 are said to be ------ .

17   If E_1 and E_2 can occur together, $P(E_1 + E_2) = \text{------}$.

18   For so-called mutually exclusive events $P(E_1E_2) = \text{------}$.

19   In obtaining the probabilities for complex events the enumeration of the outcome points is tedious. Therefore we turn to ------ analysis.

20   The total number of possible arrangements for n outcomes out of a possible n points is _____.

21   $_3P_3 =$ _____ .

22   $_4P_4$ (where two objects of one kind are indistinguishable and two objects of another kind are indistinguishable) $=$ _____ .

23   For four objects, how many possible arrangements are there for selecting three objects?

24   In general, $_nP_r =$ _____ .

25   How many *combinations* of two subjects are possible from a total of five subjects?

26   What is the mathematical relationship among $_nC_r$ and $_nP_r$ and $r!$?

CHAPTER 5

THE BINOMIAL AND
CHI-SQUARE
DISTRIBUTIONS

Two of the most widely used techniques for analyzing categorical information are those for the *binomial distribution* and the *chi-square goodness of fit
test*. Using the results of the last chapter as a basis, we now turn to the
problem of structuring behavioral inquiries for the appropriate application
of these techniques. We shall first consider the binomial distribution.

BINOMIAL DISTRIBUTION

The binomial distribution is extremely useful for analyzing responses that
are classified into two and only two categories. It is common practice to
designate one of the two categories as a "success" and the other as a
"failure." The arbitrary nature of the designations success and failure is
illustrated by the following individual dichotomous responses:

Success	*Failure*
Member of a civic club	Not a civic club member
Opposing a particular political candidate	Favoring the candidate
Receiving clinical counseling	Not receiving clinical counseling

It is clear that the list of such dichotomous responses is endless and that the
determination of which category is designated as success and which as
failure is an arbitrary decision on the part of the investigator.

Under certain assumptions about the nature of the categories, the
binomial distribution gives the probability of observing a specified number
of successes in a sample of responses. As we shall see, this knowledge, in
turn, permits us not only to anticipate the likelihood of a particular sample
result, but also to test the reasonableness of basic hypotheses made about
the population of interest. The *assumptions* underlying the binomial distribution are

1. All of the observations are independent of one another. That is, a "success" or "failure" classification of one response in no way influences the classification of any other response as a success or failure.

2. The probability of being classified as a "success" is identical for all the responses in the study.

As an example of these two assumptions, suppose that several subjects were to participate in the experiment mentioned in Chapter 4 concerning the guessing of the proper button. Recall that there were five buttons, three square ones and two round ones. Here success could be defined as the selection of the one proper button, failure as the selection of any of the other four buttons. Clearly, assumption 1 is reasonable, since the chance of any given subject's being successful in guessing the proper button would not affect the chance of any other subject's being successful. Furthermore, assumption 2 is satisfied, since the probability of a successful event, which was shown to be

$$P(\text{success}) = \tfrac{1}{5}$$

for any subject, is clearly the same for each and every participating subject. The binomial distribution may therefore be used to calculate the probability of observing a specified number of successful guesses in any sample of participating subjects. Thus we could find the chance of, say, eight subjects out of a sample of ten guessing the proper button.

There are various inquiries in the field of human behavior which can be similarly structured in accordance with the assumptions underlying the use of the binomial distribution.

DEFINITION   *Binomial Formula*

The probability of observing exactly x successes out of a sample of n independent observations (each with the same probability p of being classified in the success category) is given by the following expression:

$$P(x) = \frac{n!}{(n-x)!\,x!}\, p^x q^{n-x}$$

where $q = (1 - p)$.

Table III of Appendix A gives $P(x)$ for various values of n and p.

The rationale of the binomial formula may be seen as follows: Consider n independent observations ($O_1, O_2, \ldots, O_n$), each with a probability of success of p and probability of failure of $q = 1 - p$. That is,

Success	*Failure*
$P(O_1) = p$	$P(O_1) = 1 - p = q$
$P(O_2) = p$	$P(O_2) = 1 - p = q$
$\vdots$	$\vdots$
$P(O_n) = p$	$P(O_n) = 1 - p = q$

For the n independent observations we first determine the probability of obtaining x consecutive successes followed by $n - x$ consecutive failures. Since the observations are independent, we use an extension of formula (1) of Chapter 4 to obtain this probability, namely

$$\underbrace{p \cdot p \cdot p \ldots p}_{\substack{x \text{ of these} \\ \text{probabilities}}}\underbrace{qqq \ldots q}_{\substack{(n - x) \text{ of} \\ \text{these prob-} \\ \text{abilities}}}$$

More concisely, this probability may be written as

$$p^x q^{n-x}$$

Now the probability of obtaining precisely x successes and $n - x$ failures in some other order of occurrence is the same as for this particular order. This is because the p's and q's would merely be rearranged to correspond to the other order, e.g.,

$$ppppqqqq = ppqppqqq$$

and likewise for all other possible arrangements of the p's and q's.

Next, we calculate the total number of possible arrangements of the n observations, where x of them are alike (the p's) and $(n - x)$ of them are alike (the q's). This is a direct application of the special case of Rule I of Chapter 4; i.e.,

$$_nP_n = \frac{n!}{n_1! \, n_2!}$$

$$= \frac{n!}{(n - x)! \, x!}$$

which is the total number of possible arrangements.

We notice that all of the possible arrangements of the p's and q's are mutually exclusive. That is, if we observe one sequence of successes and failures, we cannot simultaneously observe some other sequence. Furthermore, any of the mutually exclusive sequences satisfies the conditions of the original question. Therefore, by the extension of formula (3) of Chapter 4 it is necessary to add

$$p^x q^{n-x}$$

as many times as there are different orders in which the desired result can occur. Thus the desired probability becomes

$$\frac{n!}{(n-x)!\,x!}\,p^x q^{n-x}$$

which again is the probability of exactly x successes out of n observations.

The resulting probability distribution for all possible x values is called the *binomial* or *Bernoulli distribution* because of its relationship to the binomial expansion; i.e.,

$$(q+p)^n = q^n + nq^{n-1}p + \frac{n(n-1)}{2}\,q^{n-2}p^2 + \cdots + p^n$$

$$= \sum_{x=0}^{n} \frac{n!}{x!\,(n-x)!}\,p^x q^{n-x}$$

The binomial formula aids behavioral inquiries in two ways. First, it permits us to anticipate the likelihood of a particular sample result. Second, it provides a test of the reasonableness of a basic assumption made about the population of interest. We shall now consider these two types of applications for the binomial formula.

DETERMINING THE LIKELIHOOD OF A PARTICULAR SAMPLE RESULT

The general structure for inquiries of this type is that the probability p of success on each observation is given or fixed and therefore not to be questioned (that is, "tested").* Using this given value of p, we compute from the binomial formula the probability of a specified number of successes in a sample of observations. Decisions are then made on the basis of this sample result.

As an illustration of the efficiency of the binomial formula for this type of inquiry consider the following examples.

---

* The classical "honest" coin tossing and "honest" die rolling problems are of this type, with the unquestioned values of p taken as $\frac{1}{2}$ and $\frac{1}{6}$, respectively.

EXAMPLE 1

If there are five true/false questions on a quiz, what is the chance of getting them all correct by guessing? Of getting four correct? Of three? Of two? Of one? Of none correct by guessing alone? If we let

$$C = \text{a correct answer}$$

$$W = \text{a wrong answer}$$

and answer these questions directly from the formal statement of probability given in Chapter 4, the sample space would be as shown in Table 5.1.

TABLE 5.1   SAMPLE SPACE FOR A FIVE-QUESTION TRUE/FALSE QUIZ

None correct	*One correct*	*Two correct*	*Three correct*	*Four correct*	*Five correct*
WWWWW	CWWWW	CCWWW	CCCWW	CCCCW	CCCCC
	WCWWW	CWCWW	CCWCW	CCCWC	
	WWCWW	CWWCW	CWCCW	CCWCC	
	WWWCW	CWWWC	WCCCW	CWCCC	
	WWWWC	WCCWW	CCWWC	WCCCC	
		WCWCW	CWCWC		
		WCWWC	WCCWC		
		WWCCW	CWWCC		
		WWCWC	WCWCC		
		WWWCC	WWCCC		

From the 32 possible outcome points in the sample space we can evaluate the probability of each of the events in question; namely, five correct, four correct, three correct, two correct, one correct, and none correct. From the basic definition of the probability of an event E, that is,

$$P(E) = \frac{h}{n}$$

these probabilities are, from Table 5.1, seen to be

$$P(5) = \tfrac{1}{32}, \qquad P(4) = \tfrac{5}{32}, \qquad P(3) = \tfrac{10}{32},$$

$$P(2) = \tfrac{10}{32}, \qquad P(1) = \tfrac{5}{32}, \qquad P(0) = \tfrac{1}{32}$$

Fortunately, however, this relatively tedious approach may be avoided by using the binomial formula. In this case it is clear that

$p = \tfrac{1}{2}$ (the chance of success on each question or response)

$n = 5$ (the total number of questions or responses)

and

$$x = 5, 4, 3, 2, 1, \text{ or } 0$$

depending on the particular question asked.

Thus the probability of getting all five correct by guessing is, from

$$P(x) = \frac{n!}{(n-x)!\,x!}\, p^x q^{n-x}$$

equal to

$$P(5) = \frac{5!}{0!\,5!} \left(\frac{1}{2}\right)^5 \left(\frac{1}{2}\right)^0$$

$$= (1)\left(\tfrac{1}{32}\right)(1)$$

$$= \tfrac{1}{32} = 0.031$$

which is the same as the probability obtained from the application of the formal statement of the basis for probability. Likewise,

$$P(4) = \frac{5!}{1!\,4!} \left(\frac{1}{2}\right)^4 \left(\frac{1}{2}\right)^1 = \frac{5}{32} = 0.156$$

$$P(3) = \frac{5!}{2!\,3!} \left(\frac{1}{2}\right)^3 \left(\frac{1}{2}\right)^2 = \frac{10}{32} = 0.312$$

$$P(2) = \frac{5!}{3!\,2!} \left(\frac{1}{2}\right)^2 \left(\frac{1}{2}\right)^3 = \frac{10}{32} = 0.312$$

$$P(1) = \frac{5!}{4!\,1!} \left(\frac{1}{2}\right)^1 \left(\frac{1}{2}\right)^4 = \frac{5}{32} = 0.156$$

$$P(0) = \frac{5!}{5!\,0!} \left(\frac{1}{2}\right)^0 \left(\frac{1}{2}\right)^5 = \frac{1}{32} = 0.031$$

Notice the ease with which these results may be directly obtained from Table III of Appendix A. The efficiency and simplicity of the binomial formula could be further appreciated by attempting to construct a sample space for, say, a ten-question quiz.

As a slightly more complicated case, consider the question: What is the chance of getting at least two questions correct by guessing? The conditions of this question are met, then, by getting five, four, three, or two questions correct. Since the probability is 1 (that is, it is certain to occur) that 0, 1, 2, 3, 4, or 5 will be correct and since the various possible results are mutually exclusive, the answer is simply

$$P \text{ (at least two correct)} = 1 - [P(0) + P(1)]$$

$$= 1 - [0.031 + 0.156]$$

$$= 0.813$$

EXAMPLE 2

Suppose that in a research study on the effects of fatigue on driving precision it was observed that for a group of drivers, after 18 consecutive hours on a test track, the proportion of drivers crossing over the center line in any one "stretch drive" was $\frac{1}{5}$. The "stretch drive" is a predetermined length of the test track.

From these data, what would be the probability of such a driver's never crossing over the center line in six independent "stretch drives"? Here

$p = \frac{1}{5}$ (using a relative frequency definition of probability)

$n = 6$

$x = 0$

Thus

$$P(0) = \frac{6!}{6!\,0!}\left(\frac{1}{5}\right)^0\left(\frac{4}{5}\right)^6$$

$$= 0.262$$

The impressiveness of this sample result is a matter of interpretation for the investigator.

EXAMPLE 3

What is the chance of getting at least two direct hits on a bombing mission in making 15 independent runs, if the probability of a hit on any single run is *given* as $\frac{1}{10}$? Here

$$p = \frac{1}{10}$$

$$n = 15$$

$$x = 2 \text{ or more hits}$$

Thus

$$P \text{ (at least two hits)} = 1 - [P(0) + P(1)]$$

where from Table III of Appendix A we have

$$P(0) = \frac{15!}{15!\,0!}\left(\frac{1}{10}\right)^0\left(\frac{9}{10}\right)^{15} = 0.206$$

$$P(1) = \frac{15!}{14!\,1!}\left(\frac{1}{10}\right)^1\left(\frac{9}{10}\right)^{14} = 0.343$$

Therefore

$$P \text{ (at least two hits)} = 1 - (0.206 + 0.343)$$

$$= 0.451$$

From this result various decisions might be made, such as to take about a 55 percent chance that the target will not be destroyed if it is estimated that two hits are required for such a purpose; to increase the number of "runs" to improve the chances of a hit; or perhaps to improve the intelligence information to increase the given value of p.

The second general use of the binomial formula will be considered next.

TESTING THE REASONABLENESS OF BASIC ASSUMPTIONS ABOUT THE POPULATION OF INTEREST

The general structure for inquiries of this type is that the probability p of success on each observation is only hypothesized and is therefore open to question. For example, it might be hypothesized that:

A group of individuals is evenly split on a political issue, in which case the probability of randomly selecting an individual favoring the issue is hypothesized to be $\frac{1}{2}$.

There is no tendency for preschool children to prefer one color over another, in which case the probability of such a child selecting a red object from a choice of four colors is hypothesized to be $\frac{1}{4}$.

In order to test hypotheses such as these, a sample is drawn, and on the basis of the sample results the hypothesized value of p is either accepted or rejected as being a "reasonable" value.

DEFINITION *Level of Significance*

By "reasonable" we mean that our observed sample result could be expected to occur more than a small percentage of the time if, in fact, p were the actual probability underlying the population. The exact percentage is normally placed at one, five, or infrequently ten percent. The selected percentage level is called the *level of significance* and is symbolically written as α (alpha). Thus we might have $\alpha = 1$ percent, 5 percent, or 10 percent (more commonly expressed $\alpha = 0.01$, 0.05, or 0.10 respectively).

If, on the other hand, we observe a sample result that could be expected less than α percent of the time from such a population, we tend to cast doubt on (that is, "reject") our original hypothesis about p. As an illustration, Gourevitch (1965) poses the following situation:

In a study of color preferences among pre-school children, each child is given three trials in which he is asked to choose among four objects which are identical except for color. One of the objects is red, one blue, one yellow and one green, and the order of the objects from right to left is changed on successive trials.

Suppose that our hypothesis is that there is no color preference among such children. That is, we hypothesize that the probability p of selecting any given color on a particular trial is $\frac{1}{4}$. Suppose, further, that a child chooses red on all three trials. Is there any reason to doubt the original hypothesis on the basis of the evidence? Let the level of significance be fixed at five percent (i.e., $\alpha = 0.05$).

Here we define "success" as the selection of a red object. Therefore,

$p = \frac{1}{4}$ (probability of success under our hypothesis)
$n = 3$ (number of independent trials)
$x = 3$ (the number of successes actually observed in our sample)

Thus the probability of observing what we did in our sample, under our hypothesized value of p, is

$$P(3) = \frac{3!}{0!\,3!}\left(\frac{1}{4}\right)^3\left(\frac{3}{4}\right)^0$$

$$= 0.016$$

The event, then, of observing all three trials' resulting in red selections is rather unlikely (although possible) under our assumption about p.

Now either of two possibilities exists: either the population value of p is $\frac{1}{4}$ and we just happened to observe an unusual sample, *or* the population value of p is not really $\frac{1}{4}$. We would normally take the latter course and reject our original hypothesis about p. We must realize, of course, that we could expect incorrectly to reject our original hypothesis 1.6 percent of the time in repeated experiments of this sort. Our conclusion would be, therefore, that since 0.016 is less than α (if $\alpha = 0.05$), we can no longer maintain our faith, on the basis of the data, in the assumption that no color preference exists.

The essential thing to remember is that we are using a particular sample result to make a judgment concerning the "true" population parameter p. Of course, every sample will not lead us to the same result, since there is a *distribution of possible sample results.*

The final aspect of structuring this type of inquiry, based on the sampling distribution of the number of successes, has to do with our interest in which direction the actual value of p might be from the hypothesized value of p.

In one situation, we might be interested in only the alternative possibility that individuals are actually more likely to succeed (following an experimental effort) than the hypothesized value of p would lead us to believe. Or, in another situation, we might be interested in verifying a suspicion (based on our subject matter intuition) that they are actually less likely to succeed. For example,

> Following an intensive poverty area nursery school program, we might limit our interest to the question of whether or not the chance of the participating children achieving successful scores on a reading readiness test has been significantly increased over the chance for such children in general.

> Following a neighborhood "Big Brother" program, we might wish to detect whether the chance of fatherless boys' being classified as delinquent has been significantly decreased below the chance for such boys in general.

Tests structured to answer these kinds of inquiries are termed *unidirectional tests*. Here our investigation is such that if the hypothesized value of p could not reasonably give rise to our sample result, the only alternative of interest concerns actual values of p lying in a predetermined direction from the hypothesized value.

In contrast, consider the following situations:

> A mechanized, computer-based reading program is to be installed in a school. We might be uncertain whether the chance of a successful reading performance of the participating children will be better or worse than for children in general.

> A recent news release has involved a particular political candidate. Prior to the news release it was assumed that the voters were evenly split between this candidate and another one. We are uncertain whether the popularity of the candidate is higher or lower than before the news release.

Tests structured to answer these kinds of inquiries are termed *bidirectional tests*. That is, if the hypothesized value of p could not reasonably give rise to our sample result, the actual value of p might logically lie in either direction from the hypothesized value. In this type of situation we wish to detect a significant difference regardless of the direction of the difference.

The distinction, then, between unidirectional and bidirectional tests is that in unidirectional tests our interest is restricted, even before the data is collected, to actual values of p lying on only *one* side of the hypothesized value. In bidirectional tests we are concerned about actual values of p being on *either* side of the hypothesized value.

As will be seen from the following illustration, α, the level of significance, is correspondingly either assigned entirely to the predetermined direction of interest or it is divided between the two directions that the actual value of p might be from the hypothesized value.

_____ **EXAMPLE 1**   (*Bidirectional Test*)

It is hypothesized that a particular group of individuals is evenly split on some political issue. On the basis of a sample of ten individuals what should be our decision rule concerning our hypothesized value of $p = \frac{1}{2}$? First we examine the probability of observing every possible result under the hypothesized value of p. That is, we examine the complete distribution of possible sample results x, assuming the hypothesized value of the population parameter p. In this case

$p = \frac{1}{2}$ (probability of an individual's favoring the issue)
$n = 10$
$x = 0, 1, 2, 3, 4, 5, 6, 7, 8, 9, 10$

All of the possible sampling distribution results are given in Table 5.2.

TABLE 5.2   **BINOMIAL PROBABILITIES FOR $n = 10, p = \frac{1}{2}$**
                           (TAKEN FROM TABLE III OF APPENDIX A)

$$P(0)\ \ = 0.001$$
$$P(1)\ \ = 0.010$$
$$P(2)\ \ = 0.044$$
$$P(3)\ \ = 0.117$$
$$P(4)\ \ = 0.205$$
$$P(5)\ \ = 0.246$$
$$P(6)\ \ = 0.205$$
$$P(7)\ \ = 0.117$$
$$P(8)\ \ = 0.044$$
$$P(9)\ \ = 0.010$$
$$P(10) = 0.001$$

Assuming that we have no a priori basis for suspecting that the actual value of p is either above or below $\frac{1}{2}$, we shall reject our hypothesized value of $p = \frac{1}{2}$ if either too many in our sample favor the issue or too many oppose it. Further assume that the opinions held by the individuals are independent of each other. Let the desired level of significance α be as close to 0.10 as is possible with a sample of size 10.

Now if we were to observe in a particular sample that none of the ten individuals favored the issue, we see from Table 5.2 that

$$P(0) = 0.001$$

which certainly would lead us to reject the hypothesis that $p = \frac{1}{2}$. That is, 0.001 is less than $\alpha = 0.10$. Likewise, if we observe ten out of the ten favoring the issue, we see from Table 5.2 that

$$P(10) = 0.001$$

which also would lead us to reject our assumption that $p = \frac{1}{2}$.

Proceeding in this fashion, we see that since the outcomes are mutually exclusive,

$$P(0) + P(1) + P(2) + P(8) + P(9) + P(10)$$
$$= 0.001 + 0.010 + 0.044 + 0.044 + 0.010 + 0.001$$
$$= 0.110$$

which is as close as we can come, with a sample size of 10, to our desired 0.10 level of significance. Actually, in this case, we would be working at an 0.11 level of significance.

Thus our decision rule would be: If we observe 0, 1, 2, 8, 9, or 10 favoring responses in our sample of ten responses, we would have observed an unusual result if in fact p were $\frac{1}{2}$. Therefore, our decision would be to reject our original hypothesis that $p = \frac{1}{2}$ and accept the alternative hypothesis that $p \neq \frac{1}{2}$. That is, there would be some evidence, based on the sampling distribution of x, to doubt the conjecture that the group is evenly split over the political issue.

Such a decision rule is called *bidirectional* because we are guarding against the actual value of p's being on either side of $\frac{1}{2}$.

EXAMPLE 2   *(Unidirectional Test)*

On the other hand, suppose that an intensive campaign has been launched in favor of the political issue. In this case we are not worried about the actual value of p's dropping below $\frac{1}{2}$. The only question of interest is whether or not the actual value of p has become significantly greater than $\frac{1}{2}$ (i.e., $p > \frac{1}{2}$). Let the desired level of significance α, in this case, be as close to 0.05 as is possible with a sample of size 10. Remember that the exact choice for α is arbitrary, although it is usually set at 0.01, 0.05, or infrequently at 0.10.

From an inspection of Table 5.2, we see that we shall be impressed if we observe 8, 9, or 10, since the chance of any of these mutually exclusive sample results' occurring when $p = \frac{1}{2}$ is

$$P(8) + P(9) + P(10) = 0.044 + 0.010 + 0.001$$
$$= 0.055$$

which is again as close as we can come, with a sample size of 10, to our desired 0.05 level. Our actual level of significance would be, in this case, 0.055. Notice that we did not include 7 since

$$P(7) = 0.117$$

which would, had we included it, put us far above the agreed-upon level of significance of 0.05.

Such a decision rule is called *unidirectional* because we are guarding only against the possibility of p's being on one side of $\frac{1}{2}$.

FORMAL HYPOTHESIS TESTING PROCEDURE FOR THE BINOMIAL DISTRIBUTION

The approach we have just outlined for accepting or rejecting the hypothesized value of p has been formalized into a seven-step procedure. In order to help clarify the formal procedure, the above examples are restated in terms of the seven steps.

Step 1 / STATE THE HYPOTHESIS

> Here the specific hypothesis under question and the alternative hypothesis are specifically stated. The hypothesized value of p is referred to as the *null* hypothesis, because we are conjecturing that there is no difference between our sample result and what we could reasonably expect if the hypothesis were in fact true. The *null* hypothesis is symbolically written as H_0.

<table>
<tr><td>*Example 1*
Bidirectional</td><td>*Example 2*
Unidirectional</td></tr>
<tr><td>$H_0: p = \frac{1}{2}$</td><td>$H_0: p = \frac{1}{2}$</td></tr>
</table>

> The *alternative* hypothesis is the one to be accepted if the null hypothesis H_0 is unreasonable in the light of our sample evidence. The alternative hypothesis is symbolically written as H_1.

<table>
<tr><td>*Example 1*
Bidirectional</td><td>*Example 2*
Unidirectional</td></tr>
<tr><td>$H_1: p \neq \frac{1}{2}$</td><td>$H_1: p > \frac{1}{2}$</td></tr>
</table>

Step 2 / STATE THE LEVEL OF SIGNIFICANCE α

> Here we state the risk that we are willing to take in rejecting the null hypothesis H_0 when in fact H_0 is true and we merely happened to observe an unusual, but nevertheless possible, sample result. You might ask why we should take any risk at all. Why not set $\alpha = 0$? This question will be discussed in Chapter 14. At this point, suffice it to say that widely used, workable levels of significance have been achieved by setting $\alpha = 0.01$, 0.05, or 0.10. With samples as small as ten the exact desired value of α is not possible. The values of α actually obtainable are indicated below for each of the examples.

Example 1   *Example 2*

Desired Levels of Significance

$\alpha = 0.10$ $\alpha = 0.05$

Actual Levels of Significance

$\alpha = 0.11$ $\alpha = 0.055$

Step 3 / STATE THE TEST STATISTIC

Here the statistic that we compute from our sample data is the number of successes. This is labeled x. Thus the test statistic is

x = number of successes observed out of n trials.

In this case n is 10.

Example 1   *Example 2*

x out of 10 x out of 10

Step 4 / SPECIFY THE SAMPLING DISTRIBUTION OF THE TEST STATISTIC

Here we are concerned with the binomial distribution. Therefore, x is distributed according to the binomial expression

$$P(x) = \frac{n!}{(n-x)!\,x!}\, p^x q^{n-x}$$

which is tabled in Table III of Appendix A for various values of p and n. Again in this case, $n = 10$, $p = \frac{1}{2}$, and $x = 0, 1, 2, 3, 4, 5, 6, 7, 8, 9,$ or 10.

Example 1   *Example 2*

Binomial distribution   Binomial distribution

Step 5 / SELECT THE REJECTION REGION

Here we make our decision as to which values of x would be so unusual to observe in our sample that we no longer could reasonably maintain our belief in the hypothesized value of p. The *rejection region* depends on both the alternative hypothesis and the level of significance.

Example 1   *Example 2*

$x = 0, 1, 2, 8, 9, 10$ $x = 8, 9, 10$

Step 6 / COMPUTE THE TEST STATISTIC

Here we evaluate the specified test statistic for our sample data. In this case we merely observe x, the number of successes observed out of n trials.

Example 1	*Example 2*
$x = \dfrac{0, 1, 2, 3, 4, 5, 6,}{7, 8, 9, \text{ or } 10}$	$x = \dfrac{0, 1, 2, 3, 4, 5, 6,}{7, 8, 9, \text{ or } 10}$

Step 7 / ACCEPT OR REJECT THE NULL HYPOTHESIS

The final step in the formal hypothesis testing procedure is to see if the computed test statistic of Step 6 falls in the specified rejection region of Step 5. If it does, we reject H_0 and accept the corresponding H_1. If it does not, we accept H_0.

Example 1	*Example 2*
If $x = 0, 1, 2, 8, 9,$ or 10	If $x = 8, 9,$ or 10
Reject H_0: $p = \frac{1}{2}$	Reject H_0: $p = \frac{1}{2}$
and	and
Accept H_1: $p \neq \frac{1}{2}$	Accept H_1: $p > \frac{1}{2}$
If $x = 3, 4, 5, 6, 7$	If $x = 0, 1, 2, 3, 4, 5, 6,$ or 7
Accept H_0: $p = \frac{1}{2}$	Accept H_0: $p = \frac{1}{2}$

This seven-step procedure, i.e.,

1. State the hypothesis.
2. State the level of significance α.
3. State the test statistic.
4. Specify the sampling distribution of the test statistic.
5. Select the rejection region.
6. Compute the test statistic.
7. Accept or reject the null hypothesis.

is quite general throughout the field of statistical hypothesis testing for both categorical and metric data; it is one to which we shall return repeatedly in the remaining chapters on structuring inquiries.

COMPUTATIONAL PROBLEMS IN EVALUATING THE BINOMIAL FORMULA

As the sample size increases, the computational aspects of the binomial distribution increase to a discouraging degree. However, there are, fortunately, computational aids available. First of all, tables, such as Table III of Appendix A, are available for evaluating the binomial formula. Second, there are approximations available which, under certain conditions, provide excellent substitutes for the direct application of the binomial distribution. One of these, the normal approximation, will be discussed in Chapter 14. At any rate, the computational problems should remain secondary to the problem of structuring inquiries for the legitimate application of the binomial formula.

MAXIMUM LIKELIHOOD AND THE BINOMIAL DISTRIBUTION

Suppose, in the example concerning opinions toward the political issue, that the problem is not either to accept or reject H_0: $p = \frac{1}{2} = 0.50$, as indicated in Examples 1 and 2. Suppose, instead, that the problem is to decide between two null hypotheses, e.g., H_0: $p = 0.50$ and H_0: $p = 0.40$. Our question becomes: On the basis of our sample data, is it more likely that our sample came from a population with a $p = 0.50$, or is it more likely that it came from a population with a $p = 0.40$?

Specifically, suppose that a sample of ten responses, in the above example, yielded seven favoring opinions. Is it more likely that $p = 0.50$ or that $p = 0.40$? If p were 0.50, the probability of observing seven successes would be, from Table III of Appendix A,

$$P(7) = 0.117$$

On the other hand, if p were 0.40, the probability of observing seven successes would be

$$P(7) = 0.042$$

Thus our observed sample result is more likely under the first hypothesis (i.e., H_0: $p = 0.50$) than it is under the second hypothesis (i.e., H_0: $p = 0.40$). Therefore, on the basis of the available evidence, it is more probable that the value of p underlying the population from which our sample came is 0.50 rather than 0.40. This approach is known generally as the *maximum likelihood method* of selecting one of several hypotheses.

THE CASE OF SEVERAL CATEGORIES

A common inquiry concerning categorical information involves an extension of the dichotomous classifications "success" and "failure" underlying the binomial formula. Instead of only two mutually exclusive categories, we might be interested in the same two questions as before, namely, determining the likelihood of a particular sample result, or testing the reasonableness of a basic assumption about the population of interest, where we are dealing with several such mutually exclusive categories. For multiple classifications these two questions are approached with techniques involving the *multinomial formula* and the *chi-square goodness of fit test*, respectively.

THE MULTINOMIAL FORMULA

The basic rationale underlying the use of the binomial formula in determining the likelihood of a particular sample result has been generalized to situations involving more than two categories of responses. The generalization is known as the multinomial formula.

DEFINITION *Multinomial Formula*

If events $E_1, E_2, \ldots, E_k$ are mutually exclusive and exhaustive and can occur with probabilities $p_1, p_2, \ldots, p_k$, respectively, the probability that

$$E_1 \text{ will occur } x_1 \text{ times}$$

and

$$E_2 \text{ will occur } x_2 \text{ times}$$

and

$$\vdots$$

$$E_k \text{ will occur } x_k \text{ times}$$

out of N independent responses is given by the following multinomial expression:

$$\frac{N!}{x_1!\, x_2! \ldots x_k!}\, p_1^{x_1} p_2^{x_2} \ldots p_k^{x_k}$$

where $x_1 + x_2 + \cdots + x_k = N$.

The rationale underlying the multinomial formula may be seen as follows: One particular outcome of N independent responses constituting a successful set is (in order of occurrence):

$$\overbrace{E_1 E_1 \ldots E_1}^{x_1 \text{ of these}}\ \overbrace{E_2 E_2 \ldots E_2}^{x_2 \text{ of these}} \ldots \overbrace{E_k E_k \ldots E_k}^{x_k \text{ of these}}$$

The probability of observing this particular outcome for the N independent responses may be obtained from the extension of the formula for the probability of the joint occurrence of two independent events, namely,

$$\overbrace{p_1 p_1 \ldots p_1}^{x_1 \text{ of these}}\ \overbrace{p_2 p_2 \ldots p_2}^{x_2 \text{ of these}} \ldots \overbrace{p_k p_k \ldots p_k}^{x_k \text{ of these}} = p_1^{x_1} p_2^{x_2} \ldots p_k^{x_k}$$

Clearly, there are several other outcomes of the N independent responses which also constitute a successful set. For example,

$$\overbrace{E_2 E_2 \ldots E_2}^{x_2 \text{ of these}} \quad \overbrace{E_1 E_1 \ldots E_1}^{x_1 \text{ of these}} \quad \ldots \quad \overbrace{E_k E_k \ldots E_k}^{x_k \text{ of these}}$$

and

$$\overbrace{E_2 E_2 \ldots E_2}^{x_2 \text{ of these}} \quad \overbrace{E_k E_k \ldots E_k}^{x_k \text{ of these}} \quad \ldots \quad \overbrace{E_1 E_1 \ldots E_1}^{x_1 \text{ of these}}$$

are but two other such successful sets. The question, then, is how many such sets are possible? Our answer may be obtained from the special case of Rule I concerning the total number of permutations possible, where certain outcomes are indistinguishable from others.

In our case all of the E_1's are indistinguishable from one another, as are the E_2's, the E_3's, ... etc. Therefore, applying the special case of Rule I given in Chapter 4, we have

$$_N P_N = \frac{N!}{x_1! \, x_2! \, \ldots \, x_k!}$$

Finally, it is clear that the various possible sets are mutually exclusive, since if we observe one set we cannot, at the same time, observe any other set. Therefore, applying an extension of the rule for the probability of occurrence of either of two mutually exclusive events, we arrive at the multinomial expression

$$\frac{N!}{x_1! \, x_2! \, \ldots \, x_k!} p_1^{x_1} p_2^{x_2} \ldots p_k^{x_k}$$

As an example, consider the following situation: A city is divided into *four* sections: A, B, C, D. Based on the census data, the probability of a voting citizen's coming from these areas (assuming the relative frequency definition of probability) is

Area	Given probability of coming from the specified area
A	0.20
B	0.30
C	0.40
D	0.10
	1.00

That is, 20 percent of the voting citizens are from area A, 30 percent from area B, 40 percent from C, and 10 percent from D.

The city council selects ten citizens, supposedly at random, to serve on a particular committee. What is the probability that the selections will be distributed, by area of the city, exactly as follows?

	Number of
Area	*selected citizens*
A	2
B	3
C	5
D	0

In applying the multinomial formula we have

$$x_1 = 2, \qquad x_2 = 3, \qquad x_3 = 5, \qquad x_4 = 0$$

and

$$p_1 = 0.20, \qquad p_2 = 0.30, \qquad p_3 = 0.40, \qquad p_4 = 0.10$$

and

$$N = 2 + 3 + 5 + 0$$
$$= 10$$

Therefore, from

$$\frac{N!}{x_1! \, x_2! \, \ldots \, x_k!} \, p_1{}^{x_1} p_2{}^{x_2} \ldots p_k{}^{x_k}$$

we have

$$\frac{10!}{2! \, 3! \, 5! \, 0!} \, (0.2)^2 (0.3)^3 (0.4)^5 (0.1)^0 = 0.028$$

as the probability of obtaining exactly such a distribution by chance alone when the A, B, C, and D areas represent 20, 30, 40, and 10 percent of the total population, respectively.

THE CHI-SQUARE GOODNESS OF FIT TEST

The general problem to be considered here involves comparing the frequency of occurrence of an entire set of events with some standard or criterion. For example,

Is the distribution of grades (categorized as A, B, C, D, and F) under a new modular curriculum reasonably in line with the previous grading pattern of the school?

Is it reasonable to assume that the incidence of a particular type of disease is equally distributed over eight areas (i.e., categories) of a particular city?

As a result of a federally assisted employment program, has the distribution of occupational categories undergone a significant change in a particular poverty area?

The direct application of the multinomial formula to this problem of testing the reasonableness of a basic assumption about the population of interest for several categories (in the same fashion as we used the binomial formula for two categories) would be extremely laborious. Fortunately, there is an excellent practical approximation available known as the *chi-square* (χ^2) *goodness of fit test*.

The chi-square (χ^2) goodness of fit test has remained in wide use in the behavioral sciences primarily for two reasons: its extreme simplicity and its general utility for categorical information.

_____ **DEFINITION**   *Chi-square Statistic*

The chi-square statistic χ^2 for the goodness of fit test is defined as follows:

$$\chi^2 = \sum_{j=1}^{k} \frac{(o_j - e_j)^2}{e_j}$$

This formula is very simple to work with, as will become evident from the accompanying examples. In the formula

    o_j means the observed frequency of the jth category
    e_j means the expected frequency of the jth category

and

$$\sum_{j=1}^{k}$$ simply means that we add the expression $\dfrac{(o_j - e_j)^2}{e_j}$

over all k categories. That is,

$$\chi^2 = \frac{(o_1 - e_1)^2}{e_1} + \frac{(o_2 - e_2)^2}{e_2} + \cdots + \frac{(o_k - e_k)^2}{e_k}$$

The rationale of the chi-square statistic evolves from the following notions: First, consider a set of categories or events

$$(E_1, E_2, \ldots, E_j, \ldots, E_k)$$

Each event has an observed frequency

$$(o_1, o_2, \ldots, o_j, \ldots, o_k)$$

and each event has an expected frequency

$$(e_1, e_2, \ldots, e_j, \ldots, e_k)$$

For a sample size n

$$\sum_{j=1}^{k} o_j = \sum_{j=1}^{k} e_j = n$$

The question is simply: How well do these two distributions (i.e., the observed and expected frequency distributions) of frequencies agree?

At first glance a good index of agreement would seem to be:

$$(o_1 - e_1) + (o_2 - e_2) + \cdots + (o_j - e_j) + \cdots + (o_k - e_k)$$

$$= \sum_{j=1}^{k} (o_j - e_j)$$

However, since

$$\sum_{j=1}^{k} (o_j - e_j) = \sum_{j=1}^{k} o_j + \sum_{j=1}^{k} e_j = n - n = 0$$

this is definitely not a good index of agreement, since it will always be zero no matter how poorly the two distributions agree. However, by squaring each term this objection is overcome; i.e.,

$$(o_1 - e_1)^2 + (o_2 - e_2)^2 + \cdots + (o_j - e_j)^2 + \cdots + (o_k - e_k)^2$$

$$= \sum_{j=1}^{k} (o_j - e_j)^2$$

which can be zero only when the correspondence between the two distributions is perfect and which gets large when they are quite different.

Finally, to give more weight to those categories or events where many more individuals are observed than expected, each of the terms is divided by the expected frequency; i.e.,

$$\frac{(o_1 - e_1)^2}{e_1} + \frac{(o_2 - e_2)^2}{e_2} + \cdots + \frac{(o_j - e_j)^2}{e_j} + \cdots + \frac{(o_k - e_k)^2}{e_k}$$

$$= \sum_{j=1}^{k} \frac{(o_j - e_j)^2}{e_j}$$

This expression is labeled χ^2. Thus

$$\chi^2 = \sum_{j=1}^{k} \frac{(o_j - e_j)^2}{e_j}$$

As an example of the computation of the χ^2 statistic consider the following situation:

A public health department is questioning the assumption that the incidence of a particular disease is distributed equally over eight equally populated areas of a city. To help answer this question, a simple random sample of 160 such cases is classified according to the eight areas. The results are as follows:

Area of city	*Incidence of disease*
I	31
II	23
III	19
IV	24
V	19
VI	14
VII	16
VIII	14
	160

It is clear that we would expect $\frac{160}{8}$ or 20 cases in each area if the assumption were true. The question here is: Is there reason to believe that the observed frequencies are "reasonably" in line with those expected under the assumption of equal incidence?

The observed and expected frequencies are most easily organized in the form shown in Table 5.3.

TABLE 5.3

				Area of city					
	I	II	III	IV	V	VI	VII	VIII	*Total*
Observed frequencies o_j	31	23	19	24	19	14	16	14	160
Expected frequencies e_j	20	20	20	20	20	20	20	20	160

Thus the chi-square statistic is

$$\chi^2 = \sum_{j=1}^{k} \frac{(o_j - e_j)^2}{e_j} = \frac{(31 - 20)^2}{20} + \frac{(23 - 20)^2}{20} + \cdots + \frac{(14 - 20)^2}{20} = 11.8$$

The Sampling Distribution of the Chi-Square Statistic

The mere calculation of the value of χ^2 for a sample of data is, of course, of no use to us unless we know how likely or unlikely we are to observe such a sample value. Thus if the χ^2 value of 11.8 obtained from the sample of 160 observations in our example were likely under the assumption that the category frequencies are equal for the population under study, we would have reason to accept this assumption. On the other hand, if it were highly unlikely that one would observe such a sample (one that would yield $\chi^2 = 11.8$), we would tend to cast doubt on the reasonableness of the assumption of equal frequencies.

For the present, let us assume that our assumption of equal frequencies is true. It is apparent that if another sample of 160 cases were observed, we would undoubtedly obtain some other value of χ^2, since the distribution of observed frequencies over the eight categories would probably differ from those given above. In fact, if this process were repeated again and again, we would obtain a sampling distribution of the various χ^2 values that are possible with the eight categories when all the categories are equally likely to be observed.

In order to discover the form of this sampling distribution empirically, we could artificially construct a large population of values distributed equally over eight categories. From this artificial population we could then repeatedly draw samples of size 160 and construct a frequency polygon (i.e., a sampling distribution) for the resulting χ^2 values. From such a sampling distribution we could tell whether or not particular values of χ^2 are likely or unlikely to occur from this type of population. This knowledge would, in turn, provide a basis for establishing a rejection region for the χ^2 statistic obtained from any particular sample under the assumption of equally likely frequencies in the population. That is, if we were to observe an unlikely χ^2 value we would reject our assumption of equally likely frequencies in the population. If we observed a likely or commonplace χ^2 value, we would have no justification for denying that the population under study is similar to our artificial population, where the values appear with equal frequency in the eight categories.

Fortunately, mathematicians have made the effort of constructing such artificial populations unnecessary. Tables have been prepared which give the probability of observing various χ^2 values for all practical numbers of categories. The frequencies in the categories are not entirely independent. For example, in the above situation, once the frequencies of seven of the categories are known, the eighth is fixed; the frequency is simply the difference between 160 (the sample size) and the number of observations in the first seven categories. That is, there are only seven degrees of freedom for the eight categories. In general, for k categories there are $(k - 1)$ degrees of freedom. The theoretical sampling distributions of χ^2 differ markedly when the number of categories is small. Figure 5.1 illustrates the differences for 3, 4, 5, and 6 degrees of freedom corresponding to problems dealing with 4, 5, 6, and 7 categories, respectively.*

---

* From P. G. Hoel, *Introduction to Mathematical Statistics* (2nd ed.), 1954. Reprinted by permission of John Wiley & Sons, Inc.

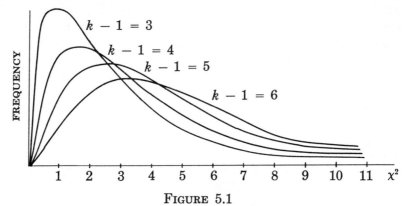

FIGURE 5.1
*Theoretical sampling distribution of
χ^2 for $k = 4, 5, 6,$ and 7 (Hoel, 1954)*

Table IV of Appendix A gives the probability of obtaining χ^2 values less than any specified value for all the practical numbers of categories. Thus, returning to our example, we have $k = 8$ categories ($k - 1 = 7$ degrees of freedom). From Table IV of Appendix A we see that 95 percent of the time ($\chi^2_{.95}$) we would expect to observe sample values of χ^2 less than 14.1 if, in fact, our assumption concerning the frequencies in the population were true. Only five percent of the time, then, would we expect to observe χ^2 values larger than 14.1 under this assumption. Likewise, 99 percent of the time we would expect to observe values less than 18.5 under this assumption, and 90 percent of the time we would expect to observe values less than 12.0.

The findings may be organized into a formal seven-step hypothesis testing procedure as follows:

Step 1 / STATE THE HYPOTHESIS

H_0: The incidence of disease is equally distributed over the eight areas.
H_1: There is a significant inequality in the incidence of the disease over the eight areas.

Step 2 / SELECT THE LEVEL OF SIGNIFICANCE α

$$\alpha = 0.05$$

Step 3 / SPECIFY THE TEST STATISTIC

$$\chi^2 = \sum_{j=1}^{k} \frac{(o_j - e_j)^2}{e_j}$$

Step 4 / SPECIFY THE DISTRIBUTION OF THE TEST STATISTIC

χ^2 is distributed as indicated in the chi-square table with $(k - 1)$ degrees of freedom. In this case $k = 8$, since there are eight areas of the city.

Step 5 / SPECIFY THE REJECTION REGION

For $\alpha = 0.05$ and $k - 1 = 7$ the critical value from Table IV of Appendix A is seen to be 14.1. Any sample value of χ^2 larger than this would be so unusual as to cause us to reject H_0.

Step 6 / COMPUTE THE TEST STATISTIC

$$\chi^2 = 11.8$$

Step 7 / ACCEPT OR REJECT THE NULL HYPOTHESIS

Since our observed sample value of $\chi^2 = 11.8$ is smaller than the critical value, we accept the hypothesis that the incidence of the disease is equally distributed over the eight areas of the city.

As a second example of the chi-square goodness of fit test, consider the following situation:

In a particular poverty area suppose that the distribution of six occupational categories was reported to be as follows:

Occupational category	Percentage
A	20
B	18
C	28
D	15
E	17
F	2
	100

Following a year's experience with a federally assisted employment program, suppose that a sample of 200 men showed the following occupational distribution:

Occupational category	Frequency
A	36
B	38
C	80
D	14
E	21
F	11
	200

Is there evidence that the federal assistance has significantly altered the distribution of the occupational categories? Again following our seven-step procedure, we have:

Step 1 / STATE THE HYPOTHESIS

H_0: No significant change has taken place in the distribution of occupational categories.
H_1: There has been a significant change.

Step 2 / SELECT THE LEVEL OF SIGNIFICANCE α

$$\alpha = 0.05$$

Step 3 / SPECIFY THE TEST STATISTIC

$$\chi^2 = \left[\sum_{j=1}^{k} \frac{(o_j - e_j)^2}{e_j} \right]$$

Step 4 / SPECIFY THE DISTRIBUTION OF THE STATISTIC

χ^2 is distributed as indicated in the chi-square table with $(k - 1)$ degrees of freedom.

Step 5 / SPECIFY THE REJECTION REGION

For $\alpha = 0.05$, with five degrees of freedom, the critical value from Table IV of Appendix A is 11.1.

Step 6 / COMPUTE THE TEST STATISTIC

The data are summarized in the form shown in Table 5.4.

TABLE 5.4

	Occupational category						
	A	B	C	D	E	F	Total
Observed, o_j	36	38	80	14	21	11	200
Expected, e_j (Based on past percentages)	40	36	56	30	34	4	200

Therefore,

$$\chi^2 = \frac{(36-40)^2}{40} + \frac{(38-36)^2}{36} + \cdots + \frac{(11-4)^2}{4}$$

$$= 36.55$$

Step 7 / ACCEPT OR REJECT THE NULL HYPOTHESIS

Reject H_0. There is a significant difference between the observed and the expected frequencies. It would be unusual to observe such a sample distribution of occupational categories if the percentages in the population were as indicated.

It is clear from the second example that the expected frequencies do not have to be equal across the categories. Thus any theoretical basis may be used for generating the expected frequencies, and in turn a sample of observations may be used either to support or to cast doubt on the reasonableness of the theory or assumption in light of the available evidence. However, it should be noted that the sampling distribution of χ^2 is based on frequencies, not percentages or proportions. Hence, although the conversion of χ^2 values obtained from percentages or proportions to χ^2 based on frequencies is straightforward, that is,

$$\chi^2_{\text{frequencies}} = N\chi^2_{\text{proportions}} = \frac{N}{100}\chi^2_{\text{percentages}}$$

it seems less confusing to work consistently from the start with observed and expected frequencies.

_____ **RULES** *for Using the Chi-square Statistic*

In using the chi-square statistic for goodness of fit tests, the following conditions should be satisfied:

1. Each sample response or observation should fall into one and only one of the specified categories.

2. The responses or observations should be independent of each other. That is, the categorization of one response should have no effect on the category in which any other response is placed.

In addition, it is generally agreed that the expected frequency in each category should be five or more. In some cases where this rule is violated, it might be possible to telescope two adjacent categories into one in order to raise the expected frequency. In general, this is not a recommended practice. There is an alternate form of the chi-square statistic, known as the *Yates correction for continuity*, that is recommended for the chi-square analysis of categorical data having only one degree of freedom.

Yates Correction for Continuity:[*]

$$\chi^2 = \sum_{j=1}^{k} \left[\frac{(|\, o_j - e_j \,| - 0.5)^2}{e_j} \right]$$

where $|\, o_j - e_j \,|$ merely means to take the absolute differences between o_j and e_j, ignoring the resulting sign.

For moderately large sample sizes the conclusions reached from the corrected and uncorrected forms of the chi-square statistic are generally comparable.

Because nothing is said about the underlying distribution of the responses in the population, the chi-square statistic is sometimes referred to as a "distribution-free" or "non-parametric" statistic. It should be remembered, however, that while the chi-square statistic is distribution-free, it is not assumption-free, as can be seen from the requirements of the above rules.

Additive Property of Chi-square Tests

A very useful characteristic of chi-square analyses is that they are additive. By this it is meant that in repeated experimentation the resulting chi-square values may be added together as well as the corresponding degrees of freedom to give a single experimental result. For example:

An experiment is repeated on three successive days with three different groups of subjects. Assume that the results of the first day yielded a value of chi-square of

$$\chi^2_1$$

---

[*] This "correction for continuity" is intended to provide a conservative adjustment for the fact that we are using the *continuous* χ^2 probability curve in making probability statements about *categorical* information.

with $k_1 - 1$ degrees of freedom. On the second day the experiment yielded a chi-square value of

$$\chi^2_2$$

with $k_2 - 1$ degrees of freedom. The third day yielded a value of chi-square of

$$\chi^2_3$$

with $k_3 - 1$ degrees of freedom.

The results of the three days of experimentation may then be pooled as follows to obtain a conclusion based on the three days of experimentation.

$$\chi^2_{\text{total}} = \chi^2_1 + \chi^2_2 + \chi^2_3$$

χ^2_{total} is distributed as indicated by the chi-square table with degrees of freedom $= (k_1 - 1) + (k_2 - 1) + (k_3 - 1)$.

This procedure may be extended to any number of experimental replications.

SUMMARY

This chapter introduces the binomial formula and its underlying rationale. The binomial formula is applied in two situations: anticipating the likelihood of a particular sample result and testing the reasonableness of a basic assumption about a population of interest. It is shown that the direct application of the binomial formula is a more efficient means of handling certain probability problems than is the formal method introduced in Chapter 4. The sampling distribution of the binomial formula is stressed in regard to utilizing sample results to test hypotheses about the population parameter p. A distinction is made between unidirectional and bidirectional tests; the concept of level of significance is introduced, and a formal seven-step procedure is presented for testing hypotheses in general, employing Table III of Appendix A. The maximum likelihood method for selecting one of several hypotheses is given.

An extension of the binomial formula to the case of several categories is made by means of the multinomial formula and the chi-square (χ^2) goodness of fit test. The nature of the χ^2 statistic is discussed in terms of its definition and sampling distribution. Finally, some working rules for goodness of fit tests are given, and the additive property of χ^2 is discussed.

Additional new terms and expressions encountered are:

Success and failure

$$p(x) = \frac{n!}{(n - x)! \, x!} p^x q^{n-x}$$

A given or fixed p

Hypothesized p

α

Distribution of possible sample results

Seven-step Procedure

1. State the hypothesis.
2. Select the level of significance α.
3. Specify the test statistic.
4. Specify the distribution of the test statistic.
5. Specify the rejection region.
6. Compute the test statistic.
7. Accept or reject the null hypothesis.

H_0 and H_1

$$\frac{N!}{x_1!\, x_2! \ldots x_k!}\, p_1{}^{x_1} p_2{}^{x_2} p_k{}^{x_k}$$

Entire set of events

$$\chi^2 = \sum_{j=1}^{k} \frac{(o_j - e_j)^2}{e_j}$$

Index of agreement
Degrees of freedom

REVIEW QUESTIONS

1   To justify the expression $p^x q^{n-x}$ in the binomial distribution, what assumption is required about the n events?

2   The total number of arrangements (each with a probability of $p^x q^{n-x}$) possible in the binomial distribution is $_nC_r$. What is true about the arrangements so that the binomial formula may be used?

3   An honest coin is thrown six times. What is the probability of getting exactly two heads? Of at least two heads?

4   In a binomial distribution with an n of 5 and a p of $\frac{1}{4}$, evaluate $p(x = 4)$.

5   In this hypothesis testing problem, n is 10 and H_0: $p = 0.60$. The level of significance is to be kept *as close to* 0.05 as possible.
   (a) State the rejection region for

$$H_1: p > 0.60$$

$$x = \text{\_ \_ \_ \_ \_ \_}$$

(b) State the rejection region for

$$H_1: p < 0.60$$

$$x = \text{------}$$

(c) State the rejection region for

$$H_1: p \neq 0.60$$

$$x = \text{------} .$$

6 A sample of 15 observations yields nine successes. Choose among the two alternative hypotheses $H_0: p = 0.50$ and $H_0: p = 0.60$ by the maximum likelihood method.

7 What assumptions are made of the events $E_1, E_2, \ldots, E_x$ in the use of the multinomial distribution?

8 Suppose the number of selected citizens in the problem discussed in the text had been as follows:

Area	Number of selected citizens
A	4
B	2
C	1
D	3

Evaluate the multinomial formula in this case.

9 What are two reasons for the widespread use of the chi-square test in the behavioral sciences?

10 When the chi-square test is used for comparing an entire set of events with some standard, such tests are called _____ tests.

11 Give two assumptions underlying the use of the chi-square distribution.

12 For six categories how many degrees of freedom are used with the chi-square goodness of fit test?

13 In 200 tosses of a coin, 115 heads and 85 tails were observed. Test the hypothesis that the coin is fair, using a level of significance of 0.05 by means of the chi-square goodness of fit test. Apply the Yates correction.

CHAPTER 6

THE NORMAL CURVE

NORMAL POPULATIONS

In Chapter 3 we saw that one effective way of describing continuous data was to construct a frequency polygon or curve. Obviously there exists an infinite variety of such frequency curves, since there is an unlimited number of sources or populations from which data might be collected.

We shall now consider one particular theoretical frequency curve known as the *normal frequency curve*. In addition to being of paramount theoretical interest to the statistician, the normal frequency curve is often approximated by empirically obtained data in the behavioral sciences. For example, such approximations are encountered in measures of human ability, such as achievement, aptitudes, and intelligence, as well as in measures of physical attributes, such as height and weight. The appropriateness of the normal frequency curve as an approximate description of the distribution of human characteristics was recognized in the first half of the nineteenth century by the Belgian statistician, Adolph Quetelet (Boring, 1957). The normal curve is sometimes also named the *Gaussian distribution* after the mathematician Gauss. The theoretical knowledge of the characteristics of normal frequency curves enables research workers to make relevant statements about a wide variety of behavioral phenomena.

It is common practice to denote the mean of a population of scores by the Greek letter mu, μ. Correspondingly, the population standard deviation is denoted by the Greek letter sigma, σ. Such descriptive population measures are termed *parameters*. Figure 6.1 illustrates the general form of all normal frequency curves constructed from population values.

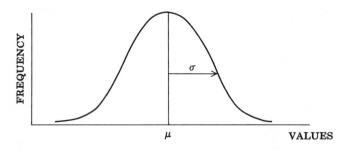

FIGURE 6.1
A normally distributed population

Although there is an infinite number of possible normal frequency curves, the two population parameters μ and σ are all that are needed completely to describe any particular normal frequency curve.

The statement that the population of values of a continuous variable (denoted X) has a normal distribution is usually expressed by means of the following notation: $X \stackrel{d}{=} N(\mu, \sigma)$, read, "The population of X values is distributed normally with a mean of μ and a standard deviation of σ." The theoretical frequency of any set of X values in a normal population is derived by means of the calculus from the equation (Young, 1962)

$$Y = \frac{1}{\sigma\sqrt{2\pi}} e^{-1/2(X-\mu/\sigma)^2}$$

where

$$Y = \text{frequency} \qquad \pi = 3.14159 \qquad e = 2.71828$$

A population giving rise to such a bell-shaped, symmetrical, normal curve, as illustrated in Figure 6.1, has many interesting characteristics. One of the most useful is the relationship of the standard deviation σ and the mean μ. For example, in a normal distribution 68.27 percent of the values fall within one standard deviation on either side of the mean; 95.45 percent of the values fall within two standard deviations, and 99.73 percent within three standard deviations of the mean. These relationships are illustrated in Figure 6.2.*

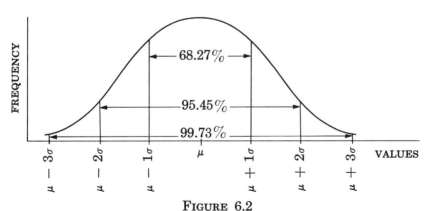

FIGURE 6.2
Relationship of the standard deviation and a normal curve

---

* Although a theoretical normal curve never touches the base axis, the total area under the curve is taken to represent 100 percent of the values when the theoretical curve is used as an approximate model for practical situations.

The practical result of this relationship is that for populations which have frequency polygons closely approximating a normal curve, it is possible to make descriptive statements concerning the frequency of occurrence of any particular range of values in the population of interest. Again, such statements are based on only the two population parameters μ and σ (e.g., $\mu \pm 1\sigma$, $\mu \pm 2\sigma$, etc.). There are two principal reasons for the prominent role played by the theoretical normal frequency curve in the behavioral sciences:

1. As mentioned, many populations of behavioral phenomena occur naturally in a form approximating a normal distribution.

2. A powerful mathematical finding, to be discussed later, known as the central limit theorem leads to the valuable result that even when a population is nonnormal in form, a sample of means drawn from such a population will tend to be normally distributed.

THE UNIT NORMAL CURVE

As with any distribution, an individual score X_i taken from a normally distributed population may be converted to a standard score Z_i by subtracting the mean μ of the population from the score and dividing the result by the standard deviation σ of the population. Thus, a standard score derived from a normal population of values is defined as

$$Z_i = \frac{X_i - \mu}{\sigma}$$

Recall, from Chapter 3, that two general properties of standard scores are (1) any distribution of standard scores follows the form of the original raw score distribution, (2) standard score distributions always have a mean of 0 and a standard deviation of 1. Therefore, the standardized scores Z_i obtained from the equation

$$Z_i = \frac{X_i - \mu}{\sigma}$$

where the X_i's are normally distributed, will not only be normally distributed but also will have a mean and standard deviation of 0 and 1, respectively. Such a theoretical distribution is called the *unit normal distribution* or *curve*. Figure 6.3 illustrates the unit normal curve corresponding to any normal population. It is important to realize that all normal populations result in this same unit normal distribution when the original values are expressed as standard scores.*

---

* The characteristics of the unit normal distribution are those of any normal distribution. Therefore, the total area under the curve is again taken to represent 100 percent of the values. For purposes of determining probabilities this total area is set equal to 1. Furthermore, 68.27, 95.45, and 99.73 percent of the values are again within ± 1, ± 2, and ± 3 standard deviation units (in this case, 1) of the mean, respectively.

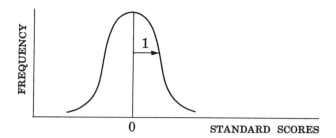

FIGURE 6.3
The unit normal curve

The statement that a set of standard scores is distributed normally with a mean of 0 and a standard deviation of 1 may be expressed as follows: $Z_i \stackrel{d}{=} N(0, 1)$. The equation from which the theoretical frequency of any set of standard scores is derived becomes

$$Y = \frac{1}{\sqrt{2\pi}} \, e^{-1/2(Z)^2}$$

As we shall see, the primary advantage of the unit normal distribution lies in the fact that statements concerning particular normal standard scores Z_i may be considered equivalent to similar statements involving the corresponding raw score values X_i in the original normal population.

We have seen that all normal populations may be converted to the unit normal distribution by means of the relationship

$$Z_i = \frac{X_i - \mu}{\sigma}$$

In order, then, to make statements about the values in any normal population we require rather complete information about the unit normal distribution. Fortunately, tables have been prepared which provide the information necessary to make such statements. One such table involving the unit normal distribution is given in Table V of Appendix A. The body of this table gives the proportion of values found between a Z score of 0 and any Z score up to 3.99. Since the total area under the unit normal curve is taken to be 1, the proportion of area contained between any two Z scores—Z_1 and Z_2—may be interpreted as the probability of observing a Z score between Z_1 and Z_2. For this reason, the unit normal distribution is also referred to as the *unit normal probability curve*.

The following examples illustrate the use of Table V of Appendix A.

EXAMPLE 1

The probability of observing a value of Z between 0 and 1.65 is illustrated in Figure 6.4. From Table V of Appendix A we see that the probability of

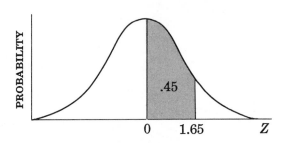

FIGURE 6.4
Unit normal probability curve

observing a value between 0 and 1.65 is 0.4505. Rounding this result to 0.45, we denote this probability as follows:

$$P(0 \leq Z \leq 1.65) = 0.45$$

Furthermore, not only does the total area under the unit normal probability curve equal one, the curve is also symmetrical. Therefore, the probability of observing a value of Z greater than zero is 0.5. Likewise, the probability of observing a value of Z less than zero is also 0.5.

From these properties of the unit normal curve, it is clear that the probability of observing a value of Z greater than 1.65 [denoted $P(Z > 1.65)$] is

$$P(Z > 1.65) = 0.5 - P(0 \leq Z \leq 1.65)$$

$$= 0.5 - 0.45$$

$$= 0.05$$

This probability, $P(Z > 1.65)$, is illustrated in Figure 6.5.

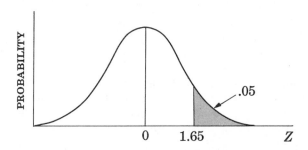

FIGURE 6.5
Unit normal probability curve

Because the unit normal probability curve is symmetrical, the probability of observing a value of Z between 0 and -1.65 [denoted $P(0 \geq Z \geq -1.65)$] is the same as the probability of observing a value of Z between 0 and $+1.65$, as illustrated in Figure 6.6. That is,

$$P(0 \geq Z \geq -1.65) = P(0 \leq Z \leq 1.65)$$
$$= 0.45$$

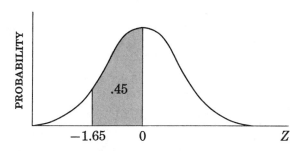

FIGURE 6.6
Unit normal probability curve

Finally, because of the property of symmetry, it is also clear that the probability of observing a value of Z less than -1.65 [denoted $P(Z < -1.65)$] is the same as the probability of observing a value of Z greater than $+1.65$. That is,

$$P(Z < -1.65) = P(Z > 1.65)$$
$$= 0.5 - P(0 \leq Z \leq 1.65)$$
$$= 0.05$$

This probability, $P(Z < -1.65)$, is illustrated in Figure 6.7.

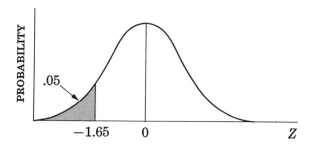

FIGURE 6.7
Unit normal probability curve

EXAMPLE 2

The probability of observing a value of Z greater than 1.96 [that is, $P(Z > 1.96)$] may be derived from Table V of Appendix A, as follows:

$$P(Z > 1.96) = 0.5 - P(0 \leq Z \leq 1.96)$$
$$= 0.5 - 0.475$$
$$= 0.025$$

Again, by symmetry, the probability of observing a value of Z less than -1.96 [that is, $P(Z < -1.96)$] is

$$P(Z < -1.96) = P(Z > 1.96)$$
$$= 0.025$$

The probabilities $P(Z > 1.96)$ and $P(Z < -1.96)$ are illustrated in Figure 6.8.

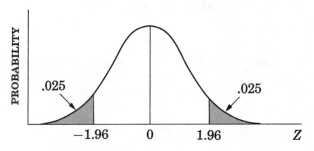

FIGURE 6.8
Unit normal probability curve

EXAMPLE 3

The probability of observing a value of Z greater than 2.33 [that is, $P(Z > 2.33)$] is, from Table V of Appendix A,

$$P(Z > 2.33) = 0.5 - P(0 \leq Z \leq 2.33)$$
$$= 0.5 - 0.4901$$

Rounding 0.4901 to 0.49, we have

$$P(Z > 2.33) = 0.01$$

This probability, $P(Z > 2.33)$, is illustrated in Figure 6.9. Of course, by symmetry, $P(Z < -2.33)$ is also 0.01.

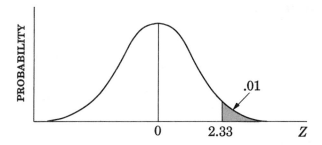

FIGURE 6.9
Unit normal probability curve

EXAMPLE 4

The probability (to three decimal places) of observing a value of Z greater than 2.58 or less than -2.58 is illustrated in Figure 6.10. This probability is thus

$$P(Z > 2.58) + P(Z < -2.58) = 0.005 + 0.005$$

$$= 0.01$$

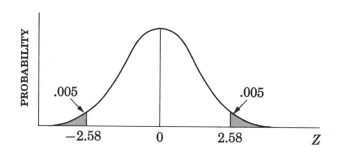

FIGURE 6.10
Unit normal probability curve

EXAMPLE 5

The probability of observing a value of Z greater than 1.28 [that is, $P(Z > 1.28)$] is

$$P(Z > 1.28) = 0.5 - P(0 \leq Z \leq 1.28)$$

$$= 0.5 - 0.3997$$

Rounding 0.3997 to 0.40, we have

$$P(Z > 1.28) = 0.10$$

This probability is illustrated in Figure 6.11. By symmetry

$$P(Z < -1.28) = P(Z > 1.28) = 0.10$$

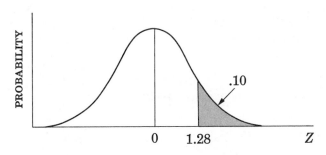

FIGURE 6.11
Unit normal probability curve

To illustrate the use of the unit normal probability curve in making statements concerning a normally distributed population consider the following problem:

A set of standardized test scores for a population of students closely approximates the theoretical normal distribution. The mean μ of the population of scores is 50, and the standard deviation σ is 10. Assume that a score of 35 is required to "pass." About what proportion of the student population passed the test?

First of all, let us treat the discrete score 35 as covering the continuous interval 34.5–35.5. The proportion sought is thus as illustrated in Figure 6.12. The standard score corresponding to the population value 34.5 is

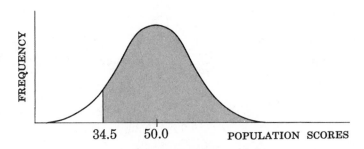

FIGURE 6.12
A normal population of scores

$$Z = \frac{34.5 - 50}{10}$$

$$= -1.55$$

Therefore, in terms of the unit normal probability curve, our desired proportion is as illustrated in Figure 6.13.

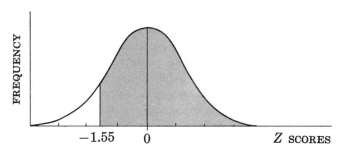

FIGURE 6.13
The unit normal probability curve

Because of the symmetry of the unit normal curve, the proportion of standard scores equal to or greater than -1.55 (that is, the probability of Z equal to or greater than -1.55) is the same as the proportion of scores less than or equal to $+1.55$. That is,

$$P(Z \geq -1.55) = P(Z \leq 1.55)$$

as shown in Figure 6.14.

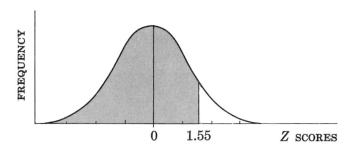

FIGURE 6.14
The unit normal probability curve

Finally, from Table V of Appendix A, we see that

$$P(Z \leq 1.55) = 0.5 + P(0 \leq Z \leq 1.55)$$

$$= 0.5 + 0.4394$$

Rounding to two decimal places, we have

$$P(Z \leq 1.55) = 0.94$$

Relating this result back to the original population of interest, we can state that about 94 percent of the population of students passed the test.

SAMPLING FROM NORMAL POPULATIONS

As in the case of the binomial distribution and behavioral research generally, we seldom have the entire normal population of interest at our disposal when we attempt to make statements about the population parameters. Practical considerations usually demand that we work with samples of data from which we make inferences about the population of interest.

A major question in behavioral inquiry concerns the interpretation of sample data. Specifically, the issue is whether a partial sampling of data provides a reasonable basis for making inferences about the population. For example, let us consider the mean of a sample that is randomly drawn from a normal population of values X_i such as is illustrated in Figure 6.15.

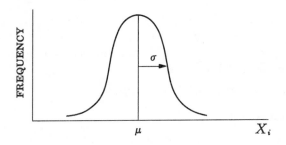

FIGURE 6.15
Normal population of X_i values

How adequate is the sample mean

$$\bar{X} = \frac{\sum_{i=1}^{N} X_i}{N}$$

in making an estimate of the population mean μ? Obviously, if the sample size includes the entire population (that is, N = population size), $\bar{X}$ will be an exact estimate of μ. Furthermore, this will always be true, no matter how many times such a sample is selected. The distribution of a set of sample means is termed the *sampling distribution of the mean*.* The sampling

---

* More properly, it is the *random sampling distribution of the mean*. Throughout the discussion here it is assumed that the samples are randomly selected from the population.

distribution of the mean, where N = population size, is therefore as illustrated in Figure 6.16. In other words, in this case there is no sampling error in estimating the population parameter μ by the sample statistic $\bar{X}$, since for each and every possible sample $\bar{X} = \mu$.

FIGURE 6.16
*Sampling distribution of the mean
where each sample size equals the population size*

At the other extreme, consider samples of size 1, in which case a sample mean is

$$\bar{X} = \frac{\sum\limits_{i=1}^{N} X_i}{N} = X_i$$

Here the sample mean is simply one of the original values in the normal population. In this case, the sampling distribution of the mean merely consists of a distribution of individual values randomly selected from the original population. The result is that, as the sampling process is continued with $N = 1$, the sampling distribution of the mean approaches the form of the original population, as illustrated in Figure 6.17. As seen from Figure 6.17, the number of possible values for a sample mean, based on a sample size of 1, is identical to the number of different values in the population.

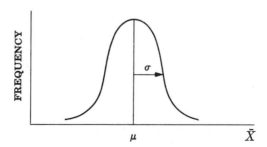

FIGURE 6.17
Sampling distribution of the mean where each sample size = 1

These two extreme cases ($N = 1$ and N = population size) point up the fact that the adequacy of a sample mean $\bar{X}$ for estimating the population mean μ is reflected by the *variability* of the sampling distribution of the mean.* The variability is, in turn, dependent on the sample size. From an intuitive point of view, this means that it is less likely for a large sample mean to deviate widely from the population mean μ than it is for a small sample mean. This general result is illustrated in Figure 6.18.

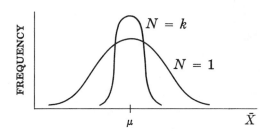

FIGURE 6.18
General form of sampling distributions of the mean
for $N = 1$ and $N = k$, where $k > 1$

The dependence of the *variability* of the sampling distribution of the mean on the *sample size* may be demonstrated by considering the data of Table 3.1 as a population of 110 values closely approximating the normal distribution. Figure 6.19 shows three sampling distributions of the mean. The first (a) is based on 100 randomly drawn samples each of size 1; the second (b) is based on 100 randomly drawn samples each of size 10, and the third (c) is based on 100 randomly drawn samples each of size 110 (i.e., N = population size).

The results of this section are all contained in the following formal theorem regarding the sampling distribution of the mean (Hoel, 1954).

THEOREM 6.1

If X is normally distributed with mean μ and standard deviation σ and random samples of size N are drawn, the sample mean $\bar{X}$ will be normally distributed with mean (expected value) μ and standard deviation (*standard error*) $\sigma/\sqrt{N}$.**

---

* The variability of the sampling distribution of the mean, as measured by the standard deviation, is termed the *standard error* of the sampling distribution of the mean. The arithmetic mean of the sampling distribution of the mean is called the *expected value* of the sampling distribution of the mean. Thus it is clear that the expected value of a sample mean is μ regardless of the sample size, even though the standard error varies with a change in sample size.

** In terms of our previous shorthand notation, this theorem may be expressed as follows: If $X \overset{d}{=} N(\mu, \sigma)$, then $\bar{X} \overset{d}{=} N(\mu, \sigma/\sqrt{N})$.

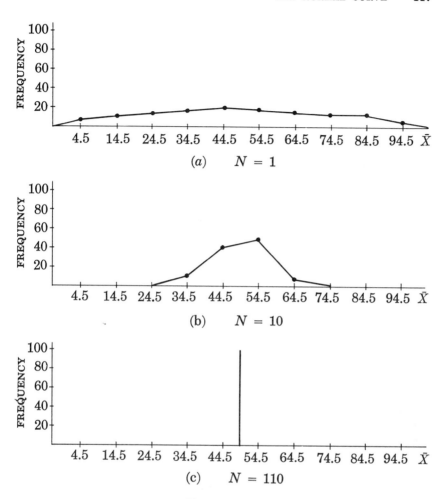

FIGURE 6.19
*An example demonstrating the dependence
of the sampling distribution of the mean on the sample size*

We shall find this theorem to be essential in structuring inquiries about population means.

SAMPLING FROM NONNORMAL POPULATIONS

So far in discussing sampling distributions of the mean we have made the assumption that our original population of values is normally distributed. Now, although a large number of variables do exhibit frequency distributions that approximate the theoretical normal curve, what can be said concerning those populations of interest that show marked deviation from the normal curve?

Another important theorem, known as the *central limit theorem*, answers our question concerning the sampling distribution of the mean from non-normal populations (Hoel, 1954).

THEOREM 6.2   *(Central Limit Theorem)*

The random sampling distribution of means drawn from any population of values (provided there is a finite mean μ and variance σ^2) will approach a normal distribution as the sample size N approaches infinity. The expected value of this sampling distribution will be μ and the *standard error* will be $\sigma/\sqrt{N}$.

TABLE   6.1   **A SET OF MEANS FOR 100 SAMPLES OF SIZE 10 RANDOMLY SELECTED FROM A RANDOM NUMBER TABLE**

Sample Number	Mean	Sample Number	Mean	Sample Number	Mean
1	3.4	35	4.8	69	5.6
2	5.3	36	3.7	70	5.3
3	4.3	37	3.7	71	2.8
4	5.0	38	3.1	72	5.8
5	4.0	39	4.5	73	4.6
6	3.9	40	3.0	74	3.4
7	3.2	41	4.1	75	4.8
8	6.1	42	4.2	76	3.7
9	5.4	43	4.2	77	4.8
10	4.7	44	4.3	78	4.6
11	4.9	45	2.7	79	4.4
12	4.0	46	3.0	80	3.9
13	4.7	47	4.6	81	4.9
14	3.8	48	5.6	82	5.1
15	4.6	49	4.0	83	4.1
16	5.2	50	5.1	84	5.9
17	4.5	51	3.2	85	4.7
18	4.6	52	3.9	86	4.8
19	4.4	53	5.4	87	4.8
20	6.1	54	4.2	88	2.6
21	4.4	55	3.7	89	3.7
22	4.1	56	3.4	90	4.7
23	5.5	57	5.3	91	5.5
24	3.2	58	6.0	92	5.0
25	4.9	59	5.6	93	4.6
26	4.1	60	4.8	94	4.6
27	3.6	61	4.6	95	3.0
28	5.0	62	4.7	96	4.9
29	4.6	63	4.8	97	4.5
30	4.6	64	3.9	98	4.3
31	4.0	65	4.5	99	5.4
32	3.9	66	4.6	100	4.5
33	3.7	67	5.3		
34	2.6	68	3.4		

The practical implication of the central limit theorem is that we may use our knowledge of the normal distribution to make statements concerning sample means randomly selected from a wide variety of populations whose exact form is unknown.

It is simple to demonstrate the central limit theorem empirically. For example, if we were to construct a frequency polygon corresponding to the random numbers of Table II in Appendix A, we would expect it to approximate the form indicated in Figure 6.20. That is, there are approximately

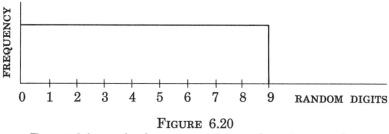

FIGURE 6.20
Expected form of a frequency polygon of random numbers

equal frequencies of each digit in the random number table. Consider drawing 100 samples of size 10 ($N = 10$ numbers) from this random number table. The means of 100 such samples are given in Table 6.1.

A frequency polygon corresponding to the means of Table 6.1 is given in Figure 6.21. Figure 6.21 illustrates the general central limit theorem, which states that even with nonnormal populations, the sample means tend toward a normal distribution.

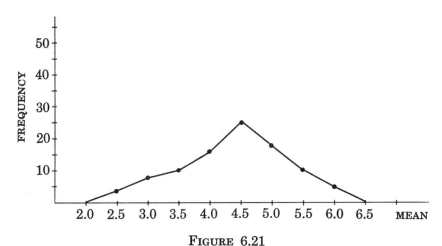

FIGURE 6.21
Frequency polygon of 100 means drawn from a random number table

THE SAMPLING DISTRIBUTION OF THE DIFFERENCE BETWEEN TWO MEANS SELECTED FROM INDEPENDENT NORMAL POPULATIONS

Another frequent type of behavioral inquiry involves the comparison of the average scores obtained in two independent populations. If complete information on each population were at our disposal, it would, indeed, be a simple matter to compare two population means μ_1 and μ_2. Normally, however, we must once again work with partial information obtained in the form of samples drawn from the populations.

We have already seen that samples drawn from a population do not generally yield means identical to the mean of the population values. If we denote the individual values in one population as X_{1i} and those in the second as X_{2i}, this means that in general

$$\bar{X}_1 \neq \mu_1 \quad \text{and} \quad \bar{X}_2 \neq \mu_2$$

for any particular pair of samples. Therefore, the difference between any two sample means $(\bar{X}_1 - \bar{X}_2)$ cannot be expected to be identical to the difference $(\mu_1 - \mu_2)$, except in the special case where each sample size exhausts the corresponding population—that is, N_1 = size of population 1 and N_2 = size of population 2, in which case

$$\bar{X}_1 = \frac{\sum_{i=1}^{N_1} X_{1i}}{N_1} = \mu_1$$

and

$$\bar{X}_2 = \frac{\sum_{i=1}^{N_2} X_{2i}}{N_2} = \mu_2$$

The following theorem is concerned with the sampling distribution of the difference between two means (Hoel, 1954).

THEOREM 6.3

If X_1 and X_2 are normally and independently distributed variables with population parameters (μ_1, σ_1) and (μ_2, σ_2), respectively, then $(\bar{X}_1 - \bar{X}_2)$ has a sampling distribution that is normally distributed with mean (*expected value*)

$$\mu_{(\bar{X}_1 - \bar{X}_2)} = \mu_1 - \mu_2$$

and standard deviation (*standard error*)

$$\sigma_{(\bar{X}_1 - \bar{X}_2)} = \sqrt{\frac{\sigma_1^2}{N_1} + \frac{\sigma_2^2}{N_2}}$$

We shall have occasion to use Theorem 6.3 in Chapter 8.

To gain an appreciation of the expected value and standard error of Theorem 6.3, consider a set of K samples, each comprised of the differences between two sample means drawn from the two independent normal populations. That is,

$$(\bar{X}_{1_1} - \bar{X}_{2_1}), (\bar{X}_{1_2} - \bar{X}_{2_2}), \ldots,$$
$$(\bar{X}_{1_j} - \bar{X}_{2_j}), \ldots, (\bar{X}_{1_K} - \bar{X}_{2_K})$$

The mean of these differences is therefore

$$\text{Mean}_{(\bar{X}_1 - \bar{X}_2)} = \frac{\sum\limits_{j=1}^{K} (\bar{X}_{1_j} - \bar{X}_{2_j})}{K}$$

$$= \frac{\sum\limits_{j=1}^{K} \bar{X}_{1_j}}{K} - \frac{\sum\limits_{j=1}^{K} \bar{X}_{2_j}}{K}$$

By Theorem 6.1, as K gets indefinitely large, these sample means approach the corresponding population means. That is, the expected value becomes

$$\mu_{(\bar{X}_1 - \bar{X}_2)} = \mu_1 - \mu_2$$

Furthermore, it is shown in Appendix E that for independent populations

$$\sigma^2_{(\bar{X}_1 - \bar{X}_2)} = \sigma^2_{\bar{X}_1} + \sigma^2_{\bar{X}_2}$$

When we apply Theorem 6.1 to each term on the right-hand side of this expression, the standard error of the mean differences $\sigma_{(\bar{X}_1 - \bar{X}_2)}$ becomes

$$\sigma_{(\bar{X}_1 - \bar{X}_2)} = \sqrt{\frac{\sigma^2_1}{N_1} + \frac{\sigma^2_2}{N_2}}$$

RESEARCH QUESTIONS BASED ON THE NORMAL CURVE

In the next few chapters we shall be considering several types of inquiries related to the problem of drawing inferences from samples of continuous behavioral responses. The theoretical normal probability curve that we have been discussing plays an essential role in these inquiries. We shall begin by asking four basic research questions; two of these questions concern the average, and two concern dispersion. Our behavioral inquiries concerning averages will be structured by asking one of two questions:

Question 1: Is our sample mean significantly different from expectation?

Question 2: Is the difference between two sample means significantly different from expectation?

Our basic inquiries concerning dispersion will likewise be structured by asking one of two questions:

Question 3: Is our sample dispersion significantly different from expectation?

Question 4: Is the difference between two sample dispersions significantly different from expectation?

The next three chapters focus on these four questions.

SUMMARY

This chapter introduces one particular theoretical frequency curve, known as the normal frequency curve. It is emphasized that although there is an infinite number of possible normal frequency curves, the two parameters μ and σ are all that are needed to describe completely any particular one. The relationship of σ to a normal curve is such that 68.27, 95.45, and 99.73 percent of the population values are contained in the interval $\mu \pm 1\sigma$, $\mu \pm 2\sigma$, and $\mu \pm 3\sigma$, respectively.

Standard scores derived from any normal population form a distribution known as the unit normal probability curve. The unit normal curve, tabled in Table V of Appendix A, is used to make probability statements about values in the original population.

The problem of sampling from normal populations leads us to Theorem 6.1, which states that if $X \overset{d}{=} N(\mu, \sigma)$, then $\bar{X} \overset{d}{=} N(\mu, \sigma/\sqrt{N})$. Sampling from nonnormal populations causes few practical problems in working with means for moderately large samples because of the central limit theorem (6.2), which states that the sample means tend to normality for a wide variety of original distribution forms.

Theorem 6.3 gives the expected value and standard error of the sampling distribution of the difference between two means selected from independent populations.

Finally, two basic research questions about central tendency and two about dispersion are presented, all of which are closely related to the theoretical normal curve.

New terms and expressions introduced in this chapter include:

Theoretical normal curve

μ

σ

Approximately normal populations

$$Z_i = \frac{X_i - \mu}{\sigma}$$

$P(Z \geq k)$, where $0 \leq k \leq 3.99$

Sampling error

Sampling distribution of the mean

Sampling from nonnormal population

Central limit theorem

Sampling distribution of the difference between two means

REVIEW QUESTIONS

1 Why do all normal populations lead to the unit normal curve when the population raw score values are converted to standard scores?

2 Since it is extremely unlikely that any practical population of values in the behavioral sciences follows exactly a normal curve, why is the normal curve stressed so heavily?

3 Find the following areas under the unit normal curve.

(a) Between $Z = 0$ and $Z = 1.70$.
(b) Between $Z = 0.93$ and $Z = 1.32$.
(c) Greater than $Z = 0.43$.
(d) Greater than $Z = -1.04$.
(e) Less than $Z = 2.04$.
(f) Less than $Z = -1.36$.

4 If we assume a normal population of scores with a mean of 50 and a standard deviation of 10, what percentage of the scores fall between a score of 65 and a score of 40? Above a score of 68?

5 What is the possible range of values for the standard error of the sampling distribution of the mean? How is the standard error related to the sample size in general?

6 If a normal population of X values has a mean of 48 and a standard deviation of 4, what are the expected value and standard error of the sampling distribution of the mean for samples of size 16?

7 Suppose that there is negative skewness in the distribution of a particular population trait with $\mu = 400$, $\sigma = 25$. If you drew 1000 random samples of 100 observations each, what would you expect the form distribution to look like? What would be the mean and standard deviation of the sampling distribution of the means (that is, the expected value and standard error)?

8   If population 1 has a mean of 100 and a standard deviation of 20, while population 2 has a mean of 50 and a standard deviation of 10, what are the expected value and the standard error of the sampling distribution of $(\bar{X}_1 - \bar{X}_2)$ if $N_1 = 40$ and $N_2 = 10$?

CHAPTER 7

TESTING HYPOTHESES
ABOUT SINGLE
POPULATION MEANS

We have seen that it is helpful to describe objectively the central tendency and dispersion of a sample of data. However, as with categorical responses, we would like to go beyond the mere description of our sample. What is more important to us is the structuring of behavioral inquiries so that we may make inferences about some population of interest.

The essential characteristic of the basic structure for inquiries concerning population means and dispersions is that a population parameter, such as μ or σ, is only *hypothesized* and therefore is open to question.* For example, it might be hypothesized that

The average score on a mathematics achievement test for a class instructed by means of a mechanized, computer-based program, is not significantly different from a national average score reported in the test manual.

The variability of I.Q.'s of children tested under a particular type of stress is not significantly different from a published value specified for children in general, such as the standard deviation of 16 I.Q. points for the Stanford-Binet test of intelligence.

In order to test hypotheses such as these, a sample of independent observations is drawn. On the basis of the sample results the hypothesized value of the population mean μ or the population standard deviation σ is either accepted or rejected as being a reasonable assumption. To clarify the term "reasonable" let us reexamine our concept of a level of significance in the light of our structure for asking questions, for example, about the population mean.

---

* The form of the structure to be followed here parallels closely the structure of Chapter 5 used to test the reasonableness of an assumption or hypothesis about p, the probability of success on a single observation.

<u>**DEFINITION**</u>   *Level of Significance*

> By "reasonable" we mean that our observed sample mean $\bar{X}$ can be expected to occur more than a small percentage of the time if, in fact, μ is the actual mean of the underlying population. The exact percentage is normally placed at one, five, or, infrequently, ten percent. The selected percentage level is called the *level of significance* and is denoted by the letter α (i.e., $\alpha = 1$ percent, 5 percent, or 10 percent, more commonly expressed as $\alpha = 0.01, 0.05,$ or 0.10 respectively).

If, on the other hand, we observe a sample mean $\bar{X}$ that could be expected less than α percent of the time from such a population, we tend to cast doubt on (that is, we "reject") our original hypothesis about μ. Two possibilities exist in this case: either the population mean is equal to μ and we just happened to observe a rare sample mean $\bar{X}$, or the population mean is not really μ. We normally take the latter course and reject our original hypothesis about μ. We must again realize that we can expect incorrectly to reject our original hypothesis about α (e.g., $\alpha = 5$ percent) percent of the time in repeated experiments of this sort.

As in the case of the binomial test discussed in Chapter 5, a distinction is made between unidirectional and bidirectional tests.* In unidirectional tests it is assumed, before the data is analyzed, that the actual value of μ may lie on only one side of the hypothesized value of μ. In bidirectional tests it is assumed beforehand that the actual value of μ of interest may lie on either side of the hypothesized value of μ.

As will be seen from the remaining examples in this chapter, α, the level of significance, is again either assigned entirely to the predetermined direction of the test or divided between the two directions that the actual value of μ might be from the hypothesized value of μ.

Consider the following illustrations of the question: Is a single sample mean significantly different from expectation?

Is the average score on a mathematics achievement test for a class instructed by means of a computer-based program significantly different from the national average score reported in the test manual? If so, we would reject the hypothesis that the published value is a reasonable descriptive measure of the average achievement of classes taught with a computer-based program.

Notice here that the word *different* implies that the actual average could logically fall on either side of the published value (bidirectional). In other words, we are uncertain whether the computer-based instruction will result in an average above or below the published value.

---

* At this point, it might be helpful for you to review the discussion of unidirectional and bidirectional tests of Chapter 5.

Is the average reading rate for a group of high-ability fifth-grade pupils significantly higher than a published national mean reading rate for fifth graders (unidirectional)? If so, we would reject the hypothesis that the published mean is a reasonable descriptive measure of the average reading rate for this type of high-ability group.

Is the average speed of a sample of cars checked during rush hour traffic significantly slower than the posted minimum speed limit (unidirectional)? If so, we would reject the hypothesis that the average speed of rush hour traffic is equal to the posted minimum limit.

The approaches taken to test these kinds of hypotheses may be classified on the basis of the size of the sample. There are a so-called *large sample* approach or theory and a *small sample* approach or theory. "Large" is generally taken to mean a sample of size 30 or more (that is, $N \geq 30$). For large samples the two approaches tend to converge. We shall first consider the large sample approach for testing hypotheses with a single sample mean.

HYPOTHESIS TESTING WITH A SINGLE LARGE SAMPLE MEAN

The question of whether or not a large sample mean differs significantly from expectation may be approached with exactly the same seven-step formal hypothesis testing procedure we discussed in Chapter 5. In practice the technique is quite straightforward, as will become evident from the examples following the discussion of our seven-step procedure.

To illustrate the seven-step procedure for testing a hypothesis about a population mean, based on data collected from a large sample, consider our example of the computer-based mathematics program.

The question was whether or not the average achievement test score for the computer-based class differed significantly from the value reported in the test manual. Suppose that we have the following data:*

The published mean   = 50
The class size N = 36
The class mean $\bar{X}$ = 52
The class standard deviation S = 10

Our question, then, is: Could this experimental mathematics class (having a mean achievement score of 52) reasonably represent a sample of students drawn from a population of potential students where the mean achievement score is equal to 50? That is, how impressive is the difference between 52 and 50? Is it large enough to cast doubt on the reasonableness

---

* The sample statistics $\bar{X}$ and S were discussed in Chapter 3.

of the assumption that 50 is an adequate descriptive measure of the mean achievement of pupils taught with the computer-based program?

Based on our sample of 36 pupils, what should be our decision rule concerning our hypothesized value of the population mean's being equal to 50?

Let us frame these questions in terms of our seven-step procedure:

Step 1 / STATE THE HYPOTHESIS

> Here the specific hypothesis under question and the alternative hypothesis are stated. The hypothesized value of the population mean μ is again referred to as the null hypothesis H_0, because we are conjecturing that there is no difference between our sample result $\bar{X}$ and what we could reasonably expect if the hypothesis were, in fact, true. That is, this sample could have reasonably come from a population of potential students where the mean achievement score is 50. In our case
>
> $$H_0: \mu = 50$$
>
> The alternative hypothesis H_1 is the one to be accepted if the null hypothesis H_0 is unreasonable in the light of our sample evidence. In our case, since we were interested (prior to the collection of the data) in whether the computer-based program might yield a mean significantly above *or* below the hypothesized value, we use the bidirectional alternative hypothesis:*
>
> $$H_1: \mu \neq 50$$

Step 2 / STATE THE LEVEL OF SIGNIFICANCE α

> Here, again, we state the risk we are willing to take in rejecting the hypothesis H_0 when in fact H_0 is true and we merely happened to observe an unusual, but nevertheless possible, sample result. Let us select a five percent level of significance. That is,
>
> $$\alpha = 0.05$$

Step 3 / STATE THE TEST STATISTIC

> The test statistic appropriate for testing a hypothesis about a population mean with a single large sample is:

---

* If the only alternative of interest was whether the actual mean was significantly *above* the published value, our unidirectional alternative hypothesis would be $H_1: \mu > 50$. Likewise, if the only alternative of interest was for the mean to be significantly *below* the published value, we would have $H_1: \mu < 50$. It should be remembered that H_0 and H_1 are established before the sample data are examined.

$$Z = \frac{\bar{X} - \mu}{\dfrac{\sigma}{\sqrt{N}}}$$

where

$\bar{X}$ = the sample mean
N = the sample size
μ = the hypothesized population mean
σ = the population standard deviation

You will notice that the test statistic Z involves the population standard deviation σ. Either σ is assumed known, or the standard deviation of our sample S is used in its place. This substitution is justified on the basis of having a large sample of 30 or more observations, in which case S is a fairly good approximation of σ. Thus in our example S may be assumed closely to approximate σ in the statistic

$$Z = \frac{\bar{X} - \mu}{\dfrac{\sigma}{\sqrt{N}}}$$

which thus becomes

$$Z = \frac{52 - 50}{\dfrac{10}{\sqrt{36}}} = \frac{2}{1.67}$$

$$= 1.20$$

An appreciation for the test statistic

$$Z = \frac{\bar{X} - \mu}{\dfrac{\sigma}{\sqrt{N}}}$$

may be gained in the following manner: First, consider a population of responses like that in Figure 7.1. Next, con-

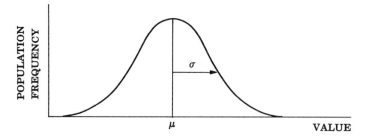

FIGURE 7.1
A population of responses

sider drawing large samples of size N repeatedly (say K samples) from this population. Compute the arithmetic mean for each sample, that is, $(\bar{X}_1, \bar{X}_2, \ldots, \bar{X}_i, \ldots, \bar{X}_K)$. These K arithmetic means *will not* all have the same value. As we saw in the last chapter, these means will form a distribution called the sampling distribution of the mean. The expected value and the standard error of the sampling distribution of the mean are from Theorem 6.1:

$$\text{Expected value} = \mu$$

$$\text{Standard error} = \frac{\sigma}{\sqrt{N}}$$

In general, the relationship between the original distribution of raw scores and the sampling distribution of arithmetic means is as shown in Figure 7.2. The important

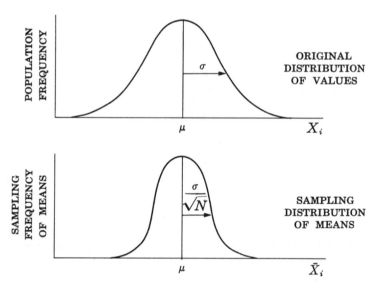

FIGURE 7.2

Comparison of original distribution of raw scores and sampling distribution of means

point is that the chance of any sample mean $\bar{X}$'s being a given distance from μ depends on σ and N. The larger σ is, the greater the possibility is that we may observe a sample mean $\bar{X}$ far removed from μ (likewise for a small N). The smaller σ is, the less likely we are to observe a sample mean far removed from μ (likewise for large N).

In order to use one table of probabilities (regardless of the values of μ, σ, or N) to determine the chance of observing a sample mean as far away, or further, from μ as we did, we *standardize the sample mean*. To standardize the sample mean, we follow the same procedure as we have previously in standardizing raw scores, whereby all distributions are reduced to one having a mean of zero and a standard deviation of one. Remember that a standard score Z_i corresponding to an original value was defined in the following manner:

$$Z_i = \frac{\text{original value} - (\text{mean of the distribution of original values})}{(\text{standard deviation of the distribution of original values})}$$

For raw (X_i) scores from a normal population the standard score conversion was therefore

$$Z_i = \frac{X_i - \mu}{\sigma}$$

However, at present we are not dealing with raw (X_i) values. We are concerned with means (i.e., $\bar{X}_1$, $\bar{X}_2$, ..., $\bar{X}_i$, ..., $\bar{X}_K$). Therefore, since the mean of the distribution of sample means (i.e., the expected value) is known to be μ and the standard deviation of the distribution of sample means (i.e., the standard error) is known to be $\sigma/\sqrt{N}$, the defining formula for the standard score corresponding to a sample mean becomes

$$Z_i = \frac{\bar{X}_i - (\text{expected value})}{(\text{standard error})} = \frac{\bar{X}_i - \mu}{\dfrac{\sigma}{\sqrt{N}}}$$

Normally the subscript i is omitted, since we are concerned with only a single mean in any given experiment. Thus we have

$$Z = \frac{\bar{X} - \mu}{\dfrac{\sigma}{\sqrt{N}}}$$

Actually, the square root of the unbiased sample variance $\hat{S}^2$ would be a more precise estimate of σ than the estimate S we are using here. However, for large samples there is little practical difference between $\hat{S}^2$ and S^2.

Step 4 / SPECIFY THE DISTRIBUTION OF THE TEST STATISTIC

The test statistic

$$Z = \frac{\bar{X} - \mu}{\dfrac{\sigma}{N}}$$

follows the unit normal probability distribution if, in fact, the null hypothesis is true. That is, in repeated sampling from a *population of responses*, the Z scores corresponding to the sample means will tend toward the normal distribution with a mean of zero and a standard deviation of one. Consider why the distribution of Z scores, where Z is defined by

$$Z = \frac{\bar{X} - \mu}{\dfrac{\sigma}{\sqrt{N}}}$$

tends toward the unit normal distribution. First of all, the distribution of the Z scores has a mean of zero and a standard deviation of one, since this is a property of all standardized distributions, as discussed in Chapter 3. The distribution of the Z's is also normal, because a standardized distribution follows the shape of the distribution of the original values and these values are sample means that tend toward a normal distribution, according to the central limit theorem.

The essential characteristic of the unit normal distribution is that the probability of our sample mean $\bar{X}$'s being a given distance (measured in standard deviation units) away from the population mean μ is the same as for the corresponding Z score's being this distance away from *zero*. In other words, we have the important result that a probability statement about a value of Z is a probability statement about $\bar{X}$, our sample mean. Probability statements about Z can be made, in turn, by referring to the unit normal probability distribution tabled in Table V of Appendix A.

Step 5 / SELECT THE REJECTION REGION

Here we make our decision as to which values of our test statistic

$$Z = \frac{\bar{X} - \mu}{\dfrac{\sigma}{\sqrt{N}}}$$

would be so unusual to observe in our sample that we no longer could reasonably maintain our belief in the hypothesized value of μ. The *rejection region* depends upon both the alternative hypothesis H_1 and the level of significance α. For our example of the experimental, computer-based mathematics program we have, from Step 1,

Alternative hypothesis, H_1: $\mu \neq 50$

Prior to the analysis of the sample data, we are uncertain whether such experimental classes have a mean achievement score above or below the published value of 50. In other words, if the experimental class mean is too far above 50 or too far below 50, we would want to declare the experimental class mean to be significantly different from the published value of 50. We have, then, a situation that calls for a bidirectional test.

Furthermore, we selected our level of significance α as

$$\alpha = 0.05$$

From our discussion of the level of significance we saw that in a bidirectional test the level of significance is divided between the two directions of the alternative hypothesis. Therefore, since we have selected an $\alpha = 0.05$, we shall assign half of α (that is, 0.025) to each direction of H_1, as illustrated in Figure 7.3. See also Figure 6.8. From Table V

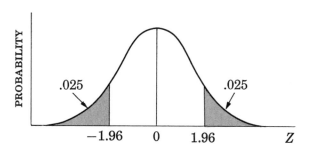

Figure 7.3
Unit normal probability curve

of Appendix A we see that the probability of observing a value of Z greater than 1.96 or less than -1.96 by chance alone when, in fact, the null hypothesis is true is 0.05.

Since $\alpha = 0.05$, a rare value of Z is taken to mean a value of Z greater than 1.96 or less than -1.96.

Remember that probability statements about Z are probability statements about our sample mean $\bar{X}$. Thus if we observe a rare value of Z, we *also* declare our observed sample mean $\bar{X}$ to be a rare value under the conditions of H_0. A rare value of $\bar{X}$ leads us, on the basis of our sample evidence, to

Reject the null hypothesis

$$H_0: \mu = 50$$

and

Accept the alternative hypothesis,

$$H_1: \mu \neq 50$$

Our *rejection region* (for $H_1: \mu = 50$ and $\alpha = 0.05$) is, therefore,

$$Z > 1.96 \quad \text{and} \quad Z < -1.96$$

for our example. Values of Z not in the *rejection region* are said to fall in the *acceptance region*.

Step 6 / COMPUTE THE TEST STATISTIC

Here we evaluate the test statistic specified in Step 3. For our example we have, again,

$$Z = \frac{\bar{X} - \mu}{\dfrac{\sigma}{\sqrt{N}}}$$

$$= \frac{52 - 50}{\dfrac{10}{\sqrt{36}}} = \frac{2}{1.67}$$

$$= 1.20$$

Recall that either σ is assumed known or the standard deviation of our large sample S is used in its place (as in the case here).

Step 7 / ACCEPT OR REJECT THE NULL HYPOTHESIS

The final step in the formal hypothesis testing procedure is to see if the computed test statistic of Step 6 falls in the *rejection region* specified in Step 5. If it does, we reject H_0 and accept the corresponding H_1. If it does not, we accept H_0.

In our case our *rejection region* is defined by

$$Z > 1.96 \quad \text{or} \quad Z < -1.96$$

while our observed test statistic resulted in

$$Z = 1.20$$

which clearly does not fall in the *rejection region*. Therefore we

Accept the null hypothesis

$$H_0: \mu = 50$$

In other words, our observed sample mean ($\bar{X} = 52$) is not significantly different from the published value of 50. There is insufficient evidence to cast doubt on the reasonableness of the assumption that 50 is an adequate descriptive measure of the mean achievement of pupils taught with the computer-based program. This experimental mathematics class (having a mean achievement score of 52) could reasonably represent a sample of students drawn from a population where the mean achievement score is equal to 50.

The formal hypothesis testing procedure for this example problem may be briefly summarized as follows:

Step 1 / STATE THE HYPOTHESIS

$$H_0: \mu = 50$$

$$H_1: \mu \neq 50$$

Step 2 / STATE THE LEVEL OF SIGNIFICANCE

$$\alpha = 0.05$$

Step 3 / STATE THE TEST STATISTIC

$$Z = \frac{\bar{X} - \mu}{\dfrac{\sigma}{\sqrt{N}}}$$

Step 4 / SPECIFY THE DISTRIBUTION OF THE TEST STATISTIC

Z follows the unit normal probability distribution [i.e., $Z \overset{d}{=} N(0, 1)$] given in Table V of Appendix A.

Step 5 / SELECT THE REJECTION REGION

The *rejection region* is

$$Z > 1.96 \quad \text{and} \quad Z < -1.96$$

Step 6 / COMPUTE THE TEST STATISTIC

$$Z = \frac{52 - 50}{\dfrac{10}{\sqrt{36}}} = 1.20$$

Step 7 / ACCEPT OR REJECT THE NULL HYPOTHESIS

Accept

$$H_0:\ \mu = 50$$

To illustrate further the seven-step procedure for testing a hypothesis about a population mean, based on data collected from a large sample, consider the two additional examples mentioned earlier in this chapter.

First, consider the question: Is the average reading rate for a group of high-ability fifth-grade pupils significantly higher than a published national mean reading rate of 200 words per minute for fifth graders? Assume the following data:

Sample size = 100
Mean reading rate of our sample $\bar{X} = 210$ words per minute
Standard deviation of our sample of reading rates $S = 25$

Our seven-step procedure is

Step 1 / STATE THE HYPOTHESIS

$$H_0:\ \mu = 200$$

$$H_1:\ \mu > 200$$

That is, we are concerned only with the question of whether this group of high-ability pupils reads significantly faster than 200 words per minute.

Step 2 / STATE THE LEVEL OF SIGNIFICANCE

Let us select a level of significance α of

$$\alpha = 0.05$$

Step 3 / STATE THE TEST STATISTIC

$$Z = \frac{\bar{X} - \mu}{\dfrac{\sigma}{\sqrt{N}}}$$

Step 4 / SPECIFY THE DISTRIBUTION OF THE TEST STATISTIC

Z follows the unit normal probability distribution.

Step 5 / SELECT THE REJECTION REGION

Corresponding to a unidirectional alternative hypothesis, such as we have here (that is, H_1: $\mu > 200$) and an $\alpha = 0.05$, the *rejection region* has already been shown in Figure 6.5 to be

$$Z > 1.65$$

That is, from Table V of Appendix A

$$P(Z > 1.65) = 0.5 - [P(0 \leq Z \leq 1.65)]$$
$$= 0.05$$

Step 6 / COMPUTE THE TEST STATISTIC

For the data in our example, we have, upon substituting S for σ,

$$Z = \frac{210 - 200}{\dfrac{25}{\sqrt{100}}} = \frac{10}{2.5}$$

$$= 4$$

Step 7 / ACCEPT OR REJECT THE NULL HYPOTHESIS

Since the test statistic for our sample clearly falls in the *rejection region*, we

Reject the null hypothesis

$$H_0\text{: } \mu = 200$$

and

Accept the alternative hypothesis

$$H_1\text{: } \mu > 200$$

Our sample mean ($\bar{X} = 210$) is significantly above the hypothesized value for the population mean ($\mu = 200$). Therefore, it is more reasonable for us to believe that the population mean reading rate for children of this type is greater than 200 (i.e., $\mu > 200$).

Finally, let us consider the question: Is the average speed of a sample of cars checked during rush hour traffic significantly slower than the posted minimum speed limit of 40 miles per hour? Assume the following:

Sample size $= 36$
Mean speed of our sample $\bar{X} = 38$ miles per hour
Standard deviation of our sample of speeds $S = 9$ miles per hour

Our seven-step procedure is

Step 1 / STATE THE HYPOTHESIS

$$H_0: \mu = 40$$

$$H_1: \mu < 40$$

That is, the only alternative of interest is whether the traffic is moving slower than the posted minimum limit of 40 miles per hour.

Step 2 / STATE THE LEVEL OF SIGNIFICANCE

Let us select a level of significance α of

$$\alpha = 0.05$$

Step 3 / STATE THE TEST STATISTIC

$$Z = \frac{\bar{X} - \mu}{\dfrac{\sigma}{\sqrt{N}}}$$

Step 4 / SPECIFY THE DISTRIBUTION OF THE TEST STATISTIC

Z follows the unit normal probability distribution.

Step 5 / SELECT THE REJECTION REGION

Corresponding to a unidirectional alternative hypothesis, such as we have here (that is, $H_1: \mu < 40$) and an $\alpha = 0.05$, the *rejection region* has already been shown in Figure 6.7 to be

$$Z < -1.65$$

That is, from Table V of Appendix A we see that

$$P(Z < -1.65) = P(Z > 1.65)$$

$$= 0.5 - [P(0 \leq Z \leq 1.65)]$$

$$= 0.05$$

Step 6 / COMPUTE THE TEST STATISTIC

For the data in our example, we have, replacing σ by S,

$$Z = \frac{38 - 40}{\dfrac{9}{\sqrt{36}}} = \frac{-2}{1.5}$$

$$= -1.33$$

Step 7 / ACCEPT OR REJECT THE NULL HYPOTHESIS

> Since the test statistic for our sample does not fall in the *rejection region*, we
>
> > Accept the null hypothesis
>
> $$H_0:\ \mu = 40$$
>
> Our observed sample mean ($\bar{X} = 38$), based on a sample of 36 cars, is not significantly below the posted minimum speed limit of 40 miles per hour. This sample of cars could reasonably represent a sample of cars drawn from a population where the mean speed is equal to 40 miles per hour.

HYPOTHESIS TESTING WITH A SINGLE SMALL SAMPLE MEAN

In behavioral research we are often confronted with the problem of having to carry out inquiries with a small number of individuals. A small sample is generally considered to be less than 30 (that is, $N < 30$). Our question is still whether or not our sample mean differs significantly from expectation. To illustrate the hypothesis testing procedure for this situation, consider again our example of the computer-based mathematics program.

The question was whether or not the average achievement test score for the computer-based class differed significantly from the value reported in the test manual. Let us only change the sample size from a large sample of 36 to a small sample of 17. Thus we have the following data:

> The published mean = 50
> The class size $N = 17$
> The class mean $\bar{X} = 52$
> The class standard deviation $S = 10$

Could this experimental mathematics class (having a mean achievement score of 52) reasonably represent a sample of students drawn from a population where the mean achievement score is equal to 50?

Let us frame this "small" sample question in terms of our seven-step procedure:

Step 1 / STATE THE HYPOTHESIS

> Our question is: Could this small sample have reasonably come from a population of students where the mean achievement score is 50? Thus our null hypothesis H_0 remains as before.
>
> $$H_0:\ \mu = 50$$

Likewise, since we were uncertain, *before the data were examined*, whether the computer-based program would yield a mean above or below the published (hypothesized) value, we use the bidirectional alternative hypothesis again.

$$H_1:\ \mu \neq 50$$

Step 2 / STATE THE LEVEL OF SIGNIFICANCE α

Let us maintain a five percent level of significance.

$$\alpha = 0.05$$

Step 3 / STATE THE TEST STATISTIC

An appropriate statistic for testing hypotheses about population means with a single small sample is known as the *Student's t statistic*. The name of this statistic stems from the fact that its properties were discovered by a mathematician named Gosset, who published his works using the name "Student." The Student's t statistic may be defined as follows:

$$t = \frac{\bar{X} - \mu}{\dfrac{S}{\sqrt{N - 1}}}$$

where

$\bar{X}$ = the sample mean
N = the sample size
μ = the hypothesized population mean
S = the sample standard deviation

Thus, for our example, we have

$$t = \frac{52 - 50}{\dfrac{10}{\sqrt{16}}}$$

$$= 0.8$$

The small sample t statistic is analogous to the large sample Z statistic. In estimating a population variance σ^2 from a sample there are two forms of the sample variance we may use: the *biased estimate* and the *unbiased estimate*.

Biased estimate

$$S^2 = \frac{\displaystyle\sum_{i=1}^{N} (X_i - \bar{X})^2}{N}$$

The square root of this biased estimate, S, is the form we have used so far in defining the sample standard deviation.

Unbiased estimate

$$\widehat{S}^2 = \frac{\sum\limits_{i=1}^{N} (X_i - \bar{X})^2}{N - 1}$$

The essential difference between S^2 and $\widehat{S}^2$ is that the expected value of $\widehat{S}^2$ is equal to σ^2, whereas the expected value of S^2 is somewhat less than σ^2. For large samples the difference between S^2 and $\widehat{S}^2$ is negligible. However, for small samples the bias might be considerable. Considering the small sample t statistic, we have

$$t = \frac{\bar{X} - \mu}{\dfrac{S}{\sqrt{N - 1}}}$$

However,

$$\widehat{S}^2 = \frac{N}{N - 1} S^2$$

or

$$\widehat{S} = \sqrt{\frac{N}{N - 1}} S$$

Therefore,

$$t = \frac{\bar{X} - \mu}{\dfrac{S}{\sqrt{N - 1}}} = \frac{\bar{X} - \mu}{\dfrac{\widehat{S}}{\sqrt{N}}}$$

which is analogous to

$$Z = \frac{\bar{X} - \mu}{\dfrac{\sigma}{\sqrt{N}}}$$

Hence for large sample sizes the value of the t statistic approaches that of the Z statistic.

Recall that the defining formula for Z involved the population standard deviation σ, which was assumed known, or the large sample standard deviation S, which was used in its place.

The defining formula for t is therefore somewhat less restrictive in the sense that no knowledge about or estimate of the population standard deviation σ is required. However, as we shall see, because of the small amount of information available we make somewhat weaker statements with the t statistic than with the Z statistic.

Step 4 / SPECIFY THE DISTRIBUTION OF THE TEST STATISTIC

For a very large value of N, the t statistic, as was pointed out in the supplementary discussion of Step 3, closely approximates that of Z. Therefore, the sampling distribution of t will approach that of the unit normal probability distribution for a large N. The total area under the t distribution curve is also symmetrical around 0 and the total area under the curve is taken to be 1. Thus the t distribution is commonly referred to as the *Student's t probability distribution*. However, for a small value of N, the Student's t probability distribution is somewhat different from the unit normal curve.

The relationship between the Z and t distributions may be clarified by referring to Tables V and VI of Appendix A. It is easily seen that the Z values correspond to the t values for infinite degrees of freedom. For example, the entry of Table VI corresponding to $t_{0.975}$ with $\nu = \infty$ is 1.96, as is the Z value of Table V, below which 97.5 percent of the cases fall. Even with $\nu = 30$ in Table VI, the difference is not great (i.e., $t = 2.04$, $Z = 1.96$). However, for small values of ν in Table VI (e.g., for $\nu = 10$, the table entry is 2.23) the discrepancy between the Z and t values becomes appreciable. In particular it has been shown that the unique form of the Student's t probability distribution depends on a quantity that is always one less than the sample size (i.e., $N - 1$), known as the *degrees of freedom*. The relationship of the sampling distribution of t and the degrees of freedom $(N - 1)$ is illustrated in Figure 7.4.* Again, as N gets large, the Student's t probability distribution approaches the Z distribution. The test statistic

$$t = \frac{\bar{X} - \mu}{\dfrac{S}{\sqrt{N - 1}}}$$

is therefore said to follow the Student's t probability distribution corresponding to $(N - 1)$ degrees of freedom if, in fact, the null hypothesis is true.

---

* The concept of degrees of freedom may be illustrated in the following way for metric data: Suppose that we know only that the arithmetic mean of three numbers is 10. How much freedom do we then have in selecting the three numbers so that their arithmetic mean is 10? Clearly, we may select any value for two of the numbers, but once these two numbers are selected, the third one must have a particular value in order that the mean remain unchanged.

For example, suppose we selected 4 and 9 as the first two numbers. Then the third number must equal 17 in order that the mean of the three numbers be 10. We have, in this case, two degrees of freedom. In general, for N numbers, we have $(N - 1)$ such degrees of freedom.

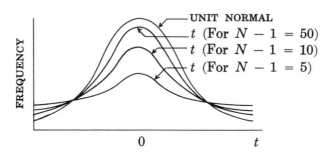

FIGURE 7.4
Sampling distribution of t for various sample sizes
contrasted with the unit normal curve

The Student's t probability distribution is interpreted in a manner similar to the unit normal probability distribution. That is, as our sample means $\bar{X}$ move away from the population mean μ, the test statistic t moves away from zero. In other words, we have the important result that a probability statement about a value of t is a probability statement about our sample mean $\bar{X}$. Probability statements about t can be made, in turn, by referring to the probability distribution of t.

The Student's t probability distribution is tabled in Table VI of Appendix A. The body of the table gives a number that has a specified probability of being greater than our observed value of t if, in fact, the null hypothesis is true. The probabilities, given across the top of the table, are 0.995, 0.99, 0.975, 0.95, 0.90, etc. The table is entered at the $\nu = N - 1$ row (referred to as $N - 1$ or ν degrees of freedom) as illustrated in the following examples using the table.

EXAMPLE 1

From Table VI of Appendix A we see that for $N - 1 = 9$ and $t_{0.95}$, the table entry is 1.83. That is, the probability of observing a value of t less than 1.83 from a sample of size 10 is 0.95. Since the total area or probability under a probability distribution is one, the probability of observing a value of t larger than 1.83 (with $N = 10$) is

$$P(t > 1.83) = 1 - P(t \leq 1.83)$$

$$= 1 - 0.95$$

$$= 0.05$$

The probability of observing a value of t greater than 1.83, for a sample of size 10, is illustrated in Figure 7.5. Since the t distribution, like the Z distribution, is symmetrical, the probability of observing a value of t greater than zero is 0.5. Likewise, the probability of observing a value of t less than zero is also 0.5.

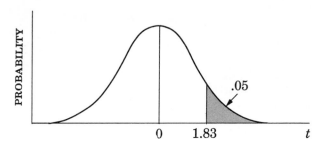

FIGURE 7.5
The t distribution for N = 10

Because the *t* distribution is symmetrical, the probability of observing a value of *t* less than −1.83 is the same as the probability of observing a value of *t* greater than +1.83. This is illustrated in Figure 7.6.

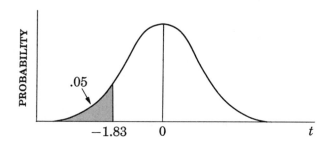

FIGURE 7.6
The t distribution for N = 10

EXAMPLE 2

By the same reasoning used in Example 1 we can see that the probability of observing a value of *t* larger than 1.86, for a sample size of 9, is 0.05. The probability of observing a value of *t* less than −1.86 is also 0.05. This is illustrated in Figure 7.7.

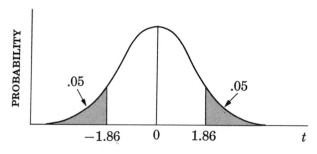

FIGURE 7.7
The t distribution for N = 9

Step 5 / SELECT THE REJECTION REGION

Recall that in a bidirectional test the level of significance α is divided between the two directions of the alternative hypothesis. Therefore, since we selected an $\alpha = 0.05$, we shall assign half of it (0.025) to each direction of H_1. From Table VI of Appendix A we see that for $N = 17$ the probability of observing a value of t less than 2.12 is 0.975. Therefore, we have the situation illustrated in Figure 7.8.

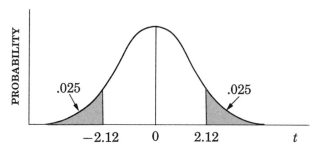

FIGURE 7.8
The t distribution for N = 17

Since $\alpha = 0.05$, a rare value of t is taken to mean a value of t greater than 2.12 or less than -2.12. Remember that probability statements about t are probability statements about our sample mean $\bar{X}$. Thus if we observe a rare value of t, we also declare our observed sample mean $\bar{X}$ to be a rare value. A rare value of $\bar{X}$ leads us, on the basis of our sample evidence, to

Reject the null hypothesis

$$H_0: \mu = 50$$

and

Accept the alternative hypothesis

$$H_1: \mu \neq 50$$

Our *rejection region* for $H_1: \mu \neq 50$, $\alpha = 0.05$, and $N = 17$ is, therefore,

$$t > 2.12 \quad \text{and} \quad t < -2.12$$

Step 6 / COMPUTE THE TEST STATISTIC

Here we evaluate the test statistic specified in Step 3. For our example we have, again,

$$t = \frac{\bar{X} - \mu}{\dfrac{S}{\sqrt{N-1}}}$$

$$= \frac{52 - 50}{\dfrac{10}{\sqrt{16}}}$$

$$= 0.8$$

Step 7 / ACCEPT OR REJECT THE NULL HYPOTHESIS

Our sample test statistic clearly does not fall in the *rejection region.* Therefore we
> Accept the null hypothesis

$$H_0: \mu = 50$$

In this case, the interpretation of the result is the same as discussed under the large sample case for this example.

The formal hypothesis testing procedure for this example problem may be briefly summarized as follows:

Step 1 / STATE THE HYPOTHESIS

$$H_0: \mu = 50$$
$$H_1: \mu \neq 50$$

Step 2 / STATE THE LEVEL OF SIGNIFICANCE

$$\alpha = 0.05$$

Step 3 / STATE THE TEST STATISTIC

$$t = \frac{\bar{X} - \mu}{\dfrac{S}{\sqrt{N-1}}}$$

Step 4 / SPECIFY THE DISTRIBUTION OF THE TEST STATISTIC

t follows the Student's t probability distribution given in Table VI of Appendix A.

Step 5 / SELECT THE REJECTION REGION

$$t > 2.12 \quad \text{and} \quad t < -2.12$$

Step 6 / COMPUTE THE TEST STATISTIC

$$t = \frac{\bar{X} - \mu}{\dfrac{S}{\sqrt{N-1}}}$$

$$= \frac{52 - 50}{\dfrac{10}{\sqrt{16}}}$$

$$= 0.8$$

Step 7 / ACCEPT OR REJECT THE NULL HYPOTHESIS

Accept

$$H_0: \mu = 50$$

To conclude our discussion of the procedure for testing a hypothesis about a population mean, based on data collected from a small sample, consider the two additional examples presented for the large sample case.

First, consider the question: Is the average reading rate for a group of high-ability fifth-grade pupils significantly higher than a published national mean reading rate of 200 words per minute for fifth-graders? Assume the following sample data:

Sample size = 26
Mean reading rate of our sample $\bar{X}$ = 210 words per minute
Standard deviation of our sample S = 25

Following our seven-step procedure for this small sample case, we have:

Step 1 / STATE THE HYPOTHESIS

$$H_0: \mu = 200$$

$$H_1: \mu > 200$$

Step 2 / STATE THE LEVEL OF SIGNIFICANCE

$$\alpha = 0.05$$

Step 3 / STATE THE TEST STATISTIC

$$t = \frac{\bar{X} - \mu}{\dfrac{S}{\sqrt{N-1}}}$$

Step 4 / SPECIFY THE DISTRIBUTION OF THE TEST STATISTIC

Student's t probability distribution.

Step 5 / SELECT THE REJECTION REGION

Since we have a unidirectional alternative hypothesis, we assign all of α to the specified direction. For a sample size of 26, we see that the probability of observing a value of t of less than 1.71 is 0.95. Therefore, our *rejection region* is $t > 1.71$, as illustrated in Figure 7.9.

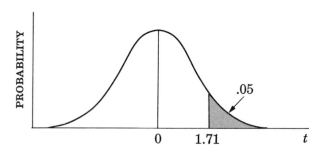

FIGURE 7.9
The t distribution for $N = 26$

Step 6 / COMPUTE THE TEST STATISTIC

$$t = \frac{210 - 200}{\dfrac{25}{\sqrt{25}}}$$

$$= 2$$

Step 7 / ACCEPT OR REJECT THE NULL HYPOTHESIS

Since the test statistic is clearly in the *rejection region*, we
Reject
$$H_0: \mu = 200$$
and
Accept
$$H_1: \mu > 200$$

The interpretation is the same as before.

Finally, consider the question: Is the average speed of a sample of cars checked during rush hour traffic significantly slower than the posted minimum speed limit of 40 miles per hour? Assume the following sample data:

Sample size = 10
Mean speed of our sample $\bar{X}$ = 38 miles per hour
Standard deviation of our sample of speeds = 9 miles per hour

Step 1 / STATE THE HYPOTHESIS

$$H_0: \mu = 40$$

$$H_1: \mu < 40$$

Step 2 / STATE THE LEVEL OF SIGNIFICANCE

$$\alpha = 0.05$$

Step 3 / STATE THE TEST STATISTIC

$$t = \frac{\bar{X} - \mu}{\dfrac{S}{\sqrt{N-1}}}$$

Step 4 / SPECIFY THE DISTRIBUTION OF THE TEST STATISTIC

Student's t probability distribution.

Step 5 / SELECT THE REJECTION REGION

Since we have a unidirectional alternative hypothesis, we assign all of α to the specified direction. For a sample of size 10 we see that the probability of observing a value of t less than 1.83 is 0.95. Since our alternative hypothesis is that $\mu < 40$, our *rejection region* is $t < -1.83$, as illustrated in Figure 7.10.

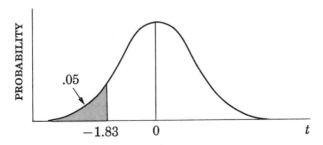

FIGURE 7.10
The t distribution for $N = 10$

Step 6 / COMPUTE THE TEST STATISTIC

$$t = \frac{38 - 40}{\dfrac{9}{\sqrt{9}}}$$

$$= -0.67$$

Step 7 / ACCEPT OR REJECT THE NULL HYPOTHESIS

Accept the null hypothesis

$$H_0: \mu = 40$$

The interpretation is as before.

INTERVAL ESTIMATION OF SINGLE POPULATION MEANS

LARGE SAMPLES

Our sample mean $\bar{X}$ is our best estimate of the value of the population mean μ. That is, the expected value of $\bar{X}$ is μ.

The sample mean $\bar{X}$ is said to be a *point estimate* of μ. The single value of our sample mean represents a point that may be taken as an estimate of the population mean. However, from random sample to random sample the sample means (that is, the $\bar{X}$'s) will not all have the same value. They will, instead, form the sampling distribution of the mean. Therefore, we cannot expect $\bar{X}$ to equal μ for every sample we might happen to select.

The mean of several random sample means will tend toward the population mean μ. However, we normally only have one sample to work with, and the probability of this particular sample mean $\bar{X}$'s being equal to the population mean μ is small indeed.

A more helpful approach is to establish a range for estimating μ instead of simply taking $\bar{X}$ as a point estimate of μ. This range is called a *confidence interval*.

To construct a confidence interval for μ, we compute an interval from our *single* sample data such that we are reasonably confident that it encompasses μ. The interpretation of a confidence interval is that if we actually had a large number of samples, a large percentage of the computed intervals would encompass μ.

We may, for example, construct a 99 percent confidence interval from our single sample data. We would correspondingly expect that if we actually had a large number of samples, 99 percent of the computed intervals would encompass μ. Ninety-five and 90 percent confidence intervals are also commonly used.* These confidence intervals are as follows:

---

* We may, of course, construct confidence intervals with any desired degree of precision.

99 Percent Confidence Interval

$$\bar{X} - 2.58 \frac{\sigma}{\sqrt{N}} \leq \mu \leq \bar{X} + 2.58 \frac{\sigma}{\sqrt{N}}$$

95 Percent Confidence Interval

$$\bar{X} - 1.96 \frac{\sigma}{\sqrt{N}} \leq \mu \leq \bar{X} + 1.96 \frac{\sigma}{\sqrt{N}}$$

90 Percent Confidence Interval

$$\bar{X} - 1.65 \frac{\sigma}{\sqrt{N}} \leq \mu \leq \bar{X} + 1.65 \frac{\sigma}{\sqrt{N}}$$

where either σ is again assumed known or the large sample standard deviation S is used in its place.

For example, let us construct 99 and 95 percent confidence intervals for the population mean μ in our example of the computer-based mathematics program. Our sample data were

The class size $N = 36$
The class mean $\bar{X} = 52$*
The class standard deviation $S = 10$

99 Percent Confidence Interval:

$$\bar{X} - 2.58 \frac{\sigma}{\sqrt{N}} \leq \mu \leq \bar{X} + 2.58 \frac{\sigma}{\sqrt{N}}$$

$$52 - 2.58 \frac{10}{\sqrt{36}} \leq \mu \leq 52 + 2.58 \frac{10}{\sqrt{36}}$$

$$47.69 \leq \mu \leq 56.31$$

95 Percent Confidence Interval:

$$\bar{X} - 1.96 \frac{\sigma}{\sqrt{N}} \leq \mu \leq \bar{X} + 1.96 \frac{\sigma}{\sqrt{N}}$$

$$52 - 1.96 \frac{10}{\sqrt{36}} \leq \mu \leq 52 + 1.96 \frac{10}{\sqrt{36}}$$

$$48.73 \leq \mu \leq 55.27$$

Notice that we pay for the greater confidence of the 99 percent confidence interval by having a wider interval. This makes intuitive sense, since we are not as sure that the population mean is between 48.73 and 55.27 as we are that it is between 47.69 and 56.31.

---

* Our best point estimate of μ is therefore $\bar{X} = 52$.

We must balance the degree of confidence desired against the usefulness of the interval width. For example, one does not have to be a statistician to be practically certain that the mean I.Q. for college students lies between 60 and 180. However, such a wide range is, of course, of little practical value in estimating the mean I.Q. A more useful statement could be made by having a 90 percent confidence interval from, say, 115 to 130.

The rationale underlying the confidence intervals given above will be demonstrated for a 95 percent confidence interval.

From Table V of Appendix A we see that the probability of Z's being between $+1.96$ and -1.96 is 0.95. This probability is illustrated in Figure 7.11. That is,

$$P(-1.96 \leq Z \leq 1.96)$$
$$= 1 - [P(Z > 1.96) + P(Z < -1.96)]$$
$$= 1 - (0.025 + 0.025)$$
$$= 0.95$$

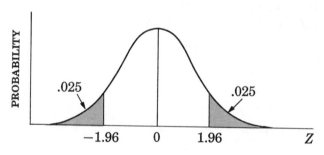

FIGURE 7.11
Unit normal probability distribution

Hence a 95 percent range for Z is

$$-1.96 \leq Z \leq 1.96$$

However,

$$Z = \frac{\bar{X} - \mu}{\dfrac{\sigma}{\sqrt{N}}}$$

Therefore,

$$-1.96 \leq \frac{\bar{X} - \mu}{\dfrac{\sigma}{\sqrt{N}}} \leq 1.96$$

or

$$-1.96 \frac{\sigma}{\sqrt{N}} \leq \bar{X} - \mu \leq 1.96 \frac{\sigma}{\sqrt{N}}$$

or

$$-\bar{X} - 1.96 \frac{\sigma}{\sqrt{N}} \leq -\mu \leq -\bar{X} + 1.96 \frac{\sigma}{\sqrt{N}}$$

Finally, rearranging signs, we have

$$\bar{X} - 1.96 \frac{\sigma}{\sqrt{N}} \leq \mu \leq \bar{X} + 1.96 \frac{\sigma}{\sqrt{N}}$$

SMALL SAMPLES

Just as we constructed confidence intervals for μ from the unit normal probability distribution, we can do so from Student's t probability distribution.

For example, let us construct a 95 percent confidence interval from the data given in our computer-based mathematics program. Our sample data are

Class size $N = 17$
Class mean $\bar{X} = 52$
Class standard deviation $S = 10$

We start by making a probability statement about t. Since our sample size is 17, we see from Table VI of Appendix A that there is a 0.05 chance of t's being greater than 2.12 or less than -2.12. That is, 95 percent of the time we would expect

$$-2.12 \leq t \leq 2.12$$

for $N = 17$.

Upon substituting our expression for t and isolating μ, we have from

$$-2.12 \leq \frac{\bar{X} - \mu}{\frac{S}{\sqrt{N-1}}} \leq 2.12$$

the interval

$$\bar{X} - 2.12 \frac{S}{\sqrt{N-1}} \leq \mu \leq \bar{X} + 2.12 \frac{S}{\sqrt{N-1}}$$

Thus for our example we have

$$52 - 2.12 \frac{10}{\sqrt{16}} \leq \mu \leq 52 + 2.12 \frac{10}{\sqrt{16}}$$

and a 95 percent confidence interval for μ based on a sample of 17 would be

$$46.70 \leq \mu \leq 57.30$$

Contrasting this confidence interval with the corresponding one constructed from the unit normal distribution or from the t distribution for $\nu = \infty$, namely

$$48.73 \leq \mu \leq 55.27$$

we see that our 95 percent confidence interval constructed from the t distribution is not as precise as it is with the unit normal distribution. This is reasonable, since we are basing our estimate on fewer observations.

SUMMARY

This chapter deals with the question of whether or not the mean of a sample of independent observations differs significantly from expectation when the underlying population mean is assumed or hypothesized to have a particular value.

The approaches to testing hypotheses about population means are classified on the basis of the sample size. For testing hypotheses about means with large sample sizes (i.e., $N \geq 30$), the statistic

$$Z = \frac{\bar{X} - \mu}{\dfrac{\sigma}{\sqrt{N}}}$$

is used with the sample value of S substituted for σ. The test statistic

$$t = \frac{\bar{X} - \mu}{\dfrac{S}{\sqrt{N - 1}}}$$

is introduced for the small sample ($N < 30$) cases. The Student's t statistic does not require knowledge of the population σ. Being less restrictive in its assumptions than the Z statistic, the Student's t statistic results in somewhat weaker statements for a given sample size.

If we repeatedly drew large samples from a normal population, the sampling distribution of the t values would approach that of the unit normal probability distribution. For any small sample size, however, the sampling distribution of t differs somewhat from the unit normal curve. The particular form of the Student's t probability distribution depends on a quantity known as the *degrees of freedom*, which is one less than the sample size. The various Student's t probability distributions are tabled in Table VI of Appendix A.

Finally, the concept of confidence intervals is discussed for both the Z and t statistics in attempting to estimate the population mean from sample data. New terms and expressions encountered in this chapter include:

Hypothesized μ
A single mean's being significantly different from expectation
Large versus small sample size
Formal hypothesis testing procedure for Z and t statistics
Degrees of freedom for metric data
Point estimate of μ
Confidence interval of μ
Large samples
Small samples

REVIEW QUESTIONS

1 The mean achievement score for a population of students has for years been equal to 55. Following an experimental program, a random sample of 100 students had a mean score of 60 and a standard deviation of 16. Test the hypothesis that the students from the experimental program are significantly better than those in the past. Assume a level of significance of 0.05.

2 Test the null hypothesis H_0: $\mu = 40$ against the alternative hypothesis H_1: $\mu \neq 40$ with $\alpha = 0.10$, $\bar{X} = 35$, $S = 16$, $N = 36$.

3 Give the *lower* and/or *upper* critical values required for significance in the following t tests:

   (a) Unidirectional (upper) with $\alpha = 0.01$ and $N = 11$.   _____
   (b) Bidirectional with $\alpha = 0.05$ and $N = 22$.   _____
   (c) Unidirectional (lower) with $\alpha = 0.10$ and $N = 41$.   _____
   (d) Bidirectional with $\alpha = 0.01$ and $N = 11$.   _____

4 Test the null hypothesis H_0: $\mu = 100$ against the alternative hypothesis H_1: $\mu < 100$ with $\alpha = 0.10$, $\bar{X} = 95$, $S = 9$, $N = 17$.

5 Test the null hypothesis H_0: $\mu = 60$ against the alternative hypothesis H_1: $\mu \neq 60$ with $\alpha = 0.05$, $\bar{X} = 75$, $S = 16$, $N = 10$.

6 Derive a 95 percent confidence limit for the population mean from the sample data of Problem 1.

7 Derive a 99 percent confidence limit for the population mean from the sample data of Problem 5.

CHAPTER 8

TESTING HYPOTHESES
ABOUT THE DIFFERENCE
BETWEEN TWO
POPULATION MEANS

The second research question, based on the normal curve, mentioned in Chapter 6 was concerned with two means, namely: Is the difference between two sample means significantly different from expectation? This second general question is perhaps the one most frequently encountered in behavioral research. Rather than comparing a sample mean with some hypothesized standard value, the problem is to compare two independent sample means. The usual experimental arrangement, involving two sample means, is the comparison of an experimental group with an independent comparable control group. One major benefit of including an independent control group is that the experimental conclusions are made comparative rather than absolute. As discussed in Chapter 2, proper control is a fundamental principle of scientific experimentation. Some examples of this type of inquiry are:

> Is the average achievement test score for a class in modern or experimental mathematics significantly different from the average achievement for a conventional class of students with comparable ability?

> Is the average reaction time for a group of experimental subjects placed under stress significantly slower than the average for a control group not subjected to stress?

> Is the average income of a group, following a federally supported vocational training program, significantly greater than the average income of a comparable group without such training?

As in the single sample case, the approaches taken to answer these kinds of questions (that is, to test the hypotheses) may be classified on the basis of the sizes of the samples. If the two sample sizes are each at least 30, we employ an approach based on the normal distribution. Otherwise, we follow a small sample approach based on the t distribution. The t distribution provides the more general method since it approaches the normal distribution as the sample sizes increase.

HYPOTHESIS TESTING WITH TWO LARGE INDEPENDENT SAMPLE MEANS

To illustrate the seven-step procedure for testing hypotheses about two population means, based on data collected from two large independent samples, assume the following data in our question concerning the comparison of the experimental and conventional mathematics classes.

Experimental class (Class 1)	*Conventional class (Class 2)*
Number of students $N_1 = 50$	Number of students $N_2 = 48$
Class mean $\bar{X}_1 = 55$	Class mean $\bar{X}_2 = 50$
Class standard deviation $S_1 = 10$	Class standard deviation $S_2 = 12$

Our question is then: Could the observed difference between the two sample means reasonably have occurred if, in fact, no difference existed between the means of two populations of potential students instructed under each curriculum? That is, how impressive is the difference between a sample mean of 55 and one of 50? Is it large enough to cast reasonable doubt on the assumption that on the average both mathematics programs are equally effective?

Our seven-step procedure is as follows:

Step 1 / STATE THE HYPOTHESIS

We are conjecturing that the mean of the potential population of students instructed with the experimental program, μ_1, is identical to the mean of the potential population of students instructed with the conventional program, μ_2. Thus our null hypothesis is

$$H_0: \mu_1 = \mu_2$$

Notice that we are not hypothesizing that the population means are equal to some absolute value, but only that they are equal to each other.

Since, in our example, we are asking only if there is a significant difference between the two programs (without regard for the direction of the difference) we use the bidirectional alternative hypothesis.*

$$H_1: \mu_1 \neq \mu_2$$

---

* If we felt that the only logical alternative to H_0 was for the experimental mathematics class to show a higher average achievement than the conventional class, our unidirectional alternative hypothesis would be $H_1: \mu_1 > \mu_2$. Of course, we could have also selected H_1 as $H_1: \mu_1 < \mu_2$. However, our example calls for a bidirectional test.

Step 2 / STATE THE LEVEL OF SIGNIFICANCE α

Let us select a level of significance of

$$\alpha = 0.05$$

Step 3 / STATE THE TEST STATISTIC

One test statistic appropriate for testing a hypothesis about two population means with two large samples is

$$Z = \frac{(\bar{X}_1 - \bar{X}_2) - (\mu_1 - \mu_2)}{\sqrt{\dfrac{\sigma_1^2}{N_1} + \dfrac{\sigma_2^2}{N_2}}}$$

where

$\bar{X}_1$ and $\bar{X}_2$ = the two sample means.
N_1 and N_2 = the two sample sizes.
μ_1 and μ_2 = the two population means.
σ_1 and σ_2 = the two population standard deviations.

Again, as in the one sample case, either σ_1 and σ_2 are assumed known or the standard deviations of our samples are used in their place. This substitution is justified on the basis of having "large" samples of observations. Thus for our example we have, under the hypothesis that $\mu_1 = \mu_2$, the following approximation:

$$Z = \frac{(\bar{X}_1 - \bar{X}_2) - (\mu_1 - \mu_2)}{\sqrt{\dfrac{S_1^2}{N_1} + \dfrac{S_2^2}{N_2}}}$$

From Theorem 6.3 recall that the sampling distribution of $(\bar{X}_1 - \bar{X}_2)$ has an expected value of $(\mu_1 - \mu_2)$ and a standard error of

$$\sqrt{\dfrac{\sigma_1^2}{N_1} + \dfrac{\sigma_2^2}{N_2}}$$

Therefore, the test statistic

$$Z = \frac{(\bar{X}_1 - \bar{X}_2) - (\mu_1 - \mu_2)}{\sqrt{\dfrac{\sigma_1^2}{N_1} + \dfrac{\sigma_2^2}{N_2}}}$$

represents a standard score corresponding to the original value $(\bar{X}_1 - \bar{X}_2)$.

Step 4 / SPECIFY THE DISTRIBUTION OF THE TEST STATISTIC

For two *independent* samples the test statistic

$$Z = \frac{(\bar{X}_1 - \bar{X}_2) - (\mu_1 - \mu_2)}{\sqrt{\dfrac{\sigma_1^2}{N_1} + \dfrac{\sigma_2^2}{N_2}}}$$

follows the unit normal probability distribution if, in fact, the null hypothesis is true.

$\bar{X}_1$ and $\bar{X}_2$ tend to be normally distributed according to the central limit theorem, and the sum or difference of scores drawn randomly from two independent normal populations tends also to be normally distributed. Since the standardization of the differences $(\bar{X}_1 - \bar{X}_2)$ does not alter the general shape of the distribution of scores, we again have a normal distribution with a mean of 0 and a standard deviation of 1. That is, Z, as defined above, follows the unit normal probability distribution.

In effect a probability statement about Z is a probability statement about $(\bar{X}_1 - \bar{X}_2)$, the difference between our two sample means. We are already familiar with the procedure for making probability statements about Z from the unit normal distribution.

Step 5 / SELECT THE REJECTION REGION

Recall that the *rejection region* depends upon both the alternative hypothesis H_1 and the level of significance α. For our example

$$H_1: \mu_1 \neq \mu_2$$

and

$$\alpha = 0.05$$

Thus if the experimental class mean were too far above or too far below the conventional class mean, we would want to declare the two programs significantly different. This bidirectional test calls for a division of the level of significance $\alpha = 0.05$. This situation is illustrated in Figure 8.1.

With $\alpha = 0.05$, a rare value of Z is taken to mean a value of Z greater than 1.96 or less than -1.96. If we observe a rare value of Z, we also declare our observed sample mean difference $(\bar{X}_1 - \bar{X}_2)$ to be a rare value. This in turn would lead us to reject H_0: $\mu_1 = \mu_2$ and accept H_1: $\mu_1 \neq \mu_2$. The *rejection region*, for our example, is therefore*

$$Z > 1.96 \quad \text{and} \quad Z < -1.96$$

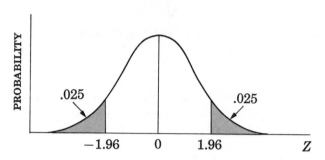

FIGURE 8.1
Unit normal probability curve

Step 6 / COMPUTE THE TEST STATISTIC

The evaluation of the test statistic is

$$Z = \frac{(\bar{X}_1 - \bar{X}_2) - (\mu_1 - \mu_2)}{\sqrt{\dfrac{\sigma_1^2}{N_1} + \dfrac{\sigma_2^2}{N_2}}}$$

$$= \frac{(55 - 50) - (0)}{\sqrt{\frac{100}{50} + \frac{144}{48}}}$$

$$= 2.24$$

Remember that either σ_1 and σ_2 are assumed known or S_1 and S_2 are used in their place (as is the case here).

Step 7 / ACCEPT OR REJECT THE NULL HYPOTHESIS

Our computed test statistic

$$Z = 2.24$$

clearly falls in the *rejection region*. Therefore, we have a statistically impressive difference between the two class means. We correspondingly reject the conjecture that the two mathematics programs are, on the average, equivalent.

---

* If our alternative hypothesis had been H_1: $\mu_1 > \mu_2$ and $\alpha = 0.05$ our *rejection region* would have been $Z > 1.65$.

Briefly summarizing the seven-step procedure, we have

Step 1 / STATE THE HYPOTHESIS

$$H_0: \mu_1 = \mu_2$$
$$H_1: \mu_1 \neq \mu_2$$

Step 2 / STATE THE LEVEL OF SIGNIFICANCE α

$$\alpha = 0.05$$

Step 3 / STATE THE TEST STATISTIC

$$Z = \frac{(\bar{X}_1 - \bar{X}_2) - (\mu_1 - \mu_2)}{\sqrt{\dfrac{\sigma_1^2}{N_1} + \dfrac{\sigma_2^2}{N_2}}}$$

Step 4 / SPECIFY THE DISTRIBUTION OF THE TEST STATISTIC

$$Z \stackrel{d}{=} N(0, 1)$$

Step 5 / SELECT THE REJECTION REGION

$$Z > 1.96 \quad \text{and} \quad Z < -1.96$$

Step 6 / COMPUTE THE TEST STATISTIC

$$Z = \frac{(55 - 50) - (0)}{\sqrt{\frac{100}{50} + \frac{144}{48}}} = 2.24$$

Step 7 / ACCEPT OR REJECT THE NULL HYPOTHESIS

Reject
$$H_0: \mu_1 = \mu_2$$
Accept
$$H_1: \mu_1 \neq \mu_2$$

HYPOTHESIS TESTING WITH TWO SMALL INDEPENDENT SAMPLE MEANS

When we are faced with a comparison of two sample means based on independent samples of less than 30 observations, our question remains the same: Is the difference between the two sample means significantly great enough to reject the conjecture that the means of the underlying populations of potential observations are identical? The small sample approach will be illustrated by means of our previous example. Only the sample sizes will be changed from large to small. Let the sample data be

Experimental class (Class 1)   *Conventional class (Class 2)*

Number of students $N_1 = 16$ Number of students $N_2 = 9$
Class mean $\bar{X}_1 = 55$ Class mean $\bar{X}_2 = 50$
Class standard deviation $S_1 = 10$ Class standard deviation $S_2 = 12$

The seven-step procedure for small samples closely approximates the previous procedure for large samples.

Step 1 / STATE THE HYPOTHESIS

$$H_0: \mu_1 = \mu_2$$

$$H_1: \mu_1 \neq \mu_2$$

Step 2 / STATE THE LEVEL OF SIGNIFICANCE α

$$\alpha = 0.05$$

Step 3 / STATE THE TEST STATISTIC

The test statistic appropriate for testing a hypothesis about two population means with data from two small samples is

$$t = \frac{(\bar{X}_1 - \bar{X}_2) - (\mu_1 - \mu_2)}{S_p\sqrt{\dfrac{1}{N_1} + \dfrac{1}{N_2}}}$$

where

$$S_p = \sqrt{\frac{N_1 S_1^2 + N_2 S_2^2}{N_1 + N_2 - 2}}$$

For large samples we have seen that an appropriate test statistic for testing the significance of the difference between two means is

$$Z = \frac{(\bar{X}_1 - \bar{X}_2) - (\mu_1 - \mu_2)}{\sqrt{\dfrac{\sigma_1^2}{N_1} + \dfrac{\sigma_2^2}{N_2}}} \tag{1}$$

The above two-sample t statistic can be shown to be analogous to this Z statistic in the following way:

In the absence of a large amount of information concerning σ_1^2 and σ_2^2, the assumption is usually made that they are equal.* Therefore, under the assumed condition of the equality of variances

$$\sigma_1^2 = \sigma_2^2 = \sigma^2$$

our Z statistic becomes

$$Z = \frac{(\bar{X}_1 - \bar{X}_2) - (\mu_1 - \mu_2)}{\sigma \sqrt{\dfrac{1}{N_1} + \dfrac{1}{N_2}}}$$

Our present problem is to estimate σ with data from our two small samples, which is done as follows: Under the assumption that $\sigma_1^2 = \sigma_2^2 = \sigma^2$ we have two estimates available: S_1^2 and S_2^2. These, however, are each biased estimates of σ^2. Hence if we were to use either sample as an unbiased estimate of σ^2 our estimate would be

$$\widehat{S}_1^2 = \left(\frac{N_1}{N_1 - 1}\right) S_1^2 \qquad \text{if we used sample 1}$$

and

$$\widehat{S}_2^2 = \left(\frac{N_2}{N_2 - 1}\right) S_2^2 \qquad \text{if we used sample 2}$$

That is, both $\widehat{S}_1^2$ and $\widehat{S}_2^2$ are unbiased estimates of σ^2.

In order that the maximum amount of information be used in estimating σ^2, the variance data from the two samples may be combined or *pooled*. The pooled sample estimate of σ^2 is denoted S_p^2 and is calculated by using a weighted average of the two individual unbiased sample estimates of σ^2. The "weights" used are the corresponding degrees of freedom for $\widehat{S}_1^2$ and $\widehat{S}_2^2$, $(N_1 - 1)$ and $(N_2 - 1)$, respectively. Therefore, the weighted average of $\widehat{S}_1^2$ and $\widehat{S}_2^2$ is

$$S_p^2 = \frac{(N_1 - 1)\,\widehat{S}_1^2 + (N_2 - 1)\,\widehat{S}_2^2}{(N_1 - 1) + (N_2 - 1)}$$

which is equivalent to

$$S_p^2 = \frac{N_1 S_1^2 + N_2 S_2^2}{N_1 + N_2 - 2}$$

---

* This assumption, known as *homoscedasticity*, may be tested by the procedures given in Chapter 9. There is increasing evidence that comparative tests, such as are discussed here, concerning means are fairly robust with respect to violations of the assumption of equality of the variances.

Therefore, the right-hand side of expression (1) becomes

$$\frac{(\bar{X}_1 - \bar{X}_2) - (\mu_1 - \mu_2)}{S_p \sqrt{\dfrac{1}{N_1} + \dfrac{1}{N_2}}}$$

which is identical to the t statistic given as the appropriate test statistic in Step 3.

Step 4 / SPECIFY THE DISTRIBUTION OF THE TEST STATISTIC

The test statistic of Step 3 follows the Student's t probability distribution with $\nu = N_1 + N_2 - 2$ degrees of freedom if, in fact, the null hypothesis is true.

As in the single sample case, we have seen that the t statistic is analogous to the Z statistic. For large sample sizes, under the conditions of the null hypothesis and equality of population variances, the sampling distribution of the two-sample t statistic closely approximates the unit normal probability distribution. With small samples, however, the approximation becomes less satisfactory. In particular, it has been shown that the specific form of the sampling distribution of the two-sample t statistic (that is, the probability distribution of t) depends upon the pooled degrees of freedom $(N_1 + N_2 - 2)$.

Step 5 / SELECT THE REJECTION REGION

From Table VI of Appendix A we see that for $N_1 = 16$ and $N_2 = 9$ ($\nu = 16 + 9 - 2 = 23$) the probability of observing a value of t less than 2.07 is 0.975. The probability, therefore, of observing a value of t greater than 2.07 is 0.025. By the symmetrical nature of the t distribution, the probability of observing a value of t less than -2.07 is also 0.025. This is illustrated in Figure 8.2.

Thus for $\alpha = 0.05$ with a bidirectional test, a rare value of t is taken to mean a value greater than 2.07 or less than -2.07. If we observe a rare value of t, we also declare our observed difference between the two sample means to be a rare value. This, in turn, would cause us to reject $H_0: \mu_1 = \mu_2$ and accept $H_1: \mu_1 \neq \mu_2$.

The *rejection region* for our example is, therefore,*

$$t > 2.07 \quad \text{and} \quad t < -2.07$$

---

* Of course, we could have a unidirectional test, where our alternative hypothesis might be $H_1: \mu_1 > \mu_2$. In such a case with $\alpha = 0.05$ our *rejection region* would be (for $N_1 + N_2 - 2 = 23$) $t > 1.71$. For $H_1: \mu_1 < \mu_2$ and $\alpha = 0.05$ our *rejection region* would be $t < -1.71$.

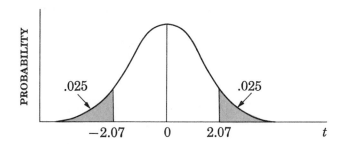

FIGURE 8.2
The t distribution for $N_1+N_2 - 2 = 23$ degrees of freedom

Step 6 / COMPUTE THE TEST STATISTIC

For our example we have, under the null hypothesis H_0: $\mu_1 = \mu_2$,

$$t = \frac{(55 - 50) - (0)}{S_p\sqrt{\frac{1}{16} + \frac{1}{9}}}$$

where

$$S_p = \sqrt{\frac{(16)(100) + (9)(144)}{16 + 9 - 2}}$$

$$= 11.22$$

Thus

$$t = \frac{5}{11.22\sqrt{\frac{1}{16} + \frac{1}{9}}} = \frac{5}{(11.22)(0.42)} = \frac{5}{4.71}$$

$$= 1.06$$

Step 7 / ACCEPT OR REJECT THE NULL HYPOTHESIS

Since the value of our test statistic is not in the *rejection region*, we

Accept the null hypothesis

$$H_0: \mu_1 = \mu_2$$

That is, we do not have sufficient evidence to reject our conjecture that, so far as the means are concerned, the samples could have both come from the same population.

Notice the change in our decision in this small sample case from the previous large sample situation. We have less confidence in a reported difference between two means when they are based on small samples than when they are based on large samples. With small samples a larger difference is required to reject the null hypothesis. It should be clear that one *should not* use large sample statistics (formulas) on small samples. The t statistic, on the other hand, is appropriate for both large and small samples.

INTERVAL ESTIMATION OF THE DIFFERENCE BETWEEN TWO POPULATION MEANS

LARGE SAMPLES

In the same manner as we constructed confidence intervals for μ in the single sample case, we can construct confidence intervals for the difference between two population means, $(\mu_1 - \mu_2)$. Let us illustrate this by constructing a 95 percent confidence interval for the difference between two population means.

We have seen that the probability of Z's being between $+1.96$ and -1.96 is 0.95. That is,

$$-1.96 \leq Z \leq 1.96$$

Upon substituting our expression for Z, we have

$$-1.96 \leq \frac{(\bar{X}_1 - \bar{X}_2) - (\mu_1 - \mu_2)}{\sqrt{\dfrac{\sigma_1^2}{N_1} + \dfrac{\sigma_2^2}{N_2}}} \leq 1.96$$

Finally, isolating $(\mu_1 - \mu_2)$, we have

$$(\bar{X}_1 - \bar{X}_2) - 1.96\sqrt{\frac{\sigma_1^2}{N_1} + \frac{\sigma_2^2}{N_2}} \leq (\mu_1 - \mu_2) \leq (\bar{X}_1 - \bar{X}_2) + 1.96\sqrt{\frac{\sigma_1^2}{N_1} + \frac{\sigma_2^2}{N_2}}$$

For example, a 95 percent confidence interval for the difference between the two population achievement means is

$$(55 - 50) - 1.96\sqrt{\tfrac{100}{50} + \tfrac{144}{48}} \leq (\mu_1 - \mu_2)$$

$$\leq (55 - 50) + 1.96\sqrt{\tfrac{100}{50} + \tfrac{144}{48}}$$

$$0.61 \leq (\mu_1 - \mu_2) \leq 9.39$$

SMALL SAMPLES

Confidence intervals may also be constructed for $(\mu_1 - \mu_2)$ from the t distribution. For example, a 95 percent confidence interval for $(\mu_1 - \mu_2)$ computed for our small sample data is as follows: A 95 percent range for t with $(N_1 + N_2 - 2) = 23$ degrees of freedom is

$$-2.07 \leq t \leq 2.07$$

Substituting our expression for t, we have

$$-2.07 \leq \frac{(\bar{X}_1 - \bar{X}_2) - (\mu_1 - \mu_2)}{S_p \sqrt{\dfrac{1}{N_1} + \dfrac{1}{N_2}}} \leq 2.07$$

Upon isolating $(\mu_1 - \mu_2)$ we have

$$(\bar{X}_1 - \bar{X}_2) - (2.07) S_p \sqrt{\frac{1}{N_1} + \frac{1}{N_2}} \leq (\mu_1 - \mu_2)$$

$$\leq (\bar{X}_1 - \bar{X}_2) + (2.07) S_p \sqrt{\frac{1}{N_1} + \frac{1}{N_2}}$$

For the data of our example, a 95 percent confidence interval for the difference between the two population means is

$$(55 - 50) - (2.07)(4.71) \leq (\mu_1 - \mu_2) \leq (55 - 50) + (2.07)(4.71)$$

$$-4.75 \leq (\mu_1 - \mu_2) \leq 14.75$$

Clearly, we cannot construct as narrow a confidence interval from two small samples as we can with two large samples.

MATCHED-PAIRS t TEST

So far in our discussion of the comparison of two means, it has been assumed that the two samples were independent. Frequently, however, the data from the two samples might be dependent. Such a situation arises, for example, when the individuals are matched or paired (e.g., by I.Q., achievement, verbal comprehension scores, etc.) prior to being assigned to the treatments. The assignment is done in such a way that one member of each pair is randomly selected for one of the treatments and all others are assigned to the second treatment. Another common experimental situation yielding dependent observations arises when the same individuals constitute both groups, as in the *before* and *after* type of study in which each individual serves as his own control.

This matching process is designed to minimize extraneous sources of variability by attempting to preselect two groups as similar as possible in order to make the comparisons more equitable (or to maintain the same group, in the case of before and after research studies). However, when the two groups are matched or made up of the same individuals, the groups can no longer be considered independent. Rather, we are dealing with samples of data that are correlated with one another. Thus the assumption of independence underlying the previous techniques of this chapter is no longer satisfied. Fortunately, there is a fairly simple technique available that is appropriate for this type of inquiry. It is known as the *matched-pairs t test*.

To illustrate the use of the matched-pairs t test, consider the following problem.*

A teacher attempts to study the effects of a new set of teaching materials on pupil "appreciation" of the United States' foreign policy by using both conventional materials and the new materials. Suppose 60 pupils are matched and paired on the basis of achievement test scores in social studies. One member of each matched pair, selected at random, is assigned to the experimental class using the new materials and the other member to the control class, which continues using the conventional material. Following the completion of this unit of study, a questionnaire form is filled out by each pupil from which he is assigned a score representing his appreciation of the United States' foreign policy. Consider, for purposes of illustration, the artificial data given in Table 8.1, which are organized in preparation for the matched-pairs t test.

The seven-step procedure for the matched-pairs t test is as follows:

Step 1 /

We hypothesize that the population means for the experimental and control groups are equivalent:

$$H_0: \mu_E = \mu_C$$

Let us select the bidirectional alternative hypothesis

$$H_1: \mu_E \neq \mu_C$$

Step 2 /

Let

$$\alpha = 0.05$$

Step 3 /

The test statistic used with the matched-pairs t test is

$$t = \frac{\bar{D}}{S_{\bar{D}}}$$

where

N = number of pairs
$\bar{D}$ = average difference in the paired scores

$$\bar{D} = \frac{\sum\limits_{i=1}^{N} D_i}{N}$$

---

* This same problem will be analyzed in a different manner in Chapter 12, wherein only the rank-ordered property of the scores is utilized in the analysis.

TABLE 8.1   ARTIFICIAL DATA ORGANIZED FOR MATCHED-PAIRS t TEST

Matched pairs	Experimental class (E)	Control class (C)	Difference $(E - C)$
1	25	10	15
2	24	11	13
3	23	12	11
4	18	19	−1
5	13	15	−2
6	25	9	16
7	15	15	0
8	12	13	−1
9	18	20	−2
10	20	11	9
11	17	18	−1
12	18	17	1
13	19	18	1
14	22	24	−2
15	24	16	8
16	11	14	−3
17	23	13	10
18	20	21	−1
19	25	6	19
20	16	17	−1
21	15	16	−1
22	16	17	−1
23	14	17	−3
24	22	14	8
25	18	11	7
26	19	14	5
27	21	14	7
28	21	22	−1
29	20	22	−2
30	20	8	12

$S_{\bar{D}}$ = standard error of the mean difference of the paired scores

$$S_{\bar{D}} = \sqrt{\frac{N \sum_{i=1}^{N} D_i^2 - (\sum_{i=1}^{N} D_i)^2}{N^2(N-1)}}$$

Since the statistic of interest is $\bar{D}$, the average of the differences of the paired scores, one approach to this problem would be to use a sample statistic of the form

$$t = \frac{\bar{D}}{\dfrac{S_D}{\sqrt{N-1}}}$$

as in the small sample case for testing hypotheses about a single sample mean (in this case, $\bar{D}$) discussed in Chapter 7. Or, alternatively, we could use a sample statistic of the form

$$t = \frac{\bar{D}}{\frac{\hat{S}_D}{\sqrt{N}}}$$

since the unbiased sample variance $\hat{S}_D{}^2$ may be expressed as

$$\hat{S}_D{}^2 = \left(\frac{N}{N-1}\right)S_D{}^2$$

Furthermore, the standard deviation of the sampling distribution of the sample mean $\bar{D}$ (from Theorem 6.1) may be estimated as:

$$S_{\bar{D}} = \frac{\hat{S}_D}{\sqrt{N}}$$

Thus our sample statistic may be expressed as follows:

$$t = \frac{\bar{D}}{S_{\bar{D}}}$$

Again, for large samples, the difference between $S_D{}^2$ and $\hat{S}_D{}^2$ is negligible.

Let us examine this test statistic more closely. The statistic of interest here is $\bar{D}$, which may also be written as

$$\bar{D} = \overline{(X_1 - X_2)}$$

However,

$$\overline{(X_1 - X_2)} = \frac{\sum_{i=1}^{N}(X_{1i} - X_{2i})}{N} = \bar{X}_1 - \bar{X}_2$$

Hence the sampling distribution of $\bar{D}$ is identical to that for $(\bar{X}_1 - \bar{X}_2)$. The expected value of this sampling distribution, $\mu_{\bar{D}}$, is thus $(\mu_1 - \mu_2)$ and, as shown in Appendix E, the standard error $\sigma_{\bar{D}}$ is

$$\sigma_{\bar{D}} = \sqrt{\sigma^2_{\bar{X}_1} + \sigma^2_{\bar{X}_2} - 2\rho\sigma_{\bar{X}_1}\sigma_{\bar{X}_2}}$$

Under our null hypothesis, the expected value of $\bar{D}$ is assumed equal to zero. Estimating the standard error with a sample of data, we have

$$S_{\bar{D}} = \sqrt{S^2_{\bar{X}_1} + S^2_{\bar{X}_2} - 2rS_{\bar{X}_1}S_{\bar{X}_2}}$$

The equivalent direct-difference method of evaluating $S_{\bar{D}}$ from a sample may be shown as follows:

D_i	$(X_{1i} - X_{2i})$
D_1	$(X_{11} - X_{21})$
D_2	$(X_{12} - X_{22})$
$\vdots$	$\vdots$
D_N	$(X_{1N} - X_{2N})$

from which

$$\bar{D} = \bar{X}_1 - \bar{X}_2$$

and

$$S_{\bar{D}}^2 = \frac{\hat{S}_D^2}{N} = \frac{\sum\limits_{i=1}^{N} (D_i - \bar{D})^2}{N(N-1)}$$

or

$$S_{\bar{D}} = \sqrt{\frac{\sum\limits_{i=1}^{N} (D_i^2 - 2D_i\bar{D} + \bar{D}^2)}{N(N-1)}}$$

which may easily be shown to be equivalent to

$$S_{\bar{D}} = \sqrt{\frac{N\sum\limits_{i=1}^{N} D_i^2 - \left(\sum\limits_{i=1}^{N} D_i\right)^2}{N^2(N-1)}}$$

Step 4 /

The test statistic

$$t = \frac{\bar{D}}{S_{\bar{D}}}$$

follows the Student's t probability distribution with $(N-1)$ degrees of freedom.

Step 5 /

Since $\alpha = 0.05$ and $N - 1 = 29$, our *rejection region* for H_1 is

$$t > 2.04 \quad \text{and} \quad t < -2.04$$

Step 6 /

From Table 8.1 we have

$$\bar{D} = \frac{15 + 13 + \cdots + (-2) + 12}{30} = 4.00$$

$$S_{\bar{D}} = \sqrt{\frac{30(1752) - (120)^2}{(30)^2(29)}}$$

$$= \sqrt{1.46}$$

$$= 1.21$$

Therefore,

$$t = \frac{\bar{D}}{S_{\bar{D}}} = \frac{4.00}{1.21} = 3.31$$

Step 7 /

Clearly, we
    Reject the null hypothesis

$$H_0: \mu_E = \mu_C$$

and
    Accept the alternative hypothesis

$$H_1: \mu_E \neq \mu_C$$

An alternative method sometimes used to help account for the initial status of the individuals in an experiment involves analyzing *gain scores*. An individual's gain score may be defined as his criterion score obtained after the completion of the experiment minus his criterion score obtained before the experiment. The mean gain score of the experimental group is then compared with that of the control group by the usual Z or t tests for independent samples. Although gain score analysis obviates the need for a direct matching of individuals across the experimental and control groups (as in the case of the matched-pairs t test discussed here), there are certain limiting assumptions underlying its use. In particular, as pointed out by Edwards (1960), the slopes of the regression lines of the "after" scores on the "before" scores in both the experimental and control groups are assumed to be approximately equal to one.

SUMMARY

This chapter deals with the question of whether or not the difference between two sample means differs significantly from expectation. Two test statistics are introduced for the case of independent samples: a Z statistic for large samples and an analogous t statistic for small samples. Confidence intervals for estimating the difference $(\mu_1 - \mu_2)$ are introduced for both large and small samples.

Finally, a test statistic

$$t = \frac{\bar{D}}{S_{\bar{D}}}$$

is presented for the special situation wherein the observations in the two groups are dependent or correlated. This technique is known as the matched-pairs t test.

Three new formulas are introduced:

$$Z = \frac{(\bar{X}_1 - \bar{X}_2) - (\mu_1 - \mu_2)}{\sqrt{\dfrac{\sigma_1^2}{N_1} + \dfrac{\sigma_2^2}{N_2}}}$$

$$t = \frac{(\bar{X}_1 - \bar{X}_2) - (\mu_1 - \mu_2)}{S_p \sqrt{\dfrac{1}{N_1} + \dfrac{1}{N_2}}}$$

where

$$S_p = \sqrt{\frac{N_1 S_1^2 + N_2 S_2^2}{N_1 + N_2 - 2}}$$

$$t = \frac{\bar{D}}{S_{\bar{D}}}$$

REVIEW QUESTIONS

1 Test the null hypothesis H_0: $\mu_1 = \mu_2$ against the alternative H_1: $\mu_1 \neq \mu_2$ with an $\alpha = 0.05$ for the following sample data: $\bar{X}_1 = 100$, $\bar{X}_2 = 95$, $S_1 = 3$, $S_2 = 4$, $N_1 = 50$, $N_2 = 37$.

2 Test the null hypothesis H_0: $\mu_1 = \mu_2$ against the alternative H_1: $\mu_1 \neq \mu_2$ with an $\alpha = 0.05$ for the following sample data: $\bar{X}_1 = 100$, $\bar{X}_2 = 95$, $S_1 = 3$, $S_2 = 4$, $N_1 = 17$, $N_2 = 10$.

3 Construct a 95 percent confidence interval for estimating $(\mu_1 - \mu_2)$ for Problem 1.

4 Construct a 95 percent confidence interval for estimating $(\mu_1 - \mu_2)$ for Problem 2.

5   Explain the differences obtained in Problems 3 and 4.

6   Test the null hypothesis $H_0: \mu_1 = \mu_2$ for the following set of paired data, against the alternative hypothesis $H_1: \mu_1 \neq \mu_2$ with $\alpha = 0.10$.

Pair	X_1	X_2
1	14	13
2	16	14
3	19	15
4	10	8
5	15	13
6	7	5
7	14	11
8	21	18
9	4	5
10	16	11

TESTING HYPOTHESES
ABOUT POPULATION
VARIANCES

HYPOTHESIS TESTING WITH A SINGLE SAMPLE VARIANCE

Although the mean is one very useful measure in testing hypotheses about populations of interest, it is not the only one. At times it may be the population dispersion that is of interest to us. The third general type of behavioral inquiry mentioned in Chapter 6 was concerned with dispersion, namely: Is a sample dispersion significantly different from expectation? The following are some examples of this type of question:

Is the variability in the I.Q.'s of a sample of children in a particular nursery school significantly different from a standard value, such as the standard deviation of 16 published for the Stanford-Binet intelligence test?

Is the variability of the reaction times for a sample of experimental subjects significantly less than some theoretical value? That is, do these experimental subjects tend to be more homogeneous in their reaction times than we would expect from our theoretical value?

Is the variability in sales volume for a sample of salesmen in a branch office, following a change in management, significantly greater than that reported for the entire sales region in the past?

To illustrate the seven-step procedure for testing a hypothesis about the dispersion of a population, consider the above question concerning the I.Q.'s of the sample of nursery school children. Suppose we have the following data:

The published variance $\sigma^2 = (16)^2 = 256$
The class size $N = 30$
The class variance $S^2 = (20)^2 = 400$

Our question, then, is: Could this sample of nursery school children (having a standard deviation of 20 I.Q. points) reasonably represent a sample of children randomly drawn from a population where the standard deviation of the I.Q. scores is equal to 16? That is, how impressive is the difference between S and σ (20 and 16) or, equivalently, between S^2 and σ^2 (400 and 256)? This type of question can be framed in terms of the following seven-step procedure:

Step 1 / STATE THE HYPOTHESIS

We are conjecturing, in our null hypothesis, that the variance of the I.Q.'s of the population of such nursery school children is equal to the published value of 256. That is,

$$H_0: \sigma^2 = 256$$

The alternative hypothesis H_1 in our problem is bidirectional, since (prior to examining our actual data) we were uncertain as to whether the sample standard deviation would fall above or below the published value. That is,

$$H_1: \sigma^2 \neq 256$$

In other words, we want to declare our result to be significantly different from the published value if our sample result is "too variable" or if it is "too homogeneous."*

Step 2 / STATE THE LEVEL OF SIGNIFICANCE α

Let us set

$$\alpha = 0.05$$

Step 3 / STATE THE TEST STATISTIC

The test statistic appropriate for testing a hypothesis about a single population variance is a chi-square (χ^2) statistic defined as follows:

$$\chi^2 = \frac{NS^2}{\sigma^2}$$

where

N = sample size
S^2 = sample variance
σ^2 = population variance

---

* As in previous situations, we also could pose unidirectional tests. Thus if we felt that the only logical alternative would be for the dispersion to be more variable than the published value, our alternative hypothesis would be $H_1: \sigma^2 > 256$. On the other hand, we could have $H_1: \sigma^2 < 256$ if we were interested only in detecting a result significantly more homogeneous than the published value.

It is clear that the statistic

$$\frac{NS^2}{\sigma^2} = \frac{(X_1 - \bar{X})^2 + (X_2 - \bar{X})^2 + \cdots + (X_N - \bar{X})^2}{\sigma^2}$$

will be large when our sample variance is much larger than the hypothesized value σ^2. Likewise, the statistic will approach zero as the sample dispersion decreases.

Step 4 / SPECIFY THE DISTRIBUTION OF THE TEST STATISTIC

The test statistic

$$\chi^2 = \frac{NS^2}{\sigma^2}$$

follows the chi-square probability distribution if, in fact, the null hypothesis is true.

If samples of size N are repeatedly selected from a normal population having a standard deviation of σ, a sampling distribution of the quantity

$$\frac{NS^2}{\sigma^2}$$

will result. It has been shown (Hoel, 1954) that the sampling distribution of NS^2/σ^2 from the normal population, $X \overset{d}{=} N(\mu, \sigma)$, follows the particular chi-square probability distribution specified by $(N - 1)$ degrees of freedom. Again, the essential characteristic of the test statistic

$$\chi^2 = \frac{NS^2}{\sigma^2}$$

for our purposes is that as S^2 gets large relative to σ^2, χ^2 increases, and as S^2 gets small relative to σ^2, χ^2 decreases.

Recall that Table IV in Appendix A gives the probability of observing values of χ^2 less than certain specified values listed in the body of the table. The table is entered at the row corresponding to $N - 1$. For example, with a sample size N of 30 we see that there is a probability of only 0.025 of observing a value of χ^2 less than 16.0. This is illustrated in Figure 9.1. Likewise, for $N = 30$, there is a probability of

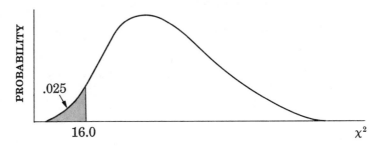

FIGURE 9.1
The chi-square distribution for N = 30

0.975 that a value of χ^2 will be less than 45.7. This is illustrated in Figure 9.2. These two results for $N = 30$ are

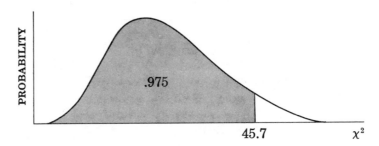

FIGURE 9.2
The chi-square distribution for N = 30

presented together in Figure 9.3. The total area under the curve is taken to be equal to 1.

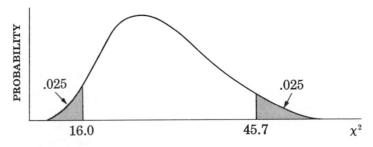

FIGURE 9.3
The chi-square distribution for N = 30

Step 5 / SELECT THE REJECTION REGION

For our bidirectional alternative hypothesis

$$H_1: \sigma^2 \neq 256$$

and $\alpha = 0.05$ a rare value of χ^2 would be seen from Table IV of Appendix A and Figure 9.3 to be a value greater than 45.7 or less than 16.0. Therefore, our *rejection region* is*

$$\chi^2 > 45.7 \quad \text{and} \quad \chi^2 < 16.0$$

Step 6 / COMPUTE THE TEST STATISTIC

$$\chi^2 = \frac{NS^2}{\sigma^2} = \frac{(30)(400)}{256} = 46.87$$

Step 7 / ACCEPT OR REJECT THE NULL HYPOTHESIS

The value of our test statistic ($\chi^2 = 46.87$) falls in the *rejection region*. Therefore, we
    Reject our null hypothesis

$$H_0: \sigma^2 = 256$$

and
    Accept our alternative hypothesis

$$H_1: \sigma^2 \neq 256$$

The difference between our sample variation and the hypothesized variation is too large to accept the conjecture that this sample could have reasonably come from a population that has a variance of 256.

Briefly summarizing our seven-step procedure, we have:

Step 1 / STATE THE HYPOTHESIS

$$H_0: \sigma^2 = 256$$

$$H_1: \sigma^2 \neq 256$$

Step 2 / STATE THE LEVEL OF SIGNIFICANCE α

$$\alpha = 0.05$$

---

* If our alternative hypothesis were unidirectional, for example, $H_1: \sigma^2 > 256$, the *rejection region* for $N = 30$ and $\alpha = 0.05$ is seen from Table IV of Appendix A to be $\chi^2 > 42.6$. For the same situation for $H_1: \sigma^2 < 256$ the *rejection region* would be $\chi^2 < 17.7$.

Step 3 / STATE THE TEST STATISTIC

$$\chi^2 = \frac{N S^2}{\sigma^2}$$

Step 4 / SPECIFY THE DISTRIBUTION OF THE TEST STATISTIC

The chi-square probability distribution corresponding to $(N - 1)$ degrees of freedom.

Step 5 / SELECT THE REJECTION REGION

$$\chi^2 > 45.7 \quad \text{and} \quad \chi^2 < 16.0$$

Step 6 / COMPUTE THE TEST STATISTIC

$$\chi^2 = 46.87$$

Step 7 / ACCEPT OR REJECT THE NULL HYPOTHESIS

Reject

$$H_0: \sigma^2 = 256$$

and
Accept

$$H_1: \sigma^2 \neq 256$$

INTERVAL ESTIMATION OF A POPULATION VARIANCE

An analogous situation exists for constructing confidence intervals for the population variance σ^2 as for the population mean μ. A 95 percent confidence interval for σ^2 based on the data of our example is constructed as follows: First construct a 95 percent range for a sample size of 30. This may be seen from Table IV of Appendix A to be

$$16 \leq \chi^2 \leq 45.7$$

Upon substituting our expression for χ^2 we have

$$16 \leq \frac{N S^2}{\sigma^2} \leq 45.7$$

Isolating σ^2, we have

$$\frac{16}{N S^2} \leq \frac{1}{\sigma^2} \leq \frac{45.7}{N S^2}$$

or

$$\frac{N S^2}{16} \geq \sigma^2 \geq \frac{N S^2}{45.7}$$

For our sample data we have

$$750.0 \geq \sigma^2 \geq 262.6$$

HYPOTHESIS TESTING WITH TWO INDEPENDENT SAMPLE VARIANCES

We shall now consider the fourth general research question of Chapter 6: Is the difference between two sample dispersions significantly different from expectation?

The comparison of two independent sample means has already been considered in Chapter 8. We shall now consider the procedure for comparing two independent sample variances to see if there is a significant difference between them. The following are some examples of this type of question:

Is the variability of reading ability scores for a third-grade class taught by means of individualized instructional devices significantly different from that of a comparable class taught by conventional methods?

Is the variability in achievement scores for a class given a series of *success experiences* significantly different from that of a class faced with a series of *failure experiences*?

Is the variability on a measure of physical skills significantly different between boys and girls?

To illustrate the procedure for comparing two variances, assume the following sample data for the question concerning the individualized reading devices.

Class taught with individualized reading devices (Class 1)

Conventional class (Class 2)

Class size $N_1 = 21$
Unbiased class variance $\hat{S}_1^2 = 36$

Class size $N_2 = 11$
Unbiased class variance $\hat{S}_2^2 = 16$

Our seven-step procedure for this type of question is

Step 1 / STATE THE HYPOTHESIS

We first conjecture that there is no difference in the variabilities of the populations of children taught under the two techniques. Thus our null hypothesis is

$$H_0: \sigma_1^2 = \sigma_2^2$$

A convention is usually maintained that the larger of the two sample variances (in our case the variance of the individualized class) is designated as $\hat{S}_1{}^2$. Thus our uni-directional alternative hypothesis is

$$H_1: \sigma_1{}^2 > \sigma_2{}^2$$

Accepting H_1 would, in essence, give support to the contention that the first sample is significantly more variable than the second sample.

Step 2 / STATE THE LEVEL OF SIGNIFICANCE α

Let us select a level of significance α of

$$\alpha = 0.05$$

Step 3 / STATE THE TEST STATISTIC

The test statistic appropriate for testing the hypothesis of equality of two population variances is

$$F = \frac{\hat{S}_1{}^2}{\hat{S}_2{}^2}$$

where $\hat{S}_1{}^2$ is the larger sample variance and $\hat{S}_2{}^2$ is the smaller sample variance.

The F statistic

$$F = \frac{\hat{S}_1{}^2}{\hat{S}_2{}^2}$$

is named after Sir Ronald Fisher, the British statistician who developed the powerful analysis of variance technique to be discussed in Chapter 10.

It is not essential that the larger of the two sample variances be designated $\hat{S}_1{}^2$; however, the task of using the corresponding table of probabilities is greatly simplified if this convention is maintained. As will be discussed in Chapter 13, the F statistic is the most general test statistic we encounter in elementary statistics, since it can be shown mathematically that the others (i.e., Z, t, χ^2) may be derived from it.

Step 4 / SPECIFY THE DISTRIBUTION OF THE TEST STATISTIC

The test statistic

$$F = \frac{\hat{S}_1{}^2}{\hat{S}_2{}^2}$$

follows the Fisher's F probability distribution if, in fact, the null hypothesis is true.

If $H_0: \sigma_1^2 = \sigma_2^2$ were actually true, and samples of size N_1 and N_2 were repeatedly drawn from populations 1 and 2, respectively, the form of the sampling distribution of

$$\frac{\widehat{S}_1^2}{\widehat{S}_2^2}$$

is known (Hoel, 1954). Although the mathematical derivation of the sampling distribution of the F statistic is beyond the scope of this book, it can be said that

$$\frac{\widehat{S}_1^2}{\widehat{S}_2^2}$$

forms a probability distribution known as the *Fisher's F probability distribution*. There are, as with the t and χ^2 statistics, several possible probability distributions for the F statistic. The particular Fisher's F probability distribution which $\widehat{S}_1^2 / \widehat{S}_2^2$ follows, if the null hypothesis is true, is determined by two values: one, the degrees of freedom $(N_1 - 1)$ corresponding to the numerator $\widehat{S}_1^2$, and the second the degrees of freedom $(N_2 - 1)$ corresponding to the denominator $\widehat{S}_2^2$.

The body of Table VII of Appendix A gives a number that has a specified probability of being exceeded by our observed value of F if, in fact, the null hypothesis is true. The probabilities are 0.05 and 0.01. The table is entered at the $N_1 - 1$ column (labeled "Degrees of freedom for greater mean square") and the $N_2 - 1$ row (labeled "Degrees of freedom for lesser mean square").

Step 5 / SELECT THE REJECTION REGION

The test statistic

$$F = \frac{\widehat{S}_1^2}{\widehat{S}_2^2}$$

is most easily handled by expressing the alternative hypothesis in the unidirectional form

$$H_1: \sigma_1^2 > \sigma_2^2$$

For $\alpha = 0.05$ we see from Table VII of Appendix A that there is only a 0.05 chance of an observed value of F's exceeding 2.77 if, in fact, $\sigma_1^2 = \sigma_2^2$ when $N_1 = 21$ and $N_2 = 11$. (That is, there is a 0.95 chance of F's being less than 2.77.) Therefore, for our example, the *rejection region* corresponding to $N_1 = 21$, $N_2 = 11$, $\alpha = 0.05$, and H_1: $\sigma_1^2 > \sigma_2^2$ is

$$F > 2.77$$

Step 6 / COMPUTE THE TEST STATISTIC

The value of the test statistic for our sample data is

$$F = \frac{\hat{S}_1^2}{\hat{S}_2^2} = \frac{36}{16} = 2.25$$

Step 7 / ACCEPT OR REJECT THE NULL HYPOTHESIS

Our sample test statistic does not fall in the *rejection region*. Thus we

Accept the null hypothesis

$$H_0: \sigma_1^2 = \sigma_2^2$$

On the basis of our sample evidence we do not have sufficient evidence to refute the conjecture that the variabilities in reading ability, for the potential groups of children instructed under the two systems, are equivalent.

The special case of testing the hypothesis $H_0: \sigma_1^2 = \sigma_2^2$ for correlated observations is encountered rather infrequently in behavioral research. An appropriate test statistic is given by McNemar (1962) for this special case.

SUMMARY OF PROCEDURES FOR TESTING HYPOTHESES CONCERNED WITH MEANS AND VARIANCES

In Chapters 7, 8, and 9 we have been concerned with four questions:

1. Is a sample mean significantly different from expectation?
2. Is the difference between two sample means significantly different from expectation?
3. Is a sample dispersion significantly different from expectation?
4. Is the difference between two sample dispersions significantly different from expectation?

These questions were all approached by means of our formal seven-step hypothesis testing procedure. These steps are summarized below for the four questions.*

---

* Only the case of independent samples is summarized here for Question 2.

Step 1 / STATE THE HYPOTHESIS

> *Null hypothesis*
> *question*   *Null hypothesis*

1	$H_0: \mu = k$ (where k is an arbitrary value)
2	$H_0: \mu_1 = \mu_2$
3	$H_0: \sigma^2 = k$
4	$H_0: \sigma_1^2 = \sigma_2^2$

> *Alternative hy-*
> *pothesis question*   *Alternative hypothesis*

1	$H_1: \mu \neq k$ or $H_1: \mu > k$ or $H_1: \mu < k$
2	$H_1: \mu_1 \neq \mu_2$ or $H_1: \mu_1 > \mu_2$ or $H_1: \mu_1 < \mu_2$
3	$H_1: \sigma^2 \neq k$ or $H_1: \sigma^2 > k$ or $H_1: \sigma^2 < k$
4	$H_1: \sigma_1^2 > \sigma_2^2$

Step 2 / STATE THE LEVEL OF SIGNIFICANCE α

Step 3 / STATE THE TEST STATISTIC

> *Question*   *Test statistic*

1      $Z = \dfrac{\bar{X} - \mu}{\dfrac{\sigma}{\sqrt{N}}}$ or $t = \dfrac{\bar{X} - \mu}{\dfrac{S}{\sqrt{N-1}}}$

2      $Z = \dfrac{\bar{X}_1 - \bar{X}_2}{\sqrt{\dfrac{\sigma_1^2}{N_1} + \dfrac{\sigma_2^2}{N_2}}}$ or $t = \dfrac{\bar{X}_1 - \bar{X}_2}{S_p \sqrt{\dfrac{1}{N_1} + \dfrac{1}{N_2}}},$

> where

$$S_p = \sqrt{\frac{N_1 S_1^2 + N_2 S_2^2}{N_1 + N_2 - 2}}$$

3      $\chi^2 = \dfrac{N S^2}{\sigma^2}$

4      $F = \dfrac{\hat{S}_1^2}{\hat{S}_2^2},$

> where S_1^2 is the larger of the two sample variances.

Step 4 / SPECIFY THE DISTRIBUTION OF THE TEST STATISTIC

Question	Probability distribution
1	Unit normal or Student's t (use the $N - 1$ row)
2	Unit normal or Student's t (use the $N_1 + N_2 - 2$ row)
3	Chi-square (use the $N - 1$ row)
4	Fisher's F (use the $N_1 - 1$ column and the $N_2 - 1$ row)

Step 5 / SELECT THE REJECTION REGION

Step 6 / COMPUTE THE TEST STATISTIC

Step 7 / ACCEPT OR REJECT THE NULL HYPOTHESIS

REVIEW QUESTIONS

1   Test the null hypothesis H_0: $\sigma^2 = 100$ against the alternative H_1: $\sigma^2 > 100$ with $\alpha = 0.05$, using the following sample data: $S^2 = 144$, $N = 25$. Against the alternative H_1: $\sigma^2 \neq 100$.

2   Test the null hypothesis H_0: $\sigma_1^2 = \sigma_2^2$ with $\alpha = 0.05$, using the following sample data:

$$\hat{S}_1^2 = 26, \qquad N_1 = 17; \qquad \hat{S}_2^2 = 24, \qquad N_2 = 14$$

For each of the following problems state the proper *test statistic* and the *appropriate degrees of freedom* if necessary.

3   The means of two treatments are to be compared on a two-tailed test. The population variances are unknown, and the sample sizes are 10 and 12.

4   Two large sample treatment means are to be compared on a two-tailed test.

5   The variance of a single sample of size 12 is hypothesized to be 14.

6   The variances of two treatments are to be compared. There are 10 individuals in each group.

Give the *lower* and/or *upper* critical values required for significance in the following tests.

7   Unidirectional t (left) at the 1% level ($N = 11$).

8   Bidirectional t at the 5% level ($N = 21$).

9   Unidirectional t (right) at the 10% level ($N = 41$).

10   Bidirectional t at the 1% level ($N = 11$).

11   Unidirectional χ^2 (left) at the 5% level ($N = 13$).

12   Bidirectional χ^2 at the 5% level ($N = 6$).

13   Unidirectional χ^2 (right) at the 1% level ($N = 11$).

14   Bidirectional χ^2 at the 1% level ($N = 11$).

15   Unidirectional F test at the 5% level, where:
$$N_1 = 11, \qquad \hat{S}_1^2 = 4$$
$$N_2 = 13, \qquad \hat{S}_2^2 = 2$$

CHAPTER 10

EXTENSIONS OF TESTS
OF HYPOTHESES ABOUT
POPULATION MEANS
AND VARIANCES

This chapter will be concerned with two extensions of the hypotheses posed in Chapters 8 and 9. First, the comparison of two independent sample means will be extended to an arbitrary number of independent sample means through a technique known as the *analysis of variance*. The comparison of two independent sample dispersions will also be extended to an arbitrary number of independent sample dispersions through the use of a test statistic known as the F_{max} *statistic*.

HYPOTHESIS TESTING WITH SEVERAL INDEPENDENT SAMPLE MEANS

THE ANALYSIS OF VARIANCE

The analysis of variance technique, developed by Fisher (1923), is an extremely versatile and powerful device for planning, analyzing, and reporting studies involving the interrelationships of several sample means. We shall consider the simplest form of this technique, known as the *one-way analysis of variance*, to extend the null hypothesis

$$H_0: \; \mu_1 = \mu_2$$

to the null hypothesis*

$$H_0: \; \mu_1 = \mu_2 = \mu_3 = \cdots = \mu_k$$

The simultaneous comparison of several independent sample means is a fairly common problem encountered in the behavioral sciences. For example, we might wish to compare:

---

*For the special case $H_0: \mu_1 = \mu_2$, the analysis of variance results are comparable to those obtained in Chapter 8.

The average achievement scores among three approaches to the presentation of material in a ninth-grade class. One approach or treatment might emphasize large class lectures, another small group discussions, and one independent study.

The average reaction times for five groups of experimental subjects, where the treatments consist of depriving the groups of sleep for different lengths of time.

The average scores on a test of creativity or divergent thinking for four groups of patients, where the treatments involve the administration of a different drug to each group.

To see how the one-way analysis of variance operates in making comparisons such as these, consider the first example given above. In order to simplify the computational aspect of the analysis, assume that only five students are randomly assigned to each of the three treatments or classroom approaches. Let the sample data and notation for these 15 students be as indicated in Table 10.1.

In general, any individual student's score is denoted X_{ti}, where

X_{ti} = the score of the ith student in the tth treatment

Thus, for example,

X_{23} = the score of the *third* student in the *second* treatment or class
= 10

The total of the scores in the tth treatment is denoted $\sum_{i=1}^{n} X_{ti}$, where

$$\sum_{i=1}^{n} X_{ti} = X_{t1} + X_{t2} + \cdots + X_{tn}$$

For example, the total of the scores in the third treatment is

$$\sum_{i=1}^{5} X_{3i} = X_{31} + X_{32} + X_{33} + X_{34} + X_{35}$$

$$= 17 + 19 + 16 + 18 + 20$$

$$= 90$$

The mean of the scores in the tth treatment is denoted $\bar{X}_t$. Therefore,

$$\bar{X}_t = \frac{\sum_{i=1}^{n} X_{ti}}{n}$$

It is easily seen that the mean of the scores in the first treatment is

$$\bar{X}_1 = \frac{\sum_{i=1}^{5} X_{1i}}{5} = \frac{10 + 12 + 9 + 11 + 13}{5} = \frac{55}{5} = 11$$

TABLE 10.1   TABULAR ARRANGEMENT OF DATA FROM THREE SAMPLES

	Class 1 Large Class Lectures			Class 2 Small Group Discussions			Class 3 Independent Study	
Student	Achievement score	Notation	Student	Achievement score	Notation	Student	Achievement score	Notation
A	10	X_{11}	F	11	X_{21}	K	17	X_{31}
B	12	X_{12}	G	13	X_{22}	L	19	X_{32}
C	9	X_{13}	H	10	X_{23}	M	16	X_{33}
D	11	X_{14}	I	12	X_{24}	N	18	X_{34}
E	13	X_{15}	J	14	X_{25}	O	20	X_{35}
$n = 5$	55	$\sum_{i=1}^{5} X_{1i}$	$n = 5$	60	$\sum_{i=1}^{5} X_{2i}$	$n = 5$	90	$\sum_{i=1}^{5} X_{3i}$

$$\bar{X}_1 = \frac{\sum_{i=1}^{5} X_{1i}}{5} = \frac{55}{5}$$

$$\bar{X}_1 = 11$$

$$\bar{X}_2 = \frac{\sum_{i=1}^{5} X_{2i}}{5} = \frac{60}{5}$$

$$\bar{X}_2 = 12$$

$$\bar{X}_3 = \frac{\sum_{i=1}^{5} X_{3i}}{5} = \frac{90}{5}$$

$$\bar{X}_3 = 18$$

The total number of scores in the entire study is denoted N. Thus in our case

$$N = n + n + n$$
$$= 5 + 5 + 5$$
$$= 15$$

The grand total of all the scores in the entire study is denoted $\sum_{t=1}^{k} \sum_{i=1}^{n} X_{ti}$, where k denotes the number of treatments. Thus the grand total is

$$\sum_{t=1}^{k} \sum_{i=1}^{n} X_{ti} = (X_{11} + X_{12} + \cdots + X_{1n}) + (X_{21} + X_{22} + \cdots + X_{2n})$$
$$+ \cdots + (X_{k1} + X_{k2} + \cdots + X_{kn})$$

For our example we have a grand total of

$$\sum_{t=1}^{3} \sum_{i=1}^{5} X_{ti} = (10 + 12 + 9 + 11 + 13) + (11 + 13 + 10 + 12 + 14)$$
$$+ (17 + 19 + 16 + 18 + 20)$$
$$= 55 + 60 + 90$$
$$= 205$$

Correspondingly, the grand or overall mean for the entire study is denoted $\bar{X}$, where

$$\bar{X} = \frac{\sum_{t=1}^{k} \sum_{i=1}^{n} X_{ti}}{N}$$

For our example, the overall mean is

$$\bar{X} = \frac{\sum_{t=1}^{3} \sum_{i=1}^{5} X_{ti}}{15} = \frac{205}{15} = 13.67$$

The seven-step procedure for comparing an arbitrary number (in our case three) of sample means by the analysis of variance technique is as follows:

Step 1 /

As a direct extension of the case of two means, we conjecture that the means for all of the potential students instructed under each approach (that is, the population means) are identical. Thus, for our example, the null hypothesis is

$$H_0\text{: } \mu_1 = \mu_2 = \mu_3$$

Our alternative hypothesis is simply that at least two of the population means are not equivalent. We thus wish to reject H_0 under any of the following conditions:

$$\mu_1 \neq \mu_2 \neq \mu_3$$

or

$$\mu_1 \neq \mu_2 = \mu_3$$

or

$$\mu_1 = \mu_2 \neq \mu_3$$

or

$$\mu_1 = \mu_3 \neq \mu_2$$

The analysis of variance is designed to detect whether or not any of these alternative conditions exist to a significant degree. If so, our conclusion is simply that it is not reasonable to assume that the three samples could have come from populations with identical means.

Step 2 /

Let us select a level of significance α of

$$\alpha = 0.05$$

Step 3 /

The test statistic appropriate for comparing an arbitrary number of sample means is

$$F = \frac{MS_T}{MS_W}$$

where MS_T, the mean square for treatments, is

$$MS_T = \frac{n \sum_{t=1}^{k} (\bar{X}_t - \bar{X})^2}{k - 1}$$

and MS_W, the mean square within treatments or groups, is

$$MS_W = \frac{\sum_{t=1}^{k} \sum_{i=1}^{n} (X_{ti} - \bar{X}_t)^2}{N - k}$$

For our example, we have

$$MS_T = \frac{5 \sum_{t=1}^{3} (\bar{X}_t - \bar{X})^2}{3 - 1}$$

$$= \frac{5[(\bar{X}_1 - \bar{X})^2 + (\bar{X}_2 - \bar{X})^2 + (\bar{X}_3 - \bar{X})^2]}{2}$$

$$= \frac{5[(11 - 13.67)^2 + (12 - 13.67)^2 + (18 - 13.67)^2]}{2}$$

$$= 71.67$$

and

$$MS_W = \frac{\sum\limits_{t=1}^{3} \sum\limits_{i=1}^{5} (X_{ti} - \bar{X}_t)^2}{15 - 3}$$

$$= \frac{[(X_{11} - \bar{X}_1)^2 + (X_{12} - \bar{X}_1)^2 + \cdots + (X_{34} - \bar{X}_3)^2 + (X_{35} - \bar{X}_3)^2]}{12}$$

$$= \frac{[(10 - 11)^2 + (12 - 11)^2 + \cdots + (18 - 18)^2 + (20 - 18)^2]}{12}$$

$$= 2.50$$

Therefore,

$$F = \frac{MS_T}{MS_W} = \frac{71.67}{2.50}$$

$$= 28.67$$

In practice, equivalent but simpler computational forms of MS_T and MS_W are used. The relationship between the defining forms and the computational forms of MS_T and MS_W are developed in Appendix C.

The following discussion is intended to provide an appreciation of the test statistic

$$F = \frac{MS_T}{MS_W}$$

Consider, again, the comparison of our three treatments. Remembering that

X_{ti} = the score of the ith individual in the tth treatment
$\bar{X}_t$ = the mean score in the tth treatment
and
$\bar{X}$ = the overall mean for the entire study

we may present graphically the results of our study involving three treatments, as illustrated in Figure 10.1.

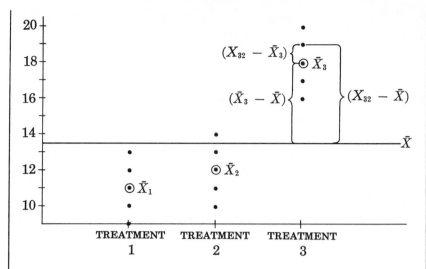

FIGURE 10.1
Graphical presentation of the data in Table 10.1

From Figure 10.1 we can see that there is another way to represent the individual, X_{ti}, scores (Johnson, 1949). That is,

$$X_{ti} = \bar{X} + (\bar{X}_t - \bar{X}) + (X_{ti} - \bar{X}_t) \qquad (1)$$

For example, consider the score of the *second* student in the *third* treatment, X_{32}.

$$X_{32} = \bar{X} + (\bar{X}_3 - \bar{X}) + (X_{32} - \bar{X}_3)$$

Upon substituting the appropriate values from Table 10.1 we have

$$19 = 13.67 + (18 - 13.67) + (19 - 18)$$

$$19 = 13.67 + 4.33 + 1$$

$$19 = 19$$

By transposing the overall mean $\bar{X}$ to the left-hand side of expression (1), we have

$$(X_{ti} - \bar{X}) = (\bar{X}_t - \bar{X}) + (X_{ti} - \bar{X}_t) \qquad (2)$$

Now, $(X_{ti} - \bar{X})$ is referred to as the *total deviation*. That is, it represents the total distance that the score of the ith student in the tth treatment is away from the overall mean. The total deviation for the score of the second student in the third treatment, X_{32}, is indicated in Figure 10.1.

$(\bar{X}_t - \bar{X})$ is referred to as the *treatment deviation*. That is, it is the distance from the mean of the tth treatment to the overall mean. The treatment deviation for the third treatment is illustrated in Figure 10.1. The term $(X_{ti} - \bar{X}_t)$ is variously referred to as the *residual, error, unexplained,* or *within-groups deviation.* We shall refer to it as the *within-groups deviation.* This deviation represents the distance that an individual score is from the corresponding treatment mean. The within-groups deviation is unexplained in the sense that we do not know why all the scores under a given treatment are not identical. It is expected that the scores would differ from treatment to treatment, but within a treatment any differences must be due to other, unaccounted for, factors. The within-groups deviation for the score of the second student in the third treatment is also indicated in Figure 10.1. Thus for X_{32} we have

$$\underset{\substack{total \\ deviation}}{(X_{32} - \bar{X})} = \underset{\substack{treatment \\ deviation}}{(\bar{X}_3 - \bar{X})} + \underset{\substack{within\text{-}groups \\ deviation}}{(X_{32} - \bar{X}_3)}$$

$$(19 - 13.67) = (18 - 13.67) + (19 - 18)$$
$$5.33 = 4.33 \qquad + 1$$
$$5.33 = 5.33$$

In general, we have the important result that the total deviation of a score for any individual can be broken down into two component parts: one part due to the particular treatment given the individual and one part that is unexplained by the treatments of our experiment.

Notice that if the treatment means were close together, the treatment deviations would all be small. Such a situation is illustrated in Figure 10.2.

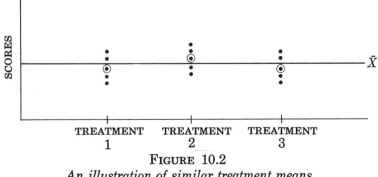

FIGURE 10.2
An illustration of similar treatment means

On the other hand, if the treatment means were not all close to one another, the treatment deviations would all be large. This situation is illustrated in Figure 10.3.

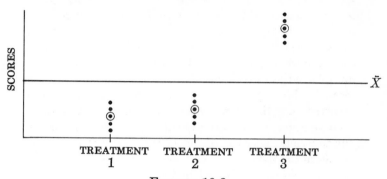

FIGURE 10.3
An illustration of dissimilar treatment means

TOTAL UNBIASED VARIANCE

By considering the scores in all of the treatments we can compute a measure of dispersion for the entire set of data. Let us take as our measure of dispersion for the total study the unbiased variance and denote it by $\hat{S}^2_{total}$. Thus the total unbiased variance $\hat{S}^2_{total}$ is

$$\hat{S}^2_{total} = \frac{\sum_{t=1}^{k} \sum_{i=1}^{n} (X_{ti} - \bar{X})^2}{N - 1}$$

The total unbiased variance for our example is, therefore,

$$\hat{S}^2_{total} = \frac{\sum_{t=1}^{3} \sum_{i=1}^{5} (X_{ti} - \bar{X})^2}{14}$$

$$= \frac{(10 - 13.67)^2 + (12 - 13.67)^2 + \cdots + (18 - 13.67)^2 + (20 - 13.67)^2}{14}$$

$$= 12.38$$

The numerator of $\hat{S}^2_{total}$, $\sum_{t=1}^{k} \sum_{i=1}^{n} (X_{ti} - \bar{X})^2$ is termed the *total sum of squares*. The denominator of $\hat{S}^2_{total}$, $N - 1$, is termed the *total degrees of freedom*.

By substitution from equation (2), the total sum of squares may be expressed as follows:

$$\sum_{t=1}^{k} \sum_{i=1}^{n} (X_{ti} - \bar{X})^2 = \sum_{t=1}^{k} \sum_{i=1}^{n} [(\bar{X}_t - \bar{X}) + (X_{ti} - \bar{X}_t)]^2$$

The right-hand side of this expression, as shown in Appendix C, may be written in the following form:

$$\sum_{t=1}^{k} \sum_{i=1}^{n} (X_{ti} - \bar{X})^2 = n \sum_{t=1}^{k} (\bar{X}_t - \bar{X})^2 + \sum_{t=1}^{k} \sum_{i=1}^{n} (X_{ti} - \bar{X}_t)^2 \qquad (3)$$

The total sum of squares is thus equal to a term involving the treatment deviation plus a term involving the within-groups deviations. The first term on the right-hand side of equation (3),

$$n \sum_{t=1}^{k} (X_t - \bar{X})^2$$

is called the *treatment sum of squares*. Notice that for treatment means close together, as in Figure 10.2, the treatment sum of squares will be very small. As the treatment means show greater differences among them, as in Figure 10.3, the treatment sum of squares will increase. Thus the larger this term becomes, the greater the evidence is for rejecting the null hypothesis that the population means are all equal.

How large must the treatment sum of squares become before we declare that a significant difference exists among the various treatment means? This depends on the dispersion of the scores within the treatments. If there is very little variability within the treatments, then even a modest difference among treatment means may prove to be significant. This situation is illustrated in Figure 10.4. On the

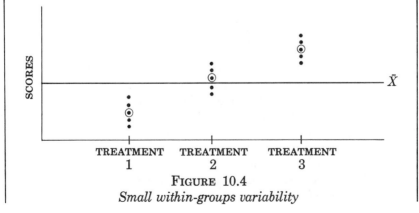

FIGURE 10.4
Small within-groups variability

other hand, if there is a great deal of unexplained variability within the treatments, the same differences among the means might not prove to be significant. This situation is illustrated in Figure 10.5. It is clear that the mean differences in Figure 10.5 are not so impressive as those in Figure 10.4, since the differences among the treatment means in Figure 10.5 are rather small relative to the variability occurring within each treatment. The essential point is that in order to declare significant differences among the treatment means, the variability within the various treatments must be taken into account.

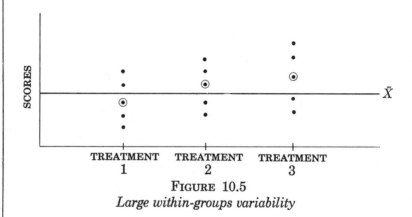

FIGURE 10.5
Large within-groups variability

The second term on the right-hand side of equation (3) reflects this within-treatment variability. This term,

$$\sum_{t=1}^{k} \sum_{i=1}^{n} (X_{ti} - \bar{X}_t)^2$$

is called the **within-groups sum of squares**. Notice that the within-groups sum of squares should be rather small in Figure 10.4 and rather large in Figure 10.5.

The distribution of the F statistic is based on the assumption that we have two independent, unbiased variance estimates. Hence the treatment sum of squares and the within-groups sum of squares are not compared directly. Instead, each term is divided by its *degrees of freedom* before they are compared.

TREATMENT DEGREES OF FREEDOM

Since there are, in general, k treatments, there are $k - 1$ degrees of freedom for treatments. In our example

$$k - 1 = 3 - 1 = 2$$

WITHIN-GROUPS DEGREES OF FREEDOM

Since there are n scores in each treatment there are $n - 1$ degrees of freedom within each treatment. Since there are k treatments, the total within-groups degree of freedom is

$$k(n - 1) = N - k$$

In our example

$$N - k = 15 - 3 = 12$$

A sum of squares divided by its corresponding degrees of freedom is called the *mean square*. Thus we have

Treatment mean square MS_T

$$= \frac{\text{treatment sum of squares}}{\text{treatment degrees of freedom}}$$

$$MS_T = \frac{n \sum_{t=1}^{k} (\bar{X}_t - \bar{X})^2}{k - 1}$$

and

Within-groups mean square MS_W

$$= \frac{\text{within-groups sum of squares}}{\text{within-groups degrees of freedom}}$$

$$MS_W = \frac{\sum_{t=1}^{k} \sum_{i=1}^{n} (X_{ti} - \bar{X}_t)^2}{N - k}$$

Suppose that there is very little difference among the treatment means relative to the unexplained variability within treatments, as in Figure 10.5. In this case the ratio MS_T/MS_W will be small.

On the other hand, for large differences among the treatment means relative to the within-groups variability with treatments, as in Figure 10.4, the ratio MS_T/MS_W will be large.

In summary, if the treatment means are far apart relative to the spread of scores within treatments, this ratio will be large. Otherwise it will be small.

Finally, as shown in Appendix C, equivalent computation forms for MS_T and MS_W are

$$MS_T = \frac{n \sum_{t=1}^{k} (\bar{X}_t - \bar{X})^2}{k-1}$$

$$= \frac{\sum_{t=1}^{k} \left[\frac{\left(\sum_{i=1}^{n} X_{ti}\right)^2}{n} \right] - \frac{\left(\sum_{t=1}^{k} \sum_{i=1}^{n} X_{ti}\right)^2}{N}}{k-1}$$

$$MS_W = \frac{\sum_{t=1}^{k} \sum_{i=1}^{n} (X_{ti} - \bar{X}_t)^2}{N-k}$$

$$= \frac{\left\{ \sum_{t=1}^{k} \sum_{i=1}^{n} X_{ti}^2 - \sum_{t=1}^{k} \left[\frac{\left(\sum_{i=1}^{n} X_{ti}\right)^2}{n} \right] \right\}}{N-k}$$

The analysis of variance is based on the assumptions that the samples are independent of one another, that the variances of the samples are homogeneous, and that the underlying populations of the samples are normally distributed. However, there is considerable agreement that the analysis of variance is quite insensitive to departures from normality and at least moderate inequities in the sample variances. The independence of the samples is, however, essential to the proper utilization of the one-way analysis of variance design discussed here.

Step 4 /

The test statistic

$$F = \frac{MS_T}{MS_W}$$

follows Fisher's F probability distribution, which is given in Table VII of Appendix A. The table is entered at the $(N - k)$ row and the $(k - 1)$ column. The interpretation of this table is the same as discussed in Chapter 9.

Step 5 /

Since we have, in our example, a row entry of

$$(N - k) = (15 - 3) = 12$$

and a column entry of

$$(k - 1) = (3 - 1) = 2$$

with

$$\alpha = 0.05$$

we see that our *rejection region* is

$$F > 3.88$$

Thus if

$$F = \frac{MS_T}{MS_W}$$

is greater than 3.88, we reject the null hypothesis

$$H_0: \ \mu_1 = \mu_2 = \mu_3$$

and accept the alternative hypothesis H_1 that the population means are not all equal.

Step 6 /

For our example, we have seen from Step 3 that the value of our test statistic is

$$F = \frac{MS_T}{MS_W}$$

$$= \frac{71.67}{2.50}$$

$$= 28.67$$

Step 7 /

Since our test statistic is clearly in the *rejection region,* we reject the null hypothesis that these three samples (large class lectures, small group discussions, and independent study) could have reasonably come from populations having identical means. The sample means,

$$\bar{X}_1 = 11$$
$$\bar{X}_2 = 12$$
$$\bar{X}_3 = 18$$

in other words, contain at least one significant difference among them.

The seven-step procedure of the one-way analysis of variance may briefly be summarized as follows for our example:

Step 1 /

$$H_0: \mu_1 = \mu_2 = \mu_3$$

H_1: The population means are not all equal

Step 2 /

$$\alpha = 0.05$$

Step 3 /

$$F = \frac{MS_T}{MS_W}$$

where

$$MS_T = \frac{n \sum_{t=1}^{3} (\bar{X}_t - \bar{X})^2}{2}$$

and

$$MS_W = \frac{\sum_{t=1}^{3} \sum_{i=1}^{5} (X_{ti} - \bar{X}_t)^2}{12}$$

Step 4 /

Fisher's F probability distribution with $(k - 1)$ and $(N - k)$ degrees of freedom.

Step 5 /

$$F > 3.88$$

Step 6 /

$$F = 28.67$$

Step 7 /

Reject

$$H_0: \mu_1 = \mu_2 = \mu_3$$

The results of a study such as this are usually reported in an analysis of variance table, as illustrated in Table 10.2.

Thus we have two applications for the F distribution. Not only does it serve to test for the equality of two dispersions, as we saw in Chapter 9, it also serves to test for the equality of several means.*

---

*Although we have restricted ourselves to equal sample sizes here, the situation involving unequal sample sizes in a one-way analysis of variance is not at all difficult to handle. (See Hays, 1963.)

TABLE 10.2   ANALYSIS OF VARIANCE TABLE

Source of variation	Degrees of freedom	Sum of squares	Mean square	F ratio	Decision
Treatments	2	143.33	71.67	28.67	Reject H_0
Within groups	12	30.00	2.50		
Total	14	173.33			

INDIVIDUAL COMPARISONS

Remember that the alternative hypothesis of the analysis of variance is simply that at least two of the population means cannot be considered equivalent. As we saw, there were several conditions that could bring this about, i.e.,

$$\mu_1 \neq \mu_2 \neq \mu_3$$

or

$$\mu_1 \neq \mu_2 = \mu_3$$

or

$$\mu_1 = \mu_2 \neq \mu_3$$

or

$$\mu_1 = \mu_3 \neq \mu_2$$

Our present concern is to explore more fully the nature of the inter-relationships of the individual sample means. There are, in general, two reasons for studying various individual comparisons as opposed to carrying out an overall analysis of variance. First of all, since a significant analysis of variance result merely tells us that at least two of the means are not equivalent, we may wish to be more precise in specifying the alternative hypothesis. Second, we may wish to proceed directly to individual comparison without first carrying out the analysis of variance. The first situation often arises in exploratory research, and the second where one is well aware that "something" significant is in the data and an omnibus statement to this effect, such as given by the analysis of variance, would do little to shed light on the particular behavioral phenomena under investigation. There are several techniques available for investigating the nature of the differences among treatments; however, the Newman-Keuls method is both quite versatile and straightforward to apply.*

Let us illustrate the use of the Newman-Keuls method of individual treatment comparisons by considering the significant results of Table 10.2.

The Newman-Keuls Method

Step 1 / ARRANGE THE TREATMENT TOTALS IN INCREASING ORDER OF MAGNITUDE

---

*See Winer (1962) for a thorough discussion of this technique.

Thus in our example we have, from the initial sample data given in Table 10.1, the ordering of Table 10.3.

TABLE   10.3   ORDERING OF TREATMENT TOTALS

	Order		
	1	*2*	*3*
Treatments in order of totals	Class 1	Class 2	Class 3
Totals	55	60	90

Step 2 / PREPARE A TABLE SHOWING THE DIFFERENCES AMONG ALL OF THE TREATMENT TOTALS

For our example we have the differences given in Table 10.4.

TABLE   10.4   DIFFERENCES AMONG TREATMENT TOTALS

	Class 1	*Class 2*	*Class 3*
Class 1	—	5	35
Class 2		—	30
Class 3			—

Step 3 / COMPUTE CRITICAL VALUES FOR TESTING THE SIGNIFICANCE OF THE DIFFERENCES BETWEEN PAIRS OF THE TREATMENTS

Here we make use of the distribution of the studentized range statistic given in Table VIII of Appendix A.

The table is entered at the *row* corresponding to the degrees of freedom for the within-groups source of variation given in the analysis of variance table (denoted $f = df$ for $S_{\bar{x}}$). From the analysis of variance results of Table 10.2

this is seen, in our case, to be 12. Therefore, we shall use row $f = 12$.

The *columns* of the table correspond to the number of steps (denoted r) between the column headings and the first row heading of Table 10.4. That is, in Table 10.4 the column heading "Class 2" is two steps away from the first row heading "Class 1." Likewise, the column heading "Class 3" is three steps away from the first row heading "Class 1." Therefore, we shall use the columns labeled $r = 2$ and $r = 3$ in Table VIII of Appendix A. The body of the table gives a so-called q *statistic* corresponding to $(1 - \alpha) = 0.99$ and $(1 - \alpha) = 0.95$. We selected $\alpha = 0.05$ [that is, $(1 - \alpha) = 0.95$ in our case]. The notation for the q statistic is

$$q_{(1-\alpha)}(r, f)$$

Each q statistic is, in turn, multiplied by

$$\sqrt{n \cdot MS_W}$$

where

$n =$ number of observations in each treatment in the analysis of variance table. In our case $n = 5$.

and

$MS_W =$ the mean square of the within-groups source of variation in the analysis of variance table. In our case $MS_W = 2.50$.

Thus for our example we have

$$\sqrt{n \cdot MS_W} = \sqrt{(5)(2.50)} = 3.54$$

The critical values for our example are presented in the form indicated in Table 10.5.

TABLE 10.5   **CRITICAL VALUES OF THE q STATISTIC**

Number of steps	2	3
$q_{0.95}(r, 12)$	3.08	3.77
$q_{0.95}(r, 12)(\sqrt{nMS_W})$	10.90	13.35

Step 4 / PREPARE A TABLE SHOWING THE SIGNIFICANT DIFFERENCES
BETWEEN TREATMENT PAIRS

A table with headings identical to those in Table 10.4 is
prepared. The significant treatment differences are indicated by a symbol as in Table 10.6. Thus from Table 10.6
we see that Class 3 is significantly higher than both Class 1

TABLE   10.6   SIGNIFICANCE OF DIFFERENCES BETWEEN
                                                          TREATMENT PAIRS

	Class 1	Class 2	Class 3
Class 1		n.s.	‡
Class 2			‡
Class 3			

and Class 2. However, Class 2 is not significantly higher
than Class 1. Our overall significant analysis of variance
result is, therefore, explained by the high scores achieved in
Class 3.

The procedure for carrying out the tests reported in
Table 10.6 has been specified in complete detail by Winer
(1962). The procedure starts in the upper right-hand corner
of Table 10.4. In our example, this corresponds to the row
heading, Class 1, and the column heading, Class 3. Class 3
is three steps away from the row heading, Class 1. The difference in the treatment totals for Class 1 and Class 3 is
seen, from Table 10.4, to be 35. The critical value for three
steps is seen, from Table 10.5, to be 13.35. Therefore, the
difference between Class 1 and Class 3 *is significant* and is
so indicated in Table 10.6.

Moving next one position to the left in the first row of
Table 10.4, we see that Class 2 is two steps away from the
row heading, Class 1. The difference in the treatment totals
for Class 1 and Class 2 is seen, from Table 10.4, to be 5.
The critical value for two steps is, from Table 10.5, 10.90.
Therefore, the difference between Class 1 and Class 2 *is not
significant.*

After completing the first row we move to the right-
hand position of the second row in Table 10.4. Class 3 is two

steps away from the second row heading, Class 2. The difference in the treatment totals for Class 2 and Class 3 is seen, from Table 10.4, to be 30. Again from Table 10.5 the critical value for two steps is 10.90; therefore, the difference between Class 2 and Class 3 *is significant* and is so indicated in Table 10.6.

Our Newman-Keuls method of investigating the significant analysis of variance results thus confirms our intuition that with $\bar{X}_1 = 11$, $\bar{X}_2 = 12$, and $\bar{X}_3 = 18$, the third class is the reason for rejecting the null hypothesis H_0: $\mu_1 = \mu_2 = \mu_3$.

TESTING THE HOMOGENEITY OF DISPERSION FOR SEVERAL INDEPENDENT SAMPLES

The analysis of variance technique was used to extend the null hypothesis

$$H_0: \mu_1 = \mu_2$$

to

$$H_0: \mu_1 = \mu_2 = \cdots = \mu_k$$

The null hypothesis concerning two population dispersions expressed either in terms of the standard deviations

$$H_0: \sigma_1 = \sigma_2$$

or in terms of the variances

$$H_0: \sigma_1{}^2 = \sigma_2{}^2$$

can also be extended to k populations. That is,

$$H_0: \sigma_1{}^2 = \sigma_2{}^2 = \cdots = \sigma_k{}^2$$

For example, in the illustrations given at the beginning of this chapter, we might be interested in comparing:

The variability, or individual differences, of achievement scores among the three approaches (large class lectures, small group discussions, and independent study) to the presentation of material in a ninth-grade class.

The variability in the reaction times for the five sleep deprivation groups.

The variability of scores on a test of creativity for the four different drug administrations.

There have been various techniques developed for testing the equality of several independent sample dispersions simultaneously. The Hartley test, the Cochran test, and the Bartlett test are all widely used. See Winer

(1962). We shall consider the Hartley test here, primarily because of its simplicity. To illustrate the Hartley test, let us assume the sample data of Table 10.7 in comparing the variability of creativity scores across the four different drug administrations.

TABLE 10.7   SUMMARY DATA FOR COMPARING FOUR VARIANCES

	Drug 1	Drug 2	Drug 3	Drug 4
Unbiased sample variance of creativity test scores	$\hat{S}_1{}^2 = 49$	$\hat{S}_2{}^2 = 50$	$\hat{S}_3{}^2 = 150$	$\hat{S}_4{}^2 = 20$
Sample sizes	$N = 13$	$N = 13$	$N = 13$	$N = 13$

The seven-step procedure for testing the equality of several independent sample variances simultaneously, using the Hartley test, is as follows:

Step 1 /

Our null hypothesis is simply that the four samples could have reasonably come from populations that have identical variances. That is,

$$H_0:\ \sigma_1{}^2 = \sigma_2{}^2 = \sigma_3{}^2 = \sigma_4{}^2$$

Our alternative hypothesis is

H_1: The four population variances are not all equal

Step 2 /

E. S. Pearson and H. O. Hartley have prepared tables for a level of significance α of 0.05 and 0.01. Let us select

$$\alpha = 0.05$$

Step 3 /

The test statistic developed by Hartley for this situation is

$$F_{max} = \frac{\hat{S}^2{}_{largest}}{\hat{S}^2{}_{smallest}}$$

where

$\hat{S}^2{}_{largest}$ = the largest unbiased sample variance in the study

$\hat{S}^2{}_{\text{smallest}}$ = the smallest unbiased sample variance in the study

Thus for our example we have

$$F_{\max} = \frac{\hat{S}^2{}_{\text{largest}}}{\hat{S}^2{}_{\text{smallest}}}$$

$$= \tfrac{150}{20}$$

$$= 7.5$$

Step 4 /

The probability distribution of the test statistic

$$F = \frac{\hat{S}^2{}_{\text{largest}}}{\hat{S}^2{}_{\text{smallest}}}$$

is given in Table IX of Appendix A. The table is entered at column k, where k is the number of variances under study. The appropriate row entry is $(N - 1)$, where N is the size of the samples (denoted df for $S_X{}^2$).* The body of the table gives a value that would be exceeded only α percent of the time if, in fact, the population variances were all identical.

Thus for our example we enter the table at column 4, since

$$k = 4$$

and at row 12, since

$$(N - 1) = 13 - 1$$

$$= 12$$

Step 5 /

Corresponding to column 4 and row 12 with $\alpha = 0.05$, the value in the body of the table is 4.79. If the population variances underlying our four samples were identical, it would be a rare event to observe a value of $F_{\max}$ (based on our sample sizes) greater than 4.79. Therefore, our *rejection region* is

$$F_{\max} > 4.79$$

Step 6 /

For our sample data

$$F_{\max} = 7.5$$

---

*In the case of unequal sample sizes, N is set equal to the largest sample size.

Step 7 /

Since the test statistic F_{max} falls in the *rejection region*, we
Reject the null hypothesis

$$H_0: \sigma_1^2 = \sigma_2^2 = \sigma_3^2 = \sigma_4^2$$

and

Accept the alternative hypothesis

H_1: The population variances are not all equal

The fluctuation in the variability of our samples
(ranging from $\hat{S}_4^2 = 20$ to $\hat{S}_3^2 = 150$) is too large to support the conjecture that the samples could have reasonably
come from populations having equal variances.

SUMMARY

This chapter has considered two null hypotheses

$$H_0: \mu_1 = \mu_2 = \cdots = \mu_k$$

and

$$H_0: \sigma_1^2 = \sigma_2^2 = \cdots = \sigma_k^2$$

The one-way analysis of variance technique is introduced as a method of
testing $H_0: \mu_1 = \mu_2 = \cdots = \mu_k$. The test statistic employed with the
analysis of variance is

$$F = \frac{MS_T}{MS_W}$$

where MS_T is an estimate of treatment variability and MS_W is an estimate
of the within-groups variability. A significant analysis of variance result
provides a signal that at least one of several alternative hypotheses is to be
preferred to the null hypothesis.

The Newman-Keuls technique is presented as one method of exploring
individual treatment comparisons. Such individual comparisons may either
follow a significant overall analysis of variance result or may be carried out
independently of it.

Finally, the Hartley test is used to test $H_0: \sigma_1^2 = \sigma_2^2 = \cdots = \sigma_k^2$.

Additional new terms and expressions introduced in this chapter include:

X_{ti}
$\bar{X}_t$
$\bar{X}$
Total deviation
Treatment deviation

Within-groups deviation
Total unbiased variance
Treatment sum of squares
Within groups sum of squares
Significance of differences between treatment pairs
F_{max}

REVIEW QUESTIONS

1 What *two* applications have been considered for the F ratio?

2 What is a check on the accuracy of the sum of squares computation in the analysis of variance?

3 State the null hypothesis for the Hartley test.

For the following two problems, give the proper *test statistic* and also the five percent critical limit:

4 The means of *four* treatments are to be compared. The number of individuals in each treatment is 10.

5 The variances of *six* treatments are to be compared. The numbers in each group are 6, 4, 3, 6, 7, 4.

6 The *treatment* variance in the analysis of variance always appears in the _____ of the F ratio.

7 Complete the analysis of variance table for the following set of data, for $\alpha = 0.01$.

Treatment 1	Treatment 2	Treatment 3
1	4	6
2	3	5

8 Apply the Newman-Keuls procedure to the results of Problem 7.

CHAPTER 11

ASSOCIATIONS
BETWEEN VARIABLES

So far each of the variables under study (e.g., incidence of disease, reaction time, intelligence, etc.) has been treated individually in testing hypotheses about frequencies, means, and variances. In this chapter we shall consider the relationship between pairs of variables, first for categorical variables and second for metric variables.

ASSOCIATIONS BETWEEN CATEGORICAL VARIABLES

Up to now we have been concerned with a single categorical variable at a time. A somewhat more interesting question is: Is there any evidence of a significant association between two such variables? For example,

Is there any significant association between the political parties of congressmen and their voting record on a particular legislative bill?

In designing a package for a new product, it might be of interest to know if there is any evidence that the color preferences of men and women are independent.

Is there any significant association between religious affiliation and type of occupation in a particular area of a city?

Of course, the list of such pairings is endless, depending on the interests of the researcher.

A slightly different form of the chi-square statistic is used for analyzing the association between categorical variables. The technique is again quite simple to apply in practice, although the rationale of its development is somewhat more involved. We shall introduce the general notation by means of two variables, one of which has two categories and the other, three categories. First of all, the *observed response frequencies* are arranged in a table form, sometimes referred to as a *contingency table,* as shown in Table 11.1. The following simplifying notation is commonly used for representing the totals:

$$N_{1.} = o_{11} + o_{12} + o_{13} \qquad N_{.1} = o_{11} + o_{21}$$

$$N_{2.} = o_{21} + o_{22} + o_{23} \qquad N_{.2} = o_{12} + o_{22}$$

$$N_{.3} = o_{13} + o_{23}$$

$$N_{..} = o_{11} + o_{12} + o_{13} + o_{21} + o_{22} + o_{23}$$

TABLE   11.1

A 2 × 3 CONTINGENCY TABLE OF OBSERVED FREQUENCIES

Variable B

		Category B_1	Category B_2	Category B_3	Totals
	Category A_1	o_{11}	o_{12}	o_{13}	$(o_{11}+o_{12}+o_{13})$
Variable A	Category A_2	o_{21}	o_{22}	o_{23}	$(o_{21}+o_{22}+o_{23})$
	Totals	$(o_{11}+o_{21})$	$(o_{12}+o_{22})$	$(o_{13}+o_{23})$	$(o_{11}+o_{12}+o_{13} +o_{21}+o_{22}+o_{23})$

Thus out of the total sample of $N_{..}$ individuals, o_{11} of them were classified into category A_1 *and* category B_1; o_{12} of them were classified into category A_1 *and* category B_2, etc. Likewise, $N_{1.}$ individuals were classified into category A_1 (regardless of their classification on variable B); $N_{.1}$ individuals were classified into category B_1 (regardless of their classification on variable A), etc.

Next, the expected response frequencies are computed and arranged in corresponding table form, as shown in Table 11.2. The values e_{11}, e_{12}, e_{13}, e_{21}, e_{22}, and e_{23} are the responses expected under the assumption that variable A and variable B are *independent*.

TABLE 11.2

**EXPECTED FREQUENCIES FOR
A 2 × 3 CONTINGENCY TABLE**

Variable B

		Category B_1	Category B_2	Category B_3	Totals
Vari-able A	Category A_1	$e_{11} = \dfrac{(N_1.)(N._1)}{N..}$	$e_{12} = \dfrac{(N_1.)(N._2)}{N..}$	$e_{13} = \dfrac{(N_1.)(N._3)}{N..}$	$N_1.$
	Category A_2	$e_{21} = \dfrac{(N_2.)(N._1)}{N..}$	$e_{22} = \dfrac{(N_2.)(N._2)}{N..}$	$e_{23} = \dfrac{(N_2.)(N._3)}{N..}$	$N_2.$
	Totals	$N._1$	$N._2$	$N._3$	$N..$

The rationale of the expected frequencies can be seen as follows: Let

A_i = event of being classified in category A_i

and

B_j = event of being classified in category B_j

where in this case

i = 1 or 2 (i.e., A_1 or A_2)

and

j = 1, 2, or 3 (i.e., B_1, B_2, or B_3)

Then, using a relative frequency definition of probability, we have

$$P(A_i) = \frac{N_i.}{N..}$$

That is,

$$P(A_1) = \frac{N_1.}{N..}, \qquad P(A_2) = \frac{N_2.}{N..}$$

Likewise,

$$P(B_j) = \frac{N._j}{N..}$$

That is,

$$P(B_1) = \frac{N_{\cdot 1}}{N_{\cdot\cdot}}, \qquad P(B_2) = \frac{N_{\cdot 2}}{N_{\cdot\cdot}}, \quad \text{and} \quad P(B_3) = \frac{N_{\cdot 3}}{N_{\cdot\cdot}}$$

Now under the assumption of independence of variable A and variable B, we have, from formula (1) of Chapter 4,

$$P(A_i \text{ and } B_j) = P(A_i)P(B_j)$$

$$= \left(\frac{N_{i\cdot}}{N_{\cdot\cdot}}\right)\left(\frac{N_{\cdot j}}{N_{\cdot\cdot}}\right)$$

as the probability that any individual will be classified in both categories A_i and B_j. Thus the number of such classifications we can expect out of a sample of $N_{\cdot\cdot}$ individuals, e_{ij}, is

$$e_{ij} = \left(\frac{N_{i\cdot}}{N_{\cdot\cdot}}\right)\left(\frac{N_{\cdot j}}{N_{\cdot\cdot}}\right)N_{\cdot\cdot}$$

$$= \frac{N_{i\cdot}N_{\cdot j}}{N_{\cdot\cdot}}$$

That is,

$$e_{11} = \frac{N_1.N_{\cdot 1}}{N_{\cdot\cdot}}, \qquad e_{12} = \frac{N_1.N_{\cdot 2}}{N_{\cdot\cdot}}, \qquad e_{13} = \frac{N_1.N_{\cdot 3}}{N_{\cdot\cdot}}$$

$$e_{21} = \frac{N_2.N_{\cdot 1}}{N_{\cdot\cdot}}, \qquad e_{22} = \frac{N_2.N_{\cdot 2}}{N_{\cdot\cdot}}, \qquad e_{23} = \frac{N_2.N_{\cdot 3}}{N_{\cdot\cdot}}$$

Therefore, if the observed responses are in fairly close agreement with the expected responses, this assumption of independence is reasonable. That is, there would not appear to be any significant association between variables A and B on the basis of the sample evidence. On the other hand, should the observed and expected responses differ widely, we would reject the assumption or hypothesis of independence, in which case we would say that there is evidence of a significant association between variables A and B.

DEFINITION   *Chi-square Statistic for a 2 × 3 Design:*

The chi-square statistic χ^2 is simply

$$\chi^2 = \frac{(o_{11} - e_{11})^2}{e_{11}} + \frac{(o_{12} - e_{12})^2}{e_{12}} + \frac{(o_{13} - e_{13})^2}{e_{13}}$$

$$+ \frac{(o_{21} - e_{21})^2}{e_{21}} + \frac{(o_{22} - e_{22})^2}{e_{22}} + \frac{(o_{23} - e_{23})^2}{e_{23}}$$

This expression may be written as

$$\chi^2 = \sum_{\text{all cells}} \left[\frac{(o_{ij} - e_{ij})^2}{e_{ij}} \right] = \sum_{i=1}^{2} \sum_{j=1}^{3} \left[\frac{(o_{ij} - e_{ij})^2}{e_{ij}} \right]$$

where i designates any row and j designates any column.

DISTRIBUTION OF THE CHI-SQUARE STATISTIC FOR A 2 × 3 DESIGN:

The above expression for χ^2 has a sampling distribution, as indicated in Table IV of Appendix A, with $(2 - 1)(3 - 1) = 2$ degrees of freedom.

For example, suppose that in a study of the association between sex and color preference a sample of 200 subjects distributed themselves as shown in Table 11.3. The basic question is: Does there appear to be any

TABLE 11.3   **CONTINGENCY TABLE FOR 2 × 3 DESIGN ARTIFICIAL DATA**

		Color Preference			
		Red	*Yellow*	*Blue*	*Totals*
Sex	Male	17	55	30	102
	Female	14	57	27	98
	Totals	31	112	57	200

significant association between color preferences of the subjects and their sex? That is, we have specifically a 2 × 3 design. The expected frequencies are, therefore, as given in Table 11.4. Thus

$$e_{11} = 15.81, \qquad e_{12} = 57.12, \qquad e_{13} = 29.07$$

$$e_{21} = 15.19, \qquad e_{22} = 54.88, \qquad e_{23} = 27.93$$

TABLE 11.4   **EXPECTED FREQUENCIES FOR DATA OF TABLE 11.3**

		Color Preference			
		Red	*Yellow*	*Blue*	*Totals*
Sex	Male	$e_{11} = \dfrac{(102)(31)}{200}$	$e_{12} = \dfrac{(102)(112)}{200}$	$e_{13} = \dfrac{(102)(57)}{200}$	102
	Female	$e_{21} = \dfrac{(98)(31)}{200}$	$e_{22} = \dfrac{(98)(112)}{200}$	$e_{23} = \dfrac{(98)(57)}{200}$	98
	Totals	31	112	57	200

We may, with this information, again use our formal hypothesis testing procedure to decide if there is a significant association between color preference and sex for this particular sample:

Step 1 / STATE THE HYPOTHESIS

H_0: Sex and color preference are independent

H_1: Sex and color preference are not independent

Step 2 / SELECT THE LEVEL OF SIGNIFICANCE

$$\alpha = 0.05$$

Step 3 / SPECIFY THE TEST STATISTIC

$$\chi^2 = \sum_{i=1}^{r} \sum_{j=1}^{c} \left[\frac{(o_{ij} - e_{ij})^2}{e_{ij}} \right]$$

Step 4 / SPECIFY THE DISTRIBUTION OF THE TEST STATISTIC

χ^2 is distributed as indicated by the chi-square table with $(r - 1)(c - 1) = (1)(2) = 2$ degrees of freedom.

Step 5 / SPECIFY THE REJECTION REGION

For $\alpha = 0.05$ and 2 degrees of freedom the critical value is seen, from Table IV of Appendix A, to be 5.99. A sample value of χ^2 greater than 5.99 would lead us to reject H_0. In such a case, the observed frequencies and expected frequencies would not be in close agreement. This, in turn, casts reasonable doubt on the assumption of independence, since this was the basis for computing the expected frequencies.

Step 6 / COMPUTE THE TEST STATISTIC

$$\chi^2 = \sum_{i=1}^{r} \sum_{j=1}^{c} \left[\frac{(o_{ij} - e_{ij})^2}{e_{ij}} \right]$$

$$= \frac{(17 - 15.81)^2}{15.81} + \frac{(55 - 57.12)^2}{57.12}$$

$$+ \frac{(30 - 29.07)^2}{29.07} + \frac{(14 - 15.19)^2}{15.19}$$

$$+ \frac{(57 - 54.88)^2}{54.88} + \frac{(27 - 27.93)^2}{27.93}$$

$$= 0.404$$

Step 7 / ACCEPT OR REJECT THE NULL HYPOTHESIS

Accept H_0.

Thus, there does not seem to be any strong indication in these data that sex and color preference are related.

It is assumed, as in the goodness of fit tests, that the individual observations are independent (i.e., unrelated or uncorrelated) of each other and that the cells of the contingency table are mutually exclusive with expected frequencies of at least five.

The above 2×3 design is easily generalized to the case where there are an arbitrary number of categories for variable A (say, r rows) and an arbitrary number of categories for variable B (say, c columns).

In general, upon repeated sampling the statistic

$$\chi^2 = \sum_{i=1}^{r} \sum_{j=1}^{c} \left[\frac{(o_{ij} - e_{ij})^2}{e_{ij}} \right]$$

has a sampling distribution that follows a chi-square probability distribution if, in fact, the two variables A and B are independent of one another. The particular chi-square probability distribution is specified by the quantity $(r-1)(c-1)$.

For the special case of analyzing a 2×2 contingency table, wherein there is only one degree of freedom, the χ^2 statistic incorporating a correction for continuity* becomes

$$\chi^2 = \sum_{i=1}^{2} \sum_{j=1}^{2} \left[\frac{(|o_{ij} - e_{ij}| - 0.5)^2}{e_{ij}} \right]$$

An equivalent, but computationally simpler, form of the χ^2 statistic corrected for continuity in a 2×2 contingency table is presented in the discussion of the median test in Chapter 12.

ASSOCIATIONS BETWEEN METRIC VARIABLES

We shall now consider the relationship between pairs of metric variables, including the prediction of one variable from another and quantifying the strength of the association between two such variables. The prediction of human behavior has always been intrinsically interesting. We might, for example, wish to predict

Industrial supervisor rating scores for employees, after on-the-job training, from selection test scores obtained at the time of the individuals' employment.

The reaction times of experimental subjects from the number of hours of sleep deprivation.

*See page 100.

Children's I.Q., as measured by a standardized instrument such as the Stanford-Binet intelligence test, from some ability that is easier to measure, such as verbal comprehension.

There are two related topics designed to help answer questions such as these: regression analysis and the correlation coefficient. Regression analysis provides us with a basis for prediction, while the correlation coefficient is a measure of the strength of association between variables.

REGRESSION ANALYSIS

The problem of predicting one variable (usually denoted Y) from another variable (usually denoted X) is known as *regression analysis*.* Generally we wish, in the behavioral sciences, to predict some future behavioral response from some known response. That is, in our examples we wish to know what the supervisor's rating score *will be*, based on the known selection test score; what the reaction time will be, based on the known amount of sleep deprivation; what the child's I.Q. *would be* (if the intelligence test were given), based on the known verbal comprehension score.

As discussed in Chapter 1, there is no absolute way of knowing what the future will actually be like. We therefore rely on experience and base our predictions on the assumption that the future relationship between two variables will resemble the past relationship. We recall again the discussion of Chapter 1; *if* the future resembles the past, *then* our experience may be of value in attempting to predict one variable from another. Otherwise, our predictions, being based on past experience, will be of little help to us. At any rate, it should be kept in mind that there is no tight statistical basis for insuring that the future will resemble the past. This is, rather, an assumption that we must live with in predicting future events.

In order to gain the experience necessary to predict one variable from another, we first collect a sample, in which both variables X and Y have already occurred. The relationship between variables X and Y in this sample is then used to construct a "prediction equation," which is, in turn, used to predict variable Y for individuals for whom only an X score is known.

To illustrate the method of analyzing a sample of known values of both variables X and Y, consider the above example concerning the industrial supervisor's rating scores. In order to minimize the computational details let us consider a sample size of 10.** The procedure is to first ad-

---

*The variable used as a predictor is termed the *independent* variable. The variable we are trying to predict is termed the *dependent* variable. Although this terminology is retained from the mathematical functional relationship between two variables, we rarely, if ever, in the behavioral sciences encounter variables that bear a perfect mathematical relationship to one another.

**Of course, our resulting prediction equation cannot be expected to be highly effective with such a small sample, since it represents a small amount of experience with the relationship of the two variables. In practice much larger samples are used.

minister the selection test to the 10 individuals, wait until the on-the-job training program is completed, and then obtain the supervisor's rating scores for these 10 employees. Let us assume that the selection test scores and the supervisor's rating scores for the 10 employees are as given in Table 11.5.

TABLE 11.5   DEPENDENT AND INDEPENDENT VARIABLES FOR
                          SAMPLE OF SIZE 10 (ARTIFICIAL DATA)

Employee	Selection test (X)	Supervisor's rating (Y)
1	10	2
2	12	4
3	11	6
4	18	16
5	13	12
6	17	12
7	16	14
8	16	10
9	13	6
10	14	8

The nature of the relationship between two variables is difficult to visualize from a straight listing such as Table 11.5. A graph of the data, termed a *scatterdiagram*, such as that presented in Figure 11.1, is much more helpful from a visual point of view.

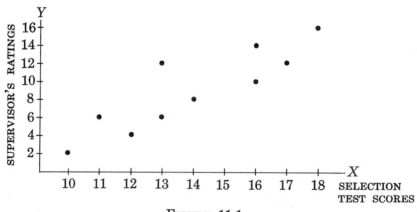

FIGURE 11.1
Scatterplot of the data in Table 11.5

As can be seen from Figure 11.1, there seems to be some tendency for the selection test scores and supervisor ratings to agree. Although the relationship is obviously not perfect, as would be the case if all of the points of Figure 11.1 fell on a single line, the lower scores do seem to be paired with the lower ratings and higher scores with higher ratings.

A fundamental question in regression analysis is how much the knowledge of variable X improves our ability to predict variable Y. To answer this question we consider the problem of predicting variable Y in the absence of any knowledge of variable X. In such a case our sample data reduces to simply the sample values of Y. When we are restricted to only the sample values of Y, the most reasonable prediction equation for estimating any individual's Y score is

$$Y_{\text{pred.}} = \bar{Y}$$

Using this prediction equation, we merely predict that all individual Y values (in our example, all the supervisor ratings) will be equal to the mean $\bar{Y}$ of our particular sample (i.e., in our case, the mean rating for the 10 employees).

The prediction equation

$$Y_{\text{pred.}} = \bar{Y}$$

is employed in the absence of any knowledge about the independent X variable for the following reasons: We saw in Chapter 6 that, in general, the expected value of the sample mean is the population mean. This holds true even if the sample size is only one. Thus the expected value of an individual Y value (i.e., a sample of size one) is μ, the mean of the population of the Y values. In turn, our best estimate of this population mean μ is the sample mean $\bar{Y}$. Hence our best prediction equation for individual Y values, based on our sample data, is

$$Y_{\text{pred.}} = \bar{Y}$$

If we employ the prediction equation

$$Y_{\text{pred.}} = \bar{Y}$$

to predict individual Y values, it is clear that we will not be right all of the time. The criterion of any prediction equation is the error in prediction resulting from its use. To illustrate this error of prediction, let us construct such a prediction equation from the sample data of Table 11.5. Thus

$$\bar{Y} = \frac{\sum\limits_{i=1}^{10} Y_i}{10}$$

$$= \frac{2 + 4 + 6 + 16 + 12 + 12 + 14 + 10 + 6 + 8}{10}$$

$$\bar{Y} = 9.0$$

Imposing, then, the prediction equation

$$Y_{\text{pred.}} = 9.0$$

on the data of Figure 11.1, we have the situation presented in Figure 11.2. As we can see from Figure 11.2, even for the sample data from which the prediction equation was developed, there is a considerable error resulting if we predict each individual's value of Y by the prediction equation

$$Y_{\text{pred.}} = \bar{Y}$$

That is, all of the sample points do not fall on, or even close to, this line.

From Figure 11.2 we see that the errors of prediction in our sample are represented by the distances that the individual Y values are from $\bar{Y}$. The measure of the overall error of prediction is generally taken to be the variance of the Y values,* which is denoted S_Y^2, where

$$S_Y^2 = \frac{\sum\limits_{i=1}^{N} (Y_i - \bar{Y})^2}{N}$$

It is clear that if all the values of Y are identical (that is, they would all fall exactly on the line $Y_{\text{pred.}} = \bar{Y}$) then S_Y^2 is zero. This simply means that there are no errors of prediction; our predictions would be correct in each and every case of our sample. On the other hand, as the distances of the Y values from $\bar{Y}$ increase (as in Figure 11.2), S_Y^2 will correspondingly increase to reflect the errors of prediction.

S_Y^2 is termed the *total variance* because it represents the largest error possible in predicting variable Y in our sample data. We have, in this case, ignored whatever information variable X might have provided in the

---

*In Chapter 3 we saw that the variance was the sum of the squared deviations of the variable divided by the number of values. In this case we have

$$S_Y^2 = \frac{\sum\limits_{i=1}^{N} (Y_i - \bar{Y})^2}{N}$$

Notice that since $Y_{\text{pred.}} = \bar{Y}$ the variance of the Y values could also be expressed

$$S_Y^2 = \frac{\sum\limits_{i=1}^{N} (Y_i - Y_{\text{pred.}})^2}{N}$$

prediction of variable Y. We can do no worse by taking variable X into account. The total variability $S_Y{}^2$ for the data of Table 11.5 is thus

$$S_Y{}^2 = \frac{\sum_{i=1}^{10} (Y_i - \bar{Y})^2}{10}$$

$$= \frac{(2 - 9)^2 + (4 - 9)^2 + \cdots + (8 - 9)^2}{10}$$

$$= 18.6$$

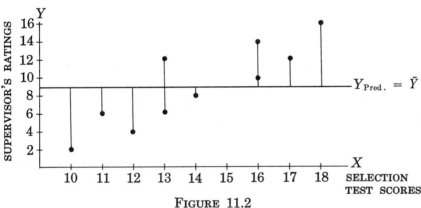

FIGURE 11.2

Illustration of the prediction equation $Y_{\text{Pred.}} = \bar{Y}$ imposed on data of Figure 11.1

Taking the total variance of our sample $S_Y{}^2$ as a criterion of our ability to predict individual values of Y without any knowledge of variable X, let us return to the fundamental question of regression analysis. Namely, by utilizing variable X, is it possible to reduce the errors of prediction? Upon examining the relationship between variables X and Y in Figure 11.1, a better-fitting line (than $Y_{\text{pred.}} = \bar{Y}$) would seem, by eye, to be something like that illustrated in Figure 11.3.

Whereas the predicted value of Y is always 9, regardless of the value of X in Figure 11.2, the predicted value of Y changes with different values of X in Figure 11.3. Thus, for example, if an individual's X score is 12 we predict his Y score, from Figure 11.3, to be 6 rather than 9. Likewise, if his X score is 17, the predicted Y score is 13.5 rather than 9.

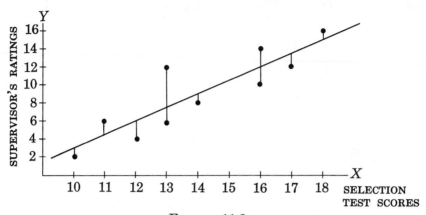

FIGURE 11.3
A straight line fitted to the data in Table 11.5

The distances from the actual sample values of Y to the fitted straight line (i.e., the errors of prediction) in Figure 11.3 are reduced considerably from those of Figure 11.2. The errors of prediction for these two lines are given in Table 11.6.

TABLE 11.6				|	A COMPARISON OF THE ERRORS OF PREDICTION FOR FIGURES 11.2 AND 11.3	
Individual	Actual rating (Y)	Predicted rating using line $Y_{pred.} = \bar{Y}$ (Fig. 11.2)	Prediction error (Fig. 11.2)	|	Predicted rating using fitted line (Fig. 11.3)	Prediction error (Fig. 11.3)
1	2	9	−7	|	3	−1
2	4	9	−5	|	6	−2
3	6	9	−3	|	4.5	1.5
4	16	9	7	|	15	1
5	12	9	3	|	7.5	4.5
6	12	9	3	|	13.5	−1.5
7	14	9	5	|	12	2
8	10	9	1	|	12	−2
9	6	9	−3	|	7.5	−1.5
10	8	9	−1	|	9	−1

The *average absolute* prediction error (i.e., if the sign or direction of the errors is ignored) for the line $Y_{pred.} = \bar{Y}$ is seen from Table 11.6 to be

Average error $(Y_{\text{pred.}} = \bar{Y})$

$$= \frac{(7) + (5) + (3) + (7) + (3) + (3) + (5) + (1) + (3) + (1)}{10}$$

$$= 3.8$$

The average absolute prediction error for the fitted line of Figure 11.3 is correspondingly

Average error (fitted line)

$$= \frac{(1) + (2) + (1.5) + (1) + (4.5) + (1.5) + (2) + (2) + (1.5) + (1)}{10}$$

$$= 1.8$$

Because the fitted line results in smaller errors, we next examine the procedure for constructing such a line.

There are various criteria for drawing or fitting a line to a set of points as in Figure 11.3. However, we shall consider only two: a line drawn freehand or by eye, and a least squares line. A line drawn by eye through the set of points is, of course, the easiest approach and for some types of applications might be adequate. The difficulty with such a line is that it is drawn subjectively, and thus the predicted values of Y would be variable from investigator to investigator. There is no standard by which one line could be judged better than another. The least squares line, on the other hand, is unique and is therefore constant for different investigators analyzing the same set of sample data.

DEFINITION *Least Squares Line*

For a set of sample data, such as in Table 11.5, the least squares line is that line for which the sum of the squares of the vertical distances from all of the Y values to the line is smaller than for any other line. Thus if D_i denotes the vertical distance from the ith Y value to the line, the least squares line* minimizes $\sum_{i=1}^{N} D_i^2$.

$$\sum_{i=1}^{N} D_i^2 = D_1^2 + D_2^2 + \cdots + D_N^2$$

---

*For a thorough discussion of the least squares criterion see Wilks (1961).

We could, of course, select any shape for our prediction line. However, we shall concentrate on the straight line. There are three reasons for restricting ourselves to a straight line at this point: First, it illustrates the theory of regression analysis perfectly well; second, it is usually adequate for a wide range of problems in the behavioral sciences; finally, a straight line can serve as a first approximation in more complicated situations.

The general equation of any straight line relating variables X and Y is

$$Y = A_0 + A_1X$$

where

$A_0 =$ the point at which the line crosses the Y axis (termed the Y intercept)

and

$A_1 =$ the slope of the line (termed the regression coefficient)

The straight line (or linear) equation

$$Y = A_0 + A_1X$$

may easily be appreciated from the following considerations: Suppose that

$Y =$ the number of chairs occupied in a room

and

$X =$ the number of individuals who have entered the room after a certain time

Thus if each person occupies one chair and X individuals enter the room, there will be X occupied chairs. This situation is illustrated by the solid line in Figure 11.4 and is represented by the equation

$$Y = X$$

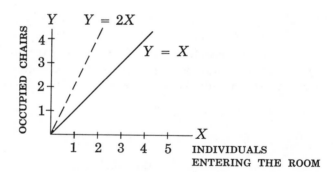

FIGURE 11.4
Graph of the equations $Y = X$ and $Y = 2X$

If, however, each individual took up two chairs, there would be $2X$ occupied chairs for every X individuals, as illustrated by the broken line in Figure 11.4, which is represented by the equation $Y = 2X$. In general, if each individual occupies A_1 chairs the equation becomes

$$Y = A_1X$$

Now suppose that there is already one chair occupied when the individuals begin entering the room. Thus if each entering individual occupies one chair and X individuals enter the room, there will be $1 + X$ occupied chairs. This situation is illustrated by the solid line in Figure 11.5 and is represented by the equation

$$Y = 1 + X$$

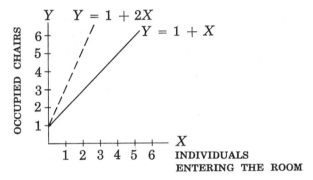

FIGURE 11.5

Graph of the equations $Y = 1 + X$ and $Y = 1 + 2X$

If however, each entering individual takes up two chairs, there would be $1 + 2X$ occupied chairs for every X individuals entering the room, as illustrated by the broken line in Figure 11.5, which is represented by the equation

$$Y = 1 + 2X$$

In general, if there are already A_0 chairs occupied and each entering individual occupies A_1 chairs, the relationship becomes

$$Y = A_0 + A_1X$$

By adopting the above straight line equation as our new prediction equation we have

$$Y_{\text{pred.}} = A_0 + A_1X$$

It is clear that we could predict the value of Y for any value of X from this equation if only we knew the Y intercept A_0 and the regression coefficient, A_1.

The unique least squares line is obtained by evaluating the following expressions for A_0 and A_1* (as will be seen from the accompanying worked examples, these rather complicated-looking expressions are actually quite straightforward to use):

$$A_0 = \frac{(\Sigma\, Y)(\Sigma\, X^2) - (\Sigma\, X)(\Sigma\, XY)}{N\, \Sigma\, X^2 - (\Sigma\, X)^2}$$

and

$$A_1 = \frac{N\, \Sigma\, XY - (\Sigma\, X)(\Sigma\, Y)}{N\, \Sigma\, X^2 - (\Sigma\, X)^2}$$

For the sample data of our example, given in Table 11.5, we have the summary results of Table 11.7. Thus, by substituting the results of Table 11.7 in the expressions for A_0 and A_1 we have

$$A_0 = \frac{(90)(2024) - (140)(1356)}{(10)(2024) - (19{,}600)}$$

$$= -12$$

and

$$A_1 = \frac{(10)(1356) - (140)(90)}{(10)(2024) - (19{,}600)}$$

$$= 1.5$$

TABLE 11.7   SUMMARY CALCULATIONS FOR THE DATA OF TABLE 11.5

$N = 10$	$\sum_{i=1}^{10} Y_i = 90$	$\sum_{i=1}^{10} X_i^2 = 2024$	$\sum_{i=1}^{10} Y_i^2 = 996$
$\sum_{i=1}^{10} X_i = 140$	$\sum_{i=1}^{10} X_i Y_i = 1356$	$(\sum_{i=1}^{10} X_i)^2 = 19{,}600$	$(\sum_{i=1}^{10} Y_i)^2 = 8100$

Therefore, our prediction equation line fitted by the method of least squares becomes

$$Y_{\text{pred.}} = A_0 + A_1 X$$

$$Y_{\text{pred.}} = -12 + 1.5X$$

This equation represents the "best" straight line, in the least squares sense, that we can use to predict values of Y from varying values of X. This is the straight line fitted to the points in Figure 11.3. Thus, for example, if an individual's X score were 10, the predicted Y value would be

---

*In order to simplify the notation in the expressions for A_0 and A_1, the subscripts and summation limits are omitted. Thus the symbols X, Y, and Σ should be interpreted as X_i, Y_i, and $\sum_{i=1}^{N}$, respectively, in every instance.

$$Y_{\text{pred.}} = -12 + (1.5)(10)$$

$$= 3$$

The predicted Y values for the 10 individuals in our sample have been given in Table 11.6. The difference between an individual's actual value of Y and the predicted value of Y for him is, again, the *error of prediction* and is indicated in Table 11.6 for all 10 individuals in our particular sample.

The defining formulas for A_0 and A_1 result from the simultaneous solution of the two equations

$$\sum_{i=1}^{N} Y_i = A_0 N + A_1 \sum_{i=1}^{N} X_i$$

$$\sum_{i=1}^{N} X_i Y_i = A_0 \sum_{i=1}^{N} X_i + A_1 \sum_{i=1}^{N} X_i^2$$

These two equations are called the *normal equations* for the least squares line. These normal equations, in turn, result from the use of the calculus to minimize the linear equation

$$Y = A_0 + A_1 X$$

with respect to both A_0 and A_1. See Wilks (1961) for a discussion of the derivation of the normal equations through the use of the calculus.

The regression coefficient A_1 indicates the slope of the line

$$Y_{\text{pred.}} = A_0 + A_1 X$$

and as such may be positive (as in our example, with $A_1 = +1.5$), negative, or zero. A negative regression coefficient simply reflects the fact that the values of Y, in our sample, tend to decrease as the values of X increase. A negative regression coefficient is illustrated in Figure 11.6.

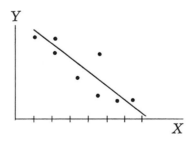

FIGURE 11.6

A graph illustrating the equation $Y_{\text{Pred.}} = A_0 + A_1 X$
where A_1 is negative

A regression coefficient of zero means that there is no slope to the line; it is horizontal to the X axis, as was the line in Figure 11.2. If $A_1 = 0$, the prediction equations

$$Y_{\text{pred.}} = \bar{Y}$$

and

$$Y_{\text{pred.}} = A_0 + A_1 X$$

are equally effective, in terms of the errors of prediction, for predicting values of Y for varying values of X.

Let us now look more carefully at the errors of prediction for these two prediction equations. The variability of the points in Figure 11.2 around the line

$$Y_{\text{pred.}} = \bar{Y}$$

was measured by $S_Y{}^2$, the variance of the Y values, and was termed the *total variance*. The total variance represents the largest errors of prediction possible. In this case, (i.e., where $A_1 = 0$) knowledge of an individual's X score is of no help in predicting his Y score.

On the other hand, in Figure 11.3, the prediction equation

$$Y_{\text{pred.}} = A_0 + A_1 X$$

where A_1 is not zero, reflects the tendency for a change in Y to accompany a change in X. However, it is clear that all of the points still do not fall on this line (although they are generally closer to this line than to the line $Y_{\text{pred.}} = \bar{Y}$ of Figure 11.2, as was shown in Table 11.6). Our question is now: Why do not the points fall on the prediction equation line

$$Y_{\text{pred.}} = A_0 + A_1 X$$

which is designed to reflect the accompaniment of variable Y by variable X? The answer is that we do not know why; it is unexplained variability. That is, we are estimating or predicting Y by the equation

$$Y_{\text{pred.}} = A_0 + A_1 X$$

and yet the relationship between X and Y is not perfect; errors of prediction result with this prediction equation. The smaller the unexplained variability, the better X and Y seem to agree, and the better is the above prediction equation. Consider, for example, Figure 11.7. In Figure 11.7 the total variability around the prediction equation

$$Y_{\text{pred.}} = \bar{Y}$$

is said to be completely explained by the relationship between X and Y expressed in the prediction equation

$$Y_{\text{pred.}} = A_0 + A_1 X$$

There is no unexplained variability, since variables X and Y agree perfectly. However, this idealized relationship between any two variables in the behavioral sciences is rare indeed. The actual relationships encountered are, at best, like that illustrated in Figure 11.3.

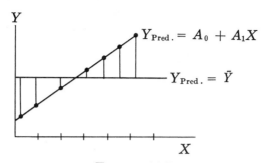

FIGURE 11.7
An illustration of the absence of unexplained variability
in predicting Y from X

The measure of this unexplained variability is defined in a manner similar to the total variance S_Y^2. Both involve the variation of the points around the respective lines. Thus, corresponding to the total variance S_Y^2, discussed on page 222, the *unexplained variance* is denoted $S^2_{Y \cdot X}$ and is expressed

$$S^2_{Y \cdot X} = \frac{\sum_{i=1}^{N} (Y_i - Y_{\text{pred.}})^2}{N} = \frac{\sum_{i=1}^{N} [Y_i - (A_0 + A_1 X_i)]^2}{N}$$

The unexplained variance* for the data of Table 11.6 is thus

$$S^2_{Y \cdot X} = \frac{\sum_{i=1}^{10} [Y_i - (-12 + 1.5 X_i)]^2}{10}$$

$$= \frac{(2 - 3)^2 + (4 - 6)^2 + \cdots + (8 - 9)^2}{10}$$

$$= 4.2$$

Thus the effectiveness of the prediction equation depends on the extent to which the total variance is explained by the equation

$$Y_{\text{pred.}} = A_0 + A_1 X$$

The better the explanation, the smaller will be the unexplained variance.

An important fact to be kept in mind in constructing a prediction equation such as we have here is that the least squares line for predicting Y from X is not the same as the least squares line for predicting X from Y.

---

* $\quad S_{Y \cdot X} = \sqrt{\dfrac{\sum_{i=1}^{N} (Y_i - Y_{\text{pred.}})^2}{N}}$ is called the *standard error of estimate of Y on X.*

These are two separate prediction problems, and the dependent and independent variables must be specified before the prediction equation is constructed. Again we are predicting either Y from X or X from Y, but both situations cannot be handled with a single line. We have adapted the convention that we are predicting Y from X in our presentation here.*

CORRELATION COEFFICIENT

It was seen in the last section that the effectiveness of the prediction equation

$$Y_{\text{pred.}} = A_0 + A_1 X$$

is reflected by the measure of the unexplained variance of our sample data $S^2_{Y \cdot X}$. However, this variability is dependent on the units of measurement used in the study. In order to obtain an index reflecting the degree of association between variables X and Y that is independent of the particular units of measurement employed for each variable (e.g., X measured in feet and Y in pounds, X measured in I.Q. units and Y in achievement test score units, etc.) we turn to the so-called *Pearson product-moment correlation coefficient*. Unless otherwise specified, the expression *correlation coefficient* will be taken to mean the coefficient to be developed in this section.

To start with, the units of measurement may be eliminated by expressing the results of the last section in proportion form. The proportion used is the extent to which the total variance is explained by the straight line relationship between X and Y given in the above prediction equation. That is, we form the ratio of the explained variance to the total variance, where

Explained variance = total variance − unexplained variance

Thus, we have

$$\frac{\text{Explained variance}}{\text{Total variance}} = \frac{\text{total variance} - \text{unexplained variance}}{\text{total variance}}$$

$$= 1 - \frac{\text{unexplained variance}}{\text{total variance}}$$

which, upon substituting the measures of these variances, S_Y^2 and $S^2_{Y \cdot X}$, becomes

$$\frac{\text{Explained variance}}{\text{Total variance}} = 1 - \frac{S^2_{Y \cdot X}}{S_Y^2}$$

---

*For a more complete discussion of this matter concerning the two prediction equations

$$Y_{\text{pred.}} = A_0 + A_1 X$$

and

$$X_{\text{pred.}} = B_0 + B_1 Y$$

see Hays (1963).

This ratio will range between one (for a perfect relationship as in Figure 11.7) and zero (if there is no linear relationship between X and Y). This ratio is termed the *coefficient of determination* and is denoted as r^2. Thus

$$r^2 = 1 - \frac{S^2_{Y \cdot X}}{S_Y^2}$$

The larger the coefficient of determination r^2, the higher the degree of relationship between X and Y.

DEFINITION   *Coefficient of Determination*

> The coefficient of determination gives the portion of the total variance that is explained or accounted for by the linear relationship between X and Y.

The coefficient of determination for the data of Table 11.5 is

$$r^2 = 1 - \frac{S^2_{Y \cdot X}}{S_Y^2}$$

$$= 1 - \frac{4.2}{18.6}$$

$$= 0.77$$

Thus 77 percent of the total variance in the sample of 10 supervisor ratings is accounted for by a linear or straight line relationship between the ratings Y and the selection test scores X.

The square root of the coefficient of determination r^2 is the well-known correlation coefficient for variables X and Y. In our example we have

$$r = \sqrt{1 - \frac{S^2_{Y \cdot X}}{S_Y^2}}$$

$$= \sqrt{0.77}$$

$$= 0.88$$

It is much more common to express the degree of relationship between two variables in terms of the correlation coefficient than in terms of the coefficient of determination. Therefore, let us consider some important characteristics of the correlation coefficient.

Characteristics of the Correlation Coefficient

1. *Sign of r.* The correlation coefficient r is given the same sign as the regression coefficient A_1. Thus by looking only at the sign of r we can tell whether the general form of the scatter diagram will be as in Figure 11.1

or 11.6. In our case, $r = 0.88$, which corresponds to the data of Figure 11.1. The coefficient of determination is, of course, always positive and therefore does not reflect the direction of the trend between X and Y.

2. *Range of r.* The range of the correlation coefficient r is

$$-1 \le r \le +1$$

A perfect correlation is represented by either

$$r = +1$$

or

$$r = -1$$

depending on the slope of the line relating the two variables. The situation in Figure 11.7, for example, clearly represents a perfect correlation, since there is no unexplained variance. That is,

$$r = \sqrt{1 - \frac{S^2_{Y \cdot X}}{S_Y{}^2}}$$

$$= \sqrt{1 - \frac{0}{S_Y{}^2}}$$

$$= \sqrt{1}$$

$$= 1$$

It should be kept in mind that a correlation coefficient of -1 also implies a perfect relationship. In general, the sign of r indicates only the nature of the regression equation, not the strength of relationship. A correlation coefficient of zero, on the other hand, indicates a total lack of relationship between X and Y. In this case the two prediction equations

$$Y_{\text{pred.}} = \bar{Y}$$

and

$$Y_{\text{pred.}} = A_0 + A_1 X$$

coincide.

3. *Interpretation of r.* The correlation coefficient r is usually interpreted through the coefficient of determination r^2. We have already seen that r^2 represents the portion of the total variance in the sample that is accounted for by the prediction equation

$$Y_{\text{pred.}} = A_0 + A_1 X$$

An alternative way to interpret r is through what is termed the *predictive efficiency* of r, indicating the percent by which r reduces the standard error of estimate. The predictive efficiency of r is denoted E_r and is expressed as

$$E_r = 100(1 - \sqrt{1 - r^2})$$

The rationale of

$$E_r = 100(1 - \sqrt{1 - r^2})$$

may be seen as follows: Since

$$r^2 = 1 - \frac{S^2_{Y \cdot X}}{S_Y^2}$$

we may express $S_{Y \cdot X}$ as a proportion of S_Y as follows:

$$\frac{S_{Y \cdot X}}{S_Y} = \sqrt{1 - r^2}$$

However, the ratio

$$\frac{S_{Y \cdot X}}{S_Y}$$

tends to zero for a high degree of relationship. To change this orientation we consider the expression

$$1 - \frac{S_{Y \cdot X}}{S_Y}$$

which tends to one for a high degree of relationship. Placing this latter expression in percentage form, we have

$$100 \left(1 - \frac{S_{Y \cdot X}}{S_Y} \right) = 100(1 - \sqrt{1 - r^2})$$

For our example

$$E_r = 100(1 - \sqrt{1 - 0.77})$$

$$= 52 \text{ percent}$$

Thus, for our example, our correlation coefficient

$$r = 0.88$$

is interpreted to mean that 77 percent of the total variance in the supervisor ratings in this sample is accounted for by the least squares line relating the ratings Y and the selection test scores X. Apparently it is, to some degree, helpful to have knowledge of the selection test scores if we wish to predict the supervisors' ratings.

Table 11.8 gives the relationship between the coefficient of determination r^2 and the correlation coefficient r for various values of r. It is seen from Table 11.8 that the portion of the total variance accounted for by the prediction equation

$$Y_{\text{pred.}} = A_0 + A_1 X$$

drops rapidly for even moderate reductions in the correlation coefficient.

TABLE 11.8   **A COMPARISON OF r AND r^2**

Correlation coefficient r	Coefficient of determination r^2
1.00	1.00
0.99	0.98
0.98	0.96
0.97	0.94
0.96	0.92
0.95	0.90
0.90	0.81
0.80	0.64
0.70	0.49
0.60	0.36
0.50	0.25

4. *Computational form of r.* The correlation coefficient for a sample of data is rarely computed in practice from the defining formula

$$r = \sqrt{1 - \frac{S^2_{Y \cdot X}}{S_Y^2}}$$

Instead, the following expression is used.* (This rather complicated-looking expression, as in the case of the formulas for A_0 and A_1, is actually quite straightforward to use, as seen from the accompanying worked example.)

$$r = \frac{N \Sigma XY - (\Sigma X)(\Sigma Y)}{\sqrt{[N \Sigma X^2 - (\Sigma X)^2][N \Sigma Y^2 - (\Sigma Y)^2]}}$$

Thus from the summary calculations of Table 11.7 we have, for our example, a correlation coefficient of

$$r = \frac{(10)(1356) - (140)(90)}{\sqrt{[(10)(2024) - (140)^2][(10)(996) - (90)^2]}}$$

$$= 0.88$$

5. *The relation of the correlation coefficient and the regression coefficient.* The definition of the regression coefficient A_1 was

$$A_1 = \frac{N \Sigma XY - (\Sigma X)(\Sigma Y)}{N \Sigma X^2 - (\Sigma X)^2}$$

which in turn may be written

$$A_1 = \frac{\Sigma (X - \bar{X})(Y - \bar{Y})}{N} \cdot \frac{1}{S_X^2}$$

---

*Again, as in the case of the expressions for A_0 and A_1, the subscripts and summation limits are omitted to simplify the notation.

Multiplying both numerator and denominator of the right-hand side by S_Y/S_Y, we have

$$A_1 = \frac{\Sigma\,(X - \bar{X})(Y - \bar{Y})}{N} \cdot \left(\frac{1}{S_X S_Y}\right)\left(\frac{S_Y}{S_X}\right)$$

However, from the definition of the correlation coefficient r we have the following relationship between A_1 and r:

$$A_1 = r\,\frac{S_Y}{S_X}$$

In our discussion of regression we have considered X as the independent variable and Y as the dependent variable. That is,

$$Y_{\text{pred.}} = A_0 + A_1 X$$

We could also reverse the roles of X and Y and develop a regression equation of the form

$$Y_{\text{pred.}} = B_0 + B_1 X$$

The equation for predicting Y from X will not, in general, be the equation for predicting X from Y. There is, however, an interesting relationship between the two regression coefficients (A_1 and B_1) and the correlation coefficient. The correlation coefficient, which will be the same regardless of which equation it is derived from, may be shown (Hays, 1963) to be

$$r = \sqrt{A_1}\,\sqrt{B_1}$$

TESTING THE SIGNIFICANCE OF A SAMPLE CORRELATION COEFFICIENT

Our prediction equation

$$Y_{\text{pred.}} = A_0 + A_1 X$$

which was the basis for defining the correlation coefficient, was constructed from sample data. Therefore, from sample to sample we can expect to observe different values for A_0, A_1, $S^2_{Y \cdot X}$, and $S_Y{}^2$. Thus there will also be different values of r. That is, r is a sample statistic, and as such cannot be expected to remain the same from sample to sample.

Typically, what we would like to do is to generalize the results of our particular study to some population of interest. We therefore consider the basic question of whether or not there is any significant degree of association between the population of Y values and the population of X values. Our procedure will be first to conjecture that there is no significant association between the two populations, as reflected by a straight line relationship.

That is, in predicting Y from X we could just as well use the equation

$$Y_{\text{pred.}} = \bar{Y}$$

as

$$Y_{\text{pred.}} = A_0 + A_1 X$$

We shall then determine whether or not our particular sample correlation coefficient was a reasonable one to observe if, in fact, there is no linear relationship between the two corresponding populations.

Thus in our example, we conjecture that there is no relationship between the scores of the population of employees given the selection test and the ratings of the population of employees given supervisor ratings.

This problem may be handled by our seven-step procedure as follows.

Step 1 /

We adopt the Greek letter rho, ρ, as a symbol of the underlying correlation coefficient. From the conjecture or assumption that there is no relationship between the two populations, our null hypothesis becomes

$$H_0: \rho = 0$$

Correspondingly, the alternative bidirectional hypothesis is that there *is* a significant correlation between the populations of scores and ratings (either positive or negative).

$$H_1: \rho \neq 0$$

Step 2 /

Let us select a level of significance α of

$$\alpha = 0.05$$

Step 3 /

The test statistic appropriate for this situation is

$$t = \frac{r\sqrt{N-2}}{\sqrt{1-r^2}}$$

Step 4 /

The test statistic

$$t = \frac{r\sqrt{N-2}}{\sqrt{1-r^2}}$$

follows the Student's t probability distribution with $N - 2$ degrees of freedom.

Step 5 /

Since we have a sample size of 10, a level of significance α of 0.05, and a bidirectional test, the *rejection region* is seen, from Table VI of Appendix A, to be

$$t > 2.31 \quad \text{and} \quad t < -2.31$$

Step 6 /

For our example we have

$$t = \frac{0.88\sqrt{8}}{\sqrt{1 - 0.77}} = \frac{2.49}{0.48}$$

$$= 5.19$$

Step 7 /

Since the value of our sample test statistic clearly falls in the *rejection region*, we

Reject the null hypothesis

$$H_0\colon \rho = 0$$

and

Accept the alternative hypothesis

$$H_1\colon \rho \neq 0$$

It is therefore unreasonable to believe that we could have observed a sample correlation coefficient such as we did (even in our very small sample) if, in fact, there were no linear relationship between the populations of scores and ratings. The selection test scores are significantly related to the supervisor ratings and hence represent a profitable source of information in the prediction of the ratings. It would, therefore, be quite helpful to use a linear prediction equation based on the principle of least squares to predict supervisor ratings from selection test scores.*

In conclusion, it should be kept clear that there is no firm statistical basis for inferring causality from a strength of relationship. Thus, even if we were to observe a perfect relationship between two variables, such as that illustrated in Figure 11.7 (that is, a situation having a correlation coefficient of 1), we cannot infer that variable X causes variable Y. It is simply that, on the basis of our sample evidence, we have reason to believe that there is a significant empirical relationship between the two variables.

---

*Tests of significance may also be made for hypothesized values of ρ other than zero and also for hypothesized values of the regression coefficient A_1 (Spiegel, 1961).

SUMMARY

This chapter has introduced the concept of the association between variables. The chi-square sampling distribution is used as a basis for studying the relationship of categorical variables and regression analysis for metric variables. The general form of the chi-square test of association is

$$\chi^2 = \sum_{i=1}^{r} \sum_{j=1}^{c} \left[\frac{(o_{ij} - e_{ij})^2}{e_{ij}} \right]$$

with $(r - 1)(c - 1)$ degrees of freedom.

The general linear regression equation for predicting y from x is

$$Y_{\text{pred.}} = A_0 + A_1 X$$

where

$$A_0 = \frac{(\Sigma\, Y)(\Sigma\, X^2) - (\Sigma\, X)(\Sigma\, XY)}{N\, \Sigma\, X^2 - (\Sigma\, X)^2}$$

and

$$A_1 = \frac{N\, \Sigma\, XY - (\Sigma\, X)(\Sigma\, Y)}{N\, \Sigma\, X^2 - (\Sigma\, X)^2}$$

The strength of association between variables X and Y is measured by the coefficient of determination r^2, where

$$r^2 = \frac{\text{explained variance}}{\text{total variance}} = 1 - \frac{S^2_{Y \cdot X}}{S_Y^2}$$

Several properties of r, known as the *Pearson product-moment correlation coefficient*, are presented.

Finally, a method is presented for testing the significance of a sample correlation coefficient.

Additional new terms and expressions of this chapter include

Contingency table
Expected response frequencies in a contingency table
Significant association
Regression analysis
   Independent variable
   Dependent variable
   Prediction equation
   Scatterplot
   Errors of prediction
   S_Y^2, total variance
   Average error
   Least squares line
   Y intercept

Positive and negative regression coefficient

$S_{Y \cdot X}$, standard error of estimate

Unexplained variance

Characteristics of the correlation coefficient r (sign, range, interpretation, computational form, relationship to A_1)

ρ

Significance test of r

REVIEW QUESTIONS

1 When the relationship between two categorical variables is studied, the data are analyzed in a _____ table.

2 In arriving at the expected frequencies for Problem 1, we "pretend" that the two variables are _____ .

3 For three categories for variable A and five categories of variable B, give the degrees of freedom for the chi-square test.

4 For r categories for variable A and c categories for variable B, give the degrees of freedom for the chi-square test.

5 For the following set of data, test the hypothesis that variable A is independent of variable B. Set $\alpha = 0.05$.

	B_1	B_2	B_3
A_1	2	1	3
A_2	3	2	4

In Questions 6 through 11, indicate whether the following statements are true or false.

6 Only a single set of measures is needed to compute a correlation coefficient.

7 In graphical representations of regression lines, negative correlations are indicated by lines running from the upper left-hand corner of the graph to the lower right-hand corner.

8   The variation of the individual scores about the regression line is known as the *unexplained* variation.

9   If the correlation between X and Y is zero, the best estimate one can make of any score on the Y distribution is the mean of the Y scores.

10 The correlation coefficient is usually interpreted through the coefficient of determination.

11 If $Y = F(X)$, Y is called the *independent* variable.

12 If the correlation between X and Y is zero, what is the best estimate one can make of any score on the Y distribution?

13 If height and weight are positively and highly correlated, what statement would be reasonable to make for an individual who is above average in height?

14 What is the ratio of explained variance to total variance called?

15 Given the following set of data, derive the regression equation, the coefficient of determination, and the correlation coefficient.

X	Y
2	3
1	2
0	0

16 As the regression coefficient A_1 approaches 0, what happens to the prediction lines $Y_{\text{pred.}} = \bar{Y}$ and $Y_{\text{pred.}} = A_0 + A_1X$?

17 If $r = 0.80$, what percentage of the variance in Y is accounted for by the least squares line relating Y and X?

18 Test the significance of the sample correlation coefficient obtained in Problem 15 against the alternative $H_1: \rho \neq 0$ with $\alpha = 0.05$.

CHAPTER 12

SOME RANK-ORDER
STATISTICS

Some types of behavioral responses are of such a nature that they can be measured more precisely than merely classifying them into mutually exclusive categories. On the other hand, because of the uncertain nature of the intervals between the scores, the arithmetic mean and variance might not be appropriate descriptive statistics. Such is the case when it is assumed only that one score represents a higher, stronger, or greater response than another score and nothing is said about the distances between any two scores—they might be close together or far apart. When phenomena are viewed in this way, they are termed rank-ordered or ordinal data. Thus behavioral responses treated as rank-ordered fall between elementary categorical data and metric data, where the ordinary rules of arithmetic and algebra apply. Rank-ordered data are generally described by the median and percentile score statistics, which do not assume the existence of constant intervals between the obtained scores. The median and percentile scores were discussed in Chapter 3.

Consider the following examples involving rank-ordered responses:

A clinical psychologist studies the effects of an experimental role-playing game on the aggressiveness of children by randomly assigning them either to a control group, involving no role-playing, or to the experimental role-playing group. The children are then all placed together in a free-play situation, and each child is given a score estimating his aggressive behavior. These aggression scores are assumed to be ordinal in nature, thereby providing a means of rank-ordering the children. The ranks of the children from each group are then compared to determine if the role-playing group shows a different aggressive tendency than the control group.

A teacher studies the effects of a new set of teaching materials on pupil understanding of the United States' foreign policy by using both conventional materials and the new materials. The pupils are then ranked together by scores obtained on a questionnaire related to this topic. Finally, the two approaches are compared by contrasting the ranks of the pupils from each group.

It is also possible to analyze the above two situations by first matching the individuals on some basis such as ability. In this case, the psychologist or the teacher would form pairs of children who have similar ability test scores obtained prior to the study. One child from each ability pairing would then be randomly selected for the experimental group, while the other would be placed in the control group.

Just as the assumptions of the scale underlying rank-ordered responses are unique, so are there unique statistical techniques appropriate for analyzing responses that are at least ordinal in nature and yet which cannot be assumed to be measured on an interval scale. This chapter will present four of the more elementary techniques for analyzing rank-ordered information: *the median test, the Mann-Whitney U test, the sign test,* and *the Wilcoxon test.*

Rank-order statistics are somewhat different from others we have considered in that, although the practical applications of the required formulas are among the simplest methods of statistical analysis, it is somewhat more difficult to gain an intuitive appreciation for their rationale. To gain this appreciation one needs to consider several extensions of the concepts of probability presented in Chapter 4. Before any extended applications with rank-ordered data are undertaken, it would be advisable to consult Siegel (1956) or Kraft and van Eeden (1968). We shall concentrate here on only the large sample cases of the above four tests with bidirectional alternative hypotheses and the situations for which these tests are appropriate.

The four rank-ordered techniques to be presented here all involve two groups (for example, a control group and an experimental group). Two of these techniques involve *dichotomous classifications* wherein a score is merely classified as being above or below another score or as being above or below a median value. The other two techniques involve what may be termed *rank classifications* whereby the actual rank-ordered position of an individual's score (or the difference score between two matched individuals) is taken into account. The latter two techniques are more powerful, when appropriate, because more of the available information is utilized. For both the coarse dichotomous classifications and the finer rank classifications two cases will be considered: independent samples and matched samples. In the case of independent samples, the subjects in each of the two groups are assumed to be randomly and independently selected from some population. In matched samples the subjects are first paired on the basis of some characteristic prior to assignment to the groups. You will recall that a frequently encountered situation of matched samples involves using the same individuals as subjects in both groups. In this way each individual serves as his own control.

Our four tests and the corresponding experimental arrangements for comparing two groups on the basis of rank-ordered information are as follows:

1. Median test. Dichotomous classifications with independent samples.

2. Mann-Whitney U test. Rank classifications with independent samples.

3. Sign test. Dichotomous classifications with matched samples.

4. Wilcoxon test. Rank classifications with matched samples.

Again, only the large sample cases will be considered here. Siegel (1956) should be consulted for the small sample cases of these situations involving two groups and their extensions to more than two groups and for situations involving unidirectional alternative hypotheses.

MEDIAN TEST

In the median test the obtained scores are used merely to identify the individuals in the study as exceeding or not exceeding the median score of the two combined groups. The samples in the two groups are assumed to be independent of one another. The large sample case of the median test, furthermore, requires that the total number of individuals in the combined groups exceed 40. To illustrate the large sample case of the median test, let us assume the artificial sample data given in Table 12.1 for the above example concerning the effect of role-playing on children's aggression.

The general seven-step hypothesis testing procedure for comparing two groups involving a large number of subjects by the median test is as follows:

Step 1 /

In this situation we make the conjecture that there is no significant difference between the two groups so far as their median values are concerned. That is, the two independent samples are assumed to come from two populations having identical medians. Hence our null hypothesis becomes

H_0: median of population 1 = median of population 2

Our alternative hypothesis is simply that the experimental and control groups are different in their median aggressive tendencies. That is,

H_1: median of population 1 $\neq$ median of population 2

Step 2 /

Let us select a level of significance $\alpha = 0.10$.

TABLE 12.1   FREE-PLAY AGGRESSION SCORES FOR COMBINED
EXPERIMENTAL AND CONTROL GROUPS (ARTIFICIAL DATA)

Experimental Group (Role-playing Experience)		Control Group (No Role-playing Experience)	
Child	Aggression score	Child	Aggression score
1	55	24	25
2	38	25	35
3	90	26	62
4	85	27	59
5	48	28	57
6	49	29	33
7	80	30	56
8	65	31	52
9	39	32	50
10	41	33	34
11	45	34	29
12	46	35	36
13	75	36	28
14	51	37	53
15	42	38	61
16	66	39	55
17	45	40	58
18	65	41	54
19	49	42	40
20	75		
21	43		
22	70		
23	44		

Step 3 /

The large sample case of the median test utilizes the following test statistic:

$$\chi^2 = \frac{N\left(\mid AD - BC \mid - \dfrac{N}{2}\right)^2}{(A + B)(C + D)(A + C)(B + D)}$$

where the letters are interpreted by means of Table 12.2. This rather complicated formula is actually an equivalent form of the χ^2 statistic, corrected for continuity, for 2 × 2 contingency tables. The present form is somewhat simpler to evaluate, however, than the form given in Chapter 11.

TABLE 12.2   ARRANGEMENT OF DATA FOR MEDIAN TEST

	Group 1	Group 2	Total
Frequency of scores exceeding the combined median	A	B	A + B
Frequency of scores not exceeding the combined median	C	D	C + D
Total	A + C	B + D	N = A + B + C + D

We expect, under our null hypothesis, that A and C, as well as B and D, would be approximately equal. That is, the expected frequencies for the A, B, C, and D cells are $(A + C)/2$, $(B + D)/2$, $(A + C)/2$, and $(B + D)/2$, respectively. In the example data of Table 12.1 the median of the 42 scores is 50.5. Therefore, our data for the median test are as shown in Table 12.3.

TABLE 12.3   MEDIAN TEST SUMMARY DATA FROM TABLE 12.1

	Experimental group	Control group	Total
Frequency of scores exceeding the combined median	A = 11	B = 10	A + B = 21
Frequency of scores not exceeding the combined median	C = 12	D = 9	C + D = 21
Total	A + C = 23	B + D = 19	N = 42

Step 4 /

The test statistic given in Step 3 follows the chi-square distribution with one degree of freedom.

Step 5 /

> With a level of significance α of 0.10 and one degree of freedom, we see from Table IV of Appendix A that the *rejection region* is
>
> $$\chi^2 > 2.71$$

Step 6 /

> From Table 12.3 we have
>
> $$\chi^2 = \frac{N\left(\,|\,AD - BC\,|\, - \dfrac{N}{2}\right)^2}{(A + B)(C + D)(A + C)(B + D)}$$
>
> $$= \frac{42\left(\,|\,(11)(9) - (10)(12)\,|\, - \dfrac{42}{2}\right)^2}{(21)(21)(23)(19)}$$
>
> $$= 0$$

Step 7 /

> Since our test statistic does not fall in the *rejection region,* we
>
> > Accept the null hypothesis
>
> > H_0: median of population 1 = median of population 2
>
> Thus we have no significant basis for casting doubt on our conjecture that the median aggression scores are equivalent for the role-playing group and the control group.
>
> It should be kept in mind that the scores (i.e., the available information) are used in a very coarse manner, in that we use them only to identify an individual as exceeding or not exceeding the overall median. In other words, we are not assuming a great deal of precision in our response measures.

MANN-WHITNEY U TEST

If we wish to treat ordinal data obtained from two independent samples in a more precise manner than merely classifying an individual as being above or below the median, we may use the Mann-Whitney U test, which takes into account the rank value of each observation. A large sample for this test is interpreted to mean that the number of individuals in the largest of the two groups exceeds 20. To illustrate the large sample case of the Mann-Whitney U test, let us again consider the artificial data of Table 12.1. It is necessary to compute the rank value of each of the 42 observations, as shown in Table 12.4. Thus child 24 is ranked number one and child 3 is ranked number 42.*

TABLE   12.4   **RANKED SCORES FOR DATA OF TABLE 12.1**

Experimental Group (Role-playing Experience)			Control Group (No Role-playing Experience)		
Child	*Aggression score*	*Rank*	*Child*	*Aggression score*	*Rank*
1	55	26.5	24	25	1
2	38	8	25	35	6
3	90	42	26	62	33
4	85	41	27	59	31
5	48	18	28	57	29
6	49	19.5	29	33	4
7	80	40	30	56	28
8	65	34.5	31	52	23
9	39	9	32	50	21
10	41	11	33	34	5
11	45	15.5	34	29	3
12	46	17	35	36	7
13	75	38.5	36	28	2
14	51	22	37	53	24
15	42	12	38	61	32
16	66	36	39	55	26.5
17	45	15.5	40	58	30
18	65	34.5	41	54	25
19	49	19.5	42	40	10
20	75	38.5			
21	43	13			
22	70	37			
23	44	14			

The seven-step procedure for the large sample Mann-Whitney U test comparison of our two independent groups by means of the ranks of the obtained scores is as follows:

Step 1 /

> We conjecture that the experimental and control groups are equally effective in creating aggressive behavior. In terms of our data we hypothesize that the rank values of the aggression scores are equivalent in the two populations from which the experimental and control samples were taken.

---

*Each of the tied scores is given the average of the ranks that would have been assigned to the tied scores had the scores all been different. When a large number of scores are tied, the procedure given by Siegel (1956) should be used.

Thus our null hypothesis is

H_0: rank values of population 1

$$= \text{rank values of population 2}$$

The bidirectional alternative hypothesis is

H_1: rank values of population 1

$$\neq \text{rank values of population 2}$$

Step 2 /

Let us retain the level of significance $\alpha = 0.10$ used in the median test of this data.

Step 3 /

The test statistic appropriate for the Mann-Whitney U test when one of the groups contains a sample size greater than 20 is

$$Z = \frac{U - \frac{N_1 N_2}{2}}{\sqrt{\frac{(N_1)(N_2)(N_1 + N_2 + 1)}{12}}}$$

where

$N_1 =$ the smaller of the two sample sizes
$N_2 =$ the larger of the two sample sizes

and

$$U = N_1 N_2 + \frac{N_1(N_1 + 1)}{2} - R_1$$

where

$R_1 =$ the sum of the ranks in the smaller of the two samples*

Thus for the data of Table 12.4 we have (since the control group contains the smaller sample)

$$R_1 = 1 + 6 + \cdots + 10$$

$$= 340.5$$

$$N_1 = 19$$

$$N_2 = 23$$

---

*Where the two samples are of equal size, the number of individuals in one of the groups is designated N_1 and R_1 is computed for these N_1 individuals.

Hence

$$U = N_1N_2 + \frac{N_1(N_1 + 1)}{2} - R_1$$

$$= (19)(23) + \frac{(19)(20)}{2} - 340.5$$

$$= 286.5$$

Therefore,

$$Z = \frac{U - \dfrac{N_1N_2}{2}}{\sqrt{\dfrac{(N_1)(N_2)(N_1 + N_2 + 1)}{12}}}$$

$$= \frac{286.5 - \dfrac{(19)(23)}{2}}{\sqrt{\dfrac{(19)(23)(19 + 23 + 1)}{12}}} = \frac{68.00}{39.57}$$

$$= 1.72$$

Step 4 /

The Z statistic follows the unit normal probability distribution.

Step 5 /

Since $\alpha = 0.10$ and we have a bidirectional alternative hypothesis, our *rejection region* is seen from Table V of Appendix A to be

$$Z > 1.65 \quad \text{and} \quad Z < -1.65$$

Step 6 /

The value of the test statistic for our sample data is

$$Z = 1.72$$

Step 7 /

Since our test statistic falls in the *rejection region*, we

Reject the null hypothesis

H_0: rank values of population 1
$\qquad\qquad\qquad$ = rank values of population 2
and
Accept the bidirectional alternative hypothesis

H_1: rank values of population 1
$\qquad\qquad\qquad$ $\neq$ rank values of population 2

Thus when we take the rank of the scores into account, we find sufficient evidence to reject our conjecture that the experimental and control groups have an equal effect on the aggression scores. The discrepancy in the conclusions of the median test and the Mann-Whitney U test for the same set of data is explained by the additional information utilized by the latter test. Also a somewhat different hypothesis is tested by the Mann-Whitney U test. A careful examination of the scores of Table 12.1 reveals that although the number of scores above the overall median is quite similar for the experimental and control groups (11 and 10, respectively, as indicated in Table 12.3), the distances of the two groups of scores above the overall median differ markedly. When we simply contrast the number of scores above and below the median for the two groups, these distances are not taken into account. Table 12.5 illustrates the difference in the pattern of distances of the two groups of scores from the overall median. This difference in the pattern of distances accounts for the significant results of the Mann-Whitney U test.

TABLE   12.5   A COMPARISON OF THE DISTRIBUTION OF SCORES
                              FOR THE TWO GROUPS OF TABLE 12.1

	Frequencies	
	---	---
Score	Experimental group (role-playing experience)	Control group (no role-playing experience)
90	1	
:		
85	1	
:		
80	1	
:		
75	2	
:		
70	1	
:		
66	1	
65	2	
:		
62		1
61		1
60		
59		1
58		1
57		1

TABLE 12.5—Continued   A COMPARISON OF THE DISTRIBUTION OF
                               SCORES FOR THE TWO GROUPS OF TABLE 12.1

| | Frequencies | |
Score	Experimental group (role-playing experience)	Control group (no role-playing experience)
56		1
55	1	1
54		1
53		1
52		1
51	1	
		Median = 50.5
50		1
49	2	
48	1	
47		
46	1	
45	2	
44	1	
43	1	
42	1	
41	1	
40		1
39	1	
38	1	
37		
36		1
35		1
34		1
33		1
:		
29		1
28		1
27		
26		
25		1

SIGN TEST

In contrast to the independent groups of the two previous tests, it often
happens that individuals are matched before being assigned to the groups.
This matching may be on the basis of I.Q., achievement, or any other
characteristic that we seek to eliminate as a variable in the comparison of
two treatments or groups. As mentioned before, the individuals may even
serve as their own control by being used in both groups. The sign test is the
most rudimentary technique for analyzing matched pairs. In the sign test,
the scores obtained are merely used to place one member of the matched

pair above or below the other member. Nothing is said about the magnitude of the difference, merely that one individual's response is above or below that of the other individual with whom he was paired. The large sample case of the sign test involves more than 25 pairs of subjects.

Consider, for purposes of illustration, the artificial matched-pair data given in Table 12.6, which were previously analyzed by means of the matched-pairs t test in Chapter 8. Recall that these data concerned the effect of new curriculum materials on the understanding of pupils of the United States' foreign policy. One member of each of the 30 pairs, selected at random, was assigned to the experimental class using the new materials and the other member to the control, which continued using the conventional material. Following the completion of this unit of study, a questionnaire form was filled out by each pupil, from which he was assigned a score representing his understanding of the United States' foreign policy.

TABLE   12.6   CRITERION SCORES FOR PAIRS OF PUPILS IN
                    EXPERIMENTAL AND CONTROL CLASSES (ARTIFICIAL DATA)

Pair	Score of pupil in experimental class (new materials)	Score of pupil in control class (conventional materials)	Sign of difference
1	25	10	+
2	24	11	+
3	23	12	+
4	18	19	−
5	13	15	−
6	25	9	+
7	15	15	0
8	12	13	−
9	18	20	−
10	20	11	+
11	17	18	−
12	18	17	+
13	19	18	+
14	22	24	−
15	24	16	+
16	11	14	−
17	23	13	+
18	20	21	−
19	25	6	+
20	16	17	−
21	15	16	−
22	16	17	−
23	14	17	−
24	22	14	+
25	18	11	+
26	19	14	+
27	21	14	+
28	21	22	−
29	20	22	−
30	20	8	+

The seven-step procedure for the large sample sign test for comparing two matched groups is as follows:

Step 1 /

In the sign test we first conjecture that the two scores within all of the potential pairs of individuals are identical; that is, that there is no difference between the two groups. Thus our null hypothesis is (for all potential matched pairs)

H_0: scores of individuals from population 1
　　= scores of individuals from population 2

Our bidirectional alternative hypothesis is thus (for all potential matched pairs)

H_1: scores of individuals from population 1
　　$\neq$ scores of individuals from population 2

Step 2 /

Let the level of significance $\alpha = 0.05$.

Step 3 /

The test statistic appropriate for the large sample case of the sign test is

$$Z = \frac{(X + 0.5) - \frac{1}{2}N}{\frac{1}{2}\sqrt{N}}$$

where

N = number of pairs in the study for which there is a difference in the scores of the two individuals within each pair*

and

X = number of positive or negative signs in the study, whichever is smaller. The sign of each pair depends on which of the two individuals has the higher score according to the following convention:

If $\begin{pmatrix} \text{score of individual} \\ \text{assigned to group 1} \end{pmatrix} > \begin{pmatrix} \text{score of individual} \\ \text{assigned to group 2} \end{pmatrix}$
then the sign of the pair is $+$

If $\begin{pmatrix} \text{score of individual} \\ \text{assigned to group 1} \end{pmatrix} < \begin{pmatrix} \text{score of individual} \\ \text{assigned to group 2} \end{pmatrix}$
then the sign of the pair is $-$

---

*In cases of ties the pair is eliminated from the analysis and N is reduced accordingly.

Thus for the data of Table 12.6 we have

$$N = 29$$

since pair number 7 is eliminated because of the tied scores, and

$$X = 14$$

since there are fewer negative signs than positive signs and there are 14 negative signs.

Step 4 /

The test statistic Z follows the unit normal probability distribution.

Step 5 /

Since $\alpha = 0.05$ and our alternative hypothesis is bidirectional, our *rejection region* is, from Table V of Appendix A,

$$Z > 1.96 \quad \text{and} \quad Z < -1.96$$

Step 6 /

The value of our test statistic Z is

$$Z = \frac{(X + 0.5) - \frac{1}{2}N}{\frac{1}{2}\sqrt{N}}$$

$$= \frac{14.5 - \frac{1}{2}(29)}{\frac{1}{2}\sqrt{29}}$$

$$= 0$$

Step 7 /

Since our test statistic does not fall in the *rejection region*, we accept the original null hypothesis that there is no difference in the effect of the two classroom materials on pupil understanding of the United States' foreign policy. Contrast this decision with the one reached with the matched-pair t test for these same data in Chapter 8. The discrepancy results from the fact that, as in the median test, we treat the response scores in a very coarse manner, in that they are used only to rank the two individuals in each pair and do not take into account the magnitude of the differences. Furthermore, the hypothesis under test is again different in each case.

WILCOXON TEST

We may, at times, wish to treat the ordinal data obtained from two matched samples in a more precise manner than merely comparing paired individuals as in the sign test. The so-called *Wilcoxon matched-pairs signed-ranks test* is designed to give more weight to pairs with large differences, whereas the sign test merely treats all differences in a similar fashion. The large sample case of the Wilcoxon test involves at least 25 pairs of subjects.

To illustrate the large sample case of the Wilcoxon test assume that it is reasonable to rank-order the differences of the scores given in Table 12.6, as well as to rank the individuals in each pair (as was done in the sign test). As shown in Table 12.7 the Wilcoxon test requires first that the differences be ranked without regard to sign (column 4).* The sign of the difference is then attached to the rank of the difference (column 5).

The seven-step procedure for the large sample Wilcoxon test for comparing two matched groups is as follows:

Step 1 /

> We conjecture that the two classes are equivalent so far as their effect on pupil understanding is concerned. In terms of the data of Table 12.7 we expect that the sum of the ranks for the positive differences will equal the sum of the ranks for the negative differences in column 5. Our null hypothesis is, therefore (for all potential matched pairs),

H_0: sum of the ranks for the positive differences

= sum of the ranks for the negative differences

The bidirectional alternative is

H_1: sum of the ranks for the positive differences

≠ sum of the ranks for the negative differences

Step 2 /

Again we shall select a level of significance $\alpha = 0.05$.

Step 3 /

> The appropriate test statistic for the large sample Wilcoxon test is

$$Z = \frac{T - \dfrac{N(N+1)}{4}}{\sqrt{\dfrac{N(N+1)(2N+1)}{24}}}$$

---

*The case of tied differences is handled as in the Mann-Whitney U test. Thus the 10 scores of value 1 in Table 12.7 each receive the average rank of 5.5.

where

N = number of pairs for which there is a difference in the scores of the two individuals within each pair. Ties are eliminated, as in the sign test.

T = the sum of the absolute values of positive ranks or the sum of the absolute values of the negative ranks, whichever sum is smaller. Thus the value of T is always positive (see Table 12.7, column 6).

TABLE   12.7   **ARRANGEMENT OF THE DATA OF TABLE 12.6 FOR ANALYSIS BY THE WILCOXON TEST**

Pair	(1) Score of pupil in exp. class (new materials)	(2) Score of pupil in control class (conv. materials)	(3) Differ- ence d	(4) Rank of d (sign ignored)	(5) Rank of d with sign attached	(6) Absolute value of like-signed ranks with smaller sum
1	25	10	15	27	27	
2	24	11	13	26	26	
3	23	12	11	24	24	
4	18	19	−1	5.5	−5.5	5.5
5	13	15	−2	12.5	−12.5	12.5
6	25	9	16	28	28	
7	15	15	0	—	—	—
8	12	13	−1	5.5	−5.5	5.5
9	18	20	−2	12.5	−12.5	12.5
10	20	11	9	22	22	
11	17	18	−1	5.5	−5.5	5.5
12	18	17	1	5.5	5.5	
13	19	18	1	5.5	5.5	
14	22	24	−2	12.5	−12.5	12.5
15	24	16	8	20.5	20.5	
16	11	14	−3	15.5	−15.5	15.5
17	23	13	10	23	23	
18	20	21	−1	5.5	−5.5	5.5
19	25	6	19	29	29	
20	16	17	−1	5.5	−5.5	5.5
21	15	16	−1	5.5	−5.5	5.5
22	16	17	−1	5.5	−5.5	5.5
23	14	17	−3	15.5	−15.5	15.5
24	22	14	8	20.5	20.5	
25	18	11	7	18.5	18.5	
26	19	14	5	17	17	
27	21	14	7	18.5	18.5	
28	21	22	−1	5.5	−5.5	5.5
29	20	22	−2	12.5	−12.5	12.5
30	20	8	12	25	25	

Total T = 125

Hence for the data of Table 12.7 we have

$$N = 29$$

Also from Table 12.7, column 6, we have

$$T = 5.5 + 12.5 + \cdots + 12.5 = 125$$

since the sum of the absolute values of the negative ranks is smaller than for the positive ranks. Therefore,

$$Z = \frac{T - \dfrac{N(N+1)}{4}}{\sqrt{\dfrac{N(N+1)(2N+1)}{24}}}$$

$$= \frac{125 - \dfrac{(29)(30)}{4}}{\sqrt{\dfrac{(29)(30)(59)}{24}}} = \frac{-92.50}{46.25}$$

$$= -2.00$$

Step 4 /

The test statistic Z follows the unit normal probability distribution.

Step 5 /

Since $\alpha = 0.05$ and we have a bidirectional alternative hypothesis, our *rejection region* is again

$$Z > 1.96 \quad \text{and} \quad Z < -1.96$$

Step 6 /

The value of our test statistic Z is

$$Z = -2.00$$

Step 7 /

Since our test statistic falls in the *rejection region*, we conclude that there is a significant difference between the effects of the experimental and the control classes on pupil understanding of the United States' foreign policy.

The discrepancy between the conclusions of the sign test and the Wilcoxon test for the same set of data is due to the fact that the Wilcoxon test takes the magnitude of the differences into account whereas the sign test does not. Thus, although the number of differences favoring each group is approximately the same (15 favoring the experimental class and 14 favoring the control class), the magnitude of the positive and negative differences differs markedly. Careful inspection of column 3 of Table 12.7 reveals that the sum of the positive differences is 142, whereas the sum of the negative differences is only 22. This fact accounts for the significant results of the Wilcoxon test.

It is clear from the examples given in this chapter that the experimental decision can depend, in part, on the selection of the test statistic. Therefore, consideration of the essential differences among the hypotheses to be tested and the underlying operational definitions for the various statistical techniques is an important aspect of selecting a method of analysis. The research worker should carefully consider the selection of a test statistic prior to the experiment in the light of the hypothesis to be tested and the operational definition of the phenomena under study rather than merely trying various post-experimental tests in a search for statistically significant results.

THE ASSOCIATION BETWEEN TWO RANK-ORDERED RESPONSES

The correlation coefficient, presented in Chapter 11, is used to assess the linear relationship between two variables that are at least interval in nature. Correspondingly, there are indices that reflect the strength of association between two rank-ordered variables. The index to be presented here is termed the *Spearman rank-ordered correlation coefficient* and is denoted r_s.*

To illustrate the computational procedure for evaluating r_s for a sample of data, consider the artificial data of Table 12.8 representing ordinal ratings for 11 children on both social maturity and self-control.

TABLE   12.8   RATINGS OF 11 CHILDREN ON SOCIAL MATURITY
                                AND SELF-CONTROL (ARTIFICIAL DATA)

Child	Rating of social maturity	Rating of self-control
1	81	47
2	40	20
3	53	36
4	60	40
5	41	24
6	30	15
7	75	43
8	66	38
9	57	37
10	59	41
11	45	22

*For other such indices see Hays (1963) or Siegel (1956).

The computation of r_s requires that each set of raw scores be converted into ranks as in Table 12.9. Ties are handled as before, by using average ranks. The difference between the two ranks for each individual is recorded in column (3) and the square of this difference in column (4).

TABLE 12.9   ARRANGEMENT OF THE DATA OF TABLE 12.8 FOR COMPUTATION OF r_s

Child	(1) Rank of social maturity rating	(2) Rank of self-control rating	(3) = (1) − (2) Difference d_i	(4) = [(1) − (2)]² d_i^2
1	11	11	0	0
2	2	2	0	0
3	5	5	0	0
4	8	8	0	0
5	3	4	−1	1
6	1	1	0	0
7	10	10	0	0
8	9	7	2	4
9	6	6	0	0
10	7	9	−2	4
11	4	3	1	1
				Total = 10

The Spearman rank-order correlation coefficient r_s is defined as follows:[*]

$$r_s = 1 - \frac{6 \sum_{i=1}^{N} d_i^2}{N^3 - N}$$

$$= 1 - \frac{6(10)}{(11)^3 - 11}$$

$$= 1 - 0.05$$

$$= 0.95$$

INTERPRETING THE SPEARMAN RANK-ORDER CORRELATION COEFFICIENT

When there are at least 10 individuals, the interpretation of r_s is generally handled in the same manner as the correlation coefficient r of Chapter 11. Therefore, following the seven-step procedure for testing the significance of a correlation coefficient given on page 238, we have, for the example data of Table 12.9,

---

[*]For a derivation of the formula for r_s, see Hays (1963).

Step 1 /

$$H_0: \rho = 0$$
$$H_1: \rho \neq 0$$

Step 2 /

Let us select a level of significance $\alpha = 0.05$.

Step 3 /

The test statistic appropriate for this situation was given as

$$t = \frac{r\sqrt{N-2}}{\sqrt{1-r^2}}$$

Interpreting r_s in the same way, we find that the test statistic becomes

$$t = \frac{r_s\sqrt{N-2}}{\sqrt{1-r_s^2}}$$

Step 4 /

The test statistic t follows the Student's t probability distribution with $N - 2$ degrees of freedom.

Step 5 /

Since $\alpha = 0.05$, $N - 2 = 9$, and we have a bidirectional alternative hypothesis, our *rejection region* is seen from Table VI of Appendix A to be

$$t > 2.26 \quad \text{and} \quad t < -2.26$$

Step 6 /

From the data of Table 12.9 we have

$$t = \frac{0.95\sqrt{11-2}}{\sqrt{1-(0.95)^2}}$$
$$= 9.13$$

Step 7 /

Since our sample test statistic clearly lies in the *rejection region*, we

Reject our null hypothesis

$$H_0: \rho = 0$$

and

Accept the alternative hypothesis

$$H_1: \rho \neq 0$$

On the basis of our sample data we conclude that there is a significant degree of association between the social maturity and the self-control ratings.

SUMMARY

This chapter has presented a very brief introduction to four of the many so-called *rank-ordered statistics* available to the behavioral scientist. The large sample cases are considered for the *median test*, the *Mann-Whitney U test*, the *sign test*, and the *Wilcoxon test*. The median and percentile scores are particularly appropriate descriptive measures for rank-ordered data.

The association between two rank-ordered responses is measured by an index known as the *Spearman rank-order correlation coefficient*.

New terms and expressions introduced include:

Dichotomous classifications
Rank classifications
Matched versus independent samples of rank-ordered responses
Tied scores given the average rank value
Rank of d
r_s

REVIEW QUESTIONS

1 Analyze the following set of data by means of the median test and the Mann-Whitney U test. Set $\alpha = 0.01$.

	Experimental group		*Control group*
1.	31	21.	14
2.	26	22.	16
3.	17	23.	25
4.	31	24.	18
5.	19	25.	40
6.	20	26.	26
7.	28	27.	22
8.	14	28.	32
9.	31	29.	16
10.	17	30.	34
11.	18	31.	29
12.	19	32.	28
13.	27	33.	20
14.	21	34.	26
15.	23	35.	27
16.	9	36.	30
17.	8	37.	31
18.	4	38.	33
19.	2	39.	34
20.	1	40.	26
		41.	24

2 Analyze the following set of data by means of the sign test and the Wilcoxon test. Set $\alpha = 0.05$.

	Experimental group	Control group
1.	4	8
2.	9	11
3.	16	14
4.	17	11
5.	9	8
6.	8	10
7.	9	11
8.	14	11
9.	11	16
10.	17	9
11.	18	8
12.	15	10
13.	11	4
14.	11	12
15.	14	13
16.	16	13
17.	16	17
18.	19	14
19.	20	14
20.	14	6
21.	15	8
22.	16	14
23.	19	17
24.	16	17
25.	14	10

3 Evaluate the Spearman rank-order correlation coefficient r_s for the following set of data. Test for the significance of r_s with $\alpha = 0.05$.

Individual	Score on test 1	Score on test 2
1	4	22
2	3	19
3	6	28
4	9	29
5	11	30
6	15	26
7	14	31
8	7	17
9	2	16
10	1	18

CHAPTER 13

SUMMARY

The use of quantitative methods in the behavioral sciences is intended to encourage the transition from private intuitive thinking to systematic public inquiry. Rather than supplanting intuition, the various statistical techniques of the previous chapters simply provide specific skills for formulating inquiries in a more precise manner. By structuring our inquiries we attempt to uncover some degree of unity in the wide variety of behavior encountered in the behavioral sciences. Knowledge of the underlying unity among individuals with regard to a particular type of behavior is, in turn, invaluable in attempting to complete the linkage from intuition to inquiry and finally to the drawing of general inferences about such behavior.

Specifically we have considered basic statistical methods for: describing behavior graphically and numerically, testing hypotheses about individual types of behavior, and studying the relationships between various types of behavior to assess the strength of behavioral associations as well as to predict one behavioral response from another.

In order to conduct objective behavioral inquiries publicly, it is necessary to distinguish between operational and literary interpretations or definitions of behavior. Essentially an operational definition defines the meaning of a concept by denoting the measuring operations involved in it. For example, the definition of intelligence as the score obtained on an intelligence test is a commonly used operational definition. Operational definitions do not necessarily coincide with "popular" or literary interpretations, and failure to recognize this distinction can easily lead to a considerable amount of confusion concerning the role of measurement and statistics in the behavioral sciences.

One helpful way of classifying the kinds of operationally defined behavioral measures is in terms of the precision with which they can be measured (e.g., nominal, ordinal, interval, and ratio scales). Regardless of the precision of our measuring instruments, there are certain fundamental principles of experimentation that distinguish experimental research from so-called *ex post facto* studies, as illustrated in Chapter 2. These principles are

1. *Control.* Basing conclusions about differences among treatments on similar groups of individuals. Proper control distinguishes a comparative inquiry from an absolute one.

2. *Randomization.* Assuring that each individual in the population has an equal opportunity of being included under any given treatment. Randomization permits the central limit theorem to operate, improves the generalizability of the results, and helps counterbalance extraneous factors not specifically controlled in the design of the experiment.

3. *Replication.* Repeating the same treatment on more than one subject. Replication provides an estimate of the experimental error against which we pit the treatment effects. Furthermore, since the sampling error in estimating a population mean from the mean of a sample of size N is

$$\sigma_{\bar{x}} = \frac{\sigma}{\sqrt{N}}$$

replication improves the precision of such an estimate.

4. *Self-containment.* Basing the conclusions of the experiment on the data of the inquiry, rather than on extra-experimental "expert" opinion. That is, the data should "speak for themselves" as a result of the investigation.

Careful attention to these experimental principles can do much to avoid confounding the particular variables under study (e.g., tasks, environments, or subjects) with other variables.

The process of data sampling forms the next critical link in the structure of our inquiries. Our interest is generally in some population characteristic, known as a *parameter,* which we estimate by computing a sample statistic. By following a general seven-step procedure for analyzing sample statistics we are able to test a wide variety of hypotheses concerning the population parameters.

REFERENCE CHARTS

Table 13.1 summarizes the methods presented in this book for describing behavioral responses.

TABLE 13.1   SUMMARY OF GRAPHICAL AND
                                              NUMERICAL DESCRIPTIVE TECHNIQUES

Categorical Variables		Metric Variables	
Graphical	Numerical	Graphical	Numerical
(1) Pie charts (2) Bar charts	(1) Frequency recordings within each classification	(1) Listing (2) Array (3) Ungrouped frequency distribution (4) Grouped frequency distribution (5) Cumulative frequency distribution (6) Histogram (7) Frequency polygon	(1) Arithmetic mean (2) Median (3) Percentile rank (4) Mode (5) Range (6) Standard deviation (7) Standard scores

Figures 13.1, 13.2, and 13.3 summarize the hypothesis testing procedures and the methods for studying the relationships between variables that have been discussed in Chapters 1 through 12.

INTERRELATIONSHIPS AMONG Z, t, χ^2 AND F

The Z, t, χ^2, and F probability distributions constitute the essence of the hypothesis testing procedures presented in this book. Although a rigorous derivation of the common properties existing among these four probability distributions requires advanced mathematical sophistication, it seems worthwhile at least to indicate certain of these interrelationships.

If we assume an underlying normal population for our observations, it can be shown that the F distribution is the most general of the four, since the others may be derived from it. Figure 13.4, adopted from Li (1964), summarizes these interrelationships.

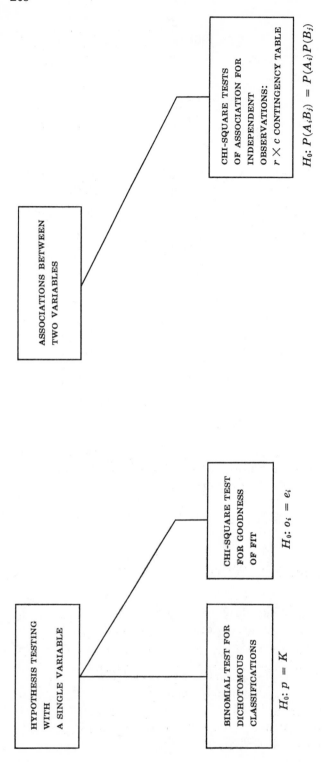

FIGURE 13.1
*Summary of procedures for testing hypotheses
and studying interrelationships of categorical variables*

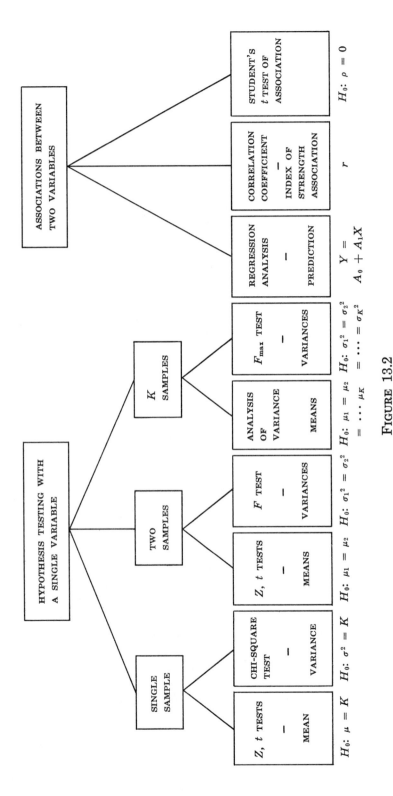

FIGURE 13.2

*Summary of procedures for testing hypotheses and studying
interrelationships of variables which may be described
by means and variances*

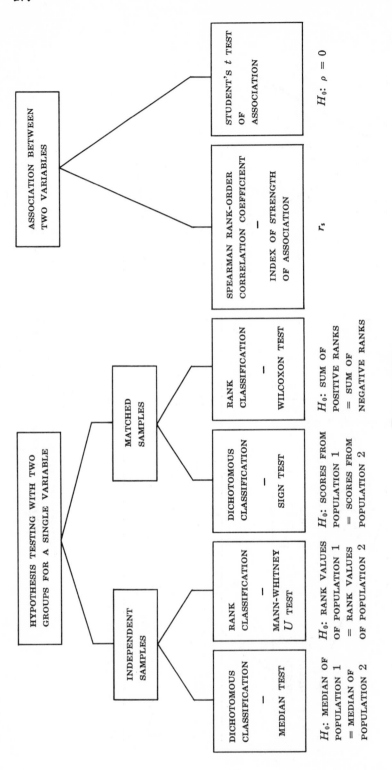

FIGURE 13.3

Summary of procedures for testing hypotheses and studying interrelationships of rank-order variables

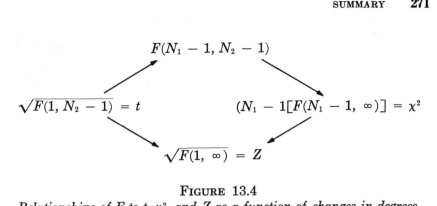

FIGURE 13.4

Relationships of F to t, x^2, and Z as a function of changes in degrees of freedom for F (the symbol ∞ denotes an infinitely large value)

---

* From C. C. Li, *Introduction to Experimental Statistics*. Copyright 1964 by McGraw-Hill Book Company. Used with permission of McGraw-Hill Book Company.

As an illustration of these relationships, consider first the following example of the relationship of F and Z.

$$P(|Z| > 1.96) = 0.05$$

Correspondingly,

$$\sqrt{F_{0.05}(1, \infty)} = \sqrt{3.84} = 1.96$$

Next consider the relation of F and t.

$$P(|t| > 2.23) = 0.05 \qquad \text{for 10 degrees of freedom}$$

Correspondingly,

$$\sqrt{F_{0.05}(1, 10)} = \sqrt{4.96} = 2.23$$

Finally, consider the relation of F and χ^2.

$$P(\chi^2 > 18.3) = 0.05 \qquad \text{for 10 degrees of freedom}$$

Correspondingly,

$$10[F_{0.05}(10, \infty)] = 10(1.83) = 18.3$$

CHAPTER 14

RELATED TOPICS

This chapter is meant to be only suggestive of topics related to and extensions of the previous categorical and metric tests rather than an exhaustive survey of the many techniques available to behavioral research workers.

CATEGORICAL VARIABLES

SAMPLE SIZE AND THE BINOMIAL DISTRIBUTION

The question of how large a sample to take is not altogether a simple one to answer. Issues of desired precision, practicality, and practical significance all come into focus on this question. The answer "No more than necessary" is of little help to us until we decide "Necessary for what purpose?"

Chart 14.1, prepared by Clopper and Pearson (1934), can be quite helpful in deciding on the sample size required to estimate the proportion of successes in a population with a specified degree of precision. It is assumed that the assumptions underlying the binomial distribution are met.

It is seen, for example, that if a sample of size 10 yields five successes (i.e., $p = 0.5$) a 95 percent confidence interval for the corresponding population parameter $\mathcal{P}$ is approximately

$$0.175 \leq \mathcal{P} \leq 0.825$$

Certainly this is not a very precise estimate. However, if we increase the sample size to 50, the 95 percent confidence interval for $\mathcal{P}$ corresponding to a sample value of $p = 0.5$ is seen to be

$$0.350 \leq \mathcal{P} \leq 0.650$$

This, of course, is a considerable improvement.

In terms of our hypothesis testing procedure with the binomial distribution it means that with a small sample size, a much more extreme result

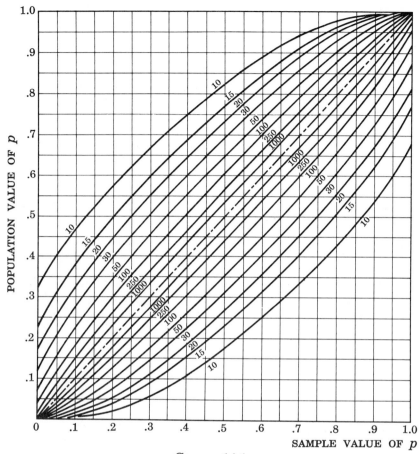

CHART 14.1

Interval estimate of population proportion P with confidence coefficient

.95 for N = 10, 15, 20, 30, 50, 100, 250, and 1000*

---

*From *Biometrika* by C. J. Clopper and E. S. Pearson, 1934. Reprinted by permission of the Biometrika Trustees.

(in terms of the sample value p) is required to reject the null hypothesis than with a larger sample. In other words, with less information, something much more dramatic or unusual must take place before we can declare any hypothesized value unreasonable.

Figure 14.1 contrasts the *acceptance regions* for sample sizes of 10 and 50 for testing the null hypothesis H_0: $p = \frac{1}{2}$ with a level of significance of five percent against the bidirectional hypothesis H_1: $p \neq \frac{1}{2}$.

Of course, at times one must utilize the subjects available, and therefore the ideal position of being able to specify the sample size is not always possible.

$n = 10$		$n = 50$	
1.00		1.00	
0.90		0.90	
0.80 ⎤	The sample estimate could	0.80	
0.70 ⎥	move in this range and we	0.70	
0.60 ⎥	would still accept	0.60 ⎤	Sample estimate could move
0.50 ⎥		0.50 ⎥	in this range and we would
0.40 ⎥	H_0: $p = \frac{1}{2}$	0.40 ⎦	still accept
0.30 ⎥		0.30	
0.20 ⎦		0.20	H_0: $p = \frac{1}{2}$
0.10		0.10	
0.00		0.00	

FIGURE 14.1

Acceptance regions for H_0: $p = \frac{1}{2}$ for $\alpha = 0.05$, $n = 10$, and $n = 50$.

THE NORMAL APPROXIMATION TO THE BINOMIAL DISTRIBUTION

In Chapter 5 it was pointed out that for large sample sizes, the direct calculation of probabilities from the binomial formula becomes quite tedious when computing facilities are not available. Fortunately, there is a method of approximating these binomial probabilities with the unit normal probability distribution.

The binomial formula

$$P(x) = \frac{n!}{x! \, (n - x)!} \, p^x q^{n-x}$$

for computing the probability of x successes out of n trials may be approximated by a standardized Z statistic defined as follows:

$$Z = \frac{x - np}{\sqrt{npq}}$$

if n is fairly large and p is fairly close to $\frac{1}{2}$.* This formula, which standardizes the number of successes, x, arises from the fact that the expected value and the standard error of x are np and $\sqrt{npq}$, respectively (see Wilks, 1961). The Z statistic follows the unit normal probability distribution of Table V in Appendix A.

Because the binomial distribution involves discrete values of x and the normal distribution is continuous, the value of x is assumed to occupy the interval $(x - 0.5)$ to $(x + 0.5)$ when the normal approximation is used. Thus our normal approximation of $p(x)$ is derived from Table V of Appendix A by finding the area between

$$Z_1 = \frac{(x - 0.5) - np}{\sqrt{npq}} \quad \text{and} \quad Z_2 = \frac{(x + 0.5) - np}{\sqrt{npq}}$$

---

*As n increases, the approximation becomes an excellent one and is quite good even for rather small values of n if p is not too far from $\frac{1}{2}$. A practical rule is for np to be at least 5 (Wilks, 1961).

To illustrate this approximation of $p(x)$, consider the data of page 77 concerning the guessing of the correct answers on five true/false questions. Here we have

$$n = 5$$

$$p = \tfrac{1}{2}$$

$$q = \tfrac{1}{2}$$

Thus, for example, the normal approximation of $p(2)$ is the area between Z_1 and Z_2, where

$$Z_1 = \frac{(x - 0.5) - np}{\sqrt{npq}} = \frac{(1.5) - 2.5}{1.12} = -0.89$$

and

$$Z_2 = \frac{(x + 0.5) - np}{\sqrt{npq}} = \frac{2.5 - 2.5}{1.12} = 0$$

The area between $Z_1 = -0.89$ and $Z_2 = 0$ is seen from Table V of Appendix A to be 0.3133, which agrees quite well with the value obtained from the direct application of the binomial formula of 0.312. That is,

$$p(2) = \frac{5!}{3!\,2!} \left(\frac{1}{2}\right)^2 \left(\frac{1}{2}\right)^3 = \frac{10}{32}$$

$$= 0.312$$

The probabilities for the other values of x may be found in a similar fashion. As a final example, suppose that we wish to evaluate the probability of one or two successes in this situation. The direct application of the binomial formula gives us

$$p(x = 1 \text{ or } 2) = p(1) + p(2)$$

$$= \frac{5!}{4!\,1!} \left(\frac{1}{2}\right)^1 \left(\frac{1}{2}\right)^4 + \frac{5!}{3!\,2!} \left(\frac{1}{2}\right)^2 \left(\frac{1}{2}\right)^3$$

$$= 0.156 + 0.312$$

$$= 0.468$$

The normal approximation is obtained by treating the two values of x as though they occupied the interval from $(1 - 0.5)$ to $(2 + 0.5)$. Thus the desired probability is approximated by finding the area of the unit normal distribution between Z_1 and Z_2, where

$$Z_1 = \frac{(1 - 0.5) - 2.5}{1.12} = -1.79$$

and

$$Z_2 = \frac{(2.5) - 2.5}{1.12} = 0$$

The probability is seen, from Table V of Appendix A, to be 0.4633, which again is in fairly close agreement with the value obtained by direct application of the binomial formula. The probability of any other set of x values may be handled in a similar fashion. Thus even for rather small values of n, the normal approximation to the binomial can be quite close.

TESTING THE SIGNIFICANCE OF THE DIFFERENCE BETWEEN TWO PROPORTIONS

The binomial formula was used to make probability statements about the number of successes in a given sample. Suppose, however, that we wish to test the significance of the difference between the proportion of successes in two separate groups. There are two cases to consider: that in which the observations in the two groups are assumed to be independent, and that in which the observations are correlated. The latter case arises when the subjects in the two groups are matched in some manner (by virtue of ability, being twins, etc.) or where the same subjects appear in both groups, as in the common *before* and *after* studies.

Independent Proportions

For purposes of illustration consider the following sample data for two independent groups:

Group 1	*Group 2*
$n_1 = 25$	$n_2 = 30$
X_1, the number of observed successes, $= 5$	X_2, the number of observed successes, $= 5$

The seven-step procedure for this situation is as follows:

Step 1 /

> We conjecture that the proportion of successes in the two groups is equivalent for the population of all potential observations. The null hypothesis is thus
>
> H_0: proportion of successes in population 1
>
> $=$ proportion of successes in population 2
>
> The alternative hypothesis may be either unidirectional or bidirectional. Let us consider the bidirectional alternative hypothesis
>
> H_1: the two population proportions are not equal

Step 2 /

> Let us select a level of significance $\alpha = 0.05$

Step 3 /

An appropriate test statistic, when the products $n_1 p_1$ and $n_2 p_2$ exceed 5, is

$$Z = \frac{p_1 - p_2}{\sigma_{p_1 - p_2}}$$

where

$$p_1 = \frac{x_1}{n_1}, \qquad p_2 = \frac{x_2}{n_2}$$

and

$$\sigma_{p_1 - p_2} = \sqrt{pq\left(\frac{1}{n_1} + \frac{1}{n_2}\right)}$$

where

$$p = \frac{n_1 p_1 + n_2 p_2}{n_1 + n_2} \quad \text{and} \quad q = 1 - p$$

Step 4 /

Z follows the unit normal probability distribution.

Step 5 /

The *rejection region* corresponding to H_1 and $\alpha = 0.05$ is

$$Z > 1.96 \quad \text{and} \quad Z < -1.96$$

Step 6 /

For our sample data we have

$$p_1 = \frac{x_1}{n_1} = \frac{5}{25} = \frac{1}{5} = 0.200$$

$$p_2 = \frac{x_2}{n_2} = \frac{5}{30} = \frac{1}{6} = 0.167$$

$$p = \frac{n_1 p_1 + n_2 p_2}{n_1 + n_2} = \frac{(25)\left(\frac{1}{5}\right) + (30)\left(\frac{1}{6}\right)}{25 + 30}$$

$$= 0.18$$

and

$$q = 1 - p = 1 - 0.18 = 0.82$$

from which

$$\sigma_{p_1 - p_2} = \sqrt{pq\left(\frac{1}{n_1} + \frac{1}{n_2}\right)} = \sqrt{(0.148)(0.073)}$$

$$= 0.105$$

Therefore,

$$Z = \frac{p_1 - p_2}{\sigma_{p_1-p_2}} = \frac{0.200 - 0.167}{0.105} = \frac{0.033}{0.105}$$

$$= 0.314$$

Step 7 /

Since our test statistic is not in the *rejection region,* we accept the null hypothesis that the proportion of successes in the two populations are equivalent.

Correlated Proportions

McNemar (1962) has developed a test statistic appropriate for testing the significance of the difference between two correlated proportions.* Such a case often arises when a program is undertaken to change the attitude of a particular group of individuals toward a particular statement or issue. As an illustration of this technique, consider the artificial data of Table 14.1 involving the responses of the same individuals both before and after exposure to an experimental treatment.

TABLE 14.1   **FORMAT OF DATA FOR THE McNEMAR TEST FOR CORRELATED PROPORTIONS**

		After Experimental Treatment		
		Disagree	Agree	
Before	Agree	$A = 16$	$B = 30$	46
Experimental				
Treatment	Disagree	$C = 34$	$D = 20$	54
		50	50	100

From Table 14.1 we see that before the experimental treatment $\frac{46}{100}$ or 0.46 of the individuals agreed with the statement. Following the experimental treatment $\frac{50}{100}$ or 0.50 of these same individuals agreed with the statement. The problem is to test the significance of the difference between the two correlated proportions 0.46 and 0.50.

The seven-step procedure for this situation is as follows:

---

*The McNemar technique is also useful in studying the agreement of two judges following the two judges' evaluation of the same subjects. See Hays (1963).

Step 1 /

> We conjecture that the proportion of individuals "agreeing"
> before and after the experimental treatment remains the
> same for the population of all potential subjects. Thus the
> null hypothesis

> H_0: proportion of "agrees" before the treatment

> = proportion of "agrees" after the treatment

> The alternative hypothesis may again be either unidirec-
> tional or bidirectional. Let us consider the bidirectional
> alternative hypothesis.

> H_1: the two proportions are not equal

Step 2 /

> Let us select a level of significance $\alpha = 0.05$.

Step 3 /

> When the frequencies of Table 14.1 are such that $A + D > 20$, an appropriate test statistic, as developed by McNemar,[*]
> is

$$Z = \frac{|D - A| - 1}{\sqrt{A + D}}$$

Step 4 /

> Z follows the unit normal probability distribution.

Step 5 /

> The *rejection region* corresponding to H_1 and $\alpha = 0.05$ is

$$Z > 1.96 \quad \text{and} \quad Z < -1.96$$

Step 6 /

> The value of the test statistic for our sample data is

$$Z = \frac{|20 - 16| - 1}{\sqrt{16 + 20}} = 0.50$$

Step 7 /

> We accept the null hypothesis that the proportion of indi-
> viduals "agreeing" with the statement has not been signif-
> icantly altered following the experimental treatment.

---

[*]A good discussion of the rationale of this statistic may be found in Edwards
(1960).

ELEMENTARY DECISION THEORY

The concepts of probability of Chapter 3 may be extended to illustrate some of the basic elements in a powerful approach to decision-making in the face of uncertainty, known as decision theory. As outlined by Chernoff and Moses (1959), the initial step in this technique is the establishment of a loss table. A loss table reflects the cost or loss incurred by taking particular available actions under various conditions. For example, our available actions might be

$$a_1 = \text{hire a potential employee}$$

or

$$a_2 = \text{reject the potential employee}$$

Correspondingly, the actual existing conditions could be considered as

$$c_1 = \text{the potential employee would be an adequate worker}$$

or

$$c_2 = \text{the potential employee would not be an adequate worker}$$

From the standpoint of the employees the best situation would be to combine a_1 with c_1. The most undesirable situation would probably be to take action a_1 when c_2 is the existing condition. For purposes of illustration, consider the loss table of Table 14.2 for this example. Thus from Table 14.2

TABLE   14.2   **LOSS TABLE**

	a_1	a_2
c_1	1	3
c_2	4	2

we see that the minimum loss involves hiring an adequate worker; the next best situation is to reject an inadequate worker. It is still more costly (i.e., a greater loss) to reject an adequate worker. However, the worst situation is the hiring of an inadequate worker.*

Once a loss table has been agreed upon, it is clear that the selection of an action would be a simple matter if only the actual condition were known. To gain some insight as to the existing condition we attempt to use our past experience by performing an experiment to see if there is some device by

---

*The units of loss are quite arbitrary and are merely used here to illustrate the relative consequences of taking a particular action in the presence of a particular condition.

which we can distinguish one condition from the other. For example, it might be our experience that three-fourths of the workers who have proved themselves adequate on the job have also passed an initial selection test. Furthermore, it might be our experience that only one-third of the workers classified as inadequate have passed this test. These past results are recorded in an experimental outcomes table such as Table 14.3. The ques-

TABLE 14.3   EXPERIMENTAL OUTCOMES

	Condition	Experimental Outcomes	
		Pass	Fail
c_1	Adequate workers	$\frac{3}{4}$	$\frac{1}{4}$
c_2	Inadequate workers	$\frac{1}{3}$	$\frac{2}{3}$

tion becomes: How can we improve the situation (i.e., minimize our losses) by administering the selection test to potential employees in attempting to detect whether they will be adequate, c_1, or inadequate, c_2, workers? In other words, what should our selection strategy be, based on our available actions and the experimental outcomes? Table 14.4 summarizes all of the possible strategies for this situation involving *actions* hire (a_1), reject (a_2)

TABLE 14.4   STRATEGIES

Strategies	Experimental Outcomes	
	Pass	Fail
S_1	a_1	a_1
S_2	a_1	a_2
S_3	a_2	a_1
S_4	a_2	a_2

and *outcomes* pass, and fail. Of the four strategies of Table 14.4 we select the one that results in the minimum expected loss. To make this selection, an average loss table is constructed, as in Table 14.5. To illustrate the calculation of the average loss figures of Table 14.5 consider strategy S_2.

TABLE 14.5   **AVERAGE LOSS TABLE**

Condition	Strategy			
	S_1	S_2	S_3	S_4
c_1	1	1.50	2.75	3
c_2	4	2.66	3.34	2

Following strategy S_2, we will take a_1 if the selection test is passed and a_2 if it is failed. Furthermore, under condition c_1 we see from Table 14.3 that we can expect to take a_1 three-fourths of the time and a_2 one-fourth of the time. Relating this relative frequency to the losses in Table 14.2, we find that we can expect to lose one unit three-fourths of the time and three units one-fourth of the time. The average expected loss is thus

$$(1)(\tfrac{3}{4}) + (3)(\tfrac{1}{4}) = 1.50$$

Under condition c_2 we can expect to take a_1 one-third of the time and a_2 two-thirds of the time. That is, we expect to lose (referring to Table 14.2) four units one-third of the time and two units two-thirds of the time. The average expected loss is thus

$$(4)(\tfrac{1}{3}) + (2)(\tfrac{2}{3}) = 2.66$$

The average losses for the other strategies are obtained in a similar fashion.

There are various criteria by which a strategy might be selected from the information of Table 14.5. A common criterion is the so-called *mini-max principle*, which results in selecting that strategy for which the maximum average loss is a minimum. From Table 14.5 we see that the maximum average loss for strategy S_2 is 2.66, which is less than the maximum average loss of any other strategy. Hence from the mini-max principle, we would follow strategy S_2. Our procedure for decision-making in the face of uncertainty will, therefore, involve administering the selection test to a potential employee. If the potential employee passes the test, he is hired; otherwise, he is rejected.

A formal structure is essential, in general, for reaching such a decision. As the number of available conditions and number of experimental outcomes increase in size, it becomes impossible intuitively to anticipate the final decision, as is the case in this simple example.

METRIC VARIABLES

STATISTICAL VERSUS PRACTICAL SIGNIFICANCE

Since there are several statistical techniques available for testing the significance of a variety of sample results, it is helpful to distinguish between statistical and practical significance. Statistical significance may be achieved in various ways in comparing two sample means, for example:

There might exist a large actual difference between the population means μ_1 and μ_2.

We might have observed a large sample difference by chance when, in fact, $\mu_1 = \mu_2$.

The sample sizes might be excessively large.

The sample variances might be artificially reduced by applying extremely rigid experimental control.

The first two conditions have been considered earlier in the general discussion of hypothesis testing. To illustrate the effect of the last two conditions, let us examine the t statistic for testing the significance of the difference between two means:

$$t = \frac{\bar{X}_1 - \bar{X}_2}{S_p \sqrt{\dfrac{1}{N_1} + \dfrac{1}{N_2}}}$$

where

$$S_p = \sqrt{\frac{N_1 S_1^2 + N_2 S_2^2}{N_1 + N_2 - 2}}$$

For fixed sample sizes it is clear that as S_1^2 and S_2^2, the sample variances, become small, t becomes large. Likewise, as N_1 and N_2 increase (for given values of S_1^2 and S_2^2), t becomes large. Thus in a sense, we may force significance through tight control or large samples. The question is: How practical is the difference between the two treatments from the standpoint of applying the statistically significant findings outside a tightly controlled laboratory setting? Hays (1963) gives a good discussion of this problem, and the procedure discussed there is helpful to follow routinely when one is analyzing data for which the above t test statistic yields a statistically significant result. The proposed formula and its interpretation are as follows:

$$\omega^2 = \frac{t^2 - 1}{t^2 + N_1 + N_2 - 1}$$

The coefficient ω^2 (omega squared) provides an estimate of the percentage of the total variability in the experiment that is accounted for by the administration of the different treatments. For example, suppose that we obtained a value of the t test statistic of 2.5 based on sample sizes of 10 and 15. From Table VI of Appendix A we see that this would clearly be statistically significant if $\alpha = 0.05$. Correspondingly, the value of ω^2 is

$$\omega^2 = \frac{t^2 - 1}{t^2 + N_1 + N_2 - 1}$$

$$= \frac{(2.5)^2 - 1}{(2.5)^2 + 10 + 15 - 1}$$

$$= 0.173$$

Thus the administration of the two treatments in this case accounts for 17.3 percent of the variance observed in the criterion measure.

Values of t that are less than one will, of course, result in a negative value of ω^2. In such a case, Hays recommends that ω^2 simply be set equal to zero.

In general, if t is statistically significant and ω^2 is moderately high, it is probably more profitable, from a practical point of view, to follow up an analysis than if only t is significant. At any rate, the notion "Make the sample sizes large enough and any difference may be considered significant" may well lead to experimental blind alleys. Again, as there are no firm rules to follow, we must turn to subject matter expertise and intuition for a balanced interpretation of the results obtained from t and ω^2.

Hays also gives an estimate of ω^2 for the one-way analysis of variance discussed in Chapter 10 as follows:

$$\text{est. } \omega^2 = \frac{SS_{\text{treatments}} - (k - 1)MS_{\text{within}}}{SS_{\text{total}} + MS_{\text{within}}}$$

Consider, for example, the artificial analysis of variance data of Table 10.2. We have, in this case,

$$\text{est. } \omega^2 = \frac{(143.33) - (2)(2.50)}{173.33 + 2.50} = 0.79$$

which is interpreted to mean that the independent variable (treatments) is estimated to account for 79 percent of the variance in the dependent variable (achievement scores). In other words, there is a strong relationship indicated between the three classroom approaches and student achievement.

SAMPLE SIZE AND TESTING HYPOTHESES ABOUT A SINGLE POPULATION MEAN

The question of how large a sample to take in testing hypotheses with a single large sample mean may be handled in the following manner.

Step 1 /

Some value, say k, is selected in such a way that we can be reasonably confident that the absolute difference between $\bar{X}$ and μ (denoted $|\bar{X} - \mu|$) does not exceed this value.

Step 2 /

Set the test statistic

$$Z = \frac{\bar{X} - \mu}{\dfrac{\sigma}{\sqrt{N}}}$$

equal to the upper limit of the corresponding confidence limit for Z. Thus if we wanted to be 95 percent confident that the difference between $\bar{X}$ and μ does not exceed k, we would have from

$$-1.96 \leq Z \leq 1.96$$

the expression

$$\frac{\bar{X} - \mu}{\dfrac{\sigma}{\sqrt{N}}} = 1.96$$

Step 3 /

Solve for N in the expression of Step 2, considering the absolute difference of $\bar{X} - \mu$. That is,

$$\sqrt{N} = \frac{1.96\sigma}{|\bar{X} - \mu|}$$

or

$$N = \left(\frac{1.96\sigma}{|\bar{X} - \mu|} \right)^2$$

where either σ is assumed known or a large sample standard deviation S is used in its place.

For example, in our computer-based mathematics class example of Chapter 7, suppose that we would like to be 95 percent confident that the absolute difference between our sample mean $\bar{X}$ and our population mean μ does not exceed two achievement score points, i.e., $k = 2$. How large a sample is required?

From our preliminary study we had the sample results

Class mean $\bar{X} = 52$
Class standard deviation $S = 10$

Therefore,

$$N = \left[\frac{1.96\,(\sigma)}{|\,\bar{X} - \mu\,|} \right]^2$$

$$= \left[\frac{1.96\,(10)}{2} \right]^2$$

$$= 96.04$$

Therefore, to be 95 percent confident that our sample mean is not more than two score points away from the population mean, we should have a sample size of at least 96.

POWER VERSUS THE LEVEL OF SIGNIFICANCE

In hypothesis testing situations a selection is made between two hypotheses: the null hypothesis H_0 and the alternative hypothesis H_1. For example, in testing a hypothesis about a population mean our two associated hypotheses, H_0 and H_1, might be

$$H_0: \mu = K$$
$$H_1: \mu > K$$

Now, in fact, H_0 might be true or it might be false. We may also, on the basis of sample data, accept H_0 or reject H_0. Table 14.6 summarizes the various conditions that can exist in this hypothesis testing situation.

TABLE 14.6 ERRORS IN HYPOTHESIS TESTING

		H_0	
		True	*False*
Decision about H_0	Accept	$1 - \alpha$	β
	Reject	α	$1 - \beta$

In Table 14.6 α denotes the probability of rejecting a true hypothesis, which, of course, is an erroneous decision. This error probability α is called the *level of significance* or *type I error*.

The symbol β (beta) denotes the probability of accepting a false hypothesis, which is also an erroneous decision. This error probability β is called a *type II error*.

The terms $(1 - \alpha)$ and $(1 - \beta)$ correspondingly denote the probability of accepting the true hypothesis and of rejecting the false hypothesis, respectively. Either of these is, of course, a correct decision. The term $(1 - \beta)$ is referred to as the *power* of the hypothesis testing procedure.

To illustrate the relationships among the error probabilities of Table 14.6, consider the following example:*

$$H_0: \mu = 200$$

$$H_1: \mu > 200$$

with a resulting decision rule based on a sample size of 100 with $\bar{X} = 210$ and $S = 25$, for $\alpha = 0.10$, as follows: If $Z > 1.28$, reject H_0 and accept H_1; otherwise, accept H_0. This decision rule is shown graphically in Figure 14.2.

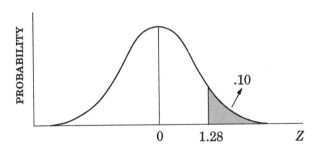

FIGURE 14.2
Rejection region in terms of Z scores for $\alpha = 0.10$

In terms of the original scores the critical value, 1.28, may be expressed

$$1.28 = \frac{\bar{X} - 200}{\frac{25}{\sqrt{100}}}$$

from which

$$\bar{X} = 203.2$$

The decision rule in terms of the original scores is shown in Figure 14.3.

---

*The discussion here applies equally well to two-sample problems.

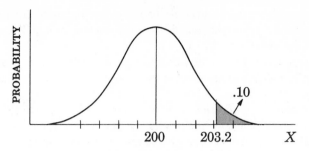

FIGURE 14.3
Rejection region in terms of original scores for α = .10

On the other hand, if we had selected an $\alpha = 0.05$ instead of 0.10, our critical Z value would have been 1.65 rather than 1.28. Correspondingly, the critical value in terms of the original scores would have been

$$1.65 = \frac{\bar{X} - 200}{\frac{25}{\sqrt{100}}}$$

from which
$$\bar{X} = 204.1$$

This decision rule for $\alpha = 0.05$, in terms of the original scores, is shown in Figure 14.4.

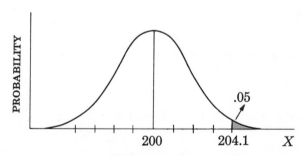

FIGURE 14.4
Rejection region in terms of original scores for α = .05

If we follow the above decision rule for $\alpha = 0.10$, any sample (coming from this population with a mean of 200) that has a mean greater than 203.2 will incorrectly result in a rejection of the null hypothesis

$$H_0: \mu = 200$$

This incorrect decision can be expected to occur 10 percent of the time in repeated experiments of this type, when in fact H_0 is true. That is, our type I error is 0.10.

Likewise, if we follow the decision rule for $\alpha = 0.05$, any sample with a mean greater than 204.1 would incorrectly reject H_0. That is, our type I error is 0.05.

A reasonable question arises at this point: Why "build in" this kind of error by specifying $\alpha = 0.01$, 0.05, or 0.10 before the analysis is undertaken? The answer becomes apparent when we consider the consequences of attempting to eliminate α. We have seen, in our example, that this type of error can easily be reduced from 0.10 to 0.05 by simply selecting a decision rule such that the critical value of Z for rejecting H_0 is 1.65 rather than 1.28.

While the reduction of a type I error might seem, at first, to be the only desirable goal, the shortcomings of this approach become apparent when we consider what would happen with these two decision rules if, in fact, H_1 were true, that is,

$$H_1: \mu > 200$$

Consider, for example, the consequences of our two decision rules based on $\alpha = 0.10$ and $\alpha = 0.05$ if the population mean were actually 202 rather than 200. In this case we would certainly like to reject

$$H_0: \mu = 200$$

First, consider the decision rule based on $\alpha = 0.10$ whereby we accept $H_0: \mu = 200$ if $\bar{X} \leq 203.2$. Of interest here is the probability of accepting $H_0: \mu = 200$ when in fact $\mu = 202$. That is, what is the type II error corresponding to the particular alternative value of $\mu = 202$? This situation is illustrated in Figure 14.5. From Table V of Appendix A it is easily seen that

$$\beta = P(X \leq 203.2) = P\left(Z \leq \frac{203.2 - 202}{\dfrac{25}{\sqrt{100}}} \right) = P(Z \leq 0.48) = 0.6844$$

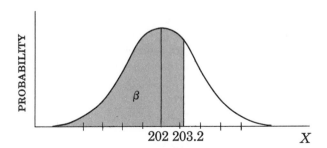

FIGURE 14.5
Acceptance region in terms of original scores for $\alpha = .10$

That is, approximately 68 percent of the time in repeated experimentation of this sort we could expect to accept H_0: $\mu = 200$ when in fact H_0 is false (i.e., $\mu = 202$). For $\alpha = 0.10$, $\beta = 0.68$, the power to reject the particular alternative H_1: $\mu = 202$ is $1 - \beta = 0.32$.

Finally, consider the decision rule based on $\alpha = 0.05$, whereby we accept H_0: $\mu = 200$ if $\bar{X} \leq 204.1$. The type II error corresponding to the particular alternative value of $\mu = 202$ is illustrated in Figure 14.6. For Figure 14.6 we have

$$\beta = P(X \leq 204.1) = P\left(Z \leq \frac{204.1 - 202}{\frac{25}{\sqrt{100}}}\right) = P(Z \leq 0.84) = 0.7996$$

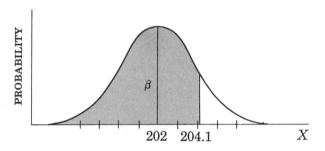

FIGURE 14.6
Acceptance region in terms of original scores for $\alpha = .05$

Thus for $\alpha = 0.05$, β is approximately 0.80, and the power to reject the particular alternative H_1: $\mu = 202$ is $1 - \beta = 0.20$.

We have seen that type I and type II errors work directly against each other. As we decrease α, β increases for a particular alternative value of μ. Correspondingly, as we decrease α, we decrease $(1 - \beta)$, the power to reject H_0, when, in fact, a particular alternative value of μ is true.

In order to achieve a reasonable balance between α, the level of significance, and $(1 - \beta)$, the power to reject alternative values of μ, it has been generally accepted that α be set at a moderate value. The values 0.01, 0.05, and 0.10 are the most widely used levels of α.

For a fixed α the power to detect alternative values of μ increases with the distance that the alternative value of μ is from the hypothesized value of μ. If we consider in the above example an alternative value for μ of 204 rather than 202, we see that the power of our test corresponding to $\alpha = 0.10$ is

$$1 - \beta = 1 - P\left(Z \leq \frac{203.2 - 204}{\frac{25}{\sqrt{100}}}\right) = 1 - P(Z \leq -0.32) = 0.6255$$

That is, the power of our test increases from about 0.32 for the alternative value of $\mu = 202$ to about 0.63 for an alternative value of $\mu = 204$. This makes intuitive sense, since the further the actual population mean is from the hypothesized value, the more likely it is that we will detect the difference.

Finally, for a fixed value of α the power may be increased by increasing the sample size, since this has the effect of reducing the standard error of the sampling distribution.* For example, had our decision rule with $\alpha = 0.10$ been based on a sample of 144 rather than 100, the critical value in terms of the original scores would have been

$$1.28 = \frac{\bar{X} - 200}{\dfrac{25}{\sqrt{144}}}$$

or

$$\bar{X} = 202.66$$

rather than 203.2. Correspondingly, the power to reject the particular alternative $H_1: \mu = 202$ would have been increased from 0.32 to approximately 0.37. That is,

$$1 - \beta = 1 - P(X \leq 202.66) = 1 - P\left(Z \leq \frac{202.66 - 202}{\dfrac{25}{\sqrt{144}}}\right)$$

$$= 1 - P(Z \leq 0.32) = 1 - 0.6255 = 0.3745$$

See Guenther (1965) for a discussion of the power of the statistical tests discussed in this book.

TWO-WAY ANALYSIS OF VARIANCE

The analysis of variance technique has been extended to cover a much wider range of situations than the single-variable case considered in Chapter 10. A complete discussion of these extensions is beyond the scope of this book. A good introduction is given by Hays (1963), and Winer (1962) presents an extremely thorough discussion of analysis of variance techniques.

The most frequently encountered extension of the analysis of variance is the analysis of two variables simultaneously. A widely used analysis of variance table for the two-variable case has the format indicated in Table 14.7.**

---

*Since the standard error of the sampling distribution for the two-sample case is smaller for correlated samples than for independent samples, it follows that tests based on correlated samples will, in general, be more powerful than tests based on independent samples for given sample sizes.

**The F ratios of Table 14.7 are formed in various ways, depending on the assumptions underlying the data collection. The case here is for the common, fixed effects design wherein no attempt is made to generalize beyond the dimensions of variables A and B included in the experiment. See Hays (1963) for a good discussion of the distinction between random and fixed effects.

TABLE 14.7   FORMAT FOR TWO-WAY ANALYSIS OF VARIANCE (FIXED EFFECTS) FOR (a) LEVELS OF VARIABLE A, (b) LEVELS OF VARIABLE B, AND (c) REPLICATIONS WITHIN EACH COMBINATION OF LEVEL A AND LEVEL B.

Source of variation	Degrees of freedom	Sum of squares	Mean square	F	Decision
Variable A	$(a-1)$	SS_A	$MS_A = \dfrac{SS_A}{a-1}$	$\dfrac{MS_A}{MS_w}$	
Variable B	$(b-1)$	SS_B	$MS_B = \dfrac{SS_B}{b-1}$	$\dfrac{MS_B}{MS_w}$	
Interaction between A and B	$(a-1)(b-1)$	SS_I	$MS_I = \dfrac{SS_I}{(a-1)(b-1)}$	$\dfrac{MS_I}{MS_w}$	
Within-groups variation	$ab(c-1)$	SS_w	$MS_w = \dfrac{SS_w}{ab(c-1)}$		

The interpretation of variables A and B is similar to that for the one-way analysis of variance. That is, if the F ratio

$$F = \frac{MS_A}{MS_W} \qquad [\text{with } (a-1) \text{ and } ab(c-1) \text{ degrees of freedom}]$$

is not significant, we conclude that there is no significant difference between the categories of variable A so far as the mean criterion scores are concerned. The same interpretation is true of variable B.

A major advantage of combining the analysis of variables A and B as shown in Table 14.7 is that a measure of the interaction between A and B is obtained. This, of course, would not be possible if variables A and B were analyzed separately. To illustrate the concept of interaction, suppose that there are two levels of variable A (A_1 and A_2) and two levels of variable B (B_1 and B_2). If there is no interaction between variables A and B, the same relative position of the two variables will be maintained on the criterion measure, regardless of the level being considered. Figure 14.7 illustrates a lack of interaction for this situation. Figure 14.8, on the other hand, illustrates the presence of interaction between variables A and B.

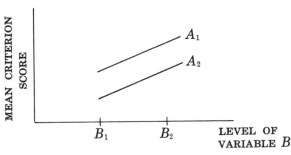

FIGURE 14.7
Illustration of a lack of interaction

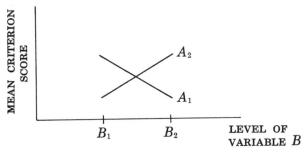

FIGURE 14.8
Illustration of a presence of interaction

From Figure 14.7, a significant result for either variable A or variable B is seen to hold true for any level of the other variable. The situation in Figure 14.8 is more complicated, however, in its interpretation, since the superiority of one level of a variable (say, A_1) over the other (A_2) depends on which level of the other variable (B) is being considered. That is, A_1 exceeds A_2 at the level B_1, but A_2 exceeds A_1 at the level B_2. Variables A and B are said to interact. The F ratio

$$F = \frac{MS_I}{MS_W} \quad \text{[with } (a-1)(b-1) \text{ and } ab(c-1) \text{ degrees of freedom]}$$

is designed to test the significance of this interaction.

The computational details of the terms in Table 14.7 will be illustrated with the following example problem: Let variable A be the presence or absence of a drug (A_1 = no drug, A_2 = drug). Let variable B be the classification of patients as anxious or not anxious (B_1 = anxious, B_2 = not anxious). Let the criterion measure be a motor-skill test score. Finally, assume that five patients are randomly assigned to the four possible combinations of variables A and B and that the data are as indicated in Table 14.8. The degrees of freedom in Table 14.7 involve the terms a, b, and c, where

a = number of levels of variable A (2 in our example)
b = number of levels of variable B (2 in our example)
c = number of individuals in each cell (5 in our example)

TABLE   14.8   **DATA ORGANIZATION FOR TWO-WAY ANALYSIS OF VARIANCE (ARTIFICIAL DATA)**

		Variable A	
		A_1	A_2
Variable B	B_1	3 7 6 4 2	1 2 2 1 0
	B_2	8 4 9 10 11	2 1 3 4 1

The sums of squares in Table 14.7 involve the term X_{ijk}, where

X_{ijk} = the motor-skill test score (criterion score) of the kth individual in the jth row and the ith column, where $i = 1, 2$ and $j = 1, 2$

The sums of squares are defined in terms of the following five expressions:

$$I = \sum_{i=1}^{a} \sum_{j=1}^{b} \sum_{k=1}^{c} X^2_{ijk}$$

$$II = \frac{\left(\sum_{i=1}^{a} \sum_{j=1}^{b} \sum_{k=1}^{c} X_{ijk} \right)^2}{abc}$$

$$III = \sum_{i=1}^{a} \left[\frac{\left(\sum_{j=1}^{b} \sum_{k=1}^{c} X_{ijk} \right)^2}{bc} \right]$$

$$IV = \sum_{j=1}^{b} \left[\frac{\left(\sum_{i=1}^{a} \sum_{k=1}^{c} X_{ijk} \right)^2}{ac} \right]$$

$$V = \sum_{i=1}^{a} \sum_{j=1}^{b} \left[\frac{\left(\sum_{k=1}^{c} X_{ijk} \right)^2}{c} \right]$$

In terms of these expressions

$$SS_A = III - II$$

$$SS_B = IV - II$$

$$SS_I = V + II - IV - III$$

$$SS_W = I - V$$

For the data of Table 14.8 we have

$$I = \sum_{i=1}^{2} \sum_{j=1}^{2} \sum_{k=1}^{5} X^2_{ijk} = 3^2 + 7^2 + \cdots + 4^2 + 1^2 = 537$$

$$II = \frac{\left(\sum_{i=1}^{2} \sum_{j=1}^{2} \sum_{k=1}^{5} X_{ijk} \right)^2}{2 \cdot 2 \cdot 5} = \frac{(3 + 7 + \cdots + 4 + 1)^2}{2 \cdot 2 \cdot 5} = \frac{81^2}{20} = 328.05$$

$$\text{III} = \sum_{i=1}^{2} \left[\frac{\left(\sum_{j=1}^{2} \sum_{k=1}^{5} X_{ijk} \right)^2}{2 \cdot 5} \right]$$

$$= \frac{(3 + 7 + \cdots + 10 + 11)^2}{2 \cdot 5} + \frac{(1 + 2 + \cdots + 4 + 1)^2}{2 \cdot 5}$$

$$= \frac{64^2}{10} + \frac{17^2}{10} = 438.50$$

$$\text{IV} = \sum_{j=1}^{2} \left[\frac{\left(\sum_{i=1}^{2} \sum_{k=1}^{5} X_{ijk} \right)^2}{2 \cdot 5} \right]$$

$$= \frac{(3 + 7 + \cdots + 1 + 0)^2}{2 \cdot 5} + \frac{(8 + 4 + \cdots + 4 + 1)^2}{2 \cdot 5}$$

$$= \frac{28^2}{10} + \frac{53^2}{10} = 359.30$$

$$\text{V} = \sum_{i=1}^{2} \sum_{j=1}^{2} \left[\frac{\left(\sum_{k=1}^{5} X_{ijk} \right)^2}{5} \right]$$

$$= \frac{(3 + 7 + 6 + 4 + 2)^2}{5} + \frac{(8 + 4 + 9 + 10 + 11)^2}{5}$$

$$+ \frac{(1 + 2 + 2 + 1 + 0)^2}{5} + \frac{(2 + 1 + 3 + 4 + 1)^2}{5} = 481.00$$

from which we have

$$SS_A = \text{III} - \text{II} = 438.50 - 328.05 = 110.45$$

$$SS_B = \text{IV} - \text{II} = 359.30 - 328.05 = 31.25$$

$$SS_I = \text{V} + \text{II} - \text{IV} - \text{III}$$

$$= 481.00 + 328.05 - 359.30 - 438.50 = 11.25$$

$$SS_W = \text{I} - \text{V} = 537 - 481.00 = 56.00$$

Therefore, our two-way analysis of variance results may be summarized as in Table 14.9, following the format of Table 14.7.

From the results of Table 14.9 we reject the hypothesis that there is no difference between the average motor-skill test scores for groups A_1 (no drug) and A_2 (drug).

TABLE 14.9 — ANALYSIS OF VARIANCE TABLE FOR THE DATA OF TABLE 14.8

Source of variation	Degrees of freedom	Sum of squares	Mean square	F	Decision
Variable A	1	110.45	110.45	31.56	*
Variable B	1	31.25	31.25	8.93	*
Interaction between A and B	1	11.25	11.25	3.21	
Within-groups variation	16	56.00	3.50		

* Results significant at the .01 level of significance (i.e., $F > 8.53$).

These averages are (from Table 14.8)

$$\bar{X}_{A_1} = \frac{3 + 7 + \cdots + 10 + 11}{10} = 6.4$$

$$\bar{X}_{A_2} = \frac{1 + 2 + \cdots + 4 + 1}{10} = 1.7$$

Simultaneously, Table 14.9 leads us to reject the hypothesis that there is no difference between the average motor-skill test scores for groups B_1 (anxious) and B_2 (not anxious). These averages are (from Table 14.8)

$$\bar{X}_{B_1} = \frac{3 + 7 + \cdots + 1 + 0}{10} = 2.8$$

$$\bar{X}_{B_2} = \frac{8 + 4 + \cdots + 4 + 1}{10} = 5.3$$

Finally, Table 14.9 leads to acceptance of the hypothesis that there is no significant interaction between the administration of the drug (or lack of it) and the characteristic of anxiety so far as the scores on the motor-skill test are concerned. This lack of significant interaction is presented graphically in Figure 14.9, where the cell means for variable A are plotted at each level of variable B.

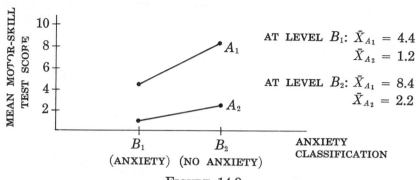

FIGURE 14.9
Diagram of interaction of data in Table 14.9

The Newman-Keuls procedure for following up significant analysis of variance results can also be extended to multiple-variable experiments of this sort. See Winer (1962).

FACTOR ANALYSIS

In Chapter 11 the correlation coefficient was presented as a means of measuring the strength of association between two variables. In attempting to explain the interrelationships among more than two variables simultaneously, we turn to a technique known as *factor analysis*. Factor analysis, originally developed by Charles Spearman and later expanded by L. L. Thurstone in *Vectors of Mind* in 1937, is a procedure for establishing so-called *reference* variables that are fewer in number than the number of original variables in the study. For example, suppose three tests were administered to a group of individuals:

1. A test of language skills.
2. A test of manual dexterity with machine tools.
3. A test of mechanical comprehension.

The association between any two of these tests can be measured by using the correlation coefficient. Let us assume that the correlation coefficient between tests 1 and 2 is 0.00; between tests 1 and 3 the correlation coefficient is 0.31, and between tests 2 and 3 the correlation coefficient is 0.95. These correlational results are usually reported together in a table called an *intercorrelation matrix*. The intercorrelational matrix for this example is given in Table 14.10. The basic question of factor analysis is: Do we really have three unique and independent traits (corresponding to the three tests), or might these results be explained by a smaller number of traits or factors (say, perhaps, a language ability and a "mechanical" ability factor)? To answer this question by means of factor analysis each correlation coefficient

TABLE 14.10   **INTERCORRELATION MATRIX**

		Test		
		1	2	3
Test	1	1.00	0.00	0.31
	2	0.00	1.00	0.95
	3	0.31	0.95	1.00

is represented by an angular notation, as follows: Let each test be represented by a line one unit long. Then from basic trigonometry, the correlation
coefficient r between any two tests may be expressed as the cosine of the
angle between the two lines. For example, for any pair of tests i and j, the
graphical representation is

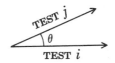

and the corresponding correlation coefficient between tests i and j is

$$r = \cos \theta$$

The graphical representation of the relationship between all pairs of
the tests in Table 14.10 is given in Figure 14.10. Now

$$\cos 90° = 0.00$$

$$\cos 72° = 0.31$$

$$\cos 18° = 0.95$$

Each of these values agrees with the corresponding correlation coefficient
of Table 14.10.

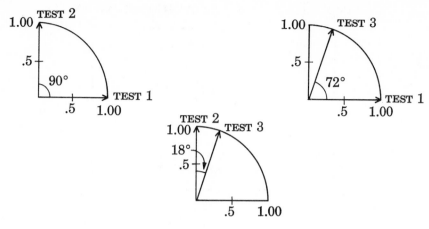

FIGURE 14.10
Graphical representation of the test pairs of Table 14.10

Furthermore, it is possible to combine all three graphical representations in a single two-dimensional figure, as illustrated by Figure 14.11. We

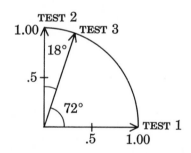

FIGURE 14.11
Graphical representation of the intercorrelation matrix of Table 14.10

have, therefore, been able to express the interrelationships among the three tests of Table 14.10 with a two-dimensional figure. That is, we have factored our intercorrelational matrix into two factors. The labeling of the two axes of Figure 14.11 is somewhat arbitrary, although "language ability" would seem to be an appropriate label for the horizontal axis and "mechanical ability" appropriate for the vertical axis in our example.

There is a large number of underlying assumptions and computational systems for handling problems of this sort, and an adequate working knowledge of factor analysis requires considerable advanced training. However, a fairly elementary introduction to this topic is given by Fruchter (1954).

TABLES

TABLE I.   **SQUARES AND SQUARE ROOTS.**

N	N^2	$\sqrt{N}$	$\sqrt{10N}$	N	N^2	$\sqrt{N}$	$\sqrt{10N}$
1.00	1.0000	1.00000	3.16228	1.50	2.2500	1.22474	3.87298
1.01	1.0201	1.00499	3.17805	1.51	2.2801	1.22882	3.88587
1.02	1.0404	1.00995	3.19374	1.52	2.3104	1.23288	3.89872
1.03	1.0609	1.01489	3.20936	1.53	2.3409	1.23693	3.91152
1.04	1.0816	1.01980	3.22490	1.54	2.3716	1.24097	3.92428
1.05	1.1025	1.02470	3.24037	1.55	2.4025	1.24499	3.93700
1.06	1.1236	1.02956	3.25576	1.56	2.4336	1.24900	3.94968
1.07	1.1449	1.03441	3.27109	1.57	2.4649	1.25300	3.96232
1.08	1.1664	1.03923	3.28634	1.58	2.4964	1.25698	3.97492
1.09	1.1881	1.04403	3.30151	1.59	2.5281	1.26095	3.98748
1.10	1.2100	1.04881	3.31662	1.60	2.5600	1.26491	4.00000
1.11	1.2321	1.05357	3.33167	1.61	2.5921	1.26886	4.01248
1.12	1.2544	1.05830	3.34664	1.62	2.6244	1.27279	4.02492
1.13	1.2769	1.06301	3.36155	1.63	2.6569	1.27671	4.03733
1.14	1.2996	1.06771	3.37639	1.64	2.6896	1.28062	4.04969
1.15	1.3225	1.07238	3.39116	1.65	2.7225	1.28452	4.06202
1.16	1.3456	1.07703	3.40588	1.66	2.7556	1.28841	4.07431
1.17	1.3689	1.08167	3.42053	1.67	2.7889	1.29228	4.08656
1.18	1.3924	1.08628	3.43511	1.68	2.8224	1.29615	4.09878
1.19	1.4161	1.09087	3.44964	1.69	2.8561	1.30000	4.11096
1.20	1.4400	1.09545	3.46410	1.70	2.8900	1.30384	4.12311
1.21	1.4641	1.10000	3.47851	1.71	2.9241	1.30767	4.13521
1.22	1.4884	1.10454	3.49285	1.72	2.9584	1.31149	4.14729
1.23	1.5129	1.10905	3.50714	1.73	2.9929	1.31529	4.15933
1.24	1.5376	1.11355	3.52136	1.74	3.0276	1.31909	4.17133
1.25	1.5625	1.11803	3.53553	1.75	3.0625	1.32288	4.18330
1.26	1.5876	1.12250	3.54965	1.76	3.0976	1.32665	4.19524
1.27	1.6129	1.12694	3.56371	1.77	3.1329	1.33041	4.20714
1.28	1.6384	1.13137	3.57771	1.78	3.1684	1.33417	4.21900
1.29	1.6641	1.13578	3.59166	1.79	3.2041	1.33791	4.23084
1.30	1.6900	1.14018	3.60555	1.80	3.2400	1.34164	4.24264
1.31	1.7161	1.14455	3.61939	1.81	3.2761	1.34536	4.25441
1.32	1.7424	1.14891	3.63318	1.82	3.3124	1.34907	4.26615
1.33	1.7689	1.15326	3.64692	1.83	3.3489	1.35277	4.27785
1.34	1.7956	1.15758	3.66060	1.84	3.3856	1.35647	4.28952
1.35	1.8225	1.16190	3.67423	1.85	3.4225	1.36015	4.30116
1.36	1.8496	1.16619	3.68782	1.86	3.4596	1.36382	4.31277
1.37	1.8769	1.17047	3.70135	1.87	3.4969	1.36748	4.32435
1.38	1.9044	1.17473	3.71484	1.88	3.5344	1.37113	4.33590
1.39	1.9321	1.17898	3.72827	1.89	3.5721	1.37477	4.34741
1.40	1.9600	1.18322	3.74166	1.90	3.6100	1.37840	4.35890
1.41	1.9881	1.18743	3.75500	1.91	3.6481	1.38203	4.37035
1.42	2.0164	1.19164	3.76829	1.92	3.6864	1.38564	4.38178
1.43	2.0449	1.19583	3.78153	1.93	3.7249	1.38924	4.39318
1.44	2.0736	1.20000	3.79473	1.94	3.7636	1.39284	4.40454
1.45	2.1025	1.20416	3.80789	1.95	3.8025	1.39642	4.41588
1.46	2.1316	1.20830	3.82099	1.96	3.8416	1.40000	4.42719
1.47	2.1609	1.21244	3.83406	1.97	3.8809	1.40357	4.43847
1.48	2.1904	1.21655	3.84708	1.98	3.9204	1.40712	4.44972
1.49	2.2201	1.22066	3.86005	1.99	3.9601	1.41067	4.46094
1.50	2.2500	1.22474	3.87298	2.00	4.0000	1.41421	4.47214
N	N^2	$\sqrt{N}$	$\sqrt{10N}$	N	N^2	$\sqrt{N}$	$\sqrt{10N}$

* From *Wiley Trigonometric Tables* (New York: John Wiley & Sons, Inc., 1945). Reprinted by permission.

TABLE I.　　　　　　　　　　　　　SQUARES AND SQUARE ROOTS.

N	N^2	$\sqrt{N}$	$\sqrt{10N}$	N	N^2	$\sqrt{N}$	$\sqrt{10N}$
2.00	4.0000	1.41421	4.47214	**2.50**	6.2500	1.58114	5.00000
2.01	4.0401	1.41774	4.48330	2.51	6.3001	1.58430	5.00999
2.02	4.0804	1.42127	4.49444	2.52	6.3504	1.58745	5.01996
2.03	4.1209	1.42478	4.50555	2.53	6.4009	1.59060	5.02991
2.04	4.1616	1.42829	4.51664	2.54	6.4516	1.59374	5.03984
2.05	4.2025	1.43178	4.52769	2.55	6.5025	1.59687	5.04975
2.06	4.2436	1.43527	4.53872	2.56	6.5536	1.60000	5.05964
2.07	4.2849	1.43875	4.54973	2.57	6.6049	1.60312	5.06952
2.08	4.3264	1.44222	4.56070	2.58	6.6564	1.60624	5.07937
2.09	4.3681	1.44568	4.57165	2.59	6.7081	1.60935	5.08920
2.10	4.4100	1.44914	4.58258	**2.60**	6.7600	1.61245	5.09902
2.11	4.4521	1.45258	4.59347	2.61	6.8121	1.61555	5.10882
2.12	4.4944	1.45602	4.60435	2.62	6.8644	1.61864	5.11859
2.13	4.5369	1.45945	4.61519	2.63	6.9169	1.62173	5.12835
2.14	4.5796	1.46287	4.62601	2.64	6.9696	1.62481	5.13809
2.15	4.6225	1.46629	4.63681	2.65	7.0225	1.62788	5.14782
2.16	4.6656	1.46969	4.64758	2.66	7.0756	1.63095	5.15752
2.17	4.7089	1.47309	4.65833	2.67	7.1289	1.63401	5.16720
2.18	4.7524	1.47648	4.66905	2.68	7.1824	1.63707	5.17687
2.19	4.7961	1.47986	4.67974	2.69	7.2361	1.64012	5.18652
2.20	4.8400	1.48324	4.69042	**2.70**	7.2900	1.64317	5.19615
2.21	4.8841	1.48661	4.70106	2.71	7.3441	1.64621	5.20577
2.22	4.9284	1.48997	4.71169	2.72	7.3984	1.64924	5.21536
2.23	4.9729	1.49332	4.72229	2.73	7.4529	1.65227	5.22494
2.24	5.0176	1.49666	4.73286	2.74	7.5076	1.65529	5.23450
2.25	5.0625	1.50000	4.74342	2.75	7.5625	1.65831	5.24404
2.26	5.1076	1.50333	4.75395	2.76	7.6176	1.66132	5.25357
2.27	5.1529	1.50665	4.76445	2.77	7.6729	1.66433	5.26308
2.28	5.1984	1.50997	4.77493	2.78	7.7284	1.66733	5.27257
2.29	5.2441	1.51327	4.78539	2.79	7.7841	1.67033	5.28205
2.30	5.2900	1.51658	4.79583	**2.80**	7.8400	1.67332	5.29150
2.31	5.3361	1.51987	4.80625	2.81	7.8961	1.67631	5.30094
2.32	5.3824	1.52315	4.81664	2.82	7.9524	1.67929	5.31037
2.33	5.4289	1.52643	4.82701	2.83	8.0089	1.68226	5.31977
2.34	5.4756	1.52971	4.83735	2.84	8.0656	1.68523	5.32917
2.35	5.5225	1.53297	4.84768	2.85	8.1225	1.68819	5.33854
2.36	5.5696	1.53623	4.85798	2.86	8.1796	1.69115	5.34790
2.37	5.6169	1.53948	4.86826	2.87	8.2369	1.69411	5.35724
2.38	5.6644	1.54272	4.87852	2.88	8.2944	1.69706	5.36656
2.39	5.7121	1.54596	4.88876	2.89	8.3521	1.70000	5.37587
2.40	5.7600	1.54919	4.89898	**2.90**	8.4100	1.70294	5.38516
2.41	5.8081	1.55242	4.90918	2.91	8.4681	1.70587	5.39444
2.42	5.8564	1.55563	4.91935	2.92	8.5264	1.70880	5.40370
2.43	5.9049	1.55885	4.92950	2.93	8.5849	1.71172	5.41295
2.44	5.9536	1.56205	4.93964	2.94	8.6436	1.71464	5.42218
2.45	6.0025	1.56525	4.94975	2.95	8.7025	1.71756	5.43139
2.46	6.0516	1.56844	4.95984	2.96	8.7616	1.72047	5.44059
2.47	6.1009	1.57162	4.96991	2.97	8.8209	1.72337	5.44977
2.48	6.1504	1.57480	4.97996	2.98	8.8804	1.72627	5.45894
2.49	6.2001	1.57797	4.98999	2.99	8.9401	1.72916	5.46809
2.50	6.2500	1.58114	5.00000	**3.00**	9.0000	1.73205	5.47723
N	N^2	$\sqrt{N}$	$\sqrt{10N}$	N	N^2	$\sqrt{N}$	$\sqrt{10N}$

TABLE I.   **SQUARES AND SQUARE ROOTS.**

N	N^2	$\sqrt{N}$	$\sqrt{10N}$	N	N^2	$\sqrt{N}$	$\sqrt{10N}$
3.00	9.0000	1.73205	5.47723	**3.50**	12.2500	1.87083	5.91608
3.01	9.0601	1.73494	5.48635	3.51	12.3201	1.87350	5.92453
3.02	9.1204	1.73781	5.49545	3.52	12.3904	1.87617	5.93296
3.03	9.1809	1.74069	5.50454	3.53	12.4609	1.87883	5.94138
3.04	9.2416	1.74356	5.51362	3.54	12.5316	1.88149	5.94979
3.05	9.3025	1.74642	5.52268	3.55	12.6025	1.88414	5.95819
3.06	9.3636	1.74929	5.53173	3.56	12.6736	1.88680	5.96657
3.07	9.4249	1.75214	5.54076	3.57	12.7449	1.88944	5.97495
3.08	9.4864	1.75499	5.54977	3.58	12.8164	1.89209	5.98331
3.09	9.5481	1.75784	5.55878	3.59	12.8881	1.89473	5.99166
3.10	9.6100	1.76068	5.56776	**3.60**	12.9600	1.89737	6.00000
3.11	9.6721	1.76352	5.57674	3.61	13.0321	1.90000	6.00833
3.12	9.7344	1.76635	5.58570	3.62	13.1044	1.90263	6.01664
3.13	9.7969	1.76918	5.59464	3.63	13.1769	1.90526	6.02495
3.14	9.8596	1.77200	5.60357	3.64	13.2496	1.90788	6.03324
3.15	9.9225	1.77482	5.61249	3.65	13.3225	1.91050	6.04152
3.16	9.9856	1.77764	5.62139	3.66	13.3956	1.91311	6.04979
3.17	10.0489	1.78045	5.63028	3.67	13.4689	1.91572	6.05805
3.18	10.1124	1.78326	5.63915	3.68	13.5424	1.91833	6.06630
3.19	10.1761	1.78606	5.64801	3.69	13.6161	1.92094	6.07454
3.20	10.2400	1.78885	5.65685	**3.70**	13.6900	1.92354	6.08276
3.21	10.3041	1.79165	5.66569	3.71	13.7641	1.92614	6.09098
3.22	10.3684	1.79444	5.67450	3.72	13.8384	1.92873	6.09918
3.23	10.4329	1.79722	5.68331	3.73	13.9129	1.93132	6.10737
3.24	10.4976	1.80000	5.69210	3.74	13.9876	1.93391	6.11555
3.25	10.5625	1.80278	5.70088	3.75	14.0625	1.93649	6.12372
3.26	10.6276	1.80555	5.70964	3.76	14.1376	1.93907	6.13188
3.27	10.6929	1.80831	5.71839	3.77	14.2129	1.94165	6.14003
3.28	10.7584	1.81108	5.72713	3.78	14.2884	1.94422	6.14817
3.29	10.8241	1.81384	5.73585	3.79	14.3641	1.94679	6.15630
3.30	10.8900	1.81659	5.74456	**3.80**	14.4400	1.94936	6.16441
3.31	10.9561	1.81934	5.75326	3.81	14.5161	1.95192	6.17252
3.32	11.0224	1.82209	5.76194	3.82	14.5924	1.95448	6.18061
3.33	11.0889	1.82483	5.77062	3.83	14.6689	1.95704	6.18870
3.34	11.1556	1.82757	5.77927	3.84	14.7456	1.95959	6.19677
3.35	11.2225	1.83030	5.78792	3.85	14.8225	1.96214	6.20484
3.36	11.2896	1.83303	5.79655	3.86	14.8996	1.96469	6.21289
3.37	11.3569	1.83576	5.80517	3.87	14.9769	1.96723	6.22093
3.38	11.4244	1.83848	5.81378	3.88	15.0544	1.96977	6.22896
3.39	11.4921	1.84120	5.82237	3.89	15.1321	1.97231	6.23699
3.40	11.5600	1.84391	5.83095	**3.90**	15.2100	1.97484	6.24500
3.41	11.6281	1.84662	5.83952	3.91	15.2881	1.97737	6.25300
3.42	11.6964	1.84932	5.84808	3.92	15.3664	1.97990	6.26099
3.43	11.7649	1.85203	5.85662	3.93	15.4449	1.98242	6.26897
3.44	11.8336	1.85472	5.86515	3.94	15.5236	1.98494	6.27694
3.45	11.9025	1.85742	5.87367	3.95	15.6025	1.98746	6.28490
3.46	11.9716	1.86011	5.88218	3.96	15.6816	1.98997	6.29285
3.47	12.0409	1.86279	5.89067	3.97	15.7609	1.99249	6.30079
3.48	12.1104	1.86548	5.89915	3.98	15.8404	1.99499	6.30872
3.49	12.1801	1.86815	5.90762	3.99	15.9201	1.99750	6.31664
3.50	12.2500	1.87083	5.91608	**4.00**	16.0000	2.00000	6.32456
N	N^2	$\sqrt{N}$	$\sqrt{10N}$	N	N^2	$\sqrt{N}$	$\sqrt{10N}$

TABLE I.   **SQUARES AND SQUARE ROOTS.**

N	N^2	$\sqrt{N}$	$\sqrt{10N}$	N	N^2	$\sqrt{N}$	$\sqrt{10N}$
4.00	16.0000	2.00000	6.32456	**4.50**	20.2500	2.12132	6.70820
4.01	16.0801	2.00250	6.33246	4.51	20.3401	2.12368	6.71565
4.02	16.1604	2.00499	6.34035	4.52	20.4304	2.12603	6.72309
4.03	16.2409	2.00749	6.34823	4.53	20.5209	2.12838	6.73053
4.04	16.3216	2.00998	6.35610	4.54	20.6116	2.13073	6.73795
4.05	16.4025	2.01246	6.36396	4.55	20.7025	2.13307	6.74537
4.06	16.4836	2.01494	6.37181	4.56	20.7936	2.13542	6.75278
4.07	16.5649	2.01742	6.37966	4.57	20.8849	2.13776	6.76018
4.08	16.6464	2.01990	6.38749	4.58	20.9764	2.14009	6.76757
4.09	16.7281	2.02237	6.39531	4.59	21.0681	2.14243	6.77495
4.10	16.8100	2.02485	6.40312	**4.60**	21.1600	2.14476	6.78233
4.11	16.8921	2.02731	6.41093	4.61	21.2521	2.14709	6.78970
4.12	16.9744	2.02978	6.41872	4.62	21.3444	2.14942	6.79706
4.13	17.0569	2.03224	6.42651	4.63	21.4369	2.15174	6.80441
4.14	17.1396	2.03470	6.43428	4.64	21.5296	2.15407	6.81175
4.15	17.2225	2.03715	6.44205	4.65	21.6225	2.15639	6.81909
4.16	17.3056	2.03961	6.44981	4.66	21.7156	2.15870	6.82642
4.17	17.3889	2.04206	6.45755	4.67	21.8089	2.16102	6.83374
4.18	17.4724	2.04450	6.46529	4.68	21.9024	2.16333	6.84105
4.19	17.5561	2.04695	6.47302	4.69	21.9961	2.16564	6.84836
4.20	17.6400	2.04939	6.48074	**4.70**	22.0900	2.16795	6.85565
4.21	17.7241	2.05183	6.48845	4.71	22.1841	2.17025	6.86294
4.22	17.8084	2.05426	6.49615	4.72	22.2784	2.17256	6.87023
4.23	17.8929	2.05670	6.50384	4.73	22.3729	2.17486	6.87750
4.24	17.9776	2.05913	6.51153	4.74	22.4676	2.17715	6.88477
4.25	18.0625	2.06155	6.51920	4.75	22.5625	2.17945	6.89202
4.26	18.1476	2.06398	6.52687	4.76	22.6576	2.18174	6.89928
4.27	18.2329	2.06640	6.53452	4.77	22.7529	2.18403	6.90652
4.28	18.3184	2.06882	6.54217	4.78	22.8484	2.18632	6.91375
4.29	18.4041	2.07123	6.54981	4.79	22.9441	2.18861	6.92098
4.30	18.4900	2.07364	6.55744	**4.80**	23.0400	2.19089	6.92820
4.31	18.5761	2.07605	6.56506	4.81	23.1361	2.19317	6.93542
4.32	18.6624	2.07846	6.57267	4.82	23.2324	2.19545	6.94262
4.33	18.7489	2.08087	6.58027	4.83	23.3289	2.19773	6.94982
4.34	18.8356	2.08327	6.58787	4.84	23.4256	2.20000	6.95701
4.35	18.9225	2.08567	6.59545	4.85	23.5225	2.20227	6.96419
4.36	19.0096	2.08806	6.60303	4.86	23.6196	2.20454	6.97137
4.37	19.0969	2.09045	6.61060	4.87	23.7169	2.20681	6.97854
4.38	19.1844	2.09284	6.61816	4.88	23.8144	2.20907	6.98570
4.39	19.2721	2.09523	6.62571	4.89	23.9121	2.21133	6.99285
4.40	19.3600	2.09762	6.63325	**4.90**	24.0100	2.21359	7.00000
4.41	19.4481	2.10000	6.64078	4.91	24.1081	2.21585	7.00714
4.42	19.5364	2.10238	6.64831	4.92	24.2064	2.21811	7.01427
4.43	19.6249	2.10476	6.65582	4.93	24.3049	2.22036	7.02140
4.44	19.7136	2.10713	6.66333	4.94	24.4036	2.22261	7.02851
4.45	19.8025	2.10950	6.67083	4.95	24.5025	2.22486	7.03562
4.46	19.8916	2.11187	6.67832	4.96	24.6016	2.22711	7.04273
4.47	19.9809	2.11424	6.68581	4.97	24.7009	2.22935	7.04982
4.48	20.0704	2.11660	6.69328	4.98	24.8004	2.23159	7.05691
4.49	20.1601	2.11896	6.70075	4.99	24.9001	2.23383	7.06399
4.50	20.2500	2.12132	6.70820	**5.00**	25.0000	2.23607	7.07107
N	N^2	$\sqrt{N}$	$\sqrt{10N}$	N	N^2	$\sqrt{N}$	$\sqrt{10N}$

TABLE I.   **SQUARES AND SQUARE ROOTS.**

N	N^2	$\sqrt{N}$	$\sqrt{10N}$	N	N^2	$\sqrt{N}$	$\sqrt{10N}$
5.00	25.0000	2.23607	7.07107	**5.50**	30.2500	2.34521	7.41620
5.01	25.1001	2.23830	7.07814	5.51	30.3601	2.34734	7.42294
5.02	25.2004	2.24054	7.08520	5.52	30.4704	2.34947	7.42967
5.03	25.3009	2.24277	7.09225	5.53	30.5809	2.35160	7.43640
5.04	25.4016	2.24499	7.09930	5.54	30.6916	2.35372	7.44312
5.05	25.5025	2.24722	7.10634	5.55	30.8025	2.35584	7.44983
5.06	25.6036	2.24944	7.11337	5.56	30.9136	2.35797	7.45654
5.07	25.7049	2.25167	7.12039	5.57	31.0249	2.36008	7.46324
5.08	25.8064	2.25389	7.12741	5.58	31.1364	2.36220	7.46994
5.09	25.9081	2.25610	7.13442	5.59	31.2481	2.36432	7.47663
5.10	26.0100	2.25832	7.14143	**5.60**	31.3600	2.36643	7.48331
5.11	26.1121	2.26053	7.14843	5.61	31.4721	2.36854	7.48999
5.12	26.2144	2.26274	7.15542	5.62	31.5844	2.37065	7.49667
5.13	26.3169	2.26495	7.16240	5.63	31.6969	2.37276	7.50333
5.14	26.4196	2.26716	7.16938	5.64	31.8096	2.37487	7.50999
5.15	26.5225	2.26936	7.17635	5.65	31.9225	2.37697	7.51665
5.16	26.6256	2.27156	7.18331	5.66	32.0356	2.37908	7.52330
5.17	26.7289	2.27376	7.19027	5.67	32.1489	2.38118	7.52994
5.18	26.8324	2.27596	7.19722	5.68	32.2624	2.38328	7.53658
5.19	26.9361	2.27816	7.20417	5.69	32.3761	2.38537	7.54321
5.20	27.0400	2.28035	7.21110	**5.70**	32.4900	2.38747	7.54983
5.21	27.1441	2.28254	7.21803	5.71	32.6041	2.38956	7.55645
5.22	27.2484	2.28473	7.22496	5.72	32.7184	2.39165	7.56307
5.23	27.3529	2.28692	7.23187	5.73	32.8329	2.39374	7.56968
5.24	27.4576	2.28910	7.23878	5.74	32.9476	2.39583	7.57628
5.25	27.5625	2.29129	7.24569	5.75	33.0625	2.39792	7.58288
5.26	27.6676	2.29347	7.25259	5.76	33.1776	2.40000	7.58947
5.27	27.7729	2.29565	7.25948	5.77	33.2929	2.40208	7.59605
5.28	27.8784	2.29783	7.26636	5.78	33.4084	2.40416	7.60263
5.29	27.9841	2.30000	7.27324	5.79	33.5241	2.40624	7.60920
5.30	28.0900	2.30217	7.28011	**5.80**	33.6400	2.40832	7.61577
5.31	28.1961	2.30434	7.28697	5.81	33.7561	2.41039	7.62234
5.32	28.3024	2.30651	7.29383	5.82	33.8724	2.41247	7.62889
5.33	28.4089	2.30868	7.30068	5.83	33.9889	2.41454	7.63544
5.34	28.5156	2.31084	7.30753	5.84	34.1056	2.41661	7.64199
5.35	28.6225	2.31301	7.31437	5.85	34.2225	2.41868	7.64853
5.36	28.7296	2.31517	7.32120	5.86	34.3396	2.42074	7.65506
5.37	28.8369	2.31733	7.32803	5.87	34.4569	2.42281	7.66159
5.38	28.9444	2.31948	7.33485	5.88	34.5744	2.42487	7.66812
5.39	29.0521	2.32164	7.34166	5.89	34.6921	2.42693	7.67463
5.40	29.1600	2.32379	7.34847	**5.90**	34.8100	2.42899	7.68115
5.41	29.2681	2.32594	7.35527	5.91	34.9281	2.43105	7.68765
5.42	29.3764	2.32809	7.36206	5.92	35.0464	2.43311	7.69415
5.43	29.4849	2.33024	7.36885	5.93	35.1649	2.43516	7.70065
5.44	29.5936	2.33238	7.37564	5.94	35.2836	2.43721	7.70714
5.45	29.7025	2.33452	7.38241	5.95	35.4025	2.43926	7.71362
5.46	29.8116	2.33666	7.38918	5.96	35.5216	2.44131	7.72010
5.47	29.9209	2.33880	7.39594	5.97	35.6409	2.44336	7.72658
5.48	30.0304	2.34094	7.40270	5.98	35.7604	2.44540	7.73305
5.49	30.1401	2.34307	7.40945	5.99	35.8801	2.44745	7.73951
5.50	30.2500	2.34521	7.41620	**6.00**	36.0000	2.44949	7.74597
N	N^2	$\sqrt{N}$	$\sqrt{10N}$	N	N^2	$\sqrt{N}$	$\sqrt{10N}$

TABLE I.   **SQUARES AND SQUARE ROOTS.**

N	N^2	$\sqrt{N}$	$\sqrt{10N}$	N	N^2	$\sqrt{N}$	$\sqrt{10N}$
6.00	36.0000	2.44949	7.74597	**6.50**	42.2500	2.54951	8.06226
6.01	36.1201	2.45153	7.75242	6.51	42.3801	2.55147	8.06846
6.02	36.2404	2.45357	7.75887	6.52	42.5104	2.55343	8.07465
6.03	36.3609	2.45561	7.76531	6.53	42.6409	2.55539	8.08084
6.04	36.4816	2.45764	7.77174	6.54	42.7716	2.55734	8.08703
6.05	36.6025	2.45967	7.77817	6.55	42.9025	2.55930	8.09321
6.06	36.7236	2.46171	7.78460	6.56	43.0336	2.56125	8.09938
6.07	36.8449	2.46374	7.79102	6.57	43.1649	2.56320	8.10555
6.08	36.9664	2.46577	7.79744	6.58	43.2964	2.56515	8.11172
6.09	37.0881	2.46779	7.80385	6.59	43.4281	2.56710	8.11788
6.10	37.2100	2.46982	7.81025	**6.60**	43.5600	2.56905	8.12404
6.11	37.3321	2.47184	7.81665	6.61	43.6921	2.57099	8.13019
6.12	37.4544	2.47386	7.82304	6.62	43.8244	2.57294	8.13634
6.13	37.5769	2.47588	7.82943	6.63	43.9569	2.57488	8.14248
6.14	37.6996	2.47790	7.83582	6.64	44.0896	2.57682	8.14862
6.15	37.8225	2.47992	7.84219	6.65	44.2225	2.57876	8.15475
6.16	37.9456	2.48193	7.84857	6.66	44.3556	2.58070	8.16088
6.17	38.0689	2.48395	7.85493	6.67	44.4889	2.58263	8.16701
6.18	38.1924	2.48596	7.86130	6.68	44.6224	2.58457	8.17313
6.19	38.3161	2.48797	7.86766	6.69	44.7561	2.58650	8.17924
6.20	38.4400	2.48998	7.87401	**6.70**	44.8900	2.58844	8.18535
6.21	38.5641	2.49199	7.88036	6.71	45.0241	2.59037	8.19146
6.22	38.6884	2.49399	7.88670	6.72	45.1584	2.59230	8.19756
6.23	38.8129	2.49600	7.89303	6.73	45.2929	2.59422	8.20366
6.24	38.9376	2.49800	7.89937	6.74	45.4276	2.59615	8.20975
6.25	39.0625	2.50000	7.90569	6.75	45.5625	2.59808	8.21584
6.26	39.1876	2.50200	7.91202	6.76	45.6976	2.60000	8.22192
6.27	39.3129	2.50400	7.91833	6.77	45.8329	2.60192	8.22800
6.28	39.4384	2.50599	7.92465	6.78	45.9684	2.60384	8.23408
6.29	39.5641	2.50799	7.93095	6.79	46.1041	2.60576	8.24015
6.30	39.6900	2.50998	7.93725	**6.80**	46.2400	2.60768	8.24621
6.31	39.8161	2.51197	7.94355	6.81	46.3761	2.60960	8.25227
6.32	39.9424	2.51396	7.94984	6.82	46.5124	2.61151	8.25833
6.33	40.0689	2.51595	7.95613	6.83	46.6489	2.61343	8.26438
6.34	40.1956	2.51794	7.96241	6.84	46.7856	2.61534	8.27043
6.35	40.3225	2.51992	7.96869	6.85	46.9225	2.61725	8.27647
6.36	40.4496	2.52190	7.97496	6.86	47.0596	2.61916	8.28251
6.37	40.5769	2.52389	7.98123	6.87	47.1969	2.62107	8.28855
6.38	40.7044	2.52587	7.98749	6.88	47.3344	2.62298	8.29458
6.39	40.8321	2.52784	7.99375	6.89	47.4721	2.62488	8.30060
6.40	40.9600	2.52982	8.00000	**6.90**	47.6100	2.62679	8.30662
6.41	41.0881	2.53180	8.00625	6.91	47.7481	2.62869	8.31264
6.42	41.2164	2.53377	8.01249	6.92	47.8864	2.63059	8.31865
6.43	41.3449	2.53574	8.01873	6.93	48.0249	2.63249	8.32466
6.44	41.4736	2.53772	8.02496	6.94	48.1636	2.63439	8.33067
6.45	41.6025	2.53969	8.03119	6.95	48.3025	2.63629	8.33667
6.46	41.7316	2.54165	8.03741	6.96	48.4416	2.63818	8.34266
6.47	41.8609	2.54362	8.04363	6.97	48.5809	2.64008	8.34865
6.48	41.9904	2.54558	8.04984	6.98	48.7204	2.64197	8.35464
6.49	42.1201	2.54755	8.05605	6.99	48.8601	2.64386	8.36062
6.50	42.2500	2.54951	8.06226	**7.00**	49.0000	2.64575	8.36660
N	N^2	$\sqrt{N}$	$\sqrt{10N}$	N	N^2	$\sqrt{N}$	$\sqrt{10N}$

TABLE I.   **SQUARES AND SQUARE ROOTS.**

N	N^2	$\sqrt{N}$	$\sqrt{10N}$	N	N^2	$\sqrt{N}$	$\sqrt{10N}$
7.00	49.0000	2.64575	8.36660	**7.50**	56.2500	2.73861	8.66025
7.01	49.1401	2.64764	8.37257	7.51	56.4001	2.74044	8.66603
7.02	49.2804	2.64953	8.37854	7.52	56.5504	2.74226	8.67179
7.03	49.4209	2.65141	8.38451	7.53	56.7009	2.74408	8.67756
7.04	49.5616	2.65330	8.39047	7.54	56.8516	2.74591	8.68332
7.05	49.7025	2.65518	8.39643	7.55	57.0025	2.74773	8.68907
7.06	49.8436	2.65707	8.40238	7.56	57.1536	2.74955	8.69483
7.07	49.9849	2.65895	8.40833	7.57	57.3049	2.75136	8.70057
7.08	50.1264	2.66083	8.41427	7.58	57.4564	2.75318	8.70632
7.09	50.2681	2.66271	8.42021	7.59	57.6081	2.75500	8.71206
7.10	50.4100	2.66458	8.42615	**7.60**	57.7600	2.75681	8.71780
7.11	50.5521	2.66646	8.43208	7.61	57.9121	2.75862	8.72353
7.12	50.6944	2.66833	8.43801	7.62	58.0644	2.76043	8.72926
7.13	50.8369	2.67021	8.44393	7.63	58.2169	2.76225	8.73499
7.14	50.9796	2.67208	8.44985	7.64	58.3696	2.76405	8.74071
7.15	51.1225	2.67395	8.45577	7.65	58.5225	2.76586	8.74643
7.16	51.2656	2.67582	8.46168	7.66	58.6756	2.76767	8.75214
7.17	51.4089	2.67769	8.46759	7.67	58.8289	2.76948	8.75785
7.18	51.5524	2.67955	8.47349	7.68	58.9824	2.77128	8.76356
7.19	51.6961	2.68142	8.47939	7.69	59.1361	2.77308	8.76926
7.20	51.8400	2.68328	8.48528	**7.70**	59.2900	2.77489	8.77496
7.21	51.9841	2.68514	8.49117	7.71	59.4441	2.77669	8.78066
7.22	52.1284	2.68701	8.49706	7.72	59.5984	2.77849	8.78635
7.23	52.2729	2.68887	8.50294	7.73	59.7529	2.78029	8.79204
7.24	52.4176	2.69072	8.50882	7.74	59.9076	2.78209	8.79773
7.25	52.5625	2.69258	8.51469	7.75	60.0625	2.78388	8.80341
7.26	52.7076	2.69444	8.52056	7.76	60.2176	2.78568	8.80909
7.27	52.8529	2.69629	8.52643	7.77	60.3729	2.78747	8.81476
7.28	52.9984	2.69815	8.53229	7.78	60.5284	2.78927	8.82043
7.29	53.1441	2.70000	8.53815	7.79	60.6841	2.79106	8.82610
7.30	53.2900	2.70185	8.54400	**7.80**	60.8400	2.79285	8.83176
7.31	53.4361	2.70370	8.54985	7.81	60.9961	2.79464	8.83742
7.32	53.5824	2.70555	8.55570	7.82	61.1524	2.79643	8.84308
7.33	53.7289	2.70740	8.56154	7.83	61.3089	2.79821	8.84873
7.34	53.8756	2.70924	8.56738	7.84	61.4656	2.80000	8.85438
7.35	54.0225	2.71109	8.57321	7.85	61.6225	2.80179	8.86002
7.36	54.1696	2.71293	8.57904	7.86	61.7796	2.80357	8.86566
7.37	54.3169	2.71477	8.58487	7.87	61.9369	2.80535	8.87130
7.38	54.4644	2.71662	8.59069	7.88	62.0944	2.80713	8.87694
7.39	54.6121	2.71846	8.59651	7.89	62.2521	2.80891	8.88257
7.40	54.7600	2.72029	8.60233	**7.90**	62.4100	2.81069	8.88819
7.41	54.9081	2.72213	8.60814	7.91	62.5681	2.81247	8.89382
7.42	55.0564	2.72397	8.61394	7.92	62.7264	2.81425	8.89944
7.43	55.2049	2.72580	8.61974	7.93	62.8849	2.81603	8.90505
7.44	55.3536	2.72764	8.62554	7.94	63.0436	2.81780	8.91067
7.45	55.5025	2.72947	8.63134	7.95	63.2025	2.81957	8.91628
7.46	55.6516	2.73130	8.63713	7.96	63.3616	2.82135	8.92188
7.47	55.8009	2.73313	8.64292	7.97	63.5209	2.82312	8.92749
7.48	55.9504	2.73496	8.64870	7.98	63.6804	2.82489	8.93308
7.49	56.1001	2.73679	8.65448	7.99	63.8401	2.82666	8.93868
7.50	56.2500	2.73861	8.66025	**8.00**	64.0000	2.82843	8.94427
N	N^2	$\sqrt{N}$	$\sqrt{10N}$	N	N^2	$\sqrt{N}$	$\sqrt{10N}$

TABLE I.

SQUARES AND SQUARE ROOTS.

N	N²	√N	√10N	N	N²	√N	√10N
8.00	64.0000	2.82843	8.94427	**8.50**	72.2500	2.91548	9.21954
8.01	64.1601	2.83019	8.94986	8.51	72.4201	2.91719	9.22497
8.02	64.3204	2.83196	8.95545	8.52	72.5904	2.91890	9.23038
8.03	64.4809	2.83373	8.96103	8.53	72.7609	2.92062	9.23580
8.04	64.6416	2.83549	8.96660	8.54	72.9316	2.92233	9.24121
8.05	64.8025	2.83725	8.97218	8.55	73.1025	2.92404	9.24662
8.06	64.9636	2.83901	8.97775	8.56	73.2736	2.92575	9.25203
8.07	65.1249	2.84077	8.98332	8.57	73.4449	2.92746	9.25743
8.08	65.2864	2.84253	8.98888	8.58	73.6164	2.92916	9.26283
8.09	65.4481	2.84429	8.99444	8.59	73.7881	2.93087	9.26823
8.10	65.6100	2.84605	9.00000	**8.60**	73.9600	2.93258	9.27362
8.11	65.7721	2.84781	9.00555	8.61	74.1321	2.93428	9.27901
8.12	65.9344	2.84956	9.01110	8.62	74.3044	2.93598	9.28440
8.13	66.0969	2.85132	9.01665	8.63	74.4769	2.93769	9.28978
8.14	66.2596	2.85307	9.02219	8.64	74.6496	2.93939	9.29516
8.15	66.4225	2.85482	9.02774	8.65	74.8225	2.94109	9.30054
8.16	66.5856	2.85657	9.03327	8.66	74.9956	2.94279	9.30591
8.17	66.7489	2.85832	9.03881	8.67	75.1689	2.94449	9.31128
8.18	66.9124	2.86007	9.04434	8.68	75.3424	2.94618	9.31665
8.19	67.0761	2.86182	9.04986	8.69	75.5161	2.94788	9.32202
8.20	67.2400	2.86356	9.05539	**8.70**	75.6900	2.94958	9.32738
8.21	67.4041	2.86531	9.06091	8.71	75.8641	2.95127	9.33274
8.22	67.5684	2.86705	9.06642	8.72	76.0384	2.95296	9.33809
8.23	67.7329	2.86880	9.07193	8.73	76.2129	2.95466	9.34345
8.24	67.8976	2.87054	9.07744	8.74	76.3876	2.95635	9.34880
8.25	68.0625	2.87228	9.08295	8.75	76.5625	2.95804	9.35414
8.26	68.2276	2.87402	9.08845	8.76	76.7376	2.95973	9.35949
8.27	68.3929	2.87576	9.09395	8.77	76.9129	2.96142	9.36483
8.28	68.5584	2.87750	9.09945	8.78	77.0884	2.96311	9.37017
8.29	68.7241	2.87924	9.10494	8.79	77.2641	2.96469	9.37550
8.30	68.8900	2.88097	9.11043	**8.80**	77.4400	2.96648	9.38083
8.31	69.0561	2.88271	9.11592	8.81	77.6161	2.96816	9.38616
8.32	69.2224	2.88444	9.12140	8.82	77.7924	2.96985	9.39149
8.33	69.3889	2.88617	9.12688	8.83	77.9689	2.97153	9.39681
8.34	69.5556	2.88791	9.13236	8.84	78.1456	2.97321	9.40213
8.35	69.7225	2.88964	9.13783	8.85	78.3225	2.97489	9.40744
8.36	69.8896	2.89137	9.14330	8.86	78.4996	2.97658	9.41276
8.37	70.0569	2.89310	9.14877	8.87	78.6769	2.97825	9.41807
8.38	70.2244	2.89482	9.15423	8.88	78.8544	2.97993	9.42338
8.39	70.3921	2.89655	9.15969	8.89	79.0321	2.98161	9.42868
8.40	70.5600	2.89828	9.16515	**8.90**	79.2100	2.98329	9.43398
8.41	70.7281	2.90000	9.17061	8.91	79.3881	2.98496	9.43928
8.42	70.8964	2.90172	9.17606	8.92	79.5664	2.98664	9.44458
8.43	71.0649	2.90345	9.18150	8.93	79.7449	2.98831	9.44987
8.44	71.2336	2.90517	9.18695	8.94	79.9236	2.98998	9.45516
8.45	71.4025	2.90689	9.19239	8.95	80.1025	2.99166	9.46044
8.46	71.5716	2.90861	9.19783	8.96	80.2816	2.99333	9.46573
8.47	71.7409	2.91033	9.20326	8.97	80.4609	2.99500	9.47101
8.48	71.9104	2.91204	9.20869	8.98	80.6404	2.99666	9.47629
8.49	72.0801	2.91376	9.21412	8.99	80.8201	2.99833	9.48156
8.50	72.2500	2.91548	9.21954	**9.00**	81.0000	3.00000	9.48683
N	N²	√N	√10N	N	N²	√N	√10N

TABLE I.   **SQUARES AND SQUARE ROOTS.**

N	N^2	$\sqrt{N}$	$\sqrt{10N}$	N	N^2	$\sqrt{N}$	$\sqrt{10N}$
9.00	81.0000	3.00000	9.48683	**9.50**	90.2500	3.08221	9.74679
9.01	81.1801	3.00167	9.49210	**9.51**	90.4401	3.08383	9.75192
9.02	81.3604	3.00333	9.49737	9.52	90.6304	3.08545	9.75705
9.03	81.5409	3.00500	9.50263	9.53	90.8209	3.08707	9.76217
9.04	81.7216	3.00666	9.50789	9.54	91.0116	3.08869	9.76729
9.05	81.9025	3.00832	9.51315	9.55	91.2025	3.09031	9.77241
9.06	82.0836	3.00998	9.51840	9.56	91.3936	3.09192	9.77753
9.07	82.2649	3.01164	9.52365	9.57	91.5849	3.09354	9.78264
9.08	82.4464	3.01330	9.52890	9.58	91.7764	3.09516	9.78775
9.09	82.6281	3.01496	9.53415	9.59	91.9681	3.09677	9.79285
9.10	82.8100	3.01662	9.53939	**9.60**	92.1600	3.09839	9.79796
9.11	82.9921	3.01828	9.54463	9.61	92.3521	3.10000	9.80306
9.12	83.1744	3.01993	9.54987	9.62	92.5444	3.10161	9.80816
9.13	83.3569	3.02159	9.55510	9.63	92.7369	3.10322	9.81326
9.14	83.5396	3.02324	9.56033	9.64	92.9296	3.10483	9.81835
9.15	83.7225	3.02490	9.56556	9.65	93.1225	3.10644	9.82344
9.16	83.9056	3.02655	9.57079	9.66	93.3156	3.10805	9.82853
9.17	84.0889	3.02820	9.57601	9.67	93.5089	3.10966	9.83362
9.18	84.2724	3.02985	9.58123	9.68	93.7024	3.11127	9.83870
9.19	84.4561	3.03150	9.58645	9.69	93.8961	3.11288	9.84378
9.20	84.6400	3.03315	9.59166	**9.70**	94.0900	3.11448	9.84886
9.21	84.8241	3.03480	9.59687	9.71	94.2841	3.11609	9.85393
9.22	85.0084	3.03645	9.60208	9.72	94.4784	3.11769	9.85901
9.23	85.1929	3.03809	9.60729	9.73	94.6729	3.11929	9.86408
9.24	85.3776	3.03974	9.61249	9.74	94.8676	3.12090	9.86914
9.25	85.5625	3.04138	9.61769	9.75	95.0625	3.12250	9.87421
9.26	85.7476	3.04302	9.62289	9.76	95.2576	3.12410	9.87927
9.27	85.9329	3.04467	9.62808	9.77	95.4529	3.12570	9.88433
9.28	86.1184	3.04631	9.63328	9.78	95.6484	3.12730	9.88939
9.29	86.3041	3.04795	9.63846	9.79	95.8441	3.12890	9.89444
9.30	86.4900	3.04959	9.64365	**9.80**	96.0400	3.13050	9.89949
9.31	86.6761	3.05123	9.64883	9.81	96.2361	3.13209	9.90454
9.32	86.8624	3.05287	9.65401	9.82	96.4324	3.13369	9.90959
9.33	87.0489	3.05450	9.65919	9.83	96.6289	3.13528	9.91464
9.34	87.2356	3.05614	9.66437	9.84	96.8256	3.13688	9.91968
9.35	87.4225	3.05778	9.66954	9.85	97.0225	3.13847	9.92472
9.36	87.6096	3.05941	9.67471	9.86	97.2196	3.14006	9.92975
9.37	87.7969	3.06105	9.67988	9.87	97.4169	3.14166	9.93479
9.38	87.9844	3.06268	9.68504	9.88	97.6144	3.14325	9.93982
9.39	88.1721	3.06431	9.69020	9.89	97.8121	3.14484	9.94485
9.40	88.3600	3.06594	9.69536	**9.90**	98.0100	3.14643	9.94987
9.41	88.5481	3.06757	9.70052	9.91	98.2081	3.14802	9.95490
9.42	88.7364	3.06920	9.70567	9.92	98.4064	3.14960	9.95992
9.43	88.9249	3.07083	9.71082	9.93	98.6049	3.15119	9.96494
9.44	89.1136	3.07246	9.71597	9.94	98.8036	3.15278	9.96995
9.45	89.3025	3.07409	9.72111	9.95	99.0025	3.15436	9.97497
9.46	89.4916	3.07571	9.72625	9.96	99.2016	3.15595	9.97998
9.47	89.6809	3.07734	9.73139	9.97	99.4009	3.15753	9.98499
9.48	89.8704	3.07896	9.73653	9.98	99.6004	3.15911	9.98999
9.49	90.0601	3.08058	9.74166	9.99	99.8001	3.16070	9.99500
9.50	90.2500	3.08221	9.74679	**10.00**	100.000	3.16228	10.0000
N	N^2	$\sqrt{N}$	$\sqrt{10N}$	N	N^2	$\sqrt{N}$	$\sqrt{10N}$

TABLE II.   **RANDOM NUMBERS**

51772	74640	42331	29044	46621
24033	23491	83587	06568	21960
45939	60173	52078	25424	11645
30586	02133	75797	45406	31041
03585	79353	81938	82322	96799
64937	03355	95863	20790	65304
15630	64759	51135	98527	62586
09448	56301	57683	30277	94623
21631	91157	77331	60710	52290
91097	17480	29414	06829	87843
50532	25496	95652	42457	73547
07136	40876	79971	54195	25708
27989	64728	10744	08396	56242
85184	73949	36601	46253	00477
54398	21154	97810	36764	32869
65544	34371	09591	07839	58892
08263	65952	85762	64236	39238
39817	67906	48236	16057	81812
62257	04077	79443	95203	02479
53298	90276	62545	21944	16530
62898	93582	04186	19640	87056
21387	76105	10863	97453	90581
55870	56974	37428	93507	94271
86707	12973	17169	88116	42187
85659	36081	50884	14070	74950
55189	00745	65253	11822	15804
41889	25439	88036	24034	67283
85418	68829	06652	41982	49159
16835	48653	71590	16159	14676
28195	27279	47152	35683	47280
76552	50020	24819	52984	76168
51817	36732	72484	94923	75936
90985	28868	99431	50995	20507
25234	09908	36574	72139	70185
11785	55261	59009	38714	38723
92843	72828	91341	84821	63886
18776	84303	99247	46149	03229
15815	63700	85915	19219	45943
30763	92486	54083	23631	05825
03878	07516	95715	02526	33537

TABLE III.   **THE BINOMIAL DISTRIBUTION.**

n	X	.01	.05	.10	.20	.30	.40	p .50	.60	.70	.80	.90	.95	.99	X
2	0	980	902	810	640	490	360	250	160	090	040	010	002	0+	0
	1	020	095	180	320	420	480	500	480	420	320	180	095	020	1
	2	0+	002	010	040	090	160	250	360	490	640	810	902	980	2
3	0	970	857	729	512	343	216	125	064	027	008	001	0+	0+	0
	1	029	135	243	384	441	432	375	288	189	096	027	007	0+	1
	2	0+	007	027	096	189	288	375	432	441	384	243	135	029	2
	3	0+	0+	001	008	027	064	125	216	343	512	729	857	970	3
4	0	961	815	656	410	240	130	062	026	008	002	0+	0+	0+	0
	1	039	171	292	410	412	346	250	154	076	026	004	0+	0+	1
	2	001	014	049	154	265	346	375	346	265	154	049	014	001	2
	3	0+	0+	004	026	076	154	250	346	412	410	292	171	039	3
	4	0+	0+	0+	002	008	026	062	130	240	410	656	815	961	4
5	0	951	774	590	328	168	078	031	010	002	0+	0+	0+	0+	0
	1	048	204	328	410	360	259	156	077	028	006	0+	0+	0+	1
	2	001	021	073	205	309	346	312	230	132	051	008	001	0+	2
	3	0+	001	008	051	132	230	312	346	309	205	073	021	001	3
	4	0+	0+	0+	006	028	077	156	259	360	410	328	204	048	4
	5	0+	0+	0+	0+	002	010	031	078	168	328	590	774	951	5
6	0	941	735	531	262	118	047	016	004	001	0+	0+	0+	0+	0
	1	057	232	354	393	303	187	094	037	010	002	0+	0+	0+	1
	2	001	031	098	246	324	311	234	138	060	015	001	0+	0+	2
	3	0+	002	015	082	185	276	312	276	185	082	015	002	0+	3
	4	0+	0+	001	015	060	138	234	311	324	246	098	031	001	4
	5	0+	0+	0+	002	010	037	094	187	303	393	354	232	057	5
	6	0+	0+	0+	0+	001	004	016	047	118	262	531	735	941	6
7	0	932	698	478	210	082	028	008	002	0+	0+	0+	0+	0+	0
	1	066	257	372	367	247	131	055	017	004	0+	0+	0+	0+	1
	2	002	041	124	275	318	261	164	077	025	004	0+	0+	0+	2
	3	0+	004	023	115	227	290	273	194	097	029	003	0+	0+	3
	4	0+	0+	003	029	097	194	273	290	227	115	023	004	0+	4
	5	0+	0+	0+	004	025	077	164	261	318	275	124	041	002	5
	6	0+	0+	0+	0+	004	017	055	131	247	367	372	257	066	6
	7	0+	0+	0+	0+	0+	002	008	028	082	210	478	698	932	7
8	0	923	663	430	168	058	017	004	001	0+	0+	0+	0+	0+	0
	1	075	279	383	336	198	090	031	008	001	0+	0+	0+	0+	1
	2	003	051	149	294	296	209	109	041	010	001	0+	0+	0+	2
	3	0+	005	033	147	254	279	219	124	047	009	0+	0+	0+	3
	4	0+	0+	005	046	136	232	273	232	136	046	005	0+	0+	4
	5	0+	0+	0+	009	047	124	219	279	254	147	033	005	0+	5
	6	0+	0+	0+	001	010	041	109	209	296	294	149	051	003	6
	7	0+	0+	0+	0+	001	008	031	090	198	336	383	279	075	7
	8	0+	0+	0+	0+	0+	001	004	017	058	168	430	663	923	8

TABLE III.   THE BINOMIAL DISTRIBUTION.

n	X	.01	.05	.10	.20	.30	.40	p .50	.60	.70	.80	.90	.95	.99	X
9	0	914	630	387	134	040	010	002	0+	0+	0+	0+	0+	0+	0
	1	083	299	387	302	156	060	018	004	0+	0+	0+	0+	0+	1
	2	003	063	172	302	267	161	070	021	004	0+	0+	0+	0+	2
	3	0+	008	045	176	267	251	164	074	021	003	0+	0+	0+	3
	4	0+	001	007	066	172	251	246	167	074	017	001	0+	0+	4
	5	0+	0+	001	017	074	167	246	251	172	066	007	001	0+	5
	6	0+	0+	0+	003	021	074	164	251	267	176	045	008	0+	6
	7	0+	0+	0+	0+	004	021	070	161	267	302	172	063	003	7
	8	0+	0+	0+	0+	0+	004	018	060	156	302	387	299	083	8
	9	0+	0+	0+	0+	0+	0+	002	010	040	134	387	630	914	9
10	0	904	599	349	107	028	006	001	0+	0+	0+	0+	0+	0+	0
	1	091	315	387	268	121	040	010	002	0+	0+	0+	0+	0+	1
	2	004	075	194	302	233	121	044	011	001	0+	0+	0+	0+	2
	3	0+	010	057	201	267	215	117	042	009	001	0+	0+	0+	3
	4	0+	001	011	088	200	251	205	111	037	006	0+	0+	0+	4
	5	0+	0+	001	026	103	201	246	201	103	026	001	0+	0+	5
	6	0+	0+	0+	006	037	111	205	251	200	088	011	001	0+	6
	7	0+	0+	0+	001	009	042	117	215	267	201	057	010	0+	7
	8	0+	0+	0+	0+	001	011	044	121	233	302	194	075	004	8
	9	0+	0+	0+	0+	0+	002	010	040	121	268	387	315	091	9
	10	0+	0+	0+	0+	0+	0+	001	006	028	107	349	599	904	10
11	0	895	569	314	086	020	004	0+	0+	0+	0+	0+	0+	0+	0
	1	099	329	384	236	093	027	005	001	0+	0+	0+	0+	0+	1
	2	005	087	213	295	200	089	027	005	001	0+	0+	0+	0+	2
	3	0+	014	071	221	257	177	081	023	004	0+	0+	0+	0+	3
	4	0+	001	016	111	220	236	161	070	017	002	0+	0+	0+	4
	5	0+	0+	002	039	132	221	226	147	057	010	0+	0+	0+	5
	6	0+	0+	0+	010	057	147	226	221	132	039	002	0+	0+	6
	7	0+	0+	0+	002	017	070	161	236	220	111	016	001	0+	7
	8	0+	0+	0+	0+	004	023	081	177	257	221	071	014	0+	8
	9	0+	0+	0+	0+	001	005	027	089	200	295	213	087	005	9
	10	0+	0+	0+	0+	0+	001	005	027	093	236	384	329	099	10
	11	0+	0+	0+	0+	0+	0+	0+	004	020	086	314	569	895	11
12	0	886	540	282	069	014	002	0+	0+	0+	0+	0+	0+	0+	0
	1	107	341	377	206	071	017	003	0+	0+	0+	0+	0+	0+	1
	2	006	099	230	283	168	064	016	002	0+	0+	0+	0+	0+	2
	3	0+	017	085	236	240	142	054	012	001	0+	0+	0+	0+	3
	4	0+	002	021	133	231	213	121	042	008	001	0+	0+	0+	4
	5	0+	0+	004	053	158	227	193	101	029	003	0+	0+	0+	5
	6	0+	0+	0+	016	079	177	226	177	079	016	0+	0+	0+	6
	7	0+	0+	0+	003	029	101	193	227	158	053	004	0+	0+	7
	8	0+	0+	0+	001	008	042	121	213	231	133	021	002	0+	8
	9	0+	0+	0+	0+	001	012	054	142	240	236	085	017	0+	9

TABLE III.   **THE BINOMIAL DISTRIBUTION.**

n	X	.01	.05	.10	.20	.30	.40	p .50	.60	.70	.80	.90	.95	.99	X
12	10	0+	0+	0+	0+	0+	002	016	064	168	283	230	099	006	10
	11	0+	0+	0+	0+	0+	0+	003	017	071	206	377	341	107	11
	12	0+	0+	0+	0+	0+	0+	0+	002	014	069	282	540	886	12
13	0	878	513	254	055	010	001	0+	0+	0+	0+	0+	0+	0+	0
	1	115	351	367	179	054	011	002	0+	0+	0+	0+	0+	0+	1
	2	007	111	245	139	045	010	001	0+	0+	0+	0+	0+	0+	2
	3	0+	021	100	246	218	111	035	006	001	0+	0+	0+	0+	3
	4	0+	003	028	154	234	184	087	024	003	0+	0+	0+	0+	4
	5	0+	0+	006	069	180	221	157	066	014	001	0+	0+	0+	5
	6	0+	0+	001	023	103	197	209	131	044	006	0+	0+	0+	6
	7	0+	0+	0+	006	044	131	209	197	103	023	001	0+	0+	7
	8	0+	0+	0+	001	014	066	157	221	180	069	006	0+	0+	8
	9	0+	0+	0+	0+	003	024	087	184	234	154	028	003	0+	9
	10	0+	0+	0+	0+	001	006	035	111	218	246	100	021	0+	10
	11	0+	0+	0+	0+	0+	001	010	045	139	268	245	111	007	11
	12	0+	0+	0+	0+	0+	0+	002	011	054	179	367	351	115	12
	13	0+	0+	0+	0+	0+	0+	0+	001	010	055	254	513	878	13
14	0	869	488	229	044	007	001	0+	0+	0+	0+	0+	0+	0+	0
	1	123	359	356	154	041	007	001	0+	0+	0+	0+	0+	0+	1
	2	008	123	257	250	113	032	006	001	0+	0+	0+	0+	0+	2
	3	0+	026	114	250	194	085	022	003	0+	0+	0+	0+	0+	3
	4	0+	004	035	172	229	155	061	014	001	0+	0+	0+	0+	4
	5	0+	0+	008	086	196	207	122	041	007	0+	0+	0+	0+	5
	6	0+	0+	001	032	126	207	183	092	023	002	0+	0+	0+	6
	7	0+	0+	0+	009	062	157	209	157	062	009	0+	0+	0+	7
	8	0+	0+	0+	002	023	092	183	207	126	032	001	0+	0+	8
	9	0+	0+	0+	0+	007	041	122	207	196	086	008	0+	0+	9
	10	0+	0+	0+	0+	001	014	061	155	229	172	035	004	0+	10
	11	0+	0+	0+	0+	0+	003	022	085	194	250	114	026	0+	11
	12	0+	0+	0+	0+	0+	001	006	032	113	250	257	123	008	12
	13	0+	0+	0+	0+	0+	0+	001	007	041	154	356	359	123	13
	14	0+	0+	0+	0+	0+	0+	0+	001	007	044	229	488	869	14
15	0	860	463	206	035	005	0+	0+	0+	0+	0+	0+	0+	0+	0
	1	130	366	343	132	031	005	0+	0+	0+	0+	0+	0+	0+	1
	2	009	135	267	231	092	022	003	0+	0+	0+	0+	0+	0+	2
	3	0+	031	129	250	170	063	014	002	0+	0+	0+	0+	0+	3
	4	0+	005	043	188	219	127	042	007	001	0+	0+	0+	0+	4
	5	0+	001	010	103	206	186	092	024	003	0+	0+	0+	0+	5
	6	0+	0+	002	043	147	207	153	061	012	001	0+	0+	0+	6
	7	0+	0+	0+	014	081	177	196	118	035	003	0+	0+	0+	7
	8	0+	0+	0+	003	035	118	196	177	081	014	0+	0+	0+	8
	9	0+	0+	0+	001	012	061	153	207	147	043	002	0+	0+	9

TABLE III.   THE BINOMIAL DISTRIBUTION.

n	X	.01	.05	.10	.20	.30	.40	p .50	.60	.70	.80	.90	.95	.99	X
15	10	0+	0+	0+	0+	003	024	092	186	206	103	010	001	0+	10
	11	0+	0+	0+	0+	001	007	042	127	219	188	043	005	0+	11
	12	0+	0+	0+	0+	0+	002	014	063	170	250	129	031	0+	12
	13	0+	0+	0+	0+	0+	0+	003	022	092	231	267	135	009	13
	14	0+	0+	0+	0+	0+	0+	0+	005	031	132	343	366	130	14
	15	0+	0+	0+	0+	0+	0+	0+	0+	005	035	206	463	860	15
16	0	851	440	185	028	003	0+	0+	0+	0+	0+	0+	0+	0+	0
	1	138	371	329	113	023	003	0+	0+	0+	0+	0+	0+	0+	1
	2	010	146	275	211	073	015	002	0+	0+	0+	0+	0+	0+	2
	3	0+	036	142	246	146	047	009	001	0+	0+	0+	0+	0+	3
	4	0+	006	051	200	204	101	028	004	0+	0+	0+	0+	0+	4
	5	0+	001	014	120	210	162	067	014	001	0+	0+	0+	0+	5
	6	0+	0+	003	055	165	198	122	039	006	0+	0+	0+	0+	6
	7	0+	0+	0+	020	101	189	175	084	019	001	0+	0+	0+	7
	8	0+	0+	0+	006	049	142	196	142	049	006	0+	0+	0+	8
	9	0+	0+	0+	001	019	084	175	189	101	020	0+	0+	0+	9
	10	0+	0+	0+	0+	006	039	122	198	165	055	003	0+	0+	10
	11	0+	0+	0+	0+	001	014	067	162	210	120	014	001	0+	11
	12	0+	0+	0+	0+	0+	004	028	101	204	200	051	006	0+	12
	13	0+	0+	0+	0+	0+	001	009	047	146	246	142	036	0+	13
	14	0+	0+	0+	0+	0+	0+	002	015	073	211	275	146	010	14
	15	0+	0+	0+	0+	0+	0+	0+	003	023	113	329	371	138	15
	16	0+	0+	0+	0+	0+	0+	0+	0+	003	028	185	440	851	16
17	0	843	418	167	023	002	0+	0+	0+	0+	0+	0+	0+	0+	0
	1	145	374	315	096	017	002	0+	0+	0+	0+	0+	0+	0+	1
	2	012	158	280	191	058	010	001	0+	0+	0+	0+	0+	0+	2
	3	001	041	156	239	125	034	005	0+	0+	0+	0+	0+	0+	3
	4	0+	008	060	209	187	080	018	002	0+	0+	0+	0+	0+	4
	5	0+	001	017	136	208	138	047	008	001	0+	0+	0+	0+	5
	6	0+	0+	004	068	178	184	094	024	003	0+	0+	0+	0+	6
	7	0+	0+	001	027	120	193	148	057	009	0+	0+	0+	0+	7
	8	0+	0+	0+	008	064	161	185	107	028	002	0+	0+	0+	8
	9	0+	0+	0+	002	028	107	185	161	064	008	0+	0+	0+	9
	10	0+	0+	0+	0+	009	057	148	193	120	027	001	0+	0+	10
	11	0+	0+	0+	0+	003	024	094	184	178	068	004	0+	0+	11
	12	0+	0+	0+	0+	001	008	047	138	208	136	017	001	0+	12
	13	0+	0+	0+	0+	0+	002	018	080	187	209	060	008	0+	13
	14	0+	0+	0+	0+	0+	0+	005	034	125	239	156	041	001	14
	15	0+	0+	0+	0+	0+	0+	001	010	058	191	280	158	012	15
	16	0+	0+	0+	0+	0+	0+	0+	002	017	096	315	374	145	16
	17	0+	0+	0+	0+	0+	0+	0+	0+	002	023	167	418	843	17

TABLE III.   **THE BINOMIAL DISTRIBUTION.**

n	X	.01	.05	.10	.20	.30	.40	p .50	.60	.70	.80	.90	.95	.99	X
18	0	835	397	150	018	002	0+	0+	0+	0+	0+	0+	0+	0+	0
	1	152	376	300	081	013	001	0+	0+	0+	0+	0+	0+	0+	1
	2	013	168	284	172	046	007	001	0+	0+	0+	0+	0+	0+	2
	3	001	047	168	230	105	025	003	0+	0+	0+	0+	0+	0+	3
	4	0+	009	070	215	168	061	012	001	0+	0+	0+	0+	0+	4
	5	0+	001	022	151	202	115	033	004	0+	0+	0+	0+	0+	5
	6	0+	0+	005	082	187	166	071	015	001	0+	0+	0+	0+	6
	7	0+	0+	001	035	138	189	121	037	005	0+	0+	0+	0+	7
	8	0+	0+	0+	012	081	173	167	077	015	001	0+	0+	0+	8
	9	0+	0+	0+	003	039	128	185	128	039	003	0+	0+	0+	9
	10	0+	0+	0+	001	015	077	167	173	081	012	0+	0+	0+	10
	11	0+	0+	0+	0+	005	037	121	189	138	035	001	0+	0+	11
	12	0+	0+	0+	0+	001	015	071	166	187	082	005	0+	0+	12
	13	0+	0+	0+	0+	0+	004	033	115	202	151	022	001	0+	13
	14	0+	0+	0+	0+	0+	001	012	061	168	215	070	009	0+	14
	15	0+	0+	0+	0+	0+	0+	003	025	105	230	168	047	001	15
	16	0+	0+	0+	0+	0+	0+	001	007	046	172	284	168	013	16
	17	0+	0+	0+	0+	0+	0+	0+	001	013	081	300	376	152	17
	18	0+	0+	0+	0+	0+	0+	0+	0+	002	018	150	397	835	18
19	0	826	377	135	014	001	0+	0+	0+	0+	0+	0+	0+	0+	0
	1	159	377	285	068	009	001	0+	0+	0+	0+	0+	0+	0+	1
	2	014	179	285	154	036	005	0+	0+	0+	0+	0+	0+	0+	2
	3	001	053	180	218	087	017	002	0+	0+	0+	0+	0+	0+	3
	4	0+	011	080	218	149	047	007	001	0+	0+	0+	0+	0+	4
	5	0+	002	027	164	192	093	022	002	0+	0+	0+	0+	0+	5
	6	0+	0+	007	095	192	145	052	008	001	0+	0+	0+	0+	6
	7	0+	0+	001	044	153	180	096	024	002	0+	0+	0+	0+	7
	8	0+	0+	0+	017	098	180	144	053	008	0+	0+	0+	0+	8
	9	0+	0+	0+	005	051	146	176	098	022	001	0+	0+	0+	9
	10	0+	0+	0+	001	022	098	176	146	051	005	0+	0+	0+	10
	11	0+	0+	0+	0+	008	053	144	180	098	017	0+	0+	0+	11
	12	0+	0+	0+	0+	002	024	096	180	153	044	001	0+	0+	12
	13	0+	0+	0+	0+	001	008	052	145	192	095	007	0+	0+	13
	14	0+	0+	0+	0+	0+	002	022	093	192	164	027	002	0+	14
	15	0+	0+	0+	0+	0+	001	007	047	149	218	080	011	0+	15
	16	0+	0+	0+	0+	0+	0+	002	017	087	218	180	053	001	16
	17	0+	0+	0+	0+	0+	0+	0+	005	036	154	285	179	014	17
	18	0+	0+	0+	0+	0+	0+	0+	001	009	068	285	377	159	18
	19	0+	0+	0+	0+	0+	0+	0+	0+	001	014	135	377	826	19
20	0	818	358	122	012	001	0+	0+	0+	0+	0+	0+	0+	0+	0
	1	165	377	270	058	007	0+	0+	0+	0+	0+	0+	0+	0+	1
	2	016	189	285	137	028	003	0+	0+	0+	0+	0+	0+	0+	2
	3	001	060	190	205	072	012	001	0+	0+	0+	0+	0+	0+	3
	4	0+	013	090	218	130	035	005	0+	0+	0+	0+	0+	0+	4

TABLE III.   **THE BINOMIAL DISTRIBUTION.**

n	X	.01	.05	.10	.20	.30	.40	p .50	.60	.70	.80	.90	.95	.99	X
20	5	0+	002	032	175	179	075	015	001	0+	0+	0+	0+	0+	5
	6	0+	0+	009	109	192	124	037	005	0+	0+	0+	0+	0+	6
	7	0+	0+	002	055	164	166	074	015	001	0+	0+	0+	0+	7
	8	0+	0+	0+	022	114	180	120	035	004	0+	0+	0+	0+	8
	9	0+	0+	0+	007	065	160	160	071	012	0+	0+	0+	0+	9
	10	0+	0+	0+	002	031	117	176	117	031	002	0+	0+	0+	10
	11	0+	0+	0+	0+	012	071	160	160	065	007	0+	0+	0+	11
	12	0+	0+	0+	0+	004	035	120	180	114	022	0+	0+	0+	12
	13	0+	0+	0+	0+	001	015	074	166	164	055	002	0+	0+	13
	14	0+	0+	0+	0+	0+	005	037	124	192	109	009	0+	0+	14
	15	0+	0+	0+	0+	0+	001	015	075	179	175	032	002	0+	15
	16	0+	0+	0+	0+	0+	0+	005	035	130	218	090	013	0+	16
	17	0+	0+	0+	0+	0+	0+	001	012	072	205	190	060	001	17
	18	0+	0+	0+	0+	0+	0+	0+	003	028	137	285	189	016	18
	19	0+	0+	0+	0+	0+	0+·	0+	0+	007	058	270	377	165	19
	20	0+	0+	0+	0+	0+	0+	0+	0+	001	012	122	358	818	20
21	0	810	341	109	009	001	0+	0+	0+	0+	0+	0+	0+	0+	0
	1	172	376	255	048	005	0+	0+	0+	0+	0+	0+	0+	0+	1
	2	017	198	284	121	022	002	0+	0+	0+	0+	0+	0+	0+	2
	3	001	066	200	192	058	009	001	0+	0+	0+	0+	0+	0+	3
	4	0+	016	100	216	113	026	003	0+	0+	0+	0+	0+	0+	4
	5	0+	003	038	183	164	059	010	001	0+	0+	0+	0+	0+	5
	6	0+	0+	011	122	188	105	026	003	0+	0+	0+	0+	0+	6
	7	0+	0+	003	065	172	149	055	009	0+	0+	0+	0+	0+	7
	8	0+	0+	001	029	129	174	097	023	002	0+	0+	0+	0+	8
	9	0+	0+	0+	010	080	168	140	050	006	0+	0+	0+	0+	9
	10	0+	0+	0+	003	041	134	168	089	018	001	0+	0+	0+	10
	11	0+	0+	0+	001	018	089	168	134	041	003	0+	0+	0+	11
	12	0+	0+	0+	0+	006	050	140	168	080	010	0+	0+	0+	12
	13	0+	0+	0+	0+	002	023	097	174	129	029	001	0+	0+	13
	14	0+	0+	0+	0+	0+	009	055	149	172	065	003	0+	0+	14
	15	0+	0+	0+	0+	0+	003	026	105	188	122	011	0+	0+	15
	16	0+	0+	0+	0+	0+	001	010	059	164	183	038	003	0+	16
	17	0+	0+	0+	0+	0+	0+	003	026	113	216	100	016	0+	17
	18	0+	0+	0+	0+	0+	0+	001	009	058	192	200	066	001	18
	19	0+	0+	0+	0+	0+	0+	0+	002	022	121	284	198	017	19
	20	0+	0+	0+	0+	0+	0+	0+	0+	005	048	255	376	172	20
	21	0+	0+	0+	0+	0+	0+	0+	0+	001	009	109	341	810	21
22	0	802	324	098	007	0+	0+	0+	0+	0+	0+	0+	0+	0+	0
	1	178	375	241	041	004	0+	0+	0+	0+	0+	0+	0+	0+	1
	2	019	207	281	107	017	001	0+	0+	0+	0+	0+	0+	0+	2
	3	001	073	208	178	047	006	0+	0+	0+	0+	0+	0+	0+	3
	4	0+	018	110	211	096	019	002	0+	0+	0+	0+	0+	0+	4

TABLE   III.   **THE BINOMIAL DISTRIBUTION.**

n	X	.01	.05	.10	.20	.30	.40	p .50	.60	.70	.80	.90	.95	.99	X
22	5	0+	003	044	190	149	046	006	0+	0+	0+	0+	0+	0+	5
	6	0+	001	014	134	181	086	018	001	0+	0+	0+	0+	0+	6
	7	0+	0+	004	077	177	131	041	005	0+	0+	0+	0+	0+	7
	8	0+	0+	001	036	142	164	076	014	001	0+	0+	0+	0+	8
	9	0+	0+	0+	014	095	170	119	034	003	0+	0+	0+	0+	9
	10	0+	0+	0+	005	053	148	154	066	010	0+	0+	0+	0+	10
	11	0+	0+	0+	001	025	107	168	107	025	001	0+	0+	0+	11
	12	0+	0+	0+	0+	010	066	154	148	053	005	0+	0+	0+	12
	13	0+	0+	0+	0+	003	034	119	170	095	014	0+	0+	0+	13
	14	0+	0+	0+	0+	001	014	076	164	142	036	001	0+	0+	14
	15	0+	0+	0+	0+	0+	005	041	131	177	077	004	0+	0+	15
	16	0+	0+	0+	0+	0+	001	018	086	181	134	014	001	0+	16
	17	0+	0+	0+	0+	0+	0+	006	046	149	190	044	003	0+	17
	18	0+	0+	0+	0+	0+	0+	002	019	096	211	110	018	0+	18
	19	0+	0+	0+	0+	0+	0+	0+	006	047	178	208	073	001	19
	20	0+	0+	0+	0+	0+	0+	0+	001	017	107	281	207	019	20
	21	0+	0+	0+	0+	0+	0+	0+	0+	004	041	241	375	178	21
	22	0+	0+	0+	0+	0+	0+	0+	0+	0+	007	098	324	802	22
23	0	794	307	089	006	0+	0+	0+	0+	0+	0+	0+	0+	0+	0
	1	184	372	226	034	003	0+	0+	0+	0+	0+	0+	0+	0+	1
	2	020	215	277	093	013	001	0+	0+	0+	0+	0+	0+	0+	2
	3	001	079	215	163	038	004	0+	0+	0+	0+	0+	0+	0+	3
	4	0+	021	120	204	082	014	001	0+	0+	0+	0+	0+	0+	4
	5	0+	004	051	194	133	035	004	0+	0+	0+	0+	0+	0+	5
	6	0+	001	017	145	171	070	012	001	0+	0+	0+	0+	0+	6
	7	0+	0+	005	088	178	113	029	003	0+	0+	0+	0+	0+	7
	8	0+	0+	001	044	153	151	058	009	0+	0+	0+	0+	0+	8
	9	0+	0+	0+	018	109	168	097	022	002	0+	0+	0+	0+	9
	10	0+	0+	0+	006	065	157	136	046	005	0+	0+	0+	0+	10
	11	0+	0+	0+	002	033	123	161	082	014	0+	0+	0+	0+	11
	12	0+	0+	0+	0+	014	082	161	123	033	002	0+	0+	0+	12
	13	0+	0+	0+	0+	005	046	136	157	065	006	0+	0+	0+	13
	14	0+	0+	0+	0+	002	022	097	168	109	018	0+	0+	0+	14
	15	0+	0+	0+	0+	0+	009	058	151	153	044	001	0+	0+	15
	16	0+	0+	0+	0+	0+	003	029	113	178	088	005	0+	0+	16
	17	0+	0+	0+	0+	0+	001	012	070	171	145	017	001	0+	17
	18	0+	0+	0+	0+	0+	0+	004	035	133	194	051	004	0+	18
	19	0+	0+	0+	0+	0+	0+	001	014	082	204	120	021	0+	19
	20	0+	0+	0+	0+	0+	0+	0+	004	038	163	215	079	001	20
	21	0+	0+	0+	0+	0+	0+	0+	001	013	093	277	215	020	21
	22	0+	0+	0+	0+	0+	0+	0+	0+	003	034	226	372	184	22
	23	0+	0+	0+	0+	0+	0+	0+	0+	0+	006	089	307	794	23

TABLE   III.   **THE BINOMIAL DISTRIBUTION.**

n	X	.01	.05	.10	.20	.30	.40	p .50	.60	.70	.80	.90	.95	.99	X
24	0	786	292	080	005	0+	0+	0+	0+	0+	0+	0+	0+	0+	0
	1	190	369	213	028	002	0+	0+	0+	0+	0+	0+	0+	0+	1
	2	022	223	272	081	010	001	0+	0+	0+	0+	0+	0+	0+	2
	3	002	086	221	149	031	003	0+	0+	0+	0+	0+	0+	0+	3
	4	0+	024	129	196	069	010	001	0+	0+	0+	0+	0+	0+	4
	5	0+	005	057	196	118	027	003	0+	0+	0+	0+	0+	0+	5
	6	0+	001	020	155	160	056	008	0+	0+	0+	0+	0+	0+	6
	7	0+	0+	006	100	176	096	021	002	0+	0+	0+	0+	0+	7
	8	0+	0+	001	053	160	136	044	005	0+	0+	0+	0+	0+	8
	9	0+	0+	0+	024	122	161	078	014	001	0+	0+	0+	0+	9
	10	0+	0+	0+	009	079	161	117	032	003	0+	0+	0+	0+	10
	11	0+	0+	0+	003	043	137	149	061	008	0+	0+	0+	0+	11
	12	0+	0+	0+	001	020	099	161	099	020	001	0+	0+	0+	12
	13	0+	0+	0+	0+	008	061	149	137	043	003	0+	0+	0+	13
	14	0+	0+	0+	0+	003	032	117	161	079	009	0+	0+	0+	14
	15	0+	0+	0+	0+	001	014	078	161	122	024	0+	0+	0+	15
	16	0+	0+	0+	0+	0+	005	044	136	160	053	001	0+	0+	16
	17	0+	0+	0+	0+	0+	002	021	096	176	100	006	0+	0+	17
	18	0+	0+	0+	0+	0+	0+	008	056	160	155	020	001	0+	18
	19	0+	0+	0+	0+	0+	0+	003	027	118	196	057	005	0+	19
	20	0+	0+	0+	0+	0+	0+	001	010	069	196	129	024	0+	20
	21	0+	0+	0+	0+	0+	0+	0+	003	031	149	221	086	002	21
	22	0+	0+	0+	0+	0+	0+	0+	001	010	081	272	223	022	22
	23	0+	0+	0+	0+	0+	0+	0+	0+	002	028	213	369	190	23
	24	0+	0+	0+	0+	0+	0+	0+	0+	0+	005	080	292	786	24
25	0	778	277	072	004	0+	0+	0+	0+	0+	0+	0+	0+	0+	0
	1	196	365	199	024	001	0+	0+	0+	0+	0+	0+	0+	0+	1
	2	024	231	266	071	007	0+	0+	0+	0+	0+	0+	0+	0+	2
	3	002	093	226	136	024	002	0+	0+	0+	0+	0+	0+	0+	3
	4	0+	027	138	187	057	007	0+	0+	0+	0+	0+	0+	0+	4
	5	0+	006	065	196	103	020	002	0+	0+	0+	0+	0+	0+	5
	6	0+	001	024	163	147	044	005	0+	0+	0+	0+	0+	0+	6
	7	0+	0+	007	111	171	080	014	001	0+	0+	0+	0+	0+	7
	8	0+	0+	002	062	165	120	032	003	0+	0+	0+	0+	0+	8
	9	0+	0+	0+	029	134	151	061	009	0+	0+	0+	0+	0+	9
	10	0+	0+	0+	012	092	161	097	021	001	0+	0+	0+	0+	10
	11	0+	0+	0+	004	054	147	133	043	004	0+	0+	0+	0+	11
	12	0+	0+	0+	001	027	114	155	076	011	0+	0+	0+	0+	12
	13	0+	0+	0+	0+	011	076	155	114	027	001	0+	0+	0+	13
	14	0+	0+	0+	0+	004	043	133	147	054	004	0+	0+	0+	14
	15	0+	0+	0+	0+	001	021	097	161	092	012	0+	0+	0+	15
	16	0+	0+	0+	0+	0+	009	061	151	134	029	0+	0+	0+	16
	17	0+	0+	0+	0+	0+	003	032	120	165	062	002	0+	0+	17
	18	0+	0+	0+	0+	0+	001	014	080	171	111	007	0+	0+	18
	19	0+	0+	0+	0+	0+	0+	005	044	147	163	024	001	0+	19

TABLE III.   **THE BINOMIAL DISTRIBUTION.**

n	X	.01	.05	.10	.20	.30	.40	p .50	.60	.70	.80	.90	.95	.99	X
25	20	0+	0+	0+	0+	0+	0+	002	020	103	196	065	006	0+	20
	21	0+	0+	0+	0+	0+	0+	0+	007	057	187	138	027	0+	21
	22	0+	0+	0+	0+	0+	0+	0+	002	024	136	226	093	002	22
	23	0+	0+	0+	0+	0+	0+	0+	0+	007	071	266	231	024	23
	24	0+	0+	0+	0+	0+	0+	0+	0+	001	024	199	365	196	24
	25	0+	0+	0+	0+	0+	0+	0+	0+	0+	004	072	277	778	25

TABLE IV.

THE CHI-SQUARE DISTRIBUTION.

PERCENTILE VALUES (χ^2_p)
for
THE CHI-SQUARE DISTRIBUTION
with ν degrees of freedom
(shaded area $=p$)

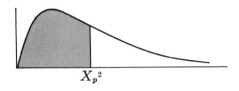

$$X_p^2$$

ν	$\chi^2_{.995}$	$\chi^2_{.99}$	$\chi^2_{.975}$	$\chi^2_{.95}$	$\chi^2_{.90}$	$\chi^2_{.75}$	$\chi^2_{.50}$	$\chi^2_{.25}$	$\chi^2_{.10}$	$\chi^2_{.05}$	$\chi^2_{.025}$	$\chi^2_{.01}$	$\chi^2_{.005}$
1	7.88	6.63	5.02	3.84	2.71	1.32	.455	.102	.0158	.0039	.0010	.0002	.0000
2	10.6	9.21	7.38	5.99	4.61	2.77	1.39	.575	.211	.103	.0506	.0201	.0100
3	12.8	11.3	9.35	7.81	6.25	4.11	2.37	1.21	.584	.352	.216	.115	.072
4	14.9	13.3	11.1	9.49	7.78	5.39	3.36	1.92	1.06	.711	.484	.297	.207
5	16.7	15.1	12.8	11.1	9.24	6.63	4.35	2.67	1.61	1.15	.831	.554	.412
6	18.5	16.8	14.4	12.6	10.6	7.84	5.35	3.45	2.20	1.64	1.24	.872	.676
7	20.3	18.5	16.0	14.1	12.0	9.04	6.35	4.25	2.83	2.17	1.69	1.24	.989
8	22.0	20.1	17.5	15.5	13.4	10.2	7.34	5.07	3.49	2.73	2.18	1.65	1.34
9	23.6	21.7	19.0	16.9	14.7	11.4	8.34	5.90	4.17	3.33	2.70	2.09	1.73
10	25.2	23.2	20.5	18.3	16.0	12.5	9.34	6.74	4.87	3.94	3.25	2.56	2.16
11	26.8	24.7	21.9	19.7	17.3	13.7	10.3	7.58	5.58	4.57	3.82	3.05	2.60
12	28.3	26.2	23.3	21.0	18.5	14.8	11.3	8.44	6.30	5.23	4.40	3.57	3.07
13	29.8	27.7	24.7	22.4	19.8	16.0	12.3	9.30	7.04	5.89	5.01	4.11	3.57
14	31.3	29.1	26.1	23.7	21.1	17.1	13.3	10.2	7.79	6.57	5.63	4.66	4.07
15	32.8	30.6	27.5	25.0	22.3	18.2	14.3	11.0	8.55	7.26	6.26	5.23	4.60
16	34.3	32.0	28.8	26.3	23.5	19.4	15.3	11.9	9.31	7.96	6.91	5.81	5.14
17	35.7	33.4	30.2	27.6	24.8	20.5	16.3	12.8	10.1	8.67	7.56	6.41	5.70
18	37.2	34.8	31.5	28.9	26.0	21.6	17.3	13.7	10.9	9.39	8.23	7.01	6.26
19	38.6	36.2	32.9	30.1	27.2	22.7	18.3	14.6	11.7	10.1	8.91	7.63	6.84
20	40.0	37.6	34.2	31.4	28.4	23.8	19.3	15.5	12.4	10.9	9.59	8.26	7.43
21	41.4	38.9	35.5	32.7	29.6	24.9	20.3	16.3	13.2	11.6	10.3	8.90	8.03
22	42.8	40.3	36.8	33.9	30.8	26.0	21.3	17.2	14.0	12.3	11.0	9.54	8.64
23	44.2	41.6	38.1	35.2	32.0	27.1	22.3	18.1	14.8	13.1	11.7	10.2	9.26
24	45.6	43.0	39.4	36.4	33.2	28.2	23.3	19.0	15.7	13.8	12.4	10.9	9.89
25	46.9	44.3	40.6	37.7	34.4	29.3	24.3	19.9	16.5	14.6	13.1	11.5	10.5
26	48.3	45.6	41.9	38.9	35.6	30.4	25.3	20.8	17.3	15.4	13.8	12.2	11.2
27	49.6	47.0	43.2	40.1	36.7	31.5	26.3	21.7	18.1	16.2	14.6	12.9	11.8
28	51.0	48.3	44.5	41.3	37.9	32.6	27.3	22.7	18.9	16.9	15.3	13.6	12.5
29	52.3	49.6	45.7	42.6	39.1	33.7	28.3	23.6	19.8	17.7	16.0	14.3	13.1
30	53.7	50.9	47.0	43.8	40.3	34.8	29.3	24.5	20.6	18.5	16.8	15.0	13.8
40	66.8	63.7	59.3	55.8	51.8	45.6	39.3	33.7	29.1	26.5	24.4	22.2	20.7
50	79.5	76.2	71.4	67.5	63.2	56.3	49.3	42.9	37.7	34.8	32.4	29.7	28.0
60	92.0	88.4	83.3	79.1	74.4	67.0	59.3	52.3	46.5	43.2	40.5	37.5	35.5
70	104.2	100.4	95.0	90.5	85.5	77.6	69.3	61.7	55.3	51.7	48.8	45.4	43.3
80	116.3	112.3	106.6	101.9	96.6	88.1	79.3	71.1	64.3	60.4	57.2	53.5	51.2
90	128.3	124.1	118.1	113.1	107.6	98.6	89.3	80.6	73.3	69.1	65.6	61.8	59.2
100	140.2	135.8	129.6	124.3	118.5	109.1	99.3	90.1	82.4	77.9	74.2	70.1	67.3

TABLE V.   **THE UNIT NORMAL DISTRIBUTION.**

AREAS
under the
STANDARD
NORMAL CURVE
from 0 to z

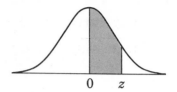

z	0	1	2	3	4	5	6	7	8	9
0.0	.0000	.0040	.0080	.0120	.0160	.0199	.0239	.0279	.0319	.0359
0.1	.0398	.0438	.0478	.0517	.0557	.0596	.0636	.0675	.0714	.0754
0.2	.0793	.0832	.0871	.0910	.0948	.0987	.1026	.1064	.1103	.1141
0.3	.1179	.1217	.1255	.1293	.1331	.1368	.1406	.1443	.1480	.1517
0.4	.1554	.1591	.1628	.1664	.1700	.1736	.1772	.1808	.1844	.1879
0.5	.1915	.1950	.1985	.2019	.2054	.2088	.2123	.2157	.2190	.2224
0.6	.2258	.2291	.2324	.2357	.2389	.2422	.2454	.2486	.2518	.2549
0.7	.2580	.2612	.2642	.2673	.2704	.2734	.2764	.2794	.2823	.2852
0.8	.2881	.2910	.2939	.2967	.2996	.3023	.3051	.3078	.3106	.3133
0.9	.3159	.3186	.3212	.3238	.3264	.3289	.3315	.3340	.3365	.3389
1.0	.3413	.3438	.3461	.3485	.3508	.3531	.3554	.3577	.3599	.3621
1.1	.3643	.3665	.3686	.3708	.3729	.3749	.3770	.3790	.3810	.3830
1.2	.3849	.3869	.3888	.3907	.3925	.3944	.3962	.3980	.3997	.4015
1.3	.4032	.4049	.4066	.4082	.4099	.4115	.4131	.4147	.4162	.4177
1.4	.4192	.4207	.4222	.4236	.4251	.4265	.4279	.4292	.4306	.4319
1.5	.4332	.4345	.4357	.4370	.4382	.4394	.4406	.4418	.4429	.4441
1.6	.4452	.4463	.4474	.4484	.4495	.4505	.4515	.4525	.4535	.4545
1.7	.4554	.4564	.4573	.4582	.4591	.4599	.4608	.4616	.4625	.4633
1.8	.4641	.4649	.4656	.4664	.4671	.4678	.4686	.4693	.4699	.4706
1.9	.4713	.4719	.4726	.4732	.4738	.4744	.4750	.4756	.4761	.4767
2.0	.4772	.4778	.4783	.4788	.4793	.4798	.4803	.4808	.4812	.4817
2.1	.4821	.4826	.4830	.4834	.4838	.4842	.4846	.4850	.4854	.4857
2.2	.4861	.4864	.4868	.4871	.4875	.4878	.4881	.4884	.4887	.4890
2.3	.4893	.4896	.4898	.4901	.4904	.4906	.4909	.4911	.4913	.4916
2.4	.4918	.4920	.4922	.4925	.4927	.4929	.4931	.4932	.4934	.4936
2.5	.4938	.4940	.4941	.4943	.4945	.4946	.4948	.4949	.4951	.4952
2.6	.4953	.4955	.4956	.4957	.4959	.4960	.4961	.4962	.4963	.4964
2.7	.4965	.4966	.4967	.4968	.4969	.4970	.4971	.4972	.4973	.4974
2.8	.4974	.4975	.4976	.4977	.4977	.4978	.4979	.4979	.4980	.4981
2.9	.4981	.4982	.4982	.4983	.4984	.4984	.4985	.4985	.4986	.4986
3.0	.4987	.4987	.4987	.4988	.4988	.4989	.4989	.4989	.4990	.4990
3.1	.4990	.4991	.4991	.4991	.4992	.4992	.4992	.4992	.4993	.4993
3.2	.4993	.4993	.4994	.4994	.4994	.4994	.4994	.4995	.4995	.4995
3.3	.4995	.4995	.4995	.4996	.4996	.4996	.4996	.4996	.4996	.4997
3.4	.4997	.4997	.4997	.4997	.4997	.4997	.4997	.4997	.4997	.4998
3.5	.4998	.4998	.4998	.4998	.4998	.4998	.4998	.4998	.4998	.4998
3.6	.4998	.4998	.4999	.4999	.4999	.4999	.4999	.4999	.4999	.4999
3.7	.4999	.4999	.4999	.4999	.4999	.4999	.4999	.4999	.4999	.4999
3.8	.4999	.4999	.4999	.4999	.4999	.4999	.4999	.4999	.4999	.4999
3.9	.5000	.5000	.5000	.5000	.5000	.5000	.5000	.5000	.5000	.5000

TABLE   VI.   **THE STUDENT'S _t_ DISTRIBUTION.**

PERCENTILE VALUES (t_p)
for
STUDENT'S t DISTRIBUTION
with ν degrees of freedom
(shaded area $= p$)

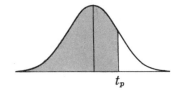

t_p

ν	$t_{.995}$	$t_{.99}$	$t_{.975}$	$t_{.95}$	$t_{.90}$	$t_{.80}$	$t_{.75}$	$t_{.70}$	$t_{.60}$	$t_{.55}$
1	63.66	31.82	12.71	6.31	3.08	1.376	1.000	.727	.325	.158
2	9.92	6.96	4.30	2.92	1.89	1.061	.816	.617	.289	.142
3	5.84	4.54	3.18	2.35	1.64	.978	.765	.584	.277	.137
4	4.60	3.75	2.78	2.13	1.53	.941	.741	.569	.271	.134
5	4.03	3.36	2.57	2.02	1.48	.920	.727	.559	.267	.132
6	3.71	3.14	2.45	1.94	1.44	.906	.718	.553	.265	.131
7	3.50	3.00	2.36	1.90	1.42	.896	.711	.549	.263	.130
8	3.36	2.90	2.31	1.86	1.40	.889	.706	.546	.262	.130
9	3.25	2.82	2.26	1.83	1.38	.883	.703	.543	.261	.129
10	3.17	2.76	2.23	1.81	1.37	.879	.700	.542	.260	.129
11	3.11	2.72	2.20	1.80	1.36	.876	.697	.540	.260	.129
12	3.06	2.68	2.18	1.78	1.36	.873	.695	.539	.259	.128
13	3.01	2.65	2.16	1.77	1.35	.870	.694	.538	.259	.128
14	2.98	2.62	2.14	1.76	1.34	.868	.692	.537	.258	.128
15	2.95	2.60	2.13	1.75	1.34	.866	.691	.536	.258	.128
16	2.92	2.58	2.12	1.75	1.34	.865	.690	.535	.258	.128
17	2.90	2.57	2.11	1.74	1.33	.863	.689	.534	.257	.128
18	2.88	2.55	2.10	1.73	1.33	.862	.688	.534	.257	.127
19	2.86	2.54	2.09	1.73	1.33	.861	.688	.533	.257	.127
20	2.84	2.53	2.09	1.72	1.32	.860	.687	.533	.257	.127
21	2.83	2.52	2.08	1.72	1.32	.859	.686	.532	.257	.127
22	2.82	2.51	2.07	1.72	1.32	.858	.686	.532	.256	.127
23	2.81	2.50	2.07	1.71	1.32	.858	.685	.532	.256	.127
24	2.80	2.49	2.06	1.71	1.32	.857	.685	.531	.256	.127
25	2.79	2.48	2.06	1.71	1.32	.856	.684	.531	.256	.127
26	2.78	2.48	2.06	1.71	1.32	.856	.684	.531	.256	.127
27	2.77	2.47	2.05	1.70	1.31	.855	.684	.531	.256	.127
28	2.76	2.47	2.05	1.70	1.31	.855	.683	.530	.256	.127
29	2.76	2.46	2.04	1.70	1.31	.854	.683	.530	.256	.127
30	2.75	2.46	2.04	1.70	1.31	.854	.683	.530	.256	.127
40	2.70	2.42	2.02	1.68	1.30	.851	.681	.529	.255	.126
60	2.66	2.39	2.00	1.67	1.30	.848	.679	.527	.254	.126
120	2.62	2.36	1.98	1.66	1.29	.845	.677	.526	.254	.126
∞	2.58	2.33	1.96	1.645	1.28	.842	.674	.524	.253	.126

Table VI is taken from Table III of R. A. Fisher & F. Yates: _Statistical Tables for Biological, Agricultural, and Medical Research_, published by Oliver & Body Ltd., Edinburgh, Scotland, and by permission of the authors and publishers.

TABLE VII.   5% (Roman Type) and 1% (Boldface Type) Points for the Distribution of F   **F DISTRIBUTION.**

Degrees of freedom for greater mean square (each cell: 5% / **1%**)

Degrees of freedom for lesser mean square	1	2	3	4	5	6	7	8	9	10	11	12	14	16	20	24	30	40	50	75	100	200	500	∞
1	161 / **4052**	200 / **4999**	216 / **5403**	225 / **5625**	230 / **5764**	234 / **5859**	237 / **5928**	239 / **5981**	241 / **6022**	242 / **6056**	243 / **6082**	244 / **6106**	245 / **6142**	246 / **6169**	248 / **6208**	249 / **6234**	250 / **6258**	251 / **6286**	252 / **6302**	253 / **6323**	253 / **6334**	254 / **6352**	254 / **6361**	254 / **6366**
2	18.51 / **98.49**	19.00 / **99.01**	19.16 / **99.17**	19.25 / **99.25**	19.30 / **99.30**	19.33 / **99.33**	19.36 / **99.34**	19.37 / **99.36**	19.38 / **99.38**	19.39 / **99.40**	19.40 / **99.41**	19.41 / **99.42**	19.42 / **99.43**	19.43 / **99.44**	19.44 / **99.45**	19.45 / **99.46**	19.46 / **99.47**	19.47 / **99.48**	19.47 / **99.48**	19.48 / **99.49**	19.49 / **99.49**	19.49 / **99.49**	19.50 / **99.50**	19.50 / **99.50**
3	10.13 / **34.12**	9.55 / **30.81**	9.28 / **29.46**	9.12 / **28.71**	9.01 / **28.24**	8.94 / **27.91**	8.88 / **27.67**	8.84 / **27.49**	8.81 / **27.34**	8.78 / **27.23**	8.76 / **27.13**	8.74 / **27.05**	8.71 / **26.92**	8.69 / **26.83**	8.66 / **26.69**	8.64 / **26.60**	8.62 / **26.50**	8.60 / **26.41**	8.58 / **26.30**	8.57 / **26.27**	8.56 / **26.23**	8.54 / **26.18**	8.54 / **26.14**	8.53 / **26.12**
4	7.71 / **21.20**	6.94 / **18.00**	6.59 / **16.69**	6.39 / **15.98**	6.26 / **15.52**	6.16 / **15.21**	6.09 / **14.98**	6.04 / **14.80**	6.00 / **14.66**	5.96 / **14.54**	5.93 / **14.45**	5.91 / **14.37**	5.87 / **14.24**	5.84 / **14.15**	5.80 / **14.02**	5.77 / **13.93**	5.74 / **13.83**	5.71 / **13.74**	5.70 / **13.69**	5.68 / **13.61**	5.66 / **13.57**	5.65 / **13.52**	5.64 / **13.48**	5.63 / **13.46**
5	6.61 / **16.26**	5.79 / **13.27**	5.41 / **12.06**	5.19 / **11.39**	5.05 / **10.97**	4.95 / **10.67**	4.88 / **10.45**	4.82 / **10.27**	4.78 / **10.15**	4.74 / **10.05**	4.70 / **9.96**	4.68 / **9.89**	4.64 / **9.77**	4.60 / **9.68**	4.56 / **9.55**	4.53 / **9.47**	4.50 / **9.38**	4.46 / **9.29**	4.44 / **9.24**	4.42 / **9.17**	4.40 / **9.13**	4.38 / **9.07**	4.37 / **9.04**	4.36 / **9.02**
6	5.99 / **13.74**	5.14 / **10.92**	4.76 / **9.78**	4.53 / **9.15**	4.39 / **8.75**	4.28 / **8.47**	4.21 / **8.26**	4.15 / **8.10**	4.10 / **7.98**	4.06 / **7.87**	4.03 / **7.79**	4.00 / **7.72**	3.96 / **7.60**	3.92 / **7.52**	3.87 / **7.39**	3.84 / **7.31**	3.81 / **7.23**	3.77 / **7.14**	3.75 / **7.09**	3.72 / **7.02**	3.71 / **6.99**	3.69 / **6.94**	3.68 / **6.90**	3.67 / **6.88**
7	5.59 / **12.25**	4.74 / **9.55**	4.35 / **8.45**	4.12 / **7.85**	3.97 / **7.46**	3.87 / **7.19**	3.79 / **7.00**	3.73 / **6.84**	3.68 / **6.71**	3.63 / **6.62**	3.60 / **6.54**	3.57 / **6.47**	3.52 / **6.35**	3.49 / **6.27**	3.44 / **6.15**	3.41 / **6.07**	3.38 / **5.98**	3.34 / **5.90**	3.32 / **5.85**	3.29 / **5.78**	3.28 / **5.75**	3.25 / **5.70**	3.24 / **5.67**	3.23 / **5.65**
8	5.32 / **11.26**	4.46 / **8.65**	4.07 / **7.59**	3.84 / **7.01**	3.69 / **6.63**	3.58 / **6.37**	3.50 / **6.19**	3.44 / **6.03**	3.39 / **5.91**	3.34 / **5.82**	3.31 / **5.74**	3.28 / **5.67**	3.23 / **5.56**	3.20 / **5.48**	3.15 / **5.36**	3.12 / **5.28**	3.08 / **5.20**	3.05 / **5.11**	3.03 / **5.06**	3.00 / **5.00**	2.98 / **4.96**	2.96 / **4.91**	2.94 / **4.88**	2.93 / **4.86**
9	5.12 / **10.56**	4.26 / **8.02**	3.86 / **6.99**	3.63 / **6.42**	3.48 / **6.06**	3.37 / **5.80**	3.29 / **5.62**	3.23 / **5.47**	3.18 / **5.35**	3.13 / **5.26**	3.10 / **5.18**	3.07 / **5.11**	3.02 / **5.00**	2.98 / **4.92**	2.93 / **4.80**	2.90 / **4.73**	2.86 / **4.64**	2.82 / **4.56**	2.80 / **4.51**	2.77 / **4.45**	2.76 / **4.41**	2.73 / **4.36**	2.72 / **4.33**	2.71 / **4.31**
10	4.96 / **10.04**	4.10 / **7.56**	3.71 / **6.55**	3.48 / **5.99**	3.33 / **5.64**	3.22 / **5.39**	3.14 / **5.21**	3.07 / **5.06**	3.02 / **4.95**	2.97 / **4.85**	2.94 / **4.78**	2.91 / **4.71**	2.86 / **4.60**	2.82 / **4.52**	2.77 / **4.41**	2.74 / **4.33**	2.70 / **4.25**	2.67 / **4.17**	2.64 / **4.12**	2.61 / **4.05**	2.59 / **4.01**	2.56 / **3.96**	2.55 / **3.93**	2.54 / **3.91**
11	4.84 / **9.65**	3.98 / **7.20**	3.59 / **6.22**	3.36 / **5.67**	3.20 / **5.32**	3.09 / **5.07**	3.01 / **4.88**	2.95 / **4.74**	2.90 / **4.63**	2.86 / **4.54**	2.82 / **4.46**	2.79 / **4.40**	2.74 / **4.29**	2.70 / **4.21**	2.65 / **4.10**	2.61 / **4.02**	2.57 / **3.94**	2.53 / **3.86**	2.50 / **3.80**	2.47 / **3.74**	2.45 / **3.70**	2.42 / **3.66**	2.41 / **3.62**	2.40 / **3.60**
12	4.75 / **9.33**	3.88 / **6.93**	3.49 / **5.95**	3.26 / **5.41**	3.11 / **5.06**	3.00 / **4.82**	2.92 / **4.65**	2.85 / **4.50**	2.80 / **4.39**	2.76 / **4.30**	2.72 / **4.22**	2.69 / **4.16**	2.64 / **4.05**	2.60 / **3.98**	2.54 / **3.86**	2.50 / **3.78**	2.46 / **3.70**	2.42 / **3.61**	2.40 / **3.56**	2.36 / **3.49**	2.35 / **3.46**	2.32 / **3.41**	2.31 / **3.38**	2.30 / **3.36**

df																								
13	4.67 / 9.07	3.80 / 6.70	3.41 / 5.74	3.18 / 5.20	3.02 / 4.86	2.92 / 4.62	2.84 / 4.44	2.77 / 4.30	2.72 / 4.19	2.67 / 4.10	2.63 / 4.02	2.60 / 3.96	2.55 / 3.85	2.51 / 3.78	2.46 / 3.67	2.42 / 3.59	2.38 / 3.51	2.34 / 3.42	2.32 / 3.37	2.28 / 3.30	2.26 / 3.27	2.24 / 3.21	2.22 / 3.18	2.21 / 3.16
14	4.60 / 8.86	3.74 / 6.51	3.34 / 5.56	3.11 / 5.03	2.96 / 4.69	2.85 / 4.46	2.77 / 4.28	2.70 / 4.14	2.65 / 4.03	2.60 / 3.94	2.56 / 3.86	2.53 / 3.80	2.48 / 3.70	2.44 / 3.62	2.39 / 3.51	2.35 / 3.43	2.31 / 3.34	2.27 / 3.26	2.24 / 3.21	2.21 / 3.14	2.19 / 3.11	2.16 / 3.06	2.14 / 3.02	2.13 / 3.00
15	4.54 / 8.68	3.68 / 6.36	3.29 / 5.42	3.06 / 4.89	2.90 / 4.56	2.79 / 4.32	2.70 / 4.14	2.64 / 4.00	2.59 / 3.89	2.55 / 3.80	2.51 / 3.73	2.48 / 3.67	2.43 / 3.56	2.39 / 3.48	2.33 / 3.36	2.29 / 3.29	2.25 / 3.20	2.21 / 3.12	2.18 / 3.07	2.15 / 3.00	2.12 / 2.97	2.10 / 2.92	2.08 / 2.89	2.07 / 2.87
16	4.49 / 8.53	3.63 / 6.23	3.24 / 5.29	3.01 / 4.77	2.85 / 4.44	2.74 / 4.20	2.66 / 4.03	2.59 / 3.89	2.54 / 3.78	2.49 / 3.69	2.45 / 3.61	2.42 / 3.55	2.37 / 3.45	2.33 / 3.37	2.28 / 3.25	2.24 / 3.18	2.20 / 3.10	2.16 / 3.01	2.13 / 2.96	2.09 / 2.89	2.07 / 2.86	2.04 / 2.80	2.02 / 2.77	2.01 / 2.75
17	4.45 / 8.40	3.59 / 6.11	3.20 / 5.18	2.96 / 4.67	2.81 / 4.34	2.70 / 4.10	2.62 / 3.93	2.55 / 3.79	2.50 / 3.68	2.45 / 3.59	2.41 / 3.52	2.38 / 3.45	2.33 / 3.35	2.29 / 3.27	2.23 / 3.16	2.19 / 3.08	2.15 / 3.00	2.11 / 2.92	2.08 / 2.86	2.04 / 2.79	2.02 / 2.76	1.99 / 2.70	1.97 / 2.67	1.96 / 2.65
18	4.41 / 8.28	3.55 / 6.01	3.16 / 5.09	2.93 / 4.58	2.77 / 4.25	2.66 / 4.01	2.58 / 3.85	2.51 / 3.71	2.46 / 3.60	2.41 / 3.51	2.37 / 3.44	2.34 / 3.37	2.29 / 3.27	2.25 / 3.19	2.19 / 3.07	2.15 / 3.00	2.11 / 2.91	2.07 / 2.83	2.04 / 2.78	2.00 / 2.71	1.98 / 2.68	1.95 / 2.62	1.93 / 2.59	1.92 / 2.57
19	4.38 / 8.18	3.52 / 5.93	3.13 / 5.01	2.90 / 4.50	2.74 / 4.17	2.63 / 3.94	2.55 / 3.77	2.48 / 3.63	2.43 / 3.52	2.38 / 3.43	2.34 / 3.36	2.31 / 3.30	2.26 / 3.19	2.21 / 3.12	2.15 / 3.00	2.11 / 2.92	2.07 / 2.84	2.02 / 2.76	2.00 / 2.70	1.96 / 2.63	1.94 / 2.60	1.91 / 2.54	1.90 / 2.51	1.88 / 2.49
20	4.35 / 8.10	3.49 / 5.85	3.10 / 4.94	2.87 / 4.43	2.71 / 4.10	2.60 / 3.87	2.52 / 3.71	2.45 / 3.56	2.40 / 3.45	2.35 / 3.37	2.31 / 3.30	2.28 / 3.23	2.23 / 3.13	2.18 / 3.05	2.12 / 2.94	2.08 / 2.86	2.04 / 2.77	1.99 / 2.69	1.96 / 2.63	1.92 / 2.56	1.90 / 2.53	1.87 / 2.47	1.85 / 2.44	1.84 / 2.42
21	4.32 / 8.02	3.47 / 5.78	3.07 / 4.87	2.84 / 4.37	2.68 / 4.04	2.57 / 3.81	2.49 / 3.65	2.42 / 3.51	2.37 / 3.40	2.32 / 3.31	2.28 / 3.24	2.25 / 3.17	2.20 / 3.07	2.15 / 2.99	2.09 / 2.88	2.05 / 2.80	2.00 / 2.72	1.96 / 2.63	1.93 / 2.58	1.89 / 2.51	1.87 / 2.47	1.84 / 2.42	1.82 / 2.38	1.81 / 2.36
22	4.30 / 7.94	3.44 / 5.72	3.05 / 4.82	2.82 / 4.31	2.66 / 3.99	2.55 / 3.76	2.47 / 3.59	2.40 / 3.45	2.35 / 3.35	2.30 / 3.26	2.26 / 3.18	2.23 / 3.12	2.18 / 3.02	2.13 / 2.94	2.07 / 2.83	2.03 / 2.75	1.98 / 2.67	1.93 / 2.58	1.91 / 2.53	1.87 / 2.46	1.84 / 2.42	1.81 / 2.37	1.80 / 2.33	1.78 / 2.31
23	4.28 / 7.88	3.42 / 5.66	3.03 / 4.76	2.80 / 4.26	2.64 / 3.94	2.53 / 3.71	2.45 / 3.54	2.38 / 3.41	2.32 / 3.30	2.28 / 3.21	2.24 / 3.14	2.20 / 3.07	2.14 / 2.97	2.10 / 2.89	2.04 / 2.78	2.00 / 2.70	1.96 / 2.62	1.91 / 2.53	1.88 / 2.48	1.84 / 2.41	1.82 / 2.37	1.79 / 2.32	1.77 / 2.28	1.76 / 2.26
24	4.26 / 7.82	3.40 / 5.61	3.01 / 4.72	2.78 / 4.22	2.62 / 3.90	2.51 / 3.67	2.43 / 3.50	2.36 / 3.36	2.30 / 3.25	2.26 / 3.17	2.22 / 3.09	2.18 / 3.03	2.13 / 2.93	2.09 / 2.85	2.02 / 2.74	1.98 / 2.66	1.94 / 2.58	1.89 / 2.49	1.86 / 2.44	1.82 / 2.36	1.80 / 2.33	1.76 / 2.27	1.74 / 2.23	1.73 / 2.21
25	4.24 / 7.77	3.38 / 5.57	2.99 / 4.68	2.76 / 4.18	2.60 / 3.86	2.49 / 3.63	2.41 / 3.46	2.34 / 3.32	2.28 / 3.21	2.24 / 3.13	2.20 / 3.05	2.16 / 2.99	2.11 / 2.89	2.06 / 2.81	2.00 / 2.70	1.96 / 2.62	1.92 / 2.54	1.87 / 2.45	1.84 / 2.40	1.80 / 2.32	1.77 / 2.29	1.74 / 2.23	1.72 / 2.19	1.71 / 2.17
26	4.22 / 7.72	3.37 / 5.53	2.89 / 4.64	2.74 / 4.14	2.59 / 3.82	2.47 / 3.59	2.39 / 3.42	2.32 / 3.29	2.27 / 3.17	2.22 / 3.09	2.18 / 3.02	2.15 / 2.96	2.10 / 2.86	2.05 / 2.77	1.99 / 2.66	1.95 / 2.58	1.90 / 2.50	1.85 / 2.41	1.82 / 2.36	1.78 / 2.28	1.76 / 2.25	1.72 / 2.19	1.70 / 2.15	1.69 / 2.13

TABLE VII.   *F* DISTRIBUTION.

5% (Roman Type) and 1% (Boldface Type) Points for the Distribution of *F*

Degrees of freedom for greater mean square

Degrees of freedom for lesser mean square	1	2	3	4	5	6	7	8	9	10	11	12	14	16	20	24	30	40	50	75	100	200	500	8
27	4.21 / **7.68**	3.35 / **5.49**	2.96 / **4.60**	2.73 / **4.11**	2.57 / **3.79**	2.46 / **3.56**	2.37 / **3.39**	2.30 / **3.26**	2.25 / **3.14**	2.20 / **3.06**	2.16 / **2.98**	2.13 / **2.93**	2.08 / **2.83**	2.03 / **2.74**	1.97 / **2.63**	1.93 / **2.55**	1.88 / **2.47**	1.84 / **2.38**	1.80 / **2.33**	1.76 / **2.25**	1.74 / **2.21**	1.71 / **2.16**	1.68 / **2.12**	1.67 / **2.10**
28	4.20 / **7.64**	3.34 / **5.45**	2.95 / **4.57**	2.71 / **4.07**	2.56 / **3.76**	2.44 / **3.53**	2.36 / **3.36**	2.29 / **3.23**	2.24 / **3.11**	2.19 / **3.03**	2.15 / **2.95**	2.12 / **2.90**	2.06 / **2.80**	2.02 / **2.71**	1.96 / **2.60**	1.91 / **2.52**	1.87 / **2.44**	1.81 / **2.35**	1.78 / **2.30**	1.75 / **2.22**	1.72 / **2.18**	1.69 / **2.13**	1.67 / **2.09**	1.65 / **2.06**
29	4.18 / **7.60**	3.33 / **5.52**	2.93 / **4.54**	2.70 / **4.04**	2.54 / **3.73**	2.43 / **3.50**	2.35 / **3.33**	2.28 / **3.20**	2.22 / **3.08**	2.18 / **3.00**	2.14 / **2.92**	2.10 / **2.87**	2.05 / **2.77**	2.00 / **2.68**	1.94 / **2.57**	1.90 / **2.49**	1.85 / **2.41**	1.80 / **2.32**	1.77 / **2.27**	1.73 / **2.19**	1.71 / **2.15**	1.68 / **2.10**	1.65 / **2.06**	1.64 / **2.03**
30	4.17 / **7.56**	3.32 / **5.39**	2.92 / **4.51**	2.69 / **4.02**	2.53 / **3.70**	2.42 / **3.47**	2.34 / **3.30**	2.27 / **3.17**	2.21 / **3.06**	2.16 / **2.98**	2.12 / **2.90**	2.09 / **2.84**	2.04 / **2.74**	1.99 / **2.66**	1.93 / **2.55**	1.89 / **2.47**	1.84 / **2.38**	1.79 / **2.29**	1.76 / **2.24**	1.72 / **2.16**	1.69 / **2.13**	1.66 / **2.07**	1.64 / **2.03**	1.62 / **2.01**
32	4.15 / **7.50**	3.30 / **5.34**	2.90 / **4.46**	2.67 / **3.97**	2.51 / **3.66**	2.40 / **3.42**	2.32 / **3.25**	2.25 / **3.12**	2.19 / **3.01**	2.14 / **2.94**	2.10 / **2.86**	2.07 / **2.80**	2.02 / **2.70**	1.97 / **2.62**	1.91 / **2.51**	1.86 / **2.42**	1.82 / **2.34**	1.76 / **2.25**	1.74 / **2.20**	1.69 / **2.12**	1.67 / **2.08**	1.64 / **2.02**	1.61 / **1.98**	1.59 / **1.96**
34	4.13 / **7.44**	3.28 / **5.29**	2.88 / **4.42**	2.65 / **3.93**	2.49 / **3.61**	2.38 / **3.38**	2.30 / **3.21**	2.23 / **3.08**	2.17 / **2.97**	2.12 / **2.89**	2.08 / **2.82**	2.05 / **2.76**	2.00 / **2.66**	1.95 / **2.58**	1.89 / **2.47**	1.84 / **2.38**	1.80 / **2.30**	1.74 / **2.21**	1.71 / **2.15**	1.67 / **2.08**	1.64 / **2.04**	1.61 / **1.98**	1.59 / **1.94**	1.57 / **1.91**
36	4.11 / **7.39**	3.26 / **5.25**	2.86 / **4.38**	2.63 / **3.89**	2.48 / **3.58**	2.36 / **3.35**	2.28 / **3.18**	2.21 / **3.04**	2.15 / **2.94**	2.10 / **2.86**	2.06 / **2.78**	2.03 / **2.72**	1.98 / **2.62**	1.93 / **2.54**	1.87 / **2.43**	1.82 / **2.35**	1.78 / **2.26**	1.72 / **2.17**	1.69 / **2.12**	1.65 / **2.04**	1.62 / **2.00**	1.59 / **1.94**	1.56 / **1.90**	1.55 / **1.87**
38	4.10 / **7.35**	3.25 / **5.21**	2.85 / **4.34**	2.62 / **3.86**	2.46 / **3.54**	2.35 / **3.32**	2.26 / **3.15**	2.19 / **3.02**	2.14 / **2.91**	2.09 / **2.82**	2.05 / **2.75**	2.02 / **2.69**	1.96 / **2.59**	1.92 / **2.51**	1.85 / **2.40**	1.80 / **2.32**	1.76 / **2.22**	1.71 / **2.14**	1.67 / **2.08**	1.63 / **2.00**	1.60 / **1.97**	1.57 / **1.90**	1.54 / **1.86**	1.53 / **1.84**
40	4.08 / **7.31**	3.23 / **5.18**	2.84 / **4.31**	2.61 / **3.83**	2.45 / **3.51**	2.34 / **3.29**	2.25 / **3.12**	2.18 / **2.99**	2.12 / **2.88**	2.07 / **2.80**	2.04 / **2.73**	2.00 / **2.66**	1.95 / **2.56**	1.90 / **2.49**	1.84 / **2.37**	1.79 / **2.29**	1.74 / **2.20**	1.69 / **2.11**	1.66 / **2.05**	1.61 / **1.97**	1.59 / **1.94**	1.55 / **1.88**	1.53 / **1.84**	1.51 / **1.81**
42	4.07 / **7.27**	3.22 / **5.15**	2.83 / **4.29**	2.59 / **3.80**	2.44 / **3.49**	2.32 / **3.26**	2.24 / **3.10**	2.17 / **2.96**	2.11 / **2.86**	2.06 / **2.77**	2.02 / **2.70**	1.99 / **2.64**	1.94 / **2.54**	1.89 / **2.46**	1.82 / **2.35**	1.78 / **2.26**	1.73 / **2.17**	1.68 / **2.08**	1.64 / **2.02**	1.60 / **1.94**	1.57 / **1.91**	1.54 / **1.85**	1.51 / **1.80**	1.49 / **1.78**
44	4.06 / **7.24**	3.21 / **5.12**	2.82 / **4.26**	2.58 / **3.78**	2.43 / **3.46**	2.31 / **3.24**	2.23 / **3.07**	2.16 / **2.94**	2.10 / **2.84**	2.05 / **2.75**	2.01 / **2.68**	1.98 / **2.62**	1.92 / **2.52**	1.88 / **2.44**	1.81 / **2.32**	1.76 / **2.24**	1.72 / **2.15**	1.66 / **2.06**	1.63 / **2.00**	1.58 / **1.92**	1.56 / **1.88**	1.52 / **1.82**	1.50 / **1.78**	1.48 / **1.75**
46	4.05 / **7.21**	3.20 / **5.10**	2.81 / **4.24**	2.57 / **3.76**	2.42 / **3.44**	2.30 / **3.22**	2.22 / **3.05**	2.14 / **2.92**	2.09 / **2.82**	2.04 / **2.73**	2.00 / **2.66**	1.97 / **2.60**	1.91 / **2.50**	1.87 / **2.42**	1.80 / **2.30**	1.75 / **2.22**	1.71 / **2.13**	1.65 / **2.04**	1.62 / **1.98**	1.57 / **1.90**	1.54 / **1.86**	1.51 / **1.80**	1.48 / **1.76**	1.46 / **1.72**

df																								
48	1.45 / 1.70	1.47 / 1.73	1.50 / 1.78	1.53 / 1.84	1.56 / 1.88	1.61 / 1.96	1.64 / 2.02	1.70 / 2.11	1.74 / 2.20	1.79 / 2.28	1.86 / 2.40	1.90 / 2.48	1.96 / 2.58	1.99 / 2.64	2.03 / 2.71	2.08 / 2.80	2.14 / 2.90	2.21 / 3.04	2.30 / 3.20	2.41 / 3.42	2.56 / 3.74	2.80 / 4.22	3.19 / 5.08	4.04 / 7.19
50	1.44 / 1.68	1.46 / 1.71	1.48 / 1.76	1.52 / 1.82	1.55 / 1.86	1.60 / 1.94	1.63 / 2.00	1.69 / 2.10	1.74 / 2.18	1.78 / 2.26	1.85 / 2.39	1.90 / 2.46	1.95 / 2.56	1.98 / 2.62	2.02 / 2.70	2.07 / 2.78	2.13 / 2.88	2.20 / 3.02	2.29 / 3.18	2.40 / 3.41	2.56 / 3.72	2.79 / 4.20	3.18 / 5.06	4.03 / 7.17
55	1.41 / 1.64	1.43 / 1.66	1.46 / 1.71	1.50 / 1.78	1.52 / 1.82	1.58 / 1.90	1.61 / 1.96	1.67 / 2.06	1.72 / 2.15	1.76 / 2.23	1.83 / 2.35	1.88 / 2.43	1.93 / 2.53	1.97 / 2.59	2.00 / 2.66	2.05 / 2.75	2.11 / 2.85	2.18 / 2.98	2.27 / 3.15	2.38 / 3.37	2.54 / 3.68	2.78 / 4.16	3.17 / 5.01	4.02 / 7.12
60	1.39 / 1.60	1.41 / 1.63	1.44 / 1.68	1.48 / 1.74	1.50 / 1.79	1.56 / 1.87	1.59 / 1.93	1.65 / 2.03	1.70 / 2.12	1.75 / 2.20	1.81 / 2.32	1.86 / 2.40	1.92 / 2.50	1.95 / 2.56	1.99 / 2.63	2.04 / 2.72	2.10 / 2.82	2.17 / 2.95	2.25 / 3.12	2.37 / 3.34	2.52 / 3.65	2.76 / 4.13	3.15 / 4.98	4.00 / 7.08
65	1.37 / 1.56	1.39 / 1.60	1.42 / 1.64	1.46 / 1.71	1.49 / 1.76	1.54 / 1.84	1.57 / 1.90	1.63 / 2.00	1.68 / 2.09	1.73 / 2.18	1.80 / 2.30	1.85 / 2.37	1.90 / 2.47	1.94 / 2.54	1.98 / 2.61	2.02 / 2.70	2.08 / 2.79	2.15 / 2.93	2.24 / 3.09	2.36 / 3.31	2.51 / 3.62	2.75 / 4.10	3.14 / 4.95	3.99 / 7.04
70	1.35 / 1.53	1.37 / 1.56	1.40 / 1.62	1.45 / 1.69	1.47 / 1.74	1.53 / 1.82	1.56 / 1.88	1.62 / 1.98	1.67 / 2.07	1.72 / 2.15	1.79 / 2.28	1.84 / 2.35	1.89 / 2.45	1.93 / 2.51	1.97 / 2.59	2.01 / 2.67	2.07 / 2.77	2.14 / 2.91	2.23 / 3.07	2.35 / 3.29	2.50 / 3.60	2.74 / 4.08	3.13 / 4.92	3.98 / 7.01
80	1.32 / 1.49	1.35 / 1.52	1.38 / 1.57	1.42 / 1.65	1.45 / 1.70	1.51 / 1.78	1.54 / 1.84	1.60 / 1.94	1.65 / 2.03	1.70 / 2.11	1.77 / 2.24	1.82 / 2.32	1.88 / 2.41	1.91 / 2.48	1.95 / 2.55	1.99 / 2.64	2.05 / 2.74	2.12 / 2.87	2.21 / 3.04	2.33 / 3.25	2.48 / 3.56	2.72 / 4.04	3.11 / 4.88	3.96 / 6.96
100	1.28 / 1.43	1.30 / 1.46	1.34 / 1.51	1.39 / 1.59	1.42 / 1.64	1.48 / 1.73	1.51 / 1.79	1.57 / 1.89	1.63 / 1.98	1.68 / 2.06	1.75 / 2.19	1.79 / 2.26	1.85 / 2.36	1.88 / 2.43	1.92 / 2.51	1.97 / 2.59	2.03 / 2.69	2.10 / 2.82	2.19 / 2.99	2.30 / 3.20	2.46 / 3.51	2.70 / 3.98	3.09 / 4.82	3.94 / 6.90
125	1.25 / 1.37	1.27 / 1.40	1.31 / 1.46	1.36 / 1.54	1.39 / 1.59	1.45 / 1.68	1.49 / 1.75	1.55 / 1.85	1.60 / 1.94	1.65 / 2.03	1.72 / 2.15	1.77 / 2.23	1.83 / 2.33	1.86 / 2.40	1.90 / 2.47	1.95 / 2.56	2.01 / 2.65	2.08 / 2.79	2.17 / 2.95	2.29 / 3.17	2.44 / 3.47	2.68 / 3.94	3.07 / 4.78	3.92 / 6.84
150	1.22 / 1.33	1.25 / 1.37	1.29 / 1.43	1.34 / 1.51	1.37 / 1.56	1.44 / 1.66	1.47 / 1.72	1.54 / 1.83	1.59 / 1.91	1.64 / 2.00	1.71 / 2.12	1.76 / 2.20	1.82 / 2.30	1.85 / 2.37	1.89 / 2.44	1.94 / 2.53	2.00 / 2.62	2.07 / 2.76	2.16 / 2.92	2.27 / 3.13	2.43 / 3.44	2.67 / 3.91	3.06 / 4.75	3.91 / 6.81
200	1.19 / 1.28	1.22 / 1.33	1.26 / 1.39	1.32 / 1.48	1.35 / 1.53	1.42 / 1.62	1.45 / 1.69	1.52 / 1.79	1.57 / 1.88	1.62 / 1.97	1.69 / 2.09	1.74 / 2.17	1.80 / 2.28	1.83 / 2.34	1.87 / 2.41	1.92 / 2.50	1.98 / 2.60	2.05 / 2.73	2.14 / 2.90	2.26 / 3.11	2.41 / 3.41	2.65 / 3.88	3.04 / 4.71	3.89 / 6.76
400	1.13 / 1.19	1.16 / 1.24	1.22 / 1.32	1.28 / 1.42	1.32 / 1.47	1.38 / 1.57	1.42 / 1.64	1.49 / 1.74	1.54 / 1.84	1.60 / 1.92	1.67 / 2.04	1.72 / 2.12	1.78 / 2.23	1.81 / 2.29	1.85 / 2.37	1.90 / 2.46	1.96 / 2.55	2.03 / 2.69	2.12 / 2.85	2.23 / 3.06	2.39 / 3.36	2.62 / 3.83	3.02 / 4.66	3.86 / 6.70
1000	1.08 / 1.11	1.13 / 1.19	1.19 / 1.28	1.26 / 1.38	1.30 / 1.44	1.36 / 1.54	1.41 / 1.61	1.47 / 1.71	1.53 / 1.81	1.58 / 1.89	1.65 / 2.01	1.70 / 2.09	1.76 / 2.20	1.80 / 2.26	1.84 / 2.34	1.89 / 2.43	1.95 / 2.53	2.02 / 2.66	2.10 / 2.82	2.22 / 3.04	2.38 / 3.34	2.61 / 3.80	3.00 / 4.62	3.85 / 6.66
∞	1.00 / 1.00	1.11 / 1.15	1.17 / 1.25	1.24 / 1.36	1.28 / 1.41	1.35 / 1.52	1.40 / 1.59	1.46 / 1.69	1.52 / 1.79	1.57 / 1.87	1.64 / 1.99	1.69 / 2.07	1.75 / 2.18	1.79 / 2.24	1.83 / 2.32	1.88 / 2.41	1.94 / 2.51	2.01 / 2.64	2.09 / 2.80	2.21 / 3.02	2.37 / 3.32	2.60 / 3.78	2.99 / 4.60	3.84 / 6.64

TABLE VIII.

DISTRIBUTION OF THE STUDENTIZED RANGE STATISTIC.

f = df for s_X	$1-\alpha$	\multicolumn{14}{c}{r = number of steps between ordered means}													
		2	3	4	5	6	7	8	9	10	11	12	13	14	15
1	.95	18.0	27.0	32.8	37.1	40.4	43.1	45.4	47.4	49.1	50.6	52.0	53.2	54.3	55.4
	.99	90.0	135	164	186	202	216	227	237	246	253	260	266	272	277
2	.95	6.09	8.3	9.8	10.9	11.7	12.4	13.0	13.5	14.0	14.4	14.7	15.1	15.4	15.7
	.99	14.0	19.0	22.3	24.7	26.6	28.2	29.5	30.7	31.7	32.6	33.4	34.1	34.8	35.4
3	.95	4.50	5.91	6.82	7.50	8.04	8.48	8.85	9.18	9.46	9.72	9.95	10.2	10.4	10.5
	.99	8.26	10.6	12.2	13.3	14.2	15.0	15.6	16.2	16.7	17.1	17.5	17.9	18.2	18.5
4	.95	3.93	5.04	5.76	6.29	6.71	7.05	7.35	7.60	7.83	8.03	8.21	8.37	8.52	8.66
	.99	6.51	8.12	9.17	9.96	10.6	11.1	11.5	11.9	12.3	12.6	12.8	13.1	13.3	13.5
5	.95	3.64	4.60	5.22	5.67	6.03	6.33	6.58	6.80	6.99	7.17	7.32	7.47	7.60	7.72
	.99	5.70	6.97	7.80	8.42	8.91	9.32	9.67	9.97	10.2	10.5	10.7	10.9	11.1	11.2
6	.95	3.46	4.34	4.90	5.31	5.63	5.89	6.12	6.32	6.49	6.65	6.79	6.92	7.03	7.14
	.99	5.24	6.33	7.03	7.56	7.97	8.32	8.61	8.87	9.10	9.30	9.49	9.65	9.81	9.95
7	.95	3.34	4.16	4.69	5.06	5.36	5.61	5.82	6.00	6.16	6.30	6.43	6.55	6.66	6.76
	.99	4.95	5.92	6.54	7.01	7.37	7.68	7.94	8.17	8.37	8.55	8.71	8.86	9.00	9.12
8	.95	3.26	4.04	4.53	4.89	5.17	5.40	5.60	5.77	5.92	6.05	6.18	6.29	6.39	6.48
	.99	4.74	5.63	6.20	6.63	6.96	7.24	7.47	7.68	7.87	8.03	8.18	8.31	8.44	8.55
9	.95	3.20	3.95	4.42	4.76	5.02	5.24	5.43	5.60	5.74	5.87	5.98	6.09	6.19	6.28
	.99	4.60	5.43	5.96	6.35	6.66	6.91	7.13	7.32	7.49	7.65	7.78	7.91	8.03	8.13
10	.95	3.15	3.88	4.33	4.65	4.91	5.12	5.30	5.46	5.60	5.72	5.83	5.93	6.03	6.11
	.99	4.48	5.27	5.77	6.14	6.43	6.67	6.87	7.05	7.21	7.36	7.48	7.60	7.71	7.81
11	.95	3.11	3.82	4.26	4.57	4.82	5.03	5.20	5.35	5.49	5.61	5.71	5.81	5.90	5.99
	.99	4.39	5.14	5.62	5.97	6.25	6.48	6.67	6.84	6.99	7.13	7.26	7.36	7.46	7.56

12	.95	3.08	3.77	4.20	4.51	4.75	4.95	5.12	5.27	5.40	5.51	5.62	5.71	5.80	5.88
	.99	4.32	5.04	5.50	5.84	6.10	6.32	6.51	6.67	6.81	6.94	7.06	7.17	7.26	7.36
13	.95	3.06	3.73	4.15	4.45	4.69	4.88	5.05	5.19	5.32	5.43	5.53	5.63	5.71	5.79
	.99	4.26	4.96	5.40	5.73	5.98	6.19	6.37	6.53	6.67	6.79	6.90	7.01	7.10	7.19
14	.95	3.03	3.70	4.11	4.41	4.64	4.83	4.99	5.13	5.25	5.36	5.46	5.55	5.64	5.72
	.99	4.21	4.89	5.32	5.63	5.88	6.08	6.26	6.41	6.54	6.66	6.77	6.87	6.96	7.05
16	.95	3.00	3.65	4.05	4.33	4.56	4.74	4.90	5.03	5.15	5.26	5.35	5.44	5.52	5.59
	.99	4.13	4.78	5.19	5.49	5.72	5.92	6.08	6.22	6.35	6.46	6.56	6.66	6.74	6.82
18	.95	2.97	3.61	4.00	4.28	4.49	4.67	4.82	4.96	5.07	5.17	5.27	5.35	5.43	5.50
	.99	4.07	4.70	5.09	5.38	5.60	5.79	5.94	6.08	6.20	6.31	6.41	6.50	6.58	6.65
20	.95	2.95	3.58	3.96	4.23	4.45	4.62	4.77	4.90	5.01	5.11	5.20	5.28	5.36	5.43
	.99	4.02	4.64	5.02	5.29	5.51	5.69	5.84	5.97	6.09	6.19	6.29	6.37	6.45	6.52
24	.95	2.92	3.53	3.90	4.17	4.37	4.54	4.68	4.81	4.92	5.01	5.10	5.18	5.25	5.32
	.99	3.96	4.54	4.91	5.17	5.37	5.54	5.69	5.81	5.92	6.02	6.11	6.19	6.26	6.33
30	.95	2.89	3.49	3.84	4.10	4.30	4.46	4.60	4.72	4.83	4.92	5.00	5.08	5.15	5.21
	.99	3.89	4.45	4.80	5.05	5.24	5.40	5.54	5.56	5.76	5.85	5.93	6.01	6.08	6.14
40	.95	2.86	3.44	3.79	4.04	4.23	4.39	4.52	4.63	4.74	4.82	4.91	4.98	5.05	5.11
	.99	3.82	4.37	4.70	4.93	5.11	5.27	5.39	5.50	5.60	5.69	5.77	5.84	5.90	5.96
60	.95	2.83	3.40	3.74	3.98	4.16	4.31	4.44	4.55	4.65	4.73	4.81	4.88	4.94	5.00
	.99	3.76	4.28	4.60	4.82	4.99	5.13	5.25	5.36	5.45	5.53	5.60	5.67	5.73	5.79
120	.95	2.80	3.36	3.69	3.92	4.10	4.24	4.36	4.48	4.56	4.64	4.72	4.78	4.84	4.90
	.99	3.70	4.20	4.50	4.71	4.87	5.01	5.12	5.21	5.30	5.38	5.44	5.51	5.56	5.61
∞	.95	2.77	3.31	3.63	3.86	4.03	4.17	4.29	4.39	4.47	4.55	4.62	4.68	4.74	4.80
	.99	3.64	4.12	4.40	4.60	4.76	4.88	4.99	5.08	5.16	5.23	5.29	5.35	5.40	5.45

From "Critical Values for Duncan's New Multiple Range Test" by H. Leon Harter, *et al.* Reproduced by permission of the senior author on behalf of his coauthors and their organization from Wright Air Development Center Technical Report 58-484. *The Probability Integrals of the Range and of the Studentized Range*, Volume 2: *Probability Integral and Percentage Points of The Studentized Range; Critical Values for Duncan's New Multiple Range Test*, by H. Leon Harter, Donald S. Clemm, and Eugene H. Guthrie.

TABLE   IX. F_{max} **DISTRIBUTION.**

df for s^2_X	$1-\alpha$	2	3	4	5	6	7	8	9	10
					$k=$number of variances					
4	.95	9.60	15.5	20.6	25.2	29.5	33.6	37.5	41.4	44.6
	.99	23.2	37.	49.	59.	69.	79.	89.	97.	106.
5	.95	7.15	10.8	13.7	16.3	18.7	20.8	22.9	24.7	26.5
	.99	14.9	22.	28.	33.	38.	42.	46.	50.	54.
6	.95	5.82	8.38	10.4	12.1	13.7	15.0	16.3	17.5	18.6
	.99	11.1	15.5	19.1	22.	25.	27.	30.	32.	34.
7	.95	4.99	6.94	8.44	9.70	10.8	11.8	12.7	13.5	14.3
	.99	8.89	12.1	14.5	16.5	18.4	20.	22.	23.	24.
8	.95	4.43	6.00	7.18	8.12	9.03	9.78	10.5	11.1	11.7
	.99	7.50	9.9	11.7	13.2	14.5	15.8	16.9	17.9	18.9
9	.95	4.03	5.34	6.31	7.11	7.80	8.41	8.95	9.45	9.91
	.99	6.54	8.5	9.9	11.1	12.1	13.1	13.9	14.7	15.3
10	.95	3.72	4.85	5.67	6.34	6.92	7.42	7.87	8.28	8.66
	.99	5.85	7.4	8.6	9.6	10.4	11.1	11.8	12.4	12.9
12	.95	3.28	4.16	4.79	5.30	5.72	6.09	6.42	6.72	7.00
	.99	4.91	6.1	6.9	7.6	8.2	8.7	9.1	9.5	9.9
15	.95	2.86	3.54	4.01	4.37	4.68	4.95	5.19	5.40	5.59
	.99	4.07	4.9	5.5	6.0	6.4	6.7	7.1	7.3	7.5
20	.95	2.46	2.95	3.29	3.54	3.76	3.94	4.10	4.24	4.37
	.99	3.32	3.8	4.3	4.6	4.9	5.1	5.3	5.5	5.6
30	.95	2.07	2.40	2.61	2.78	2.91	3.02	3.12	3.21	3.29
	.99	2.63	3.0	3.3	3.4	3.6	3.7	3.8	3.9	4.0
60	.95	1.67	1.85	1.96	2.04	2.11	2.17	2.22	2.26	2.30
	.99	1.96	2.2	2.3	2.4	2.4	2.5	2.5	2.6	2.6
∞	.95	1.00	1.00	1.00	1.00	1.00	1.00	1.00	1.00	1.00
	.99	1.00	1.00	1.00	1.00	1.00	1.00	1.00	1.00	1.00

From E. S. Pearson and H. O. Hartley (eds.), *Biometrika Tables for Statisticians*, Vol. 1, 2nd Edition (New York: Cambridge, 1958). Reprinted by permission of the Biometrika Trustees.

GROUPED DATA FORMULAS FOR THE MEAN, MEDIAN, MODE, PERCENTILE RANKS AND STANDARD DEVIATION

Rather than computing the mean, median, mode, percentile ranks, and standard deviation directly from the defining formulas in terms of the raw scores, we can approximate these values from a *grouped frequency distribution*. To illustrate the grouped data formulas, consider the data of Table 3.1 in Chapter 3. The data are first organized as follows:

Interval	f_i	U_i	$f_i U_i$	$f_i U_i^2$	Cumulative frequency
0–9	3	−4	−12	48	3
10–19	7	−3	−21	63	10
20–29	11	−2	−22	44	21
30–39	15	−1	−15	15	36
40–49	19	0	0	0	55
50–59	19	1	19	19	74
60–69	15	2	30	60	89
70–79	11	3	33	99	100
80–89	7	4	28	112	107
90–99	3	5	15	75	110
$N = 110$			Totals 55	535	

The arithmetic mean $\bar{X}$ is then computed as follows:

$$\bar{X} = C\left(\frac{\sum\limits_{i=1}^{I} f_i U_i}{N}\right) + A$$

where

N = number of cases ($N = 110$ in our example)

C = the width of the intervals, which are assumed to run from -0.5 to 9.5, 9.5 to 19.5, etc. ($C = 10$ in our example)

I = number of intervals ($I = 10$ in our example)

A = midpoint of the interval that is arbitrarily designated 0 ($A = 44.5$ in our example)

f_i = frequency of cases in the ith interval

U_i = the number of intervals that the ith interval is removed from the interval designated 0. For example, the interval (10–19) is three intervals below the interval (40–49) that is arbitrarily designated 0.

Therefore,

$$\bar{X} = 10(\tfrac{55}{110}) + 44.5$$

$$= 49.5$$

The median is calculated from the following formula:

$$\text{Median} = \text{lower real limit of median interval} + \left(\frac{\frac{N}{2} - F_{LL}}{F_M}\right)C$$

where

F_{LL} = cumulative frequency up to the lower real limit of the median interval

F_M = frequency in the median interval

Since one-half (55) of the cases are contained in or below the interval (40–49), this is the median interval, which again is assumed to run from 39.5 to 49.5. Also,

$$F_{LL} = 36$$

and

$$F_M = 19$$

Therefore

$$\text{Median} = 39.5 + \left(\frac{\frac{110}{2} - 36}{19}\right)10$$

$$= 39.5 + 10$$

$$= 49.5$$

The mode may be computed from the following formula:

$$\text{Mode} = \text{lower real limit of modal interval} + \left(\frac{D_1}{D_1 + D_2}\right)C$$

where

D_1 = the absolute difference between the frequency in the modal interval and the frequency in the interval just below the modal interval

D_2 = the absolute difference between the frequency in the modal interval and the frequency in the interval just above the modal interval

In our example there are two modal intervals, (40–49) and (50–59). Therefore, we may select either as our modal interval. Let us select the interval (40–49) as the modal interval. Then

$$D_1 = 19 - 15 = 4$$

$$D_2 = 19 - 19 = 0$$

Therefore

$$\text{Mode} = 39.5 + \left(\frac{4}{4 + 0}\right)10$$

$$= 49.5$$

Since the distribution is symmetrical, the mean, median, and mode all coincide.

The percentile rank corresponding to any particular score X may be estimated by the following formula:

$$\text{Percentile rank} = P_{LL} + \left(\frac{X - X_{LL}}{i}\right)P_i$$

where

P_{LL} = cumulative percentage at the lower real limit of the interval containing X

X = given score

X_{LL} = score at lower real limit of interval containing X

i = width of interval

P_i = percentage of cases within the interval containing X

For example, the percentile rank of a score of 65 would be estimated as follows for the data of Table 3.1 in Chapter 3:

$$\text{Percentile rank} = 50 + \left(\frac{65 - 49.5}{10}\right)17.3$$

$$= 76.8$$

The standard deviation S is computed as follows:

$$S = C\sqrt{\frac{\sum\limits_{i=1}^{I} f_i U_i^2}{N} - \left(\frac{\sum\limits_{i=1}^{I} f_i U_i}{N}\right)^2}$$

$$= 10\sqrt{\frac{535}{110} - (0.5)^2}$$

$$= 21.5$$

For a small number of intervals (less than 12) a correction factor, known as *Sheppard's correction*, may be used to adjust the standard deviation estimated from grouped data. Sheppard's correction is

$$S_C = \sqrt{S^2 - \frac{C^2}{12}}$$

DERIVATION OF COMPUTATIONAL FORMULAS FOR THE ONE-WAY ANALYSIS OF VARIANCE

$$\sum_{t=1}^{k} \sum_{i=1}^{n} [(\bar{X}_t - \bar{X}) + (X_{ti} - \bar{X}_t)]^2$$

$$= \sum_{t=1}^{k} \sum_{i=1}^{n} [(\bar{X}_t - \bar{X})^2 + 2(\bar{X}_t - \bar{X})(X_{ti} - \bar{X}_t) + (X_{ti} - \bar{X}_t)^2]$$

$$= n \sum_{t=1}^{k} (\bar{X}_t - \bar{X})^2 + 2 \sum_{t=1}^{k} (\bar{X}_t - \bar{X}) \sum_{i=1}^{n} (X_{ti} - \bar{X}_t) + \sum_{t=1}^{k} \sum_{i=1}^{n} (X_{ti} - \bar{X}_t)^2$$

However, the sum of the deviations of any set of scores about the arithmetic mean is equal to zero. Therefore, the middle term vanishes, and we have the relationship

$$\sum_{t=1}^{k} \sum_{i=1}^{n} [(\bar{X}_t - \bar{X}) + (X_{ti} - \bar{X}_t)]^2$$

$$= n \sum_{t=1}^{k} (\bar{X}_t - \bar{X})^2 + \sum_{t=1}^{k} \sum_{i=1}^{n} (X_{ti} - \bar{X}_t)^2$$

Furthermore, the two terms on the right-hand side of this relationship may be expressed as follows:

$$n \sum_{t=1}^{k} (\bar{X}_t - \bar{X})^2 = n \sum_{t=1}^{k} (\bar{X}^2_t - 2\bar{X}\bar{X}_t + \bar{X}^2)$$

$$= n \sum_{t=1}^{k} \bar{X}^2_t - 2n\bar{X} \sum_{t=1}^{k} \bar{X}_t + n \sum_{t=1}^{k} \bar{X}^2$$

$$= n \sum_{t=1}^{k} \left(\frac{\sum_{i=1}^{n} X_{ti}}{n} \right)^2 - 2n\bar{X}(k\bar{X}) + nk\bar{X}^2$$

$$= \sum_{t=1}^{k} \left[\frac{\left(\sum_{i=1}^{n} X_{ti} \right)^2}{n} \right] - nk\bar{X}^2$$

Thus

$$n \sum_{t=1} (\bar{X}_t - \bar{X})^2 = \sum_{t=1}^{k} \left[\frac{\left(\sum\limits_{i=1}^{n} X_{ti} \right)^2}{n} \right] - \frac{\left(\sum\limits_{t=1}^{k} \sum\limits_{i=1}^{n} X_{ti} \right)^2}{N}$$

where $N = nk$. Also

$$\sum_{t=1}^{k} \sum_{i=1}^{n} (X_{ti} - \bar{X}_t)^2 = \sum_{t=1}^{k} \sum_{i=1}^{n} (X^2{}_{ti} - 2\bar{X}_t X_{ti} + \bar{X}^2{}_t)$$

$$= \sum_{t=1}^{k} \sum_{i=1}^{n} X^2{}_{ti} - 2 \sum_{t=1}^{k} \bar{X}_t \sum_{i=1}^{n} X_{ti} + n \sum_{t=1}^{k} \bar{X}^2{}_t$$

$$= \sum_{t=1}^{k} \sum_{i=1}^{n} X^2{}_{ti} - 2 \sum_{t=1}^{k} \bar{X}_t n\bar{X}_t + n \sum_{t=1}^{k} \bar{X}^2{}_t$$

$$= \sum_{t=1}^{k} \sum_{i=1}^{n} X^2{}_{ti} - n \sum_{t=1}^{k} \bar{X}^2{}_t$$

Thus

$$\sum_{t=1}^{k} \sum_{i=1}^{n} (X_{ti} - \bar{X}_t)^2 = \sum_{t=1}^{k} \sum_{i=1}^{n} X^2{}_{ti} - \sum_{t=1}^{k} \left[\frac{\left(\sum\limits_{i=1}^{n} X_{ti} \right)^2}{n} \right]$$

REVIEW OF BASIC ALGEBRAIC RULES

RULE 1

$$\sum_{i=1}^{N} CX_i = C \sum_{i=1}^{N} X_i$$

RULE 2

$$\sum_{i=1}^{N} C = NC$$

RULE 3

$$\sum_{i=1}^{N} (X_i + Y_i) = \sum_{i=1}^{N} X_i + \sum_{i=1}^{N} Y_i$$

RULE 4

$$\left(\sum_{i=1}^{N} X_i\right)^2 \neq \sum_{i=1}^{N} X_i^2$$

RULE 5

$$\left(\sum_{i=1}^{N} X_i Y_i\right) \neq \left(\sum_{i=1}^{N} X_i\right)\left(\sum_{i=1}^{N} Y_i\right)$$

For example, let $X_1 = 2$, $X_2 = 3$, $X_3 = 4$, $Y_1 = 1$, $Y_2 = 3$, $Y_3 = 2$, and $C = 3$. Therefore, $N = 3$; that is, there are three values of X and three values of Y. If we recall that the symbol Σ merely means to "add up," our rules then give us:

RULE 1

$$\sum_{i=1}^{N} CX_i = C \sum_{i=1}^{N} X_i$$

$$(3)(2) + (3)(3) + (3)(4) = 3(2 + 3 + 4)$$

$$27 = 27$$

RULE 2

$$\sum_{i=1}^{N} C = NC$$

$$3 + 3 + 3 = 3(3)$$

$$9 = 9$$

RULE 3

$$\sum_{i=1}^{N} (X_i + Y_i) = \sum_{i=1}^{N} X_i + \sum_{i=1}^{N} Y_i$$

$$(2 + 1) + (3 + 3) + (4 + 2) = (2 + 3 + 4) + (1 + 3 + 2)$$

$$3 + 6 + 6 = 9 + 6$$

$$15 = 15$$

RULE 4

$$\left(\sum_{i=1}^{N} X_i\right)^2 \neq \sum_{i=1}^{N} X_i^2$$

$$(2 + 3 + 4)^2 \neq 2^2 + 3^2 + 4^2$$

$$(9)^2 \neq 4 + 9 + 16$$

$$81 \neq 29$$

RULE 5

$$\left(\sum_{i=1}^{N} X_i Y_i\right) \neq \left(\sum_{i=1}^{N} X_i\right)\left(\sum_{i=1}^{N} Y_i\right)$$

$$(2)(1) + (3)(3) + (4)(2) \neq (2 + 3 + 4)(1 + 3 + 2)$$

$$2 + 9 + 8 \neq (9)(6)$$

$$19 \neq 54$$

DEMONSTRATION OF
THE RELATIONSHIP

$$\sigma^2_{(\bar{X}_1 - \bar{X}_2)} = \sigma^2_{\bar{X}_1} + \sigma^2_{\bar{X}_2}$$

FOR INDEPENDENT
GROUPS

First of all, the mean of a sample of K mean differences of the form $(\bar{X}_1 - \bar{X}_2)$ is

Mean of $(\bar{X}_1 - \bar{X}_2)$'s = mean of $\bar{X}_1$'s $-$ mean of $\bar{X}_2$'s

For a sample of data we shall adopt the following notation to denote this relationship:

$$\overline{(\bar{X}_1 - \bar{X}_2)} = \overline{\bar{X}}_1 - \overline{\bar{X}}_2$$

The variance of a sample of K mean differences of the form $(\bar{X}_1 - \bar{X}_2)$ may then be expressed as

$$S^2_{(\bar{X}_1 - \bar{X}_2)} = \frac{\sum_{j=1}^{K} [(\bar{X}_{1j} - \bar{X}_{2j}) - (\overline{\bar{X}}_1 - \overline{\bar{X}}_2)]^2}{K}$$

$$= \frac{\sum_{j=1}^{K} [(\bar{X}_{1j} - \overline{\bar{X}}_1) - (\bar{X}_{2j} - \overline{\bar{X}}_2)]^2}{K}$$

$$= \frac{\sum_{j=1}^{K} [(\bar{X}_{1j} - \overline{\bar{X}}_1)^2 + (\bar{X}_{2j} - \overline{\bar{X}}_2)^2 - 2(\bar{X}_{1j} - \overline{\bar{X}}_1)(\bar{X}_{2j} - \overline{\bar{X}}_2)]}{K}$$

$$= \frac{\sum_{j=1}^{K} (\bar{X}_{1j} - \overline{\bar{X}}_1)^2}{K} + \frac{\sum_{j=1}^{K} (\bar{X}_{2j} - \overline{\bar{X}}_2)^2}{K} - 2\frac{\sum_{j=1}^{K} (\bar{X}_{1j} - \overline{\bar{X}}_1)(\bar{X}_{2j} - \overline{\bar{X}}_2)}{K}$$

$$= S^2_{\bar{X}_1} + S^2_{\bar{X}_2} - 2\frac{\sum_{j=1}^{K} (\bar{X}_{1j} - \overline{\bar{X}}_1)(\bar{X}_{2j} - \overline{\bar{X}}_2)}{K}$$

We shall now show that

$$\frac{\sum_{j=1}^{K} (\bar{X}_{1j} - \overline{\bar{X}}_1)(\bar{X}_{2j} - \overline{\bar{X}}_2)}{K} = rS_{\bar{x}_1}S_{\bar{x}_2}$$

where r is the correlation coefficient between the $\bar{X}_1$'s and $\bar{X}_2$'s. By the definitions of r, $S_{\bar{x}_1}$, and $S_{\bar{x}_2}$ we wish to show that

$$\frac{\sum (\bar{X}_{1j} - \overline{\bar{X}}_1)(\bar{X}_{2j} - \overline{\bar{X}}_2)}{K} = \frac{K \sum \bar{X}_{1j}\bar{X}_{2j} - (\sum \bar{X}_{1j})(\sum \bar{X}_{2j})}{\sqrt{K \sum \bar{X}^2_{1j} - (\sum \bar{X}_{1j})^2}\sqrt{K \sum \bar{X}^2_{2j} - (\sum \bar{X}_{2j})^2}}$$

$$\times \left[\sqrt{\frac{\sum (\bar{X}_{1j} - \overline{\bar{X}}_1)^2}{K}} \right]\left[\sqrt{\frac{\sum (\bar{X}_{2j} - \overline{\bar{X}}_2)^2}{K}} \right] \quad (1)$$

where $\sum$ is understood to mean $\sum_{j=1}^{K}$ in every case.

The standard deviations expressed in the brackets may be expressed as

$$\left[\sqrt{\frac{\sum \bar{X}_{1j}^2}{K} - \left(\frac{\sum \bar{X}_{1j}}{K}\right)^2} \right]\left[\sqrt{\frac{\sum \bar{X}_{2j}^2}{K} - \left(\frac{\sum \bar{X}_{2j}}{K}\right)^2} \right]$$

which is equivalent to

$$\left[\sqrt{\frac{K \sum \bar{X}_{1j}^2 - (\sum \bar{X}_{1j})^2}{K^2}} \right]\left[\sqrt{\frac{K \sum \bar{X}_{2j}^2 - (\sum \bar{X}_{2j})^2}{K^2}} \right]$$

The right-hand side of equation (1) therefore simplifies to

$$\frac{\sum \bar{X}_{1j}\bar{X}_{2j}}{K} - \frac{(\sum \bar{X}_{1j})(\sum \bar{X}_{2j})}{K^2}$$

The left-hand side of equation (1) may likewise be shown to be equal to this same expression, as follows:

$$\frac{\sum (\bar{X}_{1j} - \overline{\bar{X}}_1)(\bar{X}_{2j} - \overline{\bar{X}}_2)}{K} = \frac{\sum (\bar{X}_{1j}\bar{X}_{2j} - \bar{X}_{1j}\overline{\bar{X}}_2 - \bar{X}_{2j}\overline{\bar{X}}_1 + \overline{\bar{X}}_1\overline{\bar{X}}_2)}{K}$$

$$= \frac{\sum \bar{X}_{1j}\bar{X}_{2j}}{K} - \frac{(K\overline{\bar{X}}_1)\overline{\bar{X}}_2}{K} - \frac{(K\overline{\bar{X}}_2)(\overline{\bar{X}}_1)}{K} + \frac{K\overline{\bar{X}}_1\overline{\bar{X}}_2}{K}$$

$$= \frac{\sum \bar{X}_{1j}\bar{X}_{2j}}{K} - \overline{\bar{X}}_1\overline{\bar{X}}_2$$

$$= \frac{\sum \bar{X}_{1j}\bar{X}_{2j}}{K} - \left(\frac{\sum \bar{X}_{1j}}{K}\right)\left(\frac{\sum \bar{X}_{2j}}{K}\right)$$

$$= \frac{\sum \bar{X}_{1j}\bar{X}_{2j}}{K} - \frac{(\sum \bar{X}_{1j})(\sum \bar{X}_{2j})}{K^2}$$

Therefore,

$$S^2_{(\bar{X}_1 - \bar{X}_2)} = S^2_{\bar{X}_2} + S^2_{\bar{X}_2} - 2rS_{\bar{X}_1}S_{\bar{X}_2}$$

However, as K gets indefinitely large, these sample statistics approach the corresponding population parameters. That is,

$$\sigma^2_{(\bar{X}_1 - \bar{X}_2)} = \sigma^2_{\bar{X}_1} + \sigma^2_{\bar{X}_2} - 2\rho\sigma_{\bar{X}_1}\sigma_{\bar{X}_2}$$

If the two populations happen to be independent, that is, uncorrelated, the population correlation coefficient between the two populations of the $\bar{X}_1$'s and $\bar{X}_2$'s is zero, and the variance of the mean differences becomes

$$\sigma^2_{(\bar{X}_1 - \bar{X}_2)} = \sigma^2_{\bar{X}_1} + \sigma^2_{\bar{X}_2}$$

GLOSSARY OF SYMBOLS

a_i	The ith available action in decision theory
A_0	The Y intercept in the regression equation $Y = A_0 + A_1X$
A_1	The regression coefficient (slope) of the regression equation $Y = A_0 + A_1X$
α	Alpha; the level of significance; type I error
β	Beta; type II error
$\mid b - c \mid$	The absolute difference between b and c, which is always taken to be positive
$_nC_r$	The number of combinations of n objects taken r at a time
c_i	The ith existing condition in decision theory
χ^2	Chi-square
$\bar{D}$	Average difference in paired scores in the matched-pairs t test
E	An event in a fundamental probability experiment
e_j	The expected frequency in the jth category in a chi-square goodness of fit analysis
e_{ij}	The expected frequency in the ijth cell in a chi-square test of association between categorical variables
E_r	Predictive efficiency of the sample correlation coefficient
F	Fisher's F statistic
$F_{\max}$	The statistic used for testing the significance of differences among several sample variances
H_0	Null hypothesis
H_1	Alternative hypothesis
h	The number of outcome points defining an event in a fundamental probability experiment
L_i	The linearly derived score corresponding to the ith observation
MS_A	Treatment A mean square in two-way analysis of variance
MS_B	Treatment B mean square in two-way analysis of variance
MS_I	Interaction mean square in two-way analysis of variance
MS_T	Treatment mean square in the one-way analysis of variance
MS_W	Within-groups mean square in the analysis of variance
μ	Mu; population mean

$n!$	n factorial $[n \cdot (n-1)(n-2) \ldots (1)]$
$N_{.j}$	The marginal total for the jth column in a chi-square test of association between categorical variables
$N_{i.}$	The marginal total for the ith row in a chi-square test of association between categorical variables
$N_{..}$	The total of all observations in a chi-square test of association between categorical variables
o_j	The observed frequency in the jth category in a chi-square goodness of fit analysis
o_{ij}	The observed frequency in the ijth cell in a chi-square test of association between categorical variables
ω^2	Omega squared; the estimate of the percentage of the total experimental variability accounted for by the treatments
p	The probability of a "success" for a single observation in a binomial distribution
$P(E)$	The probability of an event E
$P(E_2 \mid E_1)$	The conditional probability of event E_2 given that event E_1 has already occurred
$P(E_1 E_2)$	The probability of the joint occurrence of events E_1 and E_2
$P(E_1 + E_2)$	The probability of the occurrence of event E_1 or E_2
nPn	The number of permutations of n objects taken n at a time
nPr	The number of permutations of n objects taken r at a time
q	The probability of a "failure" for a single observation in a binomial distribution $(q = 1 - p)$
$q_{1-\alpha}(r, f)$	The q statistic employed in the Newman-Keuls procedure
r	Sample correlation coefficient
r^2	Sample coefficient of determination
r_s	The Spearman rank-order correlation coefficient
R_1	Sum of the ranks in the smaller of the two samples in the Mann-Whitney U test
ρ	Rho; population correlation coefficient
S	Sample standard deviation
$\mathbf{s}$	The sample space of a fundamental probability experiment
S_i	The ith strategy in decision theory
S_Y^2	The variance of the dependent variable in regression analysis
$S^2_{Y \cdot X}$	Unexplained variance in regression analysis
S^2	Sample variance
S_p	The standard error of the t statistic obtained by pooling the variance data of the two samples
$\hat{S}^2_{\text{largest}}$	The largest unbiased sample variance in the Hartley test
$S_{\bar{D}}$	Standard error of the mean difference in the paired scores in the matched pairs t test
$S_{(\text{of } Z_i \text{ scores})}$	Standard deviation of the standard score distribution $[S_{(\text{of } Z_i \text{ scores})} = 1]$
$\hat{S}^2$	Unbiased sample variance

$\hat{S}^2_{\text{smallest}}$	The smallest unbiased sample variance in the Hartley test
Σ	Capital sigma; the "sum of"
$\hat{S}^2_{\text{total}}$	Total unbiased variance in the one-way analysis of variance
σ	Lowercase sigma; population standard deviation
σ^2	Population variance
$\sigma_{\bar{X}}$	Standard deviation of the theoretical sampling distribution of means
σ_{p1-p2}	The standard error of the sampling distribution of the difference between two proportions
T	The T statistic in the Wilcoxon test
T_i	A linearly derived score with the property that the mean of the T_i scores is 50 and the standard deviation is 10
t	Student's t statistic
U	The Mann-Whitney U statistic
X	The number of fewer signs in the sign test
X_i	The value of the independent variable for the ith observation (sometimes also written simply X)
X_{ti}	The score of the ith individual in the tth treatment in the one-way analysis of variance
X_{ijk}	The score of the kth individual in the (i,j)th cell in the two-way analysis of variance
$\bar{X}$	Sample mean
$\bar{X}_t$	The mean score in the tth treatment in the one-way analysis of variance
Y	A dependent variable
Y_i	The value of the dependent variable for the ith observation (sometimes also written simply Y)
$Y_{\text{pred.}}$	The predicted value of the dependent variable in regression analysis
$\bar{Y}$	The average value of the dependent variable in regression analysis
Z_i	Standard score of the ith observation (sometimes also written simply as Z)
$\bar{Z}$	Mean of the standard score distribution ($\bar{Z} = 0$)
$Z_i \overset{d}{=} N(0, 1)$	A unit normal distribution of Z scores

REFERENCES

Amrine, M., "The 1965 Congressional Inquiry into Testing—A Commentary," *The American Psychologist*, **20** (November 1965), Number 11.

Boring, E. G., *A History of Experimental Psychology*, 2nd ed. New York: Appleton-Century-Crofts, 1957.

Chernoff, H., and L. E. Moses, *Elementary Decision Theory*. New York: John Wiley & Sons, 1959.

Clopper, C. J., and E. S. Pearson, "The Use of Confidence or Fiducial Limits Illustrated in the Case of the Binomial," *Biometrika*, **26** (1934), 404–413.

Edwards, A. L., *Experimental Design in Psychological Research*. New York: Holt, Rinehart and Winston, 1960.

Ferguson, G. A., *Statistical Analysis and Psychology and Education*, 2nd ed. New York: McGraw-Hill Book Company, 1966.

Fisher, R. A., and W. A. Mackenzie, "Studies in Crop Variation II: The Manurial Response of Different Potato Varieties," *Journal of Agricultural Science*, **XIII** (1923), 311–320.

Fisher, R. A., *The Design of Experiments*, 2nd ed. London: Oliver & Boyd, 1937.

Fruchter, Benjamin, *Introduction to Factor Analysis*. New York: D. Van Nostrand Company, 1954.

Games, P. A., and G. R. Klare, *Elementary Statistics*. New York: McGraw-Hill Book Company, 1967.

Gourevitch, Vivian, *Statistical Methods: A Problem Solving Approach*. Boston: Allyn and Bacon, 1965.

Guenther, W. C., *Concepts of Statistical Inference*. New York: McGraw-Hill Book Company, 1965.

Guilford, J. P., *Fundamental Statistics in Psychology and Education*. New York: McGraw-Hill Book Company, 1965.

Hammond, K. R., and J. E. Householder, *Introduction to the Statistical Method*. New York: A. A. Knopf, 1962.

Hays, William L., *Statistics for Psychologists*. New York: Holt, Rinehart and Winston, 1963.

Hendel, C. W., Jr., *Hume, Selections*. New York: Charles Scribner's Sons, 1927.

Hoel, P. G., *Introduction to Mathematical Statistics*, 2nd ed. New York: John Wiley & Sons, 1954.

Johnson, P. O., *Statistical Methods in Research*. Englewood Cliffs, N.J.: Prentice-Hall, Inc., 1949.

Kerlinger, F. N., *Foundations of Behavioral Research*. New York: Holt, Rinehart and Winston, 1964.

Kraft, C. H., and C. van Eeden, *A Nonparametric Introduction to Statistics*. New York: The Macmillan Company, 1968.

Li, C. C., *Introduction to Experimental Statistics*. New York: McGraw-Hill Book Company, 1964.

McNemar, Q., *Psychological Statistics*, 3rd ed. New York: John Wiley & Sons, 1962.

Peterson, Roger T., "Eerie Cradle of New Specie," *National Geographic*, **131**, No. 4 (April 1967).

Seder, L. A., "The Technique of Experimenting in the Factory," *Industrial Quality Control* (March 1948).

Siegel, Sidney, *Nonparametric Statistics*. New York: McGraw-Hill Book Company, 1956.

Spiegel, M. R., *Theory and Problems of Statistics*. Schaum Publishing Co., 1961.

Torgerson, W. S., *Theory and Methods of Scaling*. New York: John Wiley & Sons, 1960.

Underwood, B. J., *Psychological Research*. New York: Appleton-Century-Crofts, 1957.

Walker, H. M., *Studies in the History of the Statistical Method*. Baltimore: The Williams and Wilkins Co., 1929.

Wilks, S. S., *Elementary Statistical Analysis*. Princeton, N.J.: Princeton University Press, 1961.

Winer, B. J., *Statistical Principles in Experimental Design*. New York: McGraw-Hill Book Company, 1962.

Young, H. D., *Statistical Treatment of Experimental Data*. New York: McGraw-Hill Book Company, 1962.

CHAPTER 3

1 continuous, discrete

2 a

3 frequency polygon

4 bimodal

5 negatively skewed

6 (a) mean
  (b) median
  (c) mode

7 right

8 mean = 6
  median = 5
  mode = 10

9 $\Sigma (X_i - \bar{X}) = \Sigma X_i - N\bar{X} = \Sigma X_i - \Sigma X_i = 0$

10 distorted by extreme values

11 $S = 0.82$

12 mean, standard deviation

13 similar

14 (a) $Z_i = 0, T_i = 50$
   (b) $Z_i = -3, T_i = 20$
   (c) $Z_i = -1, T_i = 40$

15 the shape is unaltered

16 to avoid negative scores

17   (a) $\displaystyle\sum_{i=1}^{4} 2X_i$ or $2 \displaystyle\sum_{i=1}^{4} X_i$

(b) $\displaystyle\sum_{i=19}^{22} X^2_i$

(c) $\displaystyle\sum_{i=1}^{N} (X_i - \bar{X})^2$

18   (a)   5   (d)   10
     (b)   6   (e)   30
     (c)   9   (f)   126

CHAPTER 4

1   wide range of generalizability

2   meaning of an outcome

3   sample space

4   mutually exclusive

5   in terms of outcome points h in the sample space

6   $P(E) = \dfrac{h}{n}$

7   (a) A, B, C, D
    (b)   4
    (c)   1
    (d) $\frac{1}{4}$

8   $n = 4, h = 3$

9   $n = 12, h = 3$

10   $n = 36, h = 6$

11   equally likely outcome points

12   relative frequency observed over a long series of trials

13   independent

14   $P(E_1E_2) = P(E_1)P(E_2)$

15   $P(E_1E_2) = P(E_1)P(E_2 \mid E_1)$

16   mutually exclusive

17   $P(E_1 + E_2) = P(E_1) + P(E_2) - P(E_1E_2)$

18   zero

19 combinatorial

20 $n! = n(n-1)(n-2) \ldots (1)$

21 6

22 6

23 24

24 $_nP_r = \dfrac{n!}{(n-r)!}$

25 10

26 $_nC_r = \dfrac{_nP_r}{r!}$

CHAPTER 5

1 independent and equally likely

2 mutually exclusive

3 $P(x = 2) = 0.234,$

   $P(x \geq 2) = 1 - [P(0) + P(1)] = 1 - (0.016 + 0.094) = 0.89$

4 $P(x = 4) = \dfrac{5!}{1!\,4!} \left(\dfrac{1}{4}\right)^4 \left(\dfrac{3}{4}\right)^1 = \dfrac{15}{1024} = 0.015$

5 (a) $x = 9, 10$
   (b) $x = 0, 1, 2, 3$
   (c) $x = 0, 1, 9, 10$

6 $P(x = 9) = 0.153$ for $p = 0.50$
   $P(x = 9) = 0.207$ for $p = 0.60$
   Choose $H_0: p = 0.60$

7 mutually exclusive and exhaustive

8 0.00073

9 simplicity and utility for categorical information

10 goodness of fit

11 The categories should be mutually exclusive and exhaustive; the responses should be independent of one another; expected frequencies should be five or more.

12 5

13   Step 1. H_0: coin is fair
       H_1: coin is biased

   Step 2. $\alpha = 0.05$

   Step 3. $\chi^2 = \displaystyle\sum_{j=1}^{k} \left[\frac{(|\, o_j - e_j\,| - 0.5)^2}{e_j} \right]$

   Step 4. $\chi^2 \overset{d}{=} \chi^2(k - 1$ degrees of freedom)

   Step 5. $\chi^2 > 3.84$

   Step 6. $\chi^2 = 4.20$

   Step 7. Reject H_0: coin is fair
       Accept H_1: coin is biased

CHAPTER 6

1   All standard score distributions have a mean of 0 and a standard deviation of 1. Furthermore, standard scores follow the shape of the original score distribution.

2   The approximation is fairly close in a number of cases because of the central limit theorem.

3   (a)   0.4554   (d)   0.8508
    (b)   0.0828   (e)   0.9793
    (c)   0.3336   (f)   0.0869

4   $Z_1 = \dfrac{39.5 - 50}{10} = -1.05, \qquad Z_2 = \dfrac{65.5 - 50}{10} = 1.55$

   The percentage of cases between the discrete scores 40 and 65 is thus approximately 79.25%.

   $Z_3 = \dfrac{68.5 - 50}{10} \doteq 1.85$

   The percentage of cases above the discrete score 68 is thus approximately 3.22%.

5   0 to σ. The standard error is inversely related to the sample size.

6   expected value $= 48$; standard error $= 1$

7   approximately normal; expected value $= 400$; standard error $= 2.5$

8   expected value $= 50$; standard error $= 4.47$

CHAPTER 7

1 Step 1. $H_0: \mu = 55$ Step 2. $\alpha = 0.05$ Step 3. $Z = \dfrac{\bar{X} - \mu}{\dfrac{\sigma}{\sqrt{N}}}$
   $H_1: \mu > 55$

Step 4. $Z \overset{d}{=} N(0, 1)$ Step 5. $Z > 1.65$

Step 6. $Z = \dfrac{60 - 55}{\dfrac{16}{\sqrt{100}}} = 3.12$ Step 7. Reject $H_0: \mu = 55$
Accept $H_1: \mu > 55$

2 Step 1. $H_0: \mu = 40$ Step 2. $\alpha = 0.10$ Step 3. $Z = \dfrac{\bar{X} - \mu}{\dfrac{\sigma}{\sqrt{N}}}$
   $H_1: \mu \neq 40$

Step 4. $Z \overset{d}{=} N(0, 1)$ Step 5. $Z > 1.65$ and $Z < -1.65$

Step 6. $Z = \dfrac{35 - 40}{\dfrac{16}{\sqrt{36}}} = -1.87$ Step 7. Reject $H_0: \mu = 40$
Accept $H_1: \mu \neq 40$

3 (a) $t > 2.76$
   (b) $t > 2.08$ and $t < -2.08$
   (c) $t < -1.30$
   (d) $t > 3.17$ and $t < -3.17$

4 Step 1. $H_0: \mu = 100$ Step 2. $\alpha = 0.10$ Step 3. $t = \dfrac{\bar{X} - \mu}{\dfrac{S}{\sqrt{N - 1}}}$
   $H_1: \mu < 100$

Step 4. $t \overset{d}{=} t(N - 1)$ Step 5. $t < -1.34$

Step 6. $t = \dfrac{95 - 100}{\dfrac{9}{\sqrt{16}}} = -2.22$ Step 7. Reject $H_0: \mu = 100$
Accept $H_1: \mu < 100$

5 Step 1. $H_0: \mu = 60$ Step 2. $\alpha = 0.05$ Step 3. $t = \dfrac{\bar{X} - \mu}{\dfrac{S}{\sqrt{N - 1}}}$
   $H_1: \mu \neq 60$

Step 4. $t \overset{d}{=} t(N - 1)$ Step 5. $t > 2.26$ and $t < -2.26$

Step 6. $t = \dfrac{75 - 60}{\dfrac{16}{\sqrt{9}}} = 2.81$ Step 7. Reject $H_0: \mu = 60$
Accept $H_1: \mu \neq 60$

6   $\bar{X} - 1.96 \dfrac{\sigma}{\sqrt{N}} \leq \mu \leq \bar{X} + 1.96 \dfrac{\sigma}{\sqrt{N}}$

$60 - 1.96(\tfrac{16}{10}) \leq \mu \leq 60 + 1.96(\tfrac{16}{10})$

$56.86 \leq \mu \leq 63.14$

7   $\bar{X} - 3.25 \dfrac{S}{\sqrt{N-1}} \leq \mu \leq \bar{X} + 3.25 \dfrac{S}{\sqrt{N-1}}$

$75 - 3.25(\tfrac{16}{3}) \leq \mu \leq 75 + 3.25(\tfrac{16}{3})$

$57.68 \leq \mu \leq 92.32$

CHAPTER 8

1   Step 1. $H_0: \mu_1 = \mu_2$ Step 2. $\alpha = 0.05$
    $H_1: \mu_1 \neq \mu_2$

Step 3. $Z = \dfrac{(\bar{X}_1 - \bar{X}_2) - (\mu_1 - \mu_2)}{\sqrt{\dfrac{\sigma_1^2}{N_1} + \dfrac{\sigma_2^2}{N_2}}}$ Step 4. $Z \overset{d}{=} N(0, 1)$

Step 5. $Z > 1.96$ and $Z < -1.96$ Step 6. $Z = \dfrac{(100 - 95)}{\sqrt{\tfrac{9}{50} + \tfrac{16}{37}}} = 6.41$

Step 7. Reject $H_0: \mu_1 = \mu_2$
        Accept $H_1: \mu_1 \neq \mu_2$

2   Step 1. $H_0: \mu_1 = \mu_2$ Step 2. $\alpha = 0.05$
    $H_1: \mu_1 \neq \mu_2$

Step 3. $t = \dfrac{(\bar{X}_1 - \bar{X}_2) - (\mu_1 - \mu_2)}{S_p \sqrt{\dfrac{1}{N_1} + \dfrac{1}{N_2}}}$

Step 4. $t \overset{d}{=} t(N_1 + N_2 - 2$ degrees of freedom$)$

Step 5. $t > 2.06$ and $t < -2.06$ Step 6. $t = \dfrac{(100 - 95)}{3.54\sqrt{\tfrac{1}{17} + \tfrac{1}{10}}} = 3.55$

Step 7. Reject $H_0: \mu_1 = \mu_2$
        Accept $H_1: \mu_1 \neq \mu_2$

3   $3.47 \leq (\mu_1 - \mu_2) \leq 6.53$

4   $2.10 \leq (\mu_1 - \mu_2) \leq 7.90$

5 The confidence interval in Problem 4 is based on less information; therefore, we are not as certain of the actual difference in the means of the populations. That is, the t distribution does not yield as precise an estimate as the unit normal distribution.

6 Step 1. $H_0: \mu_1 = \mu_2$ Step 2. $\alpha = 0.10$
   $H_1: \mu_1 \neq \mu_2$

Step 3. $t = \dfrac{\bar{D}}{S_{\bar{D}}}$ Step 4. $t \overset{d}{=} t(N - 1 \text{ degrees of freedom})$

Step 5. $t > 1.83$ and $t < -1.83$ Step 6. $t = \dfrac{2.30}{0.517} = 4.45$

Step 7. Reject $H_0: \mu_1 = \mu_2$
   Accept $H_1: \mu_1 \neq \mu_2$

CHAPTER 9

1 (a) Step 1. $H_0: \sigma^2 = 100$ Step 2. $\alpha = 0.05$ Step 3. $\chi^2 = \dfrac{NS^2}{\sigma^2}$
      $H_1: \sigma^2 > 100$

   Step 4. $\chi^2 \overset{d}{=} \chi^2(N - 1 \text{ degrees of freedom})$ Step 5. $\chi^2 > 36.4$

   Step 6. $\chi^2 = \dfrac{25(144)}{100} = 36$ Step 7. Accept $H_0: \sigma^2 = 100$

   (b) Step 1. $H_0: \sigma^2 = 100$ Step 2. $\alpha = 0.05$ Step 3. $\chi^2 = \dfrac{NS^2}{\sigma^2}$
      $H_1: \sigma^2 \neq 100$

   Step 4. $\chi^2 = \chi^2(N - 1 \text{ degrees of freedom})$

   Step 5. $\chi^2 > 39.4$ and $\chi^2 < 12.4$ Step 6. $\chi^2 = 36$

   Step 7. Accept $H_0: \sigma^2 = 100$

2 Step 1. $H_0: \sigma_1{}^2 = \sigma_2{}^2$ Step 2. $\alpha = 0.05$ Step 3. $F = \dfrac{\hat{S}_1{}^2}{\hat{S}_2{}^2}$
   $H_1: \sigma_1{}^2 > \sigma_2{}^2$

Step 4. $F \overset{d}{=} F(N_1 - 1, N_2 - 1 \text{ degrees of freedom})$

Step 5. $F > 2.51$ Step 6. $F = 1.08$ Step 7. Accept $H_0: \sigma_1{}^2 = \sigma_2{}^2$

3 $t = \dfrac{\bar{X}_1 - \bar{X}_2}{S_p \sqrt{\dfrac{1}{N_1} + \dfrac{1}{N_2}}}$; 20 degrees of freedom

4 Z

5   $\chi^2 = \dfrac{NS^2}{\sigma^2}$; 11 degrees of freedom

6   $F = \dfrac{\widehat{S}_1{}^2}{\widehat{S}_2{}^2}$; 9 and 9 degrees of freedom

7   $t < -2.76$

8   $t > 2.09$ and $t < -2.09$

9   $t > 1.30$

10   $t > 3.17$ and $t < -3.17$

11   $\chi^2 < 5.23$

12   $\chi^2 > 12.8$ and $\chi^2 < 0.831$

13   $\chi^2 > 23.2$

14   $\chi^2 > 25.2$ and $\chi^2 < 2.16$

15   $F > 2.76$

CHAPTER 10

1   testing the null hypothesis H_0: $\sigma_1{}^2 = \sigma_2{}^2$ (see Chapter 9)
testing the null hypothesis H_0: $\mu_1 = \mu_2 = \cdots = \mu_k$

2   The sum of squares for treatments plus the sum of squares within groups
should equal the sum of squares for all observations considered together.

3   H_0: $\sigma_1{}^2 = \sigma_2{}^2 = \cdots = \sigma_k{}^2$

4   F; $F > 2.86$

5   $F_{\max}$; $F_{\max} > 13.7$

6   numerator

7

Source of variation	Degrees of freedom	Sum of squares	Mean square	F ratio	Decision
Treatments	2	16	8	16	Accept H_0: $\mu_1 = \mu_2 = \mu_3$
Within groups	3	1.5	0.5		
Total	5	17.5		$F_{0.99}(2, 3) = 30.81$	

8

	Order		
	1	2	3
	Treatment	Treatment	Treatment
Treatments in order of totals	1	2	3
Totals	3	7	11

	Treatment 1	Treatment 2	Treatment 3
Treatment 1	—	4	8
Treatment 2		—	4
Treatment 3			—

Number of steps	2	3
$q_{0.99}(r, 3)$	8.26	10.6
$q_{0.99}(r, 3)\sqrt{nMS_W}$	8.26	10.6

	Treatment 1	Treatment 2	Treatment 3
Treatment 1		n.s.	n.s.
Treatment 2			n.s.
Treatment 3			

CHAPTER 11

1 contingency

2 independent

3 8

4 $(r - 1)(c - 1)$

5 1. H_0: A and B are independent   2. $\alpha = 0.05$
    H_1: A and B are not independent

   3. $\chi^2 = \sum_{\text{all cells}} \left[\frac{(o_{ij} - e_{ij})^2}{e_{ij}} \right]$

   4. $\chi^2 \overset{d}{=} \chi^2(r - 1, c - 1 \text{ degrees of freedom})$ 5. $\chi^2 > 5.99$

   6. $\chi^2 = 0.08$ 7. Accept H_0

6 false

7 true

8 true

9 true

10 true

11 false

12 $\bar{Y}$

13 His weight is probably also above average.

14 coefficient of determination

15 $Y = 0.17 + 1.5X$
   $r^2 = 0.96$
   $r = 0.98$

16 They tend to coincide.

17 64

18 Step 1. H_0: $\rho = 0$ Step 2. $\alpha = 0.05$
        H_1: $\rho \neq 0$

   Step 3. $t = \dfrac{r\sqrt{N - 2}}{\sqrt{1 - r^2}}$ Step 4. $t \overset{d}{=} t(N - 2 \text{ degrees of freedom})$

   Step 5. $t > 12.71$ and $t < -12.71$ Step 6. $t = 4.9$

Step 7. Accept H_0: $\rho = 0$

Notice that with such a small sample even an $r = 0.98$ is not sufficient to reject the hypothesis that the underlying population correlation is zero.

CHAPTER 12

1 (a)   median test
           combined median $= 24$

	Experimental group	Control group	Total
Frequency of scores exceeding the combined median	$A = 6$	$B = 14$	$A + B = 20$
Frequency of scores not exceeding the combined median	$C = 14$	$D = 7$	$C + D = 21$
Total	$A + C = 20$	$B + D = 21$	$N = 41$

Step 1. H_0: median of experimental group = median of control group

H_1: median of experimental group $\neq$ median of control group

Step 2. $\alpha = 0.01$

Step 3. $\chi^2 = \dfrac{N\left(|\,AD - BC\,| - \dfrac{N}{2}\right)^2}{(A + B)(C + D)(A + C)(B + D)}$

Step 4. $\chi^2 \overset{d}{=} \chi^2(1 \text{ degree of freedom})$

Step 5. $\chi^2 > 6.63$

Step 6. $\chi^2 = \dfrac{41[\,|\,(6)(7) - (14)(14)\,| - \frac{41}{2}]^2}{(20)(21)(20)(21)} = 4.14$

Step 7. Accept H_0

(b)   Mann-Whitney U test

Experimental Group		Control Group	
Score	Rank	Score	Rank
31	34.5	14	6.5
26	24.5	16	8.5
17	10.5	25	22
31	34.5	18	12.5
19	14.5	40	41
20	16.5	26	24.5
28	29.5	22	19
14	6.5	32	37
31	34.5	16	8.5
17	10.5	34	39.5
18	12.5	29	31
19	14.5	28	29.5
27	27.5	20	16.5
21	18	26	24.5
23	20	27	27.5
9	5	30	32
8	4	31	34.5
4	3	33	38
2	2	34	39.5
1	1	26	24.5
		24	21

Step 1. H_0: rank values of experimental group = rank values of control group

H_1: rank values of experimental group $\neq$ rank values of control group

Step 2. $\alpha = 0.01$

Step 3. $Z = \dfrac{U - \dfrac{N_1 N_2}{2}}{\sqrt{\dfrac{(N_1)(N_2)(N_1 + N_2 + 1)}{12}}}$

Step 4. $Z \overset{d}{=} N(0, 1)$

Step 5. $Z > 2.58$ and $Z < -2.58$

Step 6. $Z = \dfrac{306.5 - \dfrac{(20)(21)}{2}}{\sqrt{\dfrac{(20)(21)(20 + 21 + 1)}{12}}}$

$= \dfrac{96.50}{38.34}$

$= 2.52$

Step 7. Reject H_0
   Accept H_1

2 (a) Sign test

Pair	Sign of difference
1	−
2	−
3	+
4	+
5	+
6	−
7	−
8	+
9	−
10	+
11	+
12	+
13	+
14	−
15	+
16	+
17	−
18	+
19	+
20	+
21	+
22	+
23	+
24	−
25	+

Step 1. H_0: scores of experimental class = scores of control class
   H_1: scores of experimental class $\neq$ scores of control class

Step 2. $\alpha = 0.05$

Step 3. $Z = \dfrac{(X + 0.5) - \frac{1}{2}N}{\frac{1}{2}\sqrt{N}}$

Step 4. $Z \overset{d}{=} N(0, 1)$

Step 5. $Z > 1.96$ and $Z < -1.96$

Step 6. $Z = \dfrac{8.5 - \frac{1}{2}(25)}{\frac{1}{2}\sqrt{25}} = \dfrac{-4}{2.5} = -1.60$

Step 7. Accept H_0

(b)   Wilcoxon test

Pair	d	Rank of $\lvert d \rvert$	Rank of d with sign attached	Absolute value of like-signed ranks having smaller total
1	−4	14.5	−14.5	14.5
2	−2	8.5	−8.5	8.5
3	2	8.5	8.5	
4	6	19.5	19.5	
5	1	3	3	
6	−2	8.5	−8.5	8.5
7	−2	8.5	−8.5	8.5
8	3	12.5	12.5	
9	−5	17	−17	17
10	8	23.5	23.5	
11	10	25	25	
12	5	17	17	
13	7	21.5	21.5	
14	−1	3	−3	3
15	1	3	3	
16	3	12.5	12.5	
17	−1	3	−3	3
18	5	17	17	
19	6	19.5	19.5	
20	8	23.5	23.5	
21	7	21.5	21.5	
22	2	8.5	8.5	
23	2	8.5	8.5	
24	−1	3	−3	3
25	4	14.5	14.5	

Step 1. H_0: sum of ranks for positive differences = sum of ranks for negative differences

H_1: sum of ranks for positive differences $\neq$ sum of ranks for negative differences

Step 2. $\alpha = 0.05$

Step 3. $Z = \dfrac{T - \dfrac{N(N+1)}{4}}{\sqrt{\dfrac{N(N+1)(2N+1)}{24}}}$

Step 4. $Z \overset{d}{=} N(0, 1)$

Step 5. $Z > 1.96$ and $Z < -1.96$

Step 6. $Z = \dfrac{66 - \dfrac{25(26)}{4}}{\sqrt{\dfrac{(25)(26)(51)}{24}}} = \dfrac{-96.50}{37.17} = -2.60$

Step 7. Reject H_0
Accept H_1

3

Individual	Ranks of test 1	Ranks of test 2	d_i	d_i^2
1	4	5	−1	1
2	3	4	−1	1
3	5	7	−2	4
4	7	8	−1	1
5	8	9	−1	1
6	10	6	4	16
7	9	10	−1	1
8	6	2	4	16
9	2	1	1	1
10	1	3	−2	4
				46

$$r_s = 1 - \frac{6(46)}{(10)^3 - 10} = 1 - 0.28 = 0.72$$

Step 1. $H_0: \rho = 0$ Step 2. $\alpha = 0.05$ Step 3. $t = \dfrac{r_s\sqrt{N-2}}{\sqrt{1 - r_s^2}}$
$H_1: \rho \neq 0$

Step 4. $t \stackrel{d}{=} t(N - 2 \text{ degrees of freedom})$

Step 5. $t > 2.31$ and $t < -2.31$

Step 6. $t = \dfrac{0.72\sqrt{8}}{\sqrt{1 - (0.72)^2}} = \dfrac{2.04}{0.69} = 2.96$

Step 7. Reject $H_0: \rho = 0$
Accept $H_1: \rho \neq 0$

INDEX